PIANO SERVICING, TUNING, AND REBUILDING

PIANO SERVICING, TUNING, AND REBUILDING

FOR THE PROFESSIONAL, THE STUDENT, AND THE HOBBYIST

SECOND EDITION

BY ARTHUR A. REBLITZ

Lanham ◆ New York ◆ Toronto ◆ Oxford

VESTAL PRESS, Inc.

Published in the United States of America
by Vestal Press, Inc.
A wholly owned subsidary of
The Rowman & Littlefield Publishing Group, Inc.
4501 Forbes Boulevard, Suite 200
Lanham, Maryland 20706

Library of Congress Cataloging-in-Publication Data

Reblitz, Arthur A.
    Piano servicing, tuning, and rebuilding for the professional, the student,
and the hobbyist / by Arthur A. Reblitz
        p. cm.
    Includes bibliographical reference and index.
        ISBN 1-879511-02-9 (HC: acid-free paper)
        ISBN 1-879511-03-7 (Pbk.: acid-free paper)
    1. Piano—Construction. 2. Piano—Maintenance and repair. 3. Piano—
Tuning. I. Title.

ML 652.R3 1992   92-13175
786.2'1928—dc20   CIP
                                                       MN

Contents

Piano Servicing, Tuning, and Rebuilding

Preface to the Second Edition

Everyone involved with the first edition of this book has been a winner! Its enthusiastic reception by amateur and professional piano technicians alike have required umpteen printings to be made, the author has made himself famous in the field of acoustic pianos and their servicing, rebuilding, and repair, and The Vestal Press, Ltd., name has become widespread for having published the world-class treatise on the subject. One is even tempted to gloat over its success.

All these plusses are hugely satisfying, but perhaps none more personally satisfying to me than the knowledge that a lot of beautiful instruments have been kept in or put back into pristine condition through the help and guidance so clearly expressed by Art Reblitz. The refinements he's included in this new edition simply add more wonderful frosting to the cake.

Harvey N. Roehl
Vestal, New York
March 1993

TELEPHONE (212) 721-2600

STEINWAY & SONS
PIANO MAKERS
STEINWAY PLACE
LONG ISLAND CITY, N.Y. 11105

Mr. Harvey Roehl
Vestal Press
P. O. Box 97   May 21, 1976
3533 Stratford Drive
Vestal, N. Y. 13850

Dear Harvey:-

　　　This book by Arthur A. Reblitz fills a void that has
existed for too long a time. I realize that it is not possible to
cover in one volume every detail that might cause a problem in
servicing, but Mr. Reblitz' research and personal experience has
peculiarly endowed him to create a manual that can be very useful
to piano owners and piano service people everywhere.

　　　Of course, there is no way to supplant practice and
experience in acquiring any skill. This is particularly true in piano
technology. The best technicians have always learned by <u>doing</u>.
I feel, however, that this book can help the apprentice - either a
professional or an advanced amateur - to gain the kind of knowledge
that will make his practice or experience in this field more meaning-
ful. As such I recommend it highly.

John H. Steinway

s/m
John H. Steinway

Preface to the First Edition

Why this book? It's pretty easy to show with some estimates and statistics that there is plenty of room for improvement of piano service in the United States and elsewhere, and they make interesting reading.

When this book was first published in 1976, the American Music Conference judged that there were perhaps ten million pianos in American homes, businesses, and institutions — and new ones are being added at a rate of about 175,000 per year. In *The Piano Technicians Journal* about the same time, Editor James H. Burton estimates that there are about 5,000 technicians working in the U. S. who match the "Craftsman Member" qualifications of the Piano Technicians Guild, although only about half of these are members of that organization. It is further estimated, based on surveys within the Guild, that suggest that the average tuner who works full-time at the trade tunes about 750 instruments per year.

A little simple arithmetic with these figures, and it's quickly apparent that if every piano in the United States were to be tuned only once each year that it would take an army of 15 to 20 thousand technicians to do the work! This obviously means that a lot of pianos simply don't get serviced and tuned, and it also could mean that there's a lot of work available if there were a sufficient number of qualified people to do the work. And what the statistics don't show is what every good piano technician knows — that a lot of work is being done by persons who are in no way properly qualified to take money from an unsuspecting public for working on their instruments.

Against this obvious need for qualified technicians to service these many instruments, there's a surprising dearth of good published information on the subject. This book illustrates and describes many normal jobs that a technician has to do which, to the best of our knowlege, have never before been published in book form.

Fortunately, most piano technicians want to learn more about pianos and how to service them, because they know that it's a complex machine and a person can work on them for an entire lifetime and really not know everything there is to know. The active participation in workshops conducted by the Technician's Guild is ample evidence of this desire to learn more; this publisher hopes that the book will serve to assist all of those — from beginner to full-time professional — to learn whatever is in these covers that may have escaped him or her previously.

For every technician who is capable of "concert tuning and regulating" a fine grand piano to satisfy the critical demands for the public performance of a Van Cliburn or a Liberace, there are scores who would aspire to that level of technical competence. All that knowledge is not necessarily between the covers of this volume, but it's fair to say that most of it is, and the person who has mastered its contents is surely well on his way to becoming a master of his profession.

The modern piano is a surprisingly complex piece of apparatus considering that it is common in American homes, as well as elsewhere around the world. Not as complex as an automobile, perhaps, but in a way more mysterious—and certainly every bit as much of a challenge to understand and service properly. Broken down to its elements, it's a machine which behaves according to the rules of physics which pertain to it, as do all machines, and there's no reason why anyone willing to take some time to study its mechanisms can't learn to repair and tune it well. It's somewhat more complex than most machinery in the sense that it combines an unusual number of components which are subject to the vagaries of changing moisture content of the air and its temperature, as well as time itself, but there's no reason at all why a person with persistence, common sense, and a bit of mechanical aptitude cannot do this type of work.

If the insides of a piano seem a bit mysterious, perhaps it is because in past years some elements in the trade have tried to keep it that way in the mistaken notion that in so doing, those active in the field would somehow best secure their own employment. This publisher has taken quite the contrary view that the more people know about a subject, the more it will interest them; the more general interest there is about a given subject, the more everyone associated with the trade will benefit in the long run. This has proven quite true in the field of automatically played pianos. In recent years the rebuilding and servicing of these has been left almost entirely to hobbyists, and some of the finest examples of rebuilding craftsmanship imaginable have been done by people who have no intention of becoming workers in the piano trade — but who are completely content to take all the time necessary to put a one-time gorgeous instrument back to its original condition for their own personal satisfaction and enjoyment.

This book is intended to serve that market as well as those who make their living at the servicing and rebuilding of pianos, and without question the fact that thousands of hobbyists have been seeking facts about proper techniques to do this means that interest of the public in general will be strengthened where these instruments are concerned; the piano trade in general cannot but benefit as a result. This publisher is pleased to play a part in this, and hopes that this book will assist in some small way to elevate the standards of service of all pianos to their owners as well as to the music-loving public.

Harvey Roehl

Acknowledgments

The author wishes to thank the following individuals, both living and deceased, who have helped by sharing their knowledge of piano technology and in many other ways: Rick Baldassin, Nelson Barden, Bob Barns, Jerry Biasella, Q. David Bowers, James Bratton, Larry Broadmoore, Elmer Brooks (Aeolian Corporation), James Burton (past editor, *The Piano Technicians Journal*), Vince Cook (Kimball International, Inc.), Joseph Cossolini, George A. Defebaugh (Superior Imports Ltd.), Lynn Defebaugh Eames (Superior Imports, Ltd.), LaRoy Edwards (Yamaha Pianos), John Farnsworth, Chris Finger (Chris Finger Pianos), Tracy Fisher (The Piano Shop, Colorado Springs), Dan and Jerry Flanigan (The Colorado Springs Music Company), Don Galt (past technical editor, *The Piano Technicians Journal*), Donald J. Gass (The WurliTzer Company), Susan Graham (past technical editor, *The Piano Technicians Journal*), Nick Gravagne, Warren Groff (Groff Piano Company), Philip Gurlick, Henry Heller (Aeolian Corporation), Lew Herwig (The WurliTzer Company), Wayne Hicks (The Mapes Piano String Co.), John Hovancak, Jr., and Dana Johnson. Also, David Johnson and Herbert Johnson (both of Schaff Piano Supply Co.), David L. Junchen, Mike Kitner, Jack Krefting (past technical editor, *The Piano Technicians Journal*), Bob Lehrer (Aeolian Corporation), Thomas Marshall, Norman Neblett (Yamaha Pianos), Roy Newstadt (The WurliTzer Company), Jennifer Parks (Parks Piano Practitioners), Tremaine Parsons, David Ramey, Joel & Priscilla Rappaport, Calvin Rice (Schaff Piano Supply Co.), Dr. Albert Sanderson (Inventronics, Inc.), Ed Schadler (American Piano Supply Co.), Mel Septon, Don Shoffner, Willard Sims (Baldwin Piano and Organ Company), William T. Singleton, Stephen R. Smith (Dampp-Chaser Electronics Corp.), Harry J. Sohmer, Jr. (Sohmer and Co., Inc.), Richard S. Sorensen, Tom Sprague, Henry Z. Steinway and John H. Steinway (both of Steinway and Sons, Inc.), Neil Torrey, Tim Trager, John Trefz, Gerald Volk (Tuners Supply Company), Roger Weisensteiner (Kimball Piano and Organ Company), and to the many other professional technicians who have supported the Piano Technicians Guild by writing, teaching and sharing their methods, and helping to improve the quality of technicians everywhere.

Special thanks to Larry Fine (author of *The Piano Book*), Roger Hathaway, Rex Kennedy (The Piano Shop, Colorado Springs), Dr. Robert Gilson (Gilson Medical Electronics), Randy Potter (Randy Potter School of Piano Technology), Harvey Roehl, and Don Teach (Shreveport Music Co.) for reading the manuscript for the second edition and making many helpful, constructive suggestions regarding its content.

To Richard Howe and Harvey Roehl, for making their priceless collections of old literature available. Many of the fine old engravings and other illustrations were taken from their out-of-print catalogues of piano manufacturers that were out of business by the 1930's.

To John Ellingsen for his many line drawings. Some of the piano action drawings, drawn freehand, are so accurate that when the individual parts are cut out and rotated around their center pins, they actually stay in the correct relationship with each other. Also, to Robert Grunow for additional line drawings, Ginger and Donald Hein for taking and helping to pose the photographs in the section on soundboard rebuilding, to Harvey Roehl for taking many other photographs, to Willie Wilson for all photographs not otherwise attributed, and to Karen Bernardo of The Vestal Press for editing the manuscript and designing the layout.

To my wife Jeannie, for helping to proofread the manuscript at various stages to make sure nothing got lost or scrambled during the many steps between the first draft and final manuscript. To my parents, Eleanor and Fred Reblitz, for instilling in me the love of music and mechanical things at an early age, and for proofreading the manuscript for the first edition. And to my mother-in-law Grace Petzke for typing and retyping the manuscript for the first edition on a manual typewriter, before the era of home computers and word processing programs.

Finally, to Harvey Roehl for encouraging and helping the author during the writing of the first edition, and to Grace Houghton, for motivating the author to write this second one. Harvey deserves the gratitude of everyone who is interested in the piano and mechanical musical instruments, for establishing and making a success of Vestal Press. Grace deserves our appreciation for continuing the business since Harvey and his wife Marion have "retired." Without Harvey and Grace, this book would not exist.

Introduction

The piano is a complex musical instrument that uses mechanisms not found in any other device. Therefore, the piano technician must have specialized knowledge and use tools and techniques unique to the piano servicing field.

Many piano servicing problems that look difficult to the novice are really simple, given the correct tools, knowledge of procedure and some mechanical ability. Other problems are more difficult, and you shouldn't tackle them in a fine piano until you gain experience on lesser-quality instruments. This book should give the mechanically minded student the necessary knowledge of procedures and tools, with the insight to distinguish between those skills that may be put to use immediately (like regulating the soft pedal in an old upright) and those that should be practiced first (like putting new hammers in a concert grand). In addition, the author hopes that the experienced tuner-technician will be inspired to venture into new areas of repair and rebuilding that he or she has been avoiding due to lack of knowledge.

Piano tuning is a skill that is not necessarily related to musical ability. A professional musician usually analyzes tone subjectively, using a sense of relative pitch to compare one note to another: "That note sounds like G and is a little flat." The professional tuner, on the other hand, usually analyzes tone objectively, using mathematical rules to compare tones: "Note #1 is eight beats per second flat of note #2." This doesn't mean a fine ear for music doesn't help the tuner; the best

tuners use both types of listening to check their work. The fact that musical ability is not essential for piano tuning is only mentioned as a bit of encouragement to those who think they will never be able to tune a piano because they were not born with perfect pitch.

This book is divided into eight chapters. Chapter 1 introduces you to the various types and sizes of pianos made over the years. Chapter 2 describes the parts and mechanisms and explains how they work. Chapter 3 helps you to know what to look for in evaluating a piano. Chapter 4 takes you through the process of removing the action, cleaning the piano, and making minor repairs. Chapter 5 shows you how to regulate the action and pedals, to adjust everything to work as it should. Chapter 6 discusses the theory of tuning, and Chapter 7 teaches you how to tune. Chapter 8 takes you through the complete rebuilding of a piano.

No single book can discuss every facet of pianos and piano technology. This one takes you to the level at which you should be able to solve most problems associated with most pianos. It doesn't teach you how to alter the design or change the geometry of actions, redesign stringing scales, or make new soundboards and bridges. You should attempt these advanced procedures only under the guidance of someone experienced in these areas, after you have extensive experience with more ordinary piano repairing and rebuilding. Other books, listed in the

Bibliography, go into greater detail on action design, stringing scales, piano history, music theory, the science of acoustics, buying a new piano, and other topics. The Bibliography also includes books on cabinet refinishing.

Why a new edition of this book? When the Vestal Press published the first edition in 1976, the piano servicing field — at least in the United States — was one in which many professional technicians were "experienced amateurs," with little formal training or education. Since then, there have been significant developments in the field: several fine residence and correspondence schools have come into being. (The publisher and author are proud of the fact that many of them use this book as a text!) The Piano Technicians Guild has featured the world's leading independent technicians and manufacturers' representatives in regional meetings, seminars, and conventions. And many of them have written extensive articles for *The Piano Technicians Journal*, addressing topics ranging from soundboard theory and construction, action regulation, and improving tuning skills, to running a piano servicing business. Consequently, the level of piano servicing has improved significantly. The author has also had fifteen more years' experience, from concert tuning for the local symphony orchestra to completely restoring some of the most valuable orchestrions and reproducing pianos in the world to brand new condition. This new edition incorporates as much of this additional knowledge and experience as possible, while still holding the size of the book to a manageable size and keeping it within an affordable price range.

Throughout this book, most measurements are given in inches with the metric equivalent following in parentheses.

Often, the word "or" is used, as in 3/8" (or 10 mm.). This use of "or" is intended to mean that while the two dimensions are not exactly the same, each one is convenient and is precise enough for that application. When the author wrote the first edition, the spellings "whippen" and "wippen" were both in common use by other technicians. Since then, the Piano Technicians Guild, most piano manufacturers, and most other authors have standardized the spelling "wippen." To conform to convention, this edition uses that spelling throughout, although "whippen" will always seem correct to the author.

Every attempt has been made to indicate designs, processes, or brand names that are the trademarked property of specific companies by putting these names in quotes, boldface, or together with their manufacturer's names. Piano brands are obvious so they are not in quotes.

Always strive to improve your skills. Study every book and video tape you can find on pianos, piano technology, and repair — and woodworking too, if you are interested in rebuilding. Join the Piano Technicians Guild and read the *Journal*. Associate with other fine technicians. Ask a lot of questions. Try different methods and techniques, and see which ones work best for you. As you understand more and more about pianos, you'll become a better technician, you'll have more fun taking care of pianos, the quality of your piano servicing will improve, and everyone with whom you associate in the field of piano servicing — piano owners, musicians, and other technicians — will benefit.

Art Reblitz
Colorado Springs, Colorado
March 1993

PIANO SERVICING, TUNING, AND REBUILDING

Chapter One

Introduction to the Piano:
Styles, Shapes and Sizes

The piano is unique among keyboard instruments. Only the piano has hammers that strike tuned strings and rebound away from them, allowing the strings to vibrate and produce sustained musical tones. Each note has an **escapement** mechanism between the key and its hammer that releases the hammer from the key just before the hammer strikes the strings, allowing it to bounce away from the strings. The pianist may play softly or loudly by depressing the keys slowly or quickly, thus varying the intensity of the blows of the hammers on the strings.

Antique Pianos

Bartolomeo Cristofori (1655-1731) built the first practical piano that could be played either softly or loudly, with an escapement mechanism for the hammers, in the early 1700's. The name **piano** is an abbreviation of Cristofori's original name for the instrument — **piano et forte**, or soft and loud. The dramatic expressive capabilities of the piano set it apart from other keyboard instruments of Cristofori's time, including the harpsichord, in which the mechanism plucks the strings, and the clavichord, in which small brass "tangents" mounted directly on the back ends of the keys touch the strings lightly to produce a very soft, delicate tone. Because of its versatility, the piano has remained popular to this day as the fundamental keyboard instrument of both home and concert hall.

The period beginning with the invention of the piano in the 1700's and ending in the late 1800's saw much experimentation and frequent design change. Early pianos of one maker were radically different from those of another. By the late 1800's, these early designs had evolved toward an instrument whose basic features were similar to those of the modern piano. It is unusual today to find a piano manufactured prior to the 1860's or 1870's outside of a museum.

Victorian Pianos

By the late 1800's, factories were mass-producing pianos and retailing them at low enough prices that the public could afford to buy them. Piano cabinets of this period typically featured fancy carvings, fretwork, moldings, and ornate veneers. Today these instruments are known as "Victorian" pianos. Victorian pianos may be categorized into three main types: the **upright**, the **square** (also known as the **square grand**), and the **grand**. Most vertical pianos were uprights, with the strings and soundboard positioned vertically. Square pianos had a rectangular shape with the strings positioned horizontally and approximately parallel to the length of the keyboard. Grand pianos had the strings positioned horizontally, approximately at right angles to the length of the keyboard. The best Victorian uprights and grands were excellent pianos. Square pianos, despite their massive, ornate cabinets, had

lots of fancy "gingerbread."

1-3. A Victorian grand made by Steinway in 1857.

small soundboards and hammers. Their appearance was more impressive than their musical capability even when they were new. Victorian pianos used mass-produced, machine-made action parts, but replacement parts for many of these pianos have not been stocked by piano supply companies since the 1930's. Of the many Victorian pianos still in existence, the best are well worth careful restoration and preservation.

Twentieth-Century Pianos

By the early 1900's — the "Golden Age of the Piano" — the development of the piano as we know it today was practically complete. Square pianos were nearly extinct.

Grand and upright cabinets were streamlined, and "gingerbread" was eliminated. The mechanical design had progressed essentially to the point where it is today, incorporating high-tensile-strength steel wire strings strung on large heavy cast-iron frames, with large hammers and large soundboards.

A common promotional trick in the early 1900's was to call an upright an "**upright grand**" or "**cabinet grand**." Because the public tends to think of a grand as being of higher quality than a vertical, these fancy labels are meant to suggest that the piano has qualities typical of grands not found in ordinary verticals. Upon careful examination, a piano with one of these names bears no

1-2. A square piano. Still somewhat easy to find, these pianos look pretty in a Victorian setting, but are musically inferior to uprights and grands of the period.

1-4 (left). A modern Steinway concert grand.

1-6 (below). The upright action is mounted above the keyboard.

more resemblance to a grand piano than any other vertical does.

The 1930's marked the beginning of a trend toward smaller and smaller pianos. Large uprights evolved into smaller **studio uprights**, and **baby grands** less than 5'8" (173 cm.) in length became more popular. By the end of the 1940's, manufacturers mass marketed small **consoles** and smaller **spinets** to consumers who didn't have room for large, boxy uprights in their "modern" smaller apartments and homes.

1-5 (above). A large upright piano typical of those made between 1900 and 1930.

The height of the cabinet and the placement of the piano action in relation to the keyboard determine whether a vertical piano is an upright, studio upright, console, or spinet. In an upright piano the action is located a distance above the keys, requiring extensions called **stickers** to connect the keys to the action. Twentieth-century full-sized uprights nearly always have stickers.

The studio upright and console are of medium height, and usually have the action mounted directly over the keys without stickers. This is called a **direct–blow action**. The studio upright (also called the "professional upright" by many manufacturers) looks like a

1-7 (left). In most modern consoles, the action rests directly on the keys.

smaller version of a full-sized upright with a slanted front. Most studio uprights made since the 1950's are high-quality, durable pianos marketed mainly to schools, churches, and piano teachers. The console is slightly smaller than a studio upright, typically with the action made as short as possible while

1-8 (right and above). In most spinets, the drop action is partially below the keyboard.

still able to sit on top of the keys. Most console pianos have fancier cabinets, for the home market.

The spinet is the smallest vertical, usually with the action partially or completely below the keys. Most spinets have **drop actions** with **drop stickers** extending downward from the keys to connect them to the action. The tone quality of spinet pianos is inherently poor in the bass, due to the short bass strings. Also, the spinet action doesn't feel as solid as that of a console or upright because of the drop stickers. While higher-priced spinets are assembled carefully from good quality materials, average spinets are manu-

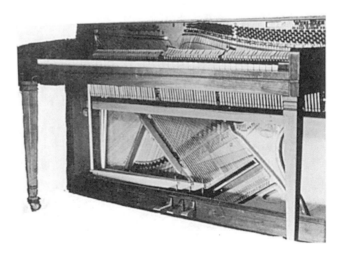

factured to satisfy consumer demand for instruments that are as small and inexpensive as possible.

Exceptions to the drop-action rule include a few spinets as short as 34" (including some Currier models) that incorporate a direct-blow **compressed action**, and certain consoles (including 40"- 41" Baldwin and Brambach models made in the late 1950's and early 1960's) that have drop actions.

In summary, a modern piano (one made since the early 1900's) is either a grand or a vertical. If a vertical, it is either an upright, a studio upright, a console, or a spinet. Most pianos made since the beginning of the 20th century use standardized action parts that are still available. A few, however, used experimental designs that are now obsolete. Millions of pianos made since the early 1900's, from the cheapest to the very best, are still around today. If a good quality piano is in a moderately good state of preservation, then it is worth repairing or restoring. Most of this book covers the servicing of modern pianos, but the text also describes specific

repairs for Victorian pianos where they differ from modern ones. The book doesn't include information on antique pianos because almost every one has its own unique design, because they are so infrequently encountered, and because their careful preservation is so important that their repair should be left to experienced technicians who specialize in historic instruments.

Player Pianos

Roll-operated player pianos have been an important part of the piano industry ever since their introduction in the 1890's. Hundreds of thousands made between 1910 and 1930, plus tens of thousands of modern pneumatic players made since the 1950's, still exist today. All piano technicians should understand at least enough about these instruments to tune and service the pianos without damaging the player mechanisms.

The first player piano was actually a **piano player** with primitive, bulky mechanisms built into a separate cabinet. Piano players, or **push-ups** as collectors call them today, were marketed between 1900 and 1905. In the words of Harvey Roehl in his book *Player Piano Treasury,* "The reason that [push-up] piano players were popular for only a few years is simply that in spite of their intrinsic worth they were . . . a clumsy contraption — clumsy to move up to the keyboard to play (great care was necessary so as not to break off the wooden fingers), a nuisance to have to take away when one wanted to play the piano by hand, and worst

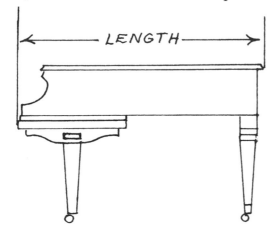

1-9. Piano sizes.

Grand Pianos, as measured from front of keyboard to back of lid, with lid closed (all dimensions approximate):

Shorter than 5'8" (173 cm.):	Baby Grand
Between 5'8" and 8'10" (173-269 cm.):	Grand
Longer than 8'10" (269) cm.):	Concert Grand

Vertical Pianos, as measured from the floor to the top of the lid (all dimensions are approximate):

Shorter than 38" (or 96.5 cm.):	Spinet
Between 38" and 44 (or 96.5 - 112 cm.):	Console
Between 44" and 51" (or 112 - 129.5 cm.):	Studio Upright or Professional Upright
Taller than 51" (or 129.5 cm.):	Upright

1-10. The most popular push-up piano player ever marketed in the United States: the Aeolian "Pianola."

of all, a device easily ignored and forgotten when once moved away from the piano."

Between 1905 and 1910 the player piano — with all the player mechanisms built into a cabinet slightly larger than an ordinary upright — replaced the push-up piano player. From then through the late 1920's, most piano companies manufactured large numbers of player pianos — so many that it is unusual today to find an ordinary non-

player piano made in the early 1920's. By the late 1920's, the radio and electronically amplified phonograph replaced the player piano as the latest home entertainment device, and player production ceased during the depression and war years of the 1930's and 1940's.

During the late 1950's, the public rediscovered player pianos, and several companies began manufacturing them again. Many old players had quit working, and it became all too common for piano technicians to rip out and discard the player mechanisms for no more reason than to make the piano action more accessible for servicing. Ironically, technicians destroyed many fine-quality old players while the public was eagerly buying inferior quality newer ones through the 1960's and 1970's. Fortunately, most technicians now realize that an old player piano is well worth preserving.

By 1914, several companies had **reproducing pianos** on the market that played with realistic expression by using specially recorded rolls and mechanisms. The most important brands in the United States — the Ampico, Duo-Art, and Welte-Mignon — were

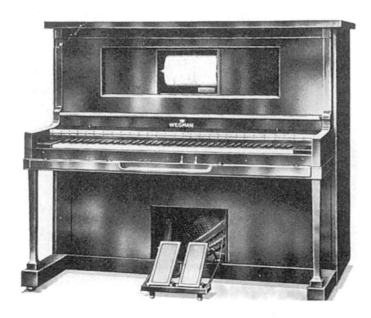

1-11. A typical 88-note upright player piano of the teens and twenties. Many hundreds of thousands still exist today.

1-12 (left). A Steinway Duo-Art grand reproducing piano of the 1920's, which plays automatically with lifelike expression.

1-13 (above). A Seeburg style KT keyboardless orchestrion, containing piano, mandolin attachment, and traps. This was one of the most popular orchestrions ever sold in America, but only a few hundred of them exist today.

installed in most brands of grand and upright pianos until the early 1930's. Much more rare and valuable than ordinary player pianos, enough reproducing pianos still exist today that conscientious piano technicians need to take the time to learn something about them. It is especially tragic when an ignorant tuner removes and discards the mechanisms from a rare reproducing piano such as a Steinway Duo-Art or Mason & Hamlin Ampico, considering their desirability to collectors today.

From the late 1800's through the late 1920's, the **coin–operated piano** and **orchestrion** (containing piano and additional instruments such as xylophones, organ pipes, and drums) were popular in public places. Today, these are even more rare and valuable than reproducing pianos. Their restoration should be attempted only by someone who has enough experience to do the work without damaging any of the parts.

1-14 (right). An extremely rare and beautiful Cremona style J orchestrion, circa 1913, restored in the author's shop in 1987. Its Egyptian-style case — with beautiful art glass, carved falcons and sphinxes — contains piano, mandolin attachment, organ pipes, orchestra bells, drums, and traps. Orchestrions are rare and valuable, and it is important for the technician to become expert at both piano work and pneumatic mechanisms before attempting their repair (Sanfilippo collection).

Player Piano Servicing and Rebuilding — the companion volume to this one by the same author — thoroughly covers the repair and restoration of player pianos.

Contemporary Trends

Throughout the 1970's and 1980's, the piano market changed dramatically when electronic keyboards began replacing inexpensive, low-quality pianos. Some manufacturers who specialized in mass marketing inexpensive pianos went out of business or sold out to other companies. Simultaneously, the demand for large uprights increased enough to enable several companies to put higher-quality large verticals back into production. So many electronic pianos are now in use that musicians often use the term "acoustic piano" to denote a conventional non-electronic instrument.

Electronic Pianos

Beginning in the late 1950's, several companies marketed mechanical/electronic pianos that were more portable than acoustic pianos and could be played through either loudspeakers or headphones. Some of these instruments stayed in tune longer than acoustic pianos. Since their introduction, the most popular brands marketed in America have been Baldwin, Kawai, Rhodes, WurliTzer, and Yamaha. Each of them incorporates a mechanical action with hammers and dampers. The tone is produced by tuned reeds in the WurliTzer; by strings but no soundboard in the Baldwin, Kawai, and Yamaha; and by tuned bars in the Rhodes. In all brands, vibration is sensed by electronic pickups and then amplified.

Servicing a mechanical/electronic piano often includes repairing the electronic components, a subject that is beyond the scope of this book. The same basic operating principles, and repair and regulating techniques for the keys and actions of acoustic pianos, are applicable to the mechanical parts of mechanical/electronic pianos. To obtain specific regulating and repair information for any of these instruments, consult the manufacturer or a technician who specializes in their repair.

In recent years, totally electronic pianos (or "electronic keyboards") without mechanical actions have become more sophisticated, less expensive, and more widely marketed. Their keyboards simulate the touch or "feel" of an acoustic piano, including the capability for both soft and loud playing. They have a variety of sounds — various piano tones, harpsichord, etc. — controlled by switches or stop tabs. Many are MIDI (Musical Instrument Digital Interface) compatible, meaning that it is possible to connect them with other sophisticated electronic and computerized musical instruments. Because of their electronic inner workings, their servicing is also outside the scope of this book.

Chapter Two

Inside Information:
The Names of Parts and How They Work

This chapter presents the names and functions of the important parts in a piano. A quick overview introduces the basic parts; then each part is discussed in greater detail, explaining what its function is and how it works. Many topics are treated more thoroughly in later chapters. While this chapter, for example, explains what the function of a pinblock is and how an action works, the chapter on restoration explains the advantages and disadvantages of various types of pinblock materials, and the chapters on regulating and repairing cover many more details on all aspects of piano actions. This chapter provides you with the fundamentals and vocabulary for a clear understanding of the later chapters.

Major Parts

A piano's foundation is its **frame**, or **skeleton** in a grand, usually made of wood, but sometimes made of a combination of timbers and steel or iron bars. The frame or skeleton is visible from the back of a vertical piano and from the bottom of a grand. It helps to support the tons of tension exerted by the stretched steel piano strings and to hold the cabinet together. In a grand piano, the shorter **inner rim** and taller **outer rim** glued around it form the main part of the cabinet. The inner rim, visible from the bottom, has the soundboard and pinblock attached to its top edge. The outer rim extends several inches farther upward and,

with the lid, provides an enclosure for the plate and strings.

The **soundboard** is a large wooden diaphragm that the strings cause to vibrate, thus increasing their volume. It is glued to

2-1. The wooden frame of a large upright, viewed from the front, with the pinblock installed, before installation of the soundboard.

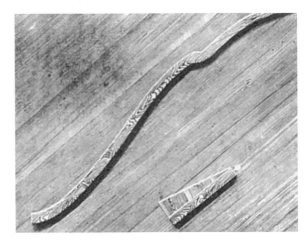

2-2 (left). The frame and rim of a small grand piano as viewed from the bottom with the soundboard and keybed installed. Larger grands have more wooden posts to withstand the tremendous tension of the strings. The inner rim in this piano is lighter color while the outer rim has a dark finish on it. The perimeter of the soundboard is glued to the top edge of the inner rim.

2-3 (above). Front view of upright soundboard with long treble bridge and shorter bass bridge attached.

the inner rim in a grand, or the **liner** in a vertical, around its edges only. This leaves the largest possible area free to vibrate. The front of the soundboard in a vertical or top in a grand, has wooden **bridges** attached to it, connecting it to the strings. The back of the soundboard has wooden **ribs** glued to it which add strength and help the soundboard maintain its proper shape.

Mounted above the soundboard in a vertical piano (and in front of it in a grand) is the **pinblock.** To the novice, this is a mysterious part of a piano because most of it is invisible in the fully assembled piano. The cast-iron **plate** fits over the pinblock and soundboard, as illustrated. Anchored in holes in the pinblock and protruding through the plate are steel **tuning pins.** One end of each string is attached to a tuning pin. From there, each string passes through various guides on the plate and over the soundboard bridges to a steel **hitch pin** embedded firmly in the plate.

If all strings were of the same thickness and under the same tension, high C would be about two inches (51 mm.) long, and low C would have to be over twenty feet (over 6

2-4. Rear view of upright soundboard, with ribs glued in place.

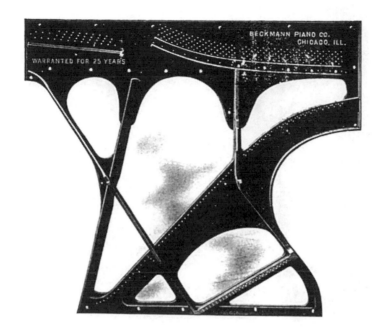

2-5 (left). A cast-iron plate for a large upright piano.

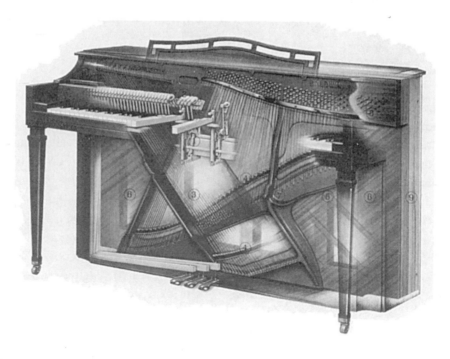

2-6. Basic construction of the vertical piano: (1) action, (2) hammers, (3) strings, (4) bridges, (5) ribs, (6) soundboard, (7) plate, (8) pinblock, (9) back, (10) cabinet.

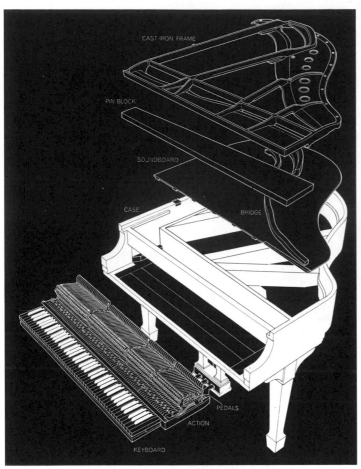

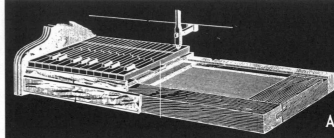

2-7 (left). Exploded view of a grand piano, showing basic construction. Copyright © 1965 by Scientific American, Inc., from "The Physics of the Piano" by E. Donnell Blackham.

2-8 (above). The vertical piano keybed.

m.) long. In an actual piano of practical length, the bass strings have wrappings of copper or iron wire wound around the core wire to make them heavier. The extra weight of the wrapping or **winding** slows the vibration of the wire to the correct rate without adding excessive stiffness. These strings are manufactured on a special machine that resembles a lathe.

In a vertical piano, the frame, soundboard, bridges, and pinblock form the **back.** With the plate and strings installed, this unit becomes the **strung back,** ready to be installed in the **cabinet.** In a grand piano, the **rim** contains these parts, and it also forms the main body of the cabinet.

Securely fastened to the rim or cabinet is the **keybed,** which provides firm support for the **keyboard** and **action.** The keybed is

made of thick planks solidly fastened together. It is either constructed in one large, glued-together piece, usually with expansion joints, or utilizing a heavy frame with lighter inset panels. The keybed is screwed and sometimes glued to the cabinet.

Sitting on the keybed is the action, which is a series of levers starting with the key — the link with your finger — and ending with the hammer, the felt-covered piece of wood that strikes the string to produce the tone. The action enables you to play loudly or softly and to repeat notes as quickly or slowly as the music dictates. If a piano hammer were attached directly to the back end of a key, the hammer would hit the string and stay there when the key was depressed, damping out the vibration and sound. Instead, all piano actions have some type of

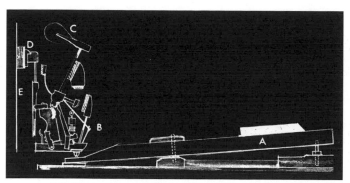

2-9. Basic parts of the vertical piano action: (A) key, (B) escapement, (C) hammer, (D) damper, (E) string.

escapement mechanism for each key that allows the hammer to be released just before it hits the string. After the escapement releases the hammer, it continues to move under its own inertia, strikes the string, and rebounds. When the key is released, the action returns to its original position and resets itself for another cycle.

For each key and hammer in the piano, except in the high treble, there is also a **damper**. When the key is at rest, the felt damper rests on the key's strings, preventing them from vibrating. When the key is depressed, the damper lifts from the strings, allowing them to vibrate. When the key is released, the damper returns to the strings, deadening the vibrations and stopping the sound. In the high treble, the main body of tone dies away so quickly that no dampers are necessary to prevent one note from blurring into the next. The high treble also lends a little extra brilliance to the tone quality of the piano by the sympathetic vibrations of these undamped strings.

Most pianos have two or three pedals. The right pedal is always the **sustaining pedal**. It raises all of the dampers at once, allowing all notes that you play as well as the sympathetic vibrations of all unstruck strings to continue sounding after the keys are released.

The left pedal is always some type of **soft pedal**. In vertical pianos and some inexpensive grands, it moves the hammers at rest closer to the strings, decreasing the distance that they travel, and thus their striking force. In good-quality grands, the soft pedal, or **una corda pedal**, shifts the entire action sideways. This causes the treble hammers to hit only two of their three strings, mellowing the tone quality and diminishing the volume.

If a piano has a third pedal, it is always between these two. In most good-quality grands and a few fine-quality verticals, this is the **sostenuto** pedal. It sustains only those notes whose keys you hold down *prior to* and *while* you push the pedal down; it doesn't sustain any notes played after the pedal is depressed. The sostenuto enables you to hold down certain keys with your fingers, sustain their sound with the pedal, release the keys, and then play other notes without having them sustained and blurred with the previous notes. In a way, the sostenuto is almost like a third hand for advanced pianists, useful for playing sophisticated classical and popular music.

In medium-priced and inexpensive grands and a few verticals, the middle pedal is the **bass sustaining pedal**. This type of pedal lifts only the bass dampers, allowing you to play one or more bass notes, and while the pedal sustains them, use both hands in the treble without blurring the sound of the treble notes. Musically speaking, this pedal is a cheap substitute for a sostenuto pedal.

In some verticals, the middle pedal is a **practice pedal**, which lowers a thick piece of felt between the hammers and strings, muffling the tone. In others, the middle pedal is coupled to the left-hand soft pedal, or connected to nothing at all.

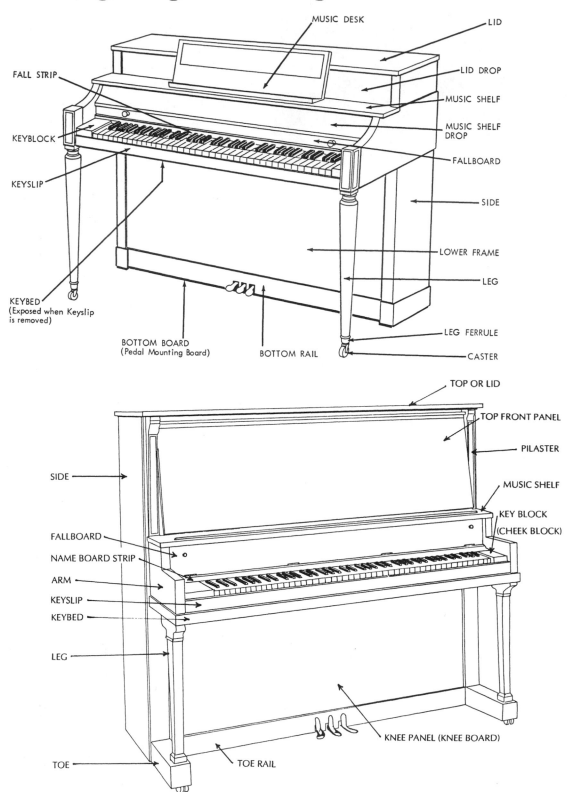

MUSIC DESK

LID

FALL STRIP

LID DROP

MUSIC SHELF

MUSIC SHELF DROP

KEYBLOCK

FALLBOARD

KEYSLIP

SIDE

LOWER FRAME

LEG

KEYBED
(Exposed when Keyslip is removed)

LEG FERRULE

BOTTOM BOARD
(Pedal Mounting Board)

BOTTOM RAIL

CASTER

TOP OR LID

TOP FRONT PANEL

PILASTER

SIDE

MUSIC SHELF

KEY BLOCK
(CHEEK BLOCK)

FALLBOARD

NAME BOARD STRIP

ARM

KEYSLIP

KEYBED

LEG

KNEE PANEL (KNEE BOARD)

TOE

TOE RAIL

2-10. Vertical piano cabinet nomenclature. For a very thorough treatment of this subject, refer to Merle Mason's *Piano Parts and Their Functions,* listed in the Bibliography.

16

2-11. Richard Schoolmaster gluing ribs to a new soundboard for a small grand piano in the now defunct Aeolian-American piano factory. The long, wooden clamping bars, or go-bars, each exert up to 200 lb. of clamping force.

Details of Construction

The Soundboard and Bridges

The ideal wood for a soundboard is Sitka spruce planed to about 3/8" (9.5 mm.) thick. This wood has the ideal balance of stiffness and flexibility. Softer wood absorbs vibrations like a sponge while harder wood is too rigid to vibrate properly.

Soundboard makers glue spruce boards about four to six inches wide (10-15 cm.) side-by-side, making a blank of the desired width. The blank is cut to the right size, planed to the proper thickness, and dried to a low moisture content. Then it is placed face down on concave supports, and ribs are glued to the back side running approximately at right angles to the grain of the soundboard. Clamping pressure forces the board and ribs to assume the shape of the concave supports. Viewed from the front, this convex shape is the **crown** of the board.

After the glue is dry, factory technicians (known as **operators**) attach the bridges to the front of the soundboard. The entire assembly is then glued to the inner rim (grand) or soundboard liner (vertical) of the piano. As the new dry board absorbs moisture from the atmosphere, it swells and bows upward a little more, gaining additional crown. The crowned shape helps to maintain compression within the soundboard, making it more vibrant, and keeping it from caving in under pressure from the strings.

In modern grands, the inner rim is made of hardwood, which forms the best foundation for maximum soundboard efficiency and a brilliant tone in the high treble. Many Victorian grands made through the late 1800's had softer inner rims, which contributed to a dull-sounding high treble. Most solid spruce soundboards in modern pianos are thinner around the perimeter for greater flexibility, except around the top end of the treble bridge where greater stiffness is desirable. Steinway's name for a soundboard with this shape is the **diaphragmatic soundboard.**

2-12. A new Mason & Hamlin 9' (274 cm.) concert grand inner rim prior to installation of soundboard and outer rim, showing the *tension resonator.*

2-13. Soundboard buttons.

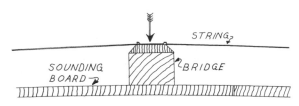

2-14. Ideally, strings have downbearing against the string, in the direction of the arrow. Note the soundboard crown and the angle of the string passing over the top of the bridge.

Extremes of humidity and dryness cause a solid spruce soundboard to expand and contract, and may cause cracks along the grain. To avoid this problem, some manufacturers use **laminated** (plywood) soundboards, which are guaranteed not to crack for the life of the piano. In small spinets and consoles, the tone quality is approximately the same whether the soundboard is solid spruce or plywood. In larger pianos a solid spruce board sounds better, even when cracked, unless loose glue joints at the ribs, liner or rim cause it to rattle or buzz.

Mason & Hamlin pianos incorporate a device known as the **tension resonator,** invented by Richard Gertz in 1900. This assembly of rods and turnbuckles prevents the rim from spreading, helping the soundboard to maintain its crown for a long time. Some Cable pianos (and possibly other brands) also use a less elaborate version of the tension resonator. The technician should never adjust the turnbuckles, except possibly during major restoration that includes extensive soundboard repair or replacement.

Some pianos have a wooden bar or strip called a **harmonic trap** attached to the back of several ribs. The trap helps to suppress undesirable harmonics, ringing, and other extraneous sounds.

Bridges are made of hardwood — usually hard maple or beech — and are fastened to the front of the soundboard with glue and screws. Each screw head passes through a wooden washer called a **soundboard button** that prevents the screw from cracking the soundboard.

In order for piano strings to vibrate the soundboard efficiently, they must press on the bridges with slight downward pressure called **downbearing**. The amount of crown in the board and the amount of downbearing directly influence tone quality and volume. Too little bearing causes a long-sustained but weak tone, while too much causes a loud tone that fades away quickly. To some extent, the more crown a soundboard has, the more downbearing the strings should have on it.

To conserve space and fit the longest possible bass strings into a cabinet, modern pianos have the bass strings crossing diagonally over the treble strings in an **overstrung** pattern. The treble and bass bridges are separate in most overstrung pianos, although in many large grands, the two bridges are connected to help strengthen the soundboard.

The top of the bridge has rows of copper-plated steel **bridge pins,** staggered and inserted at angles, which give the strings **side bearing** and hold them tightly so that they will solidly contact the bridge and pass their vibrations through it into the soundboard. To permit the most efficient transmis-

2-15. Left, a Broadwood grand piano made in the late 1800s with straight stringing. Below, line drawing showing how the bass strings cross over the treble strings in an overstrung piano. This design allows maximum string length in a given cabinet size.

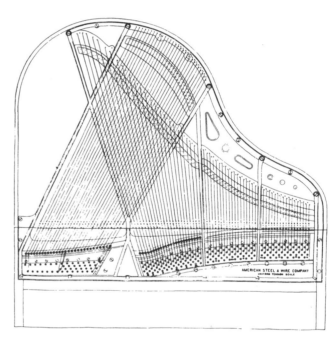

sion of string vibrations into the soundboard, the bridge is only as large as necessary in order to hold the bridge pins in place without cracking. In a good-quality piano, the bridge edges have notches precisely located along the center line of the pins, and perpendicular to the length of the strings, so that the pins effectively terminate the vibrating portion of the strings at the same length in all planes of rotation, and all strings of each unison have exactly the same length.

Treble bridges can be solid, laminated, or have a horizontally oriented top layer called a **cap**. Steinway and Baldwin grand pianos incorporate laminated bridges with the layers of wood oriented vertically; Steinway adds a cap, while Baldwin doesn't. Most average quality pianos have solid wood bridges — either capped or uncapped — with the grain of the main body of the bridge oriented vertically. All of these types of bridges transmit vibration well from the strings into the

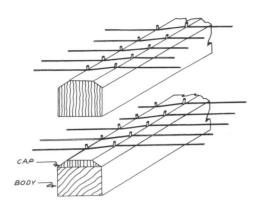

2-16. Uncapped and capped solid wood bridges.

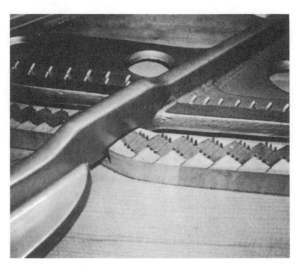

2-18. This upright bridge is notched for the plate strut, seriously weakening the bridge and soundboard, and contributing to tuning instability and loss of crown.

soundboard. Solid wood bridges crack more often than laminated ones do if they are subjected to wide swings of humidity and dryness, or if the strings have too much side bearing on the bridge pins. Laminated bridges with the layers oriented horizontally don't transmit vibration as well.

For the best bass tone quality, the bass strings should be as long as possible, with the bass bridge located close to the bottom of an upright or the back rim of a grand. Unfortunately, the soundboard doesn't vibrate well near the edge. To maximize bass string length without having the bass bridge glued too near the edge of the soundboard, many pianos have the bridge mounted on a **shelf** or **apron** that transmits the string vibrations to a more flexible part of the board.

In high quality pianos, the plate braces, or **struts**, pass over the bridges. In small and inexpensive pianos, the treble bridge has a large notch to allow the strut to pass through it without touching. This notch weakens the bridge and soundboard, causing tuning instability in the strings immediately surrounding it. The soundboard also may eventually lose its crown in the area of the notch, with consequent loss of downbearing and tone quality. Some pianos have a piece of wood glued behind the notch on the back of the sound-

2-17. An offset or shelf bass bridge in a Seeburg upright.

2-19. This grand plate strut passes over the top of the bridge, eliminating the need for notching.

board which supposedly compensates somewhat for this weakness.

The Pinblock

The **pinblock** is a laminated hardwood plank, with the grain of the various layers running at different angles to each other to support the tuning pins without cracking. The pins usually extend into the pinblock about 1¼" (32 mm.) deep. The block must hold them tightly enough to keep them from turning under string tension, but not so tightly that they can't be turned smoothly by the tuner. Many old uprights have three ¼" (6.4 mm.) layers of hard maple backed by one thicker layer. Most grands and modern verticals have five or more layers, each layer ³/16" to ¼" (4.8 — 6.4 mm.) thick. Baldwin and a few other manufacturers usc pinblock material known as "Falconwood™" which has many very thin layers (see illus. 2-21.) Chapter 8 includes further discussion of various types of pinblock material.

In all vertical pianos the pinblock is glued to the front surface of the back structure. The bottom edge of the pinblock overhangs the front of the top of the soundboard, as

seen at the extreme treble end of the piano in illus. 2-6. This overhang mates with a flange cast into the back of the plate. Large screws hold the plate to the pinblock and back frame structure. This forms a sandwich, with the pinblock supported by the tuning pin area of the plate, the flange and back frame, but not by the soundboard. The better the parts fit together, the better the piano will stay in tune. This arrangement helps distribute the string tension evenly over the entire pinblock into the frame and plate, resulting in the best tuning stability and greatest structural integrity. With the cabinet sides glued to the back, and the keybed and bottom installed, the entire structure strengthens the back against twisting.

In many older uprights, including most Victorian uprights, the plate only comes up to the bottom of the pinblock. Technicians call this type of piano a **half plate** or **three-quarter plate** piano. Although the top of the plate does help to support the string tension, the screws and glue hold the pinblock to the back frame. Some piano builders installed a separate plate over the pinblock to help keep it from coming unglued. In the 1890's, some manufacturers believed that three-quarter

2-20 (left). A small piece of conventional grand piano pinblock blank, showing the cross-grain laminations of hard maple.

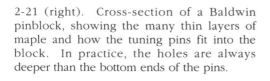

2-21 (right). Cross-section of a Baldwin pinblock, showing the many thin layers of maple and how the tuning pins fit into the block. In practice, the holes are always deeper than the bottom ends of the pins.

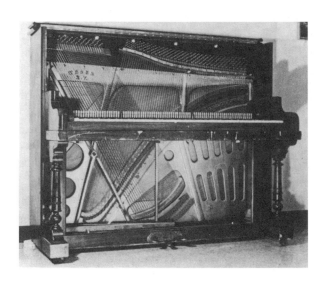

2-22. A beautiful Victorian Weber upright with action removed to illustrate the three-quarter plate. The pinblock in this piano has survived the years better than most normally do.

2-23. The plate with pinblock attached, removed from a small grand piano, and viewed from the bottom.

plate pianos sounded better than full plate pianos. This was possibly due to the smaller plate absorbing less vibration. But the greater durability provided by a full plate offset the slight loss — if any — in tone quality; eventually the full plate won out. As piano manufacturers made further improvements, any loss there might have been in tone quality was more than regained by the employment of higher tension stringing scales and other design improvements.

In a grand piano, the skeleton ends under the front edge of the soundboard, leaving a large cavity for the action (see illus. 2-7). A grand plate lacks the heavy support behind the pinblock provided by the back structure in an upright. So the grand plate must be much heavier in this area with a much larger flange extending down to support the entire thickness of the pinblock.

In a good-quality piano, the back edge of the pinblock mates closely with the flange for tuning stability. If the pinblock fits poorly,

the piano won't stay in tune as well. At worst, if the pinblock touches the flange only at a "high point" near the middle, it will rock back and forth during tuning, making it impossible to fine-tune the piano. In many grands, several long screws fasten the ends of the pinblock to the inner rim, and many small ones hold it tightly to the plate. Other grands have the pinblock attached only to the plate, and not the rim. In this type, the plate, pinblock, and strings may be lifted out of the piano in one piece by simply removing the perimeter screws, loosening the strings, and lifting them off the bridge. Some Mason & Hamlins also have the front of the block glued to the stretcher. Steinway grands have the front edge of the pinblock glued and doweled to the stretcher, and the ends of the block mortised into the rim and glued to it, all contributing to greater tuning stability.

Many Victorian grands have a three-quarter plate, with the pinblock mortised into the rim. In some of these pianos, the top of the

2-24. Looking up under the bottom of the pinblock in a small Cable grand, as viewed from the area normally occupied by the action.

pinblock slopes downward from the cornice to the plate. Replacing a sloped pinblock is much more difficult than replacing a simple modern one.

The Plate

Older Victorian pianos made prior to the introduction of large one-piece castings have an assembly of steel bars and plates bolted together. These are strong enough to support the string tension of those instruments, which is much lower than that in modern pianos. All modern pianos have a single piece cast-iron plate designed to support many tons of string tension, with the help of the wooden frame. (Exceptions are a few rare pianos made in the 1930's and 1940's with cast aluminum plates). Cast-iron is brittle and has little tensile strength, but it has enormous compressive strength, and it is this quality that makes it so useful for piano plates. The average upright or medium-sized grand has about 230 strings, each under about 160 pounds (72.7 kg.) of tension, with the combined pull totaling approximately eighteen tons (16,300 kg.). The tension in a concert grand is close to thirty tons (27,180 kg.).

In any piano, the plate must hold everything together under enormous compression, opposing the high tension of the strings. At the same time, it must permit the strings and soundboard to vibrate freely without absorbing and deadening too much of the vibration. To support the string tension without deadening the tone, the plate touches the soundboard around its perimeter only where the screws fasten it to the inner rim; it doesn't touch the soundboard anywhere else.

In most modern grand pianos, dowels or large screws in the inner rim support the plate around its perimeter, holding it up off the soundboard and allowing for some adjustment of downbearing; other large screws hold it down. In Baldwin grands having the threaded perimeter-bolt plate suspension system, the holes in the plate are threaded, and the plate is suspended by large hex-head bolts threaded through the plate and into the inner rim.

In vertical pianos, the plate rests on the entire face of the pinblock and the perimeter of the soundboard. Some verticals have wooden shims between the perimeter of the plate and the soundboard. Others have small lugs cast into the back of the plate only where the screws go through it, reducing the contact area between cast-iron and soundboard. In some older Victorian grands, shims support the plate under its entire perimeter, deadening the tone somewhat.

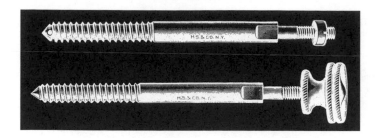

2-25. Nose bolts, with two styles of nuts.

Most pianos, both vertical and grand, also have one or more **nose bolts** and nuts. These support the midsection of the plate, where it would bend or break if left unsupported. The factory technician who installs the plate in the piano adjusts the height of each nose bolt so the plate doesn't bend when the nut is tight. Some grands also have an additional nose bolt attached to a hollow iron casting called a **bell** or **plate-rim support** under the high treble part of the soundboard. Fastened to the rim and extending inward, the bell supports the plate in an area where there is no other support for a nose bolt. *The purpose of the nose bolts is to support the plate, not to give the tuner a means of bending the plate down to increase downbearing on the bridges.*

The plate has a variety of guide pins and other supports to hold the strings in place. The upright plate usually has a **v-bar** or **bearing bar** formed into the casting. This bar terminates the speaking length of the treble strings at the top end. Firm contact at the termination point of the speaking length is necessary for good tone quality. The **pressure bar** holds the strings against the v-bar with enough force to prevent buzzing or other undesirable noises. It also keeps the strings from slipping sideways. Taut steel wire sometimes deforms the cast-iron of the v-bar. To prevent this problem, some pianos

2-26. Left: Plate support bolts (A) and nose bolts (B) in a Chickering grand. These support the plate so that it doesn't touch the soundboard. Right: a wooden shim between the plate and soundboard in an old Seeburg upright.

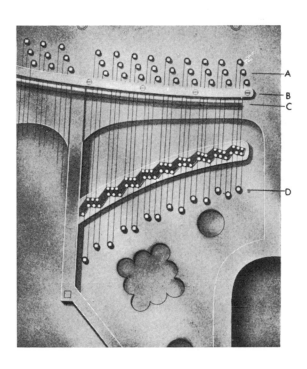

2-27. Details of the vertical piano plate: (A) tuning pins, (B) pressure bar, (C) V-bar, (D) hitch pins.

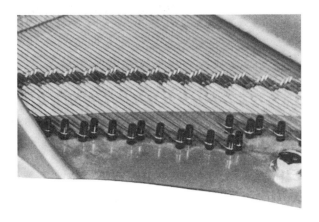

2-28. Baldwin "Acu-Just" hitch pins.

have a nickel-plated steel rod called the **bearing wire** resting in a groove in the v-bar. The bearing wire forms the termination point for the strings.

The treble strings pass over the treble bridge and then loop around **hitch pins.** These are steel pins inserted tightly into holes drilled in the plate at an angle to hold the strings against the plate. In many older pianos, a strip of felt dresses the plate near the edge, inboard of the hitch pins where the strings rest on it, to suppress undesirable noise. Since this felt holds moisture, causing rust in high humidity areas, most newer pianos have no felt here. Baldwin pianos made after the late 1960's have hitch pins made of slotted tubular steel and mounted at a 90° angle to the strings. Called "**Acu-Just**" hitch pins, they allow the height of each string to be adjusted separately for optimum downbearing.

In most vertical pianos, the plate has a **bass top bridge** or **nut**, which supports the top ends of the bass strings under the tuning pins. The top bridge is usually part of the plate casting; it has guide pins that terminate the speaking length of the strings and keep them spaced correctly. Partial plate pianos have a separate wood or metal bass top bridge piece attached to the face of the pinblock. The bass top bridge is thick enough to provide clearance for the bass strings where they cross over the treble strings. The strings have enough downbearing on the bass top bridge so a pressure bar is usually unnecessary. In most pianos, each individual bass string is attached to its own hitch pin with a loop tied in the end of the wire.

Some vertical pianos have individual fittings called **agraffes** screwed into threaded holes in the plate; each agraffe holds the strings for one note. The agraffes take the place of the pressure bar, and provide a more solid termination point for the speaking lengths of the strings, contributing to better tone quality and tuning stability.

In a grand piano, the hammers try to push the strings upward, so the termination

2-29. Agraffes for single, double, and three-string unisons.

point must hold them firmly in place. (This is in contrast to a vertical piano, in which the v-bar simply provides a rest for the strings.) Good-quality grand plates have agraffes for this purpose throughout most of the scale, with a **capo bar** in the highest section where there isn't enough room for agraffes. The capo bar holds the strings down from above like a huge pressure bar. Less expensive grands have a capo bar throughout, with no agraffes.

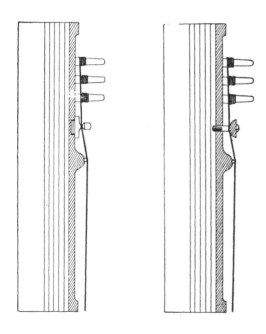

2-30. Cross-sections of vertical pianos fitted with agraffes (left) and a pressure bar (right).

Downbearing

The right amount of string downbearing on the bridges is critical to good tone quality. The height of string-bearing surfaces on the plate — the v-bar, agraffe, capo bar, and hitch pin areas — in relation to the height of the bridges determines the amount of downbearing. With too much downbearing, the tone is loud but of short duration; with too little, the tone has a longer sustain time but is thin and weak. Excessive downbearing on the bass bridge can restrict the movement of the soundboard so much that it actually deadens the tone of the high treble.

Even the most careful plate casting methods traditionally have produced plates whose dimensions, while very similar, were not identical from one plate to the next. Also, soundboards have tended to vary from one piano to the next in their amount of crown after being installed. These two significant variables make it necessary for a fine-quality piano to have its string downbearing adjusted during installation of the plate. In the finest-quality instruments, each bridge or bridge cap is left unnotched and a little

2-31. The capo bar, an integral part of many grand plates.

thicker than necessary (in the dimension from soundboard to string-bearing surface), until after the plate is installed. Then the factory technician holds test strings in place temporarily to find the correct bridge height for optimum downbearing. Finally, the technician carefully planes the bridge or cap to the finished height, finishes the notches, drills the bridge pin holes, and installs the pins. The piano is finally ready to be strung. In most medium priced and inexpensive pianos, the factory technician installs and finishes the bridge before installing the plate. The technician then adjusts the plate height for optimum downbearing by adjusting the height of the perimeter supports and nose bolts. In any piano, it is important for the plate to be supported uniformly without any high or low spots, so that nothing bends or twists when the technician tightens the plate screws.

In grands having the pinblock attached only to the plate, or screwed but not glued to the inner rim, shims are inserted between the bottom of the block and the top of the inner rim for a tight fit after the correct plate height is determined. In fine-quality grands with the pinblock glued or doweled to the stretcher or rim, the installer shapes the pinblock and glues it to the case after determining the plate height, because once the pinblock is glued in, its height is no longer adjustable. The assembly procedure involves installing and removing the plate several times to ensure that everything has the best possible fit. Vertical pianos have little flexibility of downbearing adjustment, due to the large surface area of the pinblock and the large number of screws holding the plate to it.

During the 1980's several manufacturers introduced a vacuum-casting process, resulting in plate castings that are more uniform from one to the next than was possible with traditional casting techniques. Combined with careful selection of wood for soundboards and careful humidity control during soundboard manufacture, the precision plate castings provide more uniform and predictable tonal results in pianos with mass produced, machine made bridges.

The Tuning Pins

Tuning pins come in various sizes and several types, including blued steel, nickel-plated, and combination nickel-plated/blued. Each pin has fine threads on the portion held by the pinblock. The top end has a hole called the **eye** to hold the end of the music wire, and a tapered square head to fit a tuning lever. Most old pianos have blued steel tuning pins, which rust if exposed to high humidity. Nickel-plated pins don't rust as easily but don't hold as tightly in the pinblock because the plating makes the fine threads dull. The best pins are combination nickel-plated/blued, with plating on the exposed end, and unplated blued threads. Some pins have rolled threads that are smooth, and others have cut threads that are rougher. Rough threads might hold a little tighter in a new pinblock, but with frequent tuning, rough threads could conceivably wear out the pinblock sooner.

Each string is wound neatly around the tuning pin three times, forming three neat coils. The end of the wire, bent over and inserted into the eye of the pin, is called the **becket.** In many inexpensive pianos the end of the wire extends out from the opposite side of the pin and is bent over. This locks the wire to the pin and keeps it from slipping out of the pin during high speed mass-production processes. This extra bend makes it harder to remove the broken piece of wire from a tuning pin when the string breaks. In high-quality pianos, the well-formed beckets don't slip, even without the extra bend.

In some pianos, the plate has oversized holes for the tuning pins to pass through. In others, wood **tuning pin bushings** line the holes and fit snugly around the pins. These bushings provide a little extra tightness and support for the pins, helping to keep them from flexing or bending, particularly during tuning.

Modern Bösendorfer grands have tapered tuning pin holes in the pinblock, with regular cylindrical tuning pins. If it becomes necessary to drive the pins a little deeper to tighten them in an older piano, the tapered holes add a little extra grip.

In the early 1900's, Mason & Hamlin built many pianos — both grands and verticals — known today as **screw stringers**, in which each string is tied to a threaded hook instead of a tuning pin. The hooks are mounted in a metal supporting framework. Each hook has an adjustable tuning nut, and the strings are tuned by turning the nuts with a special Mason & Hamlin tuning wrench.

A few old WurliTzer vertical pianos have a thinner-than-usual back, with the tuning pin holes drilled all the way through. The back ends of the pins are split and have wedges driven into them. Presumably by driving the wedges in, the pins can be tightened. This feature was used only for a short time and is encountered only rarely today.

Another oddity is the Wegman piano built in the early 1900's, with no tuning pin holes in the pinblock. Instead, the plate webbing in the tuning pin area is thicker than usual, and each tuning pin hole in the plate is slightly oblong, with the lower end (in an upright) narrower than the tuning pin. The stubby tuning pins are anchored tightly in place by the string tension locking them into the plate holes.

The Strings

The **pitch** of a musical tone is expressed in **hertz**, or **hz** —named after the nineteenth-century German physisist Heinrich Hertz — the number of cycles per second of the sound waves producing it. Simple laws of physics dictate that several factors influence

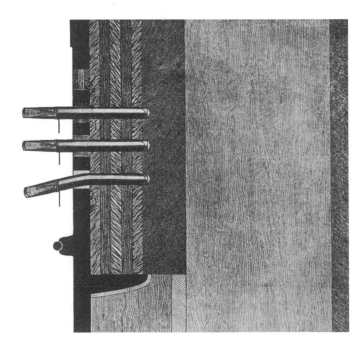

2-32. A greatly exaggerated drawing showing the merits of tuning pin bushings. The upper two pins have them, and the lower pin doesn't.

the fundamental pitch of a vibrating string, including its length, diameter, tension, density, and stiffness. The pitch goes down as the length *increases*, the diameter *increases*, or the tension *decreases*. In our musical scale, the pitch in hz of any note is twice that of the same note an octave lower, or half that of the same note an octave higher. The note A above middle C vibrates at 440 hz.

Theoretically, if a piano had all plain steel strings of the same diameter, with each string under the same tension, and the strings for high C had their usual length of approximately two inches, low C — seven octaves lower — would have to be seven times as long, or over twenty-one feet long, making the piano impractical to build and house. Or, if a piano had a practical length, with high C about two inches and the lowest bass string six or eight feet long, with all the strings of the same diameter, then the lowest strings would need far less tension, causing them to have a very weak, soft tone with badly out-of-tune harmonics. Or, if the same piano had high C about two inches long and the lowest bass strings six or eight feet long, with all strings under the same tension, then the diameter of solid bass strings would have to be so large that they would act and sound more like steel rods or bars than vibrating strings, due to excessive stiffness. Also, it would be impractical to put a solid wire of that large a diameter under enough tension to achieve the desired pitch.

For a bass string to have enough mass to produce a low pitch under high tension without being too long or stiff, the plain steel core wire has one or two windings of copper wire wrapped around it. The windings enable bass strings in large pianos to have enough mass, tension, and flexibility to produce a powerful sound with good tone quality; they enable small pianos to produce at least some semblance of piano tone.

The string maker wraps the winding on the core wire in a machine resembling a lathe, which holds the core wire under tension so the winding will stay tight after the technician installs the new string in the piano and pulls it up to pitch. Most string makers flatten or **swage** the core wire of wound strings under the ends of the winding. This helps to keep the ends from coming loose and buzzing or rattling. Some wound strings have hexagonal core wire, which helps the entire winding to stay tight. The lowest bass notes with one thick string per note have **double wound strings**, with two layers of winding. Higher bass notes having two or three strings per note have **single wound strings** with just one layer. The technician who strings the piano gives each wound string a twist in the direction of the winding before placing it on its hitch pin, to tighten the winding on the core, although in some modern factories this step is omitted.

Some bass strings have windings of soft, pliable iron or steel wire, copper-plated steel

HITCH PIN   START OF WINDING   END OF WINDING

2-33. A double-wound bass string.

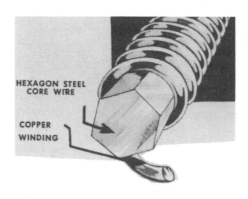

2-34. Detail of bass string with hexagonal core wire.

wire, or aluminum wire. Steel and aluminum have less mass than copper, so these windings have to be larger than copper windings to have the same weight. A steel-wound bass string under the same tension as a copper-wound string of the same weight and core wire diameter has a different tone quality due to its larger size. The soft steel windings eventually rust and become pitted when exposed to humidity. Copper plating retards deterioration, but eventually the thin copper becomes so oxidized that the underlying steel rusts anyway. Aluminum windings also corrode. All fine-quality pianos made today have bass strings wound with solid copper wire.

A well-designed scale should have a smooth tonal transition from a full, rich low bass to a brilliant, clear high treble. Generally, wire diameter and tension decrease from bass to treble. Piano makers refer to single, double, and three-string bass notes as **monochord, bichord,** and **trichord unisons,** respectively. The section from the lowest note on the treble bridge to about F below middle C is the **tenor** range of a piano. To provide the smoothest sounding transition from wound bass strings to plain steel treble strings, many fine-quality pianos have small-diameter-wound trichord unisons in the tenor.

The size of the plain steel treble strings also decreases gradually from low to high notes, although the difference in size isn't as noticeable to the eye as it is with the wound bass strings. In an average piano, the diameter of the plain steel treble strings decreases from approximately .044" (#19½) for the lowest notes, to approximately .031" (#13) for the highest.

Single string bass notes have the highest tension — over 300 pounds per string in a large piano. Going upward through the bass section, the tension decreases, with the plain steel trichord unisons averaging about 160 pounds tension per string in the treble of an average piano. The tension increases a little in the high treble in some pianos.

In some spinet pianos with poor bass tone quality due to their very short bass strings, the scale designers purposely degrade the tone quality of the tenor section by using unusually thick music wire. This makes the transition from bass to treble less obvious. In the least expensive of these little pianos, manufacturers use two-string plain wire unisons from the low end of the treble bridge almost up to middle C. This makes tuning very difficult, due to the stiffness of the thick wire and the jump in wire thickness from the bichord to trichord unisons in the middle of the temperament octave.

When designing a new piano, scale designers begin with the desired cabinet size and then design the string specifications. The cabinet size dictates the maximum length of the low A bass string, experience dictates that high C should be about 2⅛" (54 mm.) long, the wire's tensile strength and elastic limit dictate the practical limits of string tension, tradition dictates that A-440 is the standard pitch for the tuning scale, and musical taste influences how bright or mellow the tone quality should be. Keeping these factors

30

in mind, the scale designer then works with all variables: the length, tension, and diameter of each string, the dimensions of the bass string windings, and the lengths of the individual non-speaking segments of each string, such as the distance from the tuning pin to agraffe, bridge to hitch pin, etc.

Scale design also takes into account many other elements, including the point at which each hammer strikes the strings, and the dimensions, mass, and hardness of the hammers. These factors, plus the consideration that the hammers should be in as straight a line as possible, all play a role in the design of the plate, bridges, and soundboard. To get an inkling of the vast number of different scale designs used throughout the history of the piano, examine the string lengths and diameters in any hundred different old pianos.

In some pianos, the string tension jumps around wildly from one note or group of notes to the next, as can be seen when it is plotted on a graph. In others, there is a smooth curve, or somewhat straight line with steps, or a combination of these.

Stringing Arrangements

In the treble of most pianos, each piece of music wire starts at one tuning pin, goes around a hitch pin, and returns to the next tuning pin, with one piece of wire forming two "strings." As mentioned above, each group of strings forming one note is a unison. Since each treble unison has three strings, and each piece of wire forms two strings, it takes *three* whole pieces of wire to make up *two* unisons, or two notes (see illus. 2-27). This scheme works if each treble section has an even number of notes. If a particular section in a piano has an odd number of three-string unisons, then the last wire in the section, which forms only one string, is tied

to its hitch pin. This often occurs next to the mid-treble plate strut.

Many pianos have more complicated stringing configurations, with some treble strings looped around two hitch pins, some looped around one pin, and others individually tied, for convenience of spacing. Some pianos have the two outer strings of each unison formed of a single piece of wire looped around a huge hitch pin, with the center string tied to an ordinary hitch pin located just inboard of the huge one. Other pianos have a separate string and hitch pin for every tuning pin, with every treble string individually tied.

Every wound string has its own machine-made loop and individual hitch pin. It might seem like tying every treble string individually ought to be a good idea too, as this should eliminate any slippage of wire around the hitch pins during tuning. In reality, the string tension changes so little during fine tuning that the friction between the wire and hitch pin keeps the string from slipping any significant amount. Individually tied treble strings do have one advantage in that when one breaks, there are still two left for that unison.

Many high quality pianos have a **duplex stringing scale**, or simply **duplex scale**. Instead of muting the non-speaking segments at either or both ends of the strings with stringing braid or understring cloth, the manufacturer leaves these segments unmuted so they can vibrate sympathetically, to add to the brilliance of the tone. Duplex string segments near the tuning pins are called the **front duplex**, and those near the hitch pins are called the **back duplex** or **aliquot** segments. In some pianos, the plate has adjustable bars or plates called **aliquot bars.**

A very rarely encountered design is **aliquot stringing**. Aliquot strings are extra strings that are tunable but mounted above the line of the regular strings and not struck by the hammers. They vibrate sympathetically with the ordinary strings, supposedly enhancing the tone.

Several types of felt and cloth may embellish the piano strings and plate. **Understring cloth** or **understring felt** on the plate acts as a cushion for the non-speaking portions of strings to prevent them from vibrating against the plate. **Stringing braid** woven in and out of non-speaking string segments prevents them from vibrating sympathetically. Some manufacturers use little cloth washers called **hitch pin punchings** on the hitch pins under the strings in some pianos. These alter downbearing slightly, or sometimes just make the piano look more colorful.

2-35. Two types of back duplex scales illustrating Steinway aliquot plates (A) and Mason & Hamlin aliquot bars (B).

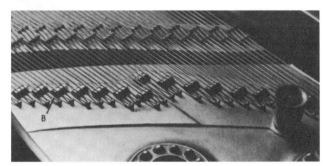

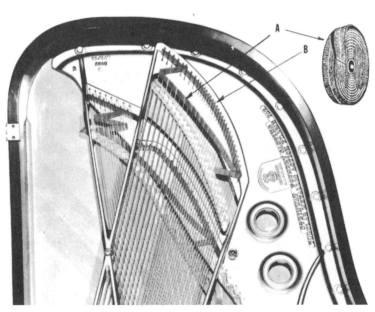

2-36. Stringing braid (A) and understring felt (B).

The Keybed

The **keybed** is a sandwich of large boards glued together. Its laminated construction helps it to remain flat through changes of humidity and temperature. If the keybed were to warp, it would change the relative positions of the action parts, throwing them out of the precise adjustment necessary for the action to work properly. The vertical piano keybed has three or four large screws at each end that fasten it to the cabinet arms, and one or two smaller screws that anchor the back edge to supports cast into the piano plate. The grand keybed has several large screws, and sometimes glue, holding it to the bottom of the rim.

The Key Frame

The **key frame** sits on the keybed and holds the keys (and action, in a grand) in place. It usually has three long rails running from one side of the piano to the other: the **back rail,** which supports the back ends of the keys at rest, the **balance rail,** which forms the pivot or fulcrum for the keys, and the **front rail,** which supports the front ends of the keys when you play them. Several slats running from front to back usually hold the long rails together, so you can remove the whole key frame from the piano in one piece.

In most grands, the key frame merely rests on the keybed without being screwed

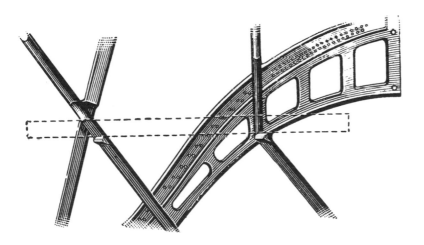

2-37 (above). The dotted lines show how the vertical piano keybed rests on projections cast into the plate.

2-38 (right). Bottom view of upright keybed with piano laid on its back.

down, to enable the una corda soft pedal to shift the entire key frame and action sideways so the treble hammers will hit only two of their three strings. The bottom of the grand key frame has adjustable **glides**, to minimize friction between key frame and keybed when the action shifts sideways. Each front corner of the key frame has a pin projecting out sideways, held down by a slotted plate or block attached to or under the key block. This plate or block holds the key frame down snugly against the keybed while still permitting sideways movement. A few inexpensive grands, and most player grands, with no una corda pedal have the key frame screwed down to the keybed.

The vertical key frame is fastened to the keybed with flat head screws. The height of the balance rail is adjustable, with paper or veneer shims inserted between the balance rail and slats. Some vertical piano key frames also have leveling screws, used for regulating balance rail height.

The key frame has two types of pins that hold the keys in position: **balance rail pins** and **front rail pins**. These smooth, unthreaded, nickel-plated steel or solid brass pins fit tightly in the holes in the key frame. The balance rail pins are round in cross section, and they extend all the way through the tops of the keys. The front rail pins are shorter and oval in cross section, and extend only part way up into the front ends of the keys. The pins keep the keys spaced evenly, unless the keys become warped.

Each balance rail pin has a cloth **balance rail punching**, on which the key rests at its pivot point. Under the cloth punching are paper or cardboard punchings of various thicknesses, for regulating the height of the keys to make them all perfectly level. Each front rail pin has a larger cloth **front rail punching** which cushions the key when you play it. The cloth front rail punching also has paper or cardboard punchings under it, to regulate how far the keys move or **travel** from their rest point to their fully depressed position. The back rail has a strip of **back rail cloth**, actually a thickly woven felt, glued to it, providing a cushion for the back ends of the keys at rest.

Modern Steinway pianos have little half-round pieces of wood covered with thin action cloth, called **balance rail bearings,**

2-39. A Cable grand key frame viewed from below, showing adjustable glides under the balance rail and a hold-down pin at one end of the front rail. The dark area in the back rail surrounds a notch where the una corda lever engages to push the key frame and action sideways.

instead of conventional balance rail punchings. Paper punchings under the bearings regulate the precise height of the keys. Steinway's name for this system, along with the key weighting system they use, is the **accelerated action.**

The various cloth strips and punchings used on the key frame and in the keys and action provide firm pivot, rest, and stop points. They also prevent various pieces of wood from clicking or knocking when coming into contact with each other.

The Keys

To make a keyboard, the manufacturer glues several straight grained sugar pine boards together, and then cuts this blank into eighty-eight individual keys. Sugar pine is strong enough to withstand hard playing, stable enough not to warp during moderate humidity changes, and lightweight enough to

have little inertia, allowing quick repetition. White keys have ivory or plastic **keytops,** and usually have plastic fronts. Sharps have keytops made of ebony or another hardwood that is dyed black, or plastic.

Ivory has always had a reputation for being the ideal covering for white keys, as it is somewhat porous, causing it to have a different feel than plastic. At the time of this writing, the importation of ivory into the United States is illegal, due to the waning world population of elephants and the cruel way in which they are still being killed by poachers. Several varieties of plastic replacement keytops are available, and as manufacturers develop better substitutes for ivory, supply companies will offer them for sale.

Each key has two cloth-bushed holes, one for each guide pin. The balance rail hole is the same diameter as the pin *only at the very bottom of the key.* The rest of the hole is larger, permitting the key to pivot without

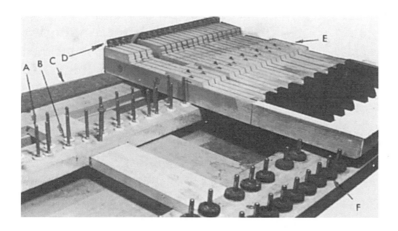

2-40 (left). Details of the key frame and keys: (A) balance rail pin, (B) balance rail punching, (C) back rail cloth, (D) capstan screw, (E) key button, (F) front rail punching.

2-41. Top right: two types of capstan screws. Bottom right: a key button.

binding. The top of each key in a good quality piano has a wooden **key button** glued over the balance point. The button has a precisely shaped and bushed rectangular hole, enhancing the stability of movement of the key. The hole for the front rail pin, toward the front of the bottom of the key, also has a precise rectangular shape and firm cloth bushings, which permit the key to move up and down without binding or knocking. The sides of the front rail pins are flat, to contact a larger area of bushing cloth than they would if they were round; this spreads the wear over a larger surface.

Inexpensive pianos sometimes have no key buttons, and have the balance rail pin bushings glued into slots in the tops of the keys. The absence of buttons allows keys to feel spongy, as they have a greater tendency to rock sideways a bit, particularly after their bushings wear or become packed down.

The back end of each key usually has a **capstan screw** or **capstan**, which is the contact point between the key and the action. The capstan has a gently rounded, polished head to minimize friction between key and action, and has holes or square sides to accept a wrench for adjustment (see illus. 2-41). The best capstans are solid brass, which stays smooth because it never rusts; less expensive capstans are brass-plated steel. As the plating wears off, the steel body is exposed to the cloth cushion on the action part; the cushion holds a certain amount of moisture, causing the capstan to become pitted. Some pianos have other types of capstans, discussed later in this chapter under the heading "Upright Action Variations."

The Hammers

A piano hammer has a hard wood **molding** and one or two layers of very hard, dense wool felt: the **underfelt** and **outer felt**. The underfelt, if present, is harder and usually brightly colored. All hammers in a set are the same width, but they gradually decrease in diameter from bass to treble. Good quality hammer felt is neither too hard — which would produce a tinny sound — nor too soft — which would cause a dull, mushy sound. The best hammer felt has long fibers oriented parallel to the strings. Inferior hammers made with short fibers or fibers oriented perpendicular to the strings, develop grooves much faster as the strings cut through the felt.

The hammer manufacturer begins with one long piece of wooden molding and one long piece of felt — either a single layer or laminated — that is thicker down the middle than at the edges. The manufacturer of the molding cuts the wood into individual pieces, and the hammer maker clamps them back together into long sections. A hydraulic or mechanical press then wraps and glues the felt around the moldings under tremendous pressure. After the glue dries, the manufacturer slices the felt into individual hammers. Gluing the hard felt around the wooden molding creates both compression inside the hammer and tension around the outside, to create the right amount of resilience for good tone. In many sets of treble hammers, **twist-tied staples** or **"T-wires"** help to hold the felt to the molding. But with modern waterproof glue, the staples aren't as important as they were in pianos of the 1800's and early 1900's. If the piano builder or restorer wishes, the hammer manufacturer applies a colored "reinforcing" liquid to the felt, which adds stiffness and helps to hold the felt in its proper shape.

The Vertical Action

The vertical piano action has a framework of three or four cast-iron or die cast action brackets and several hardwood rails (or aluminum rails, in many modern pianos), which support all the other action parts. The bottom of each bracket has a socket that rests on a **bottom ball bolt** screwed into the keybed. The top of each bracket has a fork or an eye that slips over an **action bracket bolt** screwed into the pinblock through an oversize hole in the plate. Each top action bracket bolt has a shoulder and a nut to hold the action in place. The entire action can be removed from the piano in one piece by removing the three or four nuts, disconnecting the dowels that connect it to the pedals (if necessary), and lifting it out.

The names of the various rails reflect their functions. The **main rail** holds most of the movable action parts for each individual note. Wherever the action parts attach to the rail, it has a tongue that mates with grooves in the action parts, keeping them aligned. The **lower action rail** (or **sticker rail**) supports the stickers. **Regulating rail posts** hold the **letoff rail** (or **regulating rail**) to the main rail; the letoff rail holds an adjustable **regulating screw** for each note. The **hammer rail** has a thick, soft piece of cloth glued to it, which serves as a rest for the hammers. Hammer rail **hooks** or **swings** connect the rail to the action brackets and

2-42 (right). An array of treble and bass upright hammers mounted on their shank with one glued onto its hammer butt. These particular hammers have no underfelt, staples, or colored reinforcing liquid. Note also that the artist did not draw the screw hole in the flange.

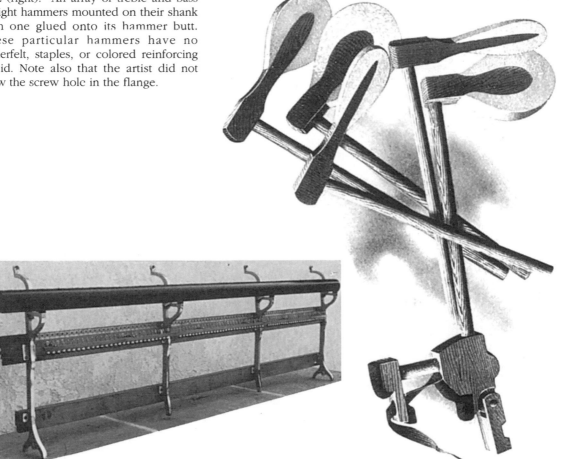

2-43 (above). The upright action skeleton.

permit it to move the hammers closer to or farther from the strings. The hammer rail swing holes in the action brackets have cloth bushings.

The **spring rail** holds one spring for each hammer and has a felt strip glued to the front to hold the springs tight and to keep the damper wires from clicking against it. The **damper lift rod** isn't a rail, but it affects all the dampers, so it is part of the main body of the action. It swings from **damper lift**

rod hooks or **swings**. The swings pivot from felt-lined metal clips screwed to the back of the main rail. The main rail has an action cloth or felt pad glued to the back near each clip, to provide a rest cushion for the lift rod.

Most of the action's moving parts swing from little hinges called **flanges**, screwed to the rails with special **flange screws**.

A **center pin** holds each flange and action part together. This little pin fits tightly

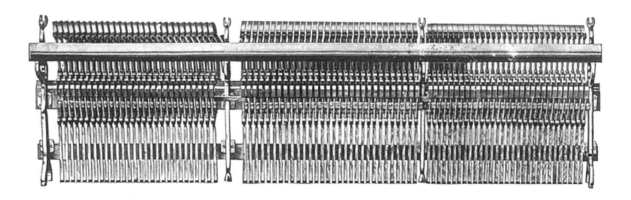

2-44. Front view of the upright action. From top to bottom, the main parts are the hammers, hammer rail, shanks, butts, backchecks, bridle straps, wippens, and stickers.

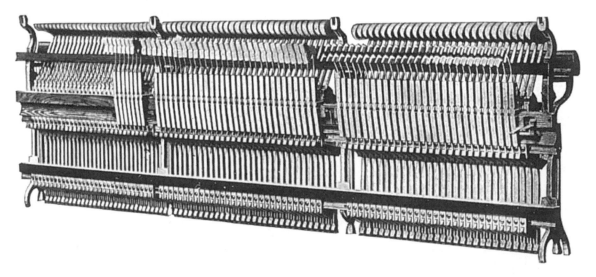

2-45. Rear view of the action. After memorizing the parts in illustration 2-47, you should have no trouble finding the dampers, spoons, and sticker flanges, or even the damper lift rod and some hammer butt springs.

in the wood of one part, and rotates in the cloth-bushed holes of the other part. The center pin must fit perfectly to allow free movement of the action part without any wobble. Some flanges, like the jack flange, are glued in place instead of being screwed down. Other parts are pinned together without a flange. Illustration 2-53 shows various types of flanges.

The movable action parts, of which there is one complete set for each key in the piano, may be broken down into three main assemblies per note: the **wippen** (including the **sticker** in full-size uprights, or **inverted sticker** in drop actions), **hammer**, and **damper** assemblies.

The sticker conveys motion from the key to the wippen. The wippen conveys motion from the sticker through the jack to the hammer butt, and the hammer hits the strings. The wippen also causes the damper to be lifted away from the strings, allowing the strings to ring until they stop vibrating or you release the key or sustaining pedal.

How the Upright Action Works

When you depress the front end of a key slowly, it pivots on the balance rail and the back end goes up. The key lifts the sticker and wippen. The wippen pushes the jack, which pushes the hammer butt. The hammer butt pivots on its own flange and moves the hammer toward the strings. When the hammer is halfway toward the strings, the spoon engages with the damper lever, lifting the damper off the strings. When the hammer is almost to the strings, the jack toe bumps into the regulating button. As the wippen continues moving up, the jack pivots on its flange and slips out from under the hammer butt. The hammer continues under its own inertia to the string, hits the string, and instantly rebounds. The backcheck catches the catcher and holds it in this position while you hold down the key.

When you release the key, the wippen drops, and the backcheck releases the catcher. The butt spring pushes on the hammer butt until the hammer shank returns to its resting place on the hammer rail cloth. The damper spring returns the damper to the strings, and the jack spring returns the jack under the butt, ready for the next repetition. This entire sequence occurs in a fraction of a second, allowing you to repeat notes rapidly. (See diagrams on page 41.)

The bridle straps keep the jacks from dropping and getting jammed under the bottom of the hammer butts when you remove the action from the piano.

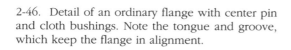

2-46. Detail of an ordinary flange with center pin and cloth bushings. Note the tongue and groove, which keep the flange in alignment.

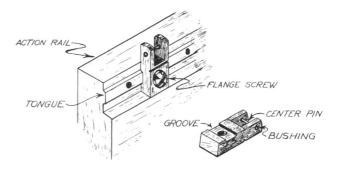

ACTION RAIL

TONGUE

FLANGE SCREW

GROOVE

CENTER PIN

BUSHING

Cross Section of the Upright Action

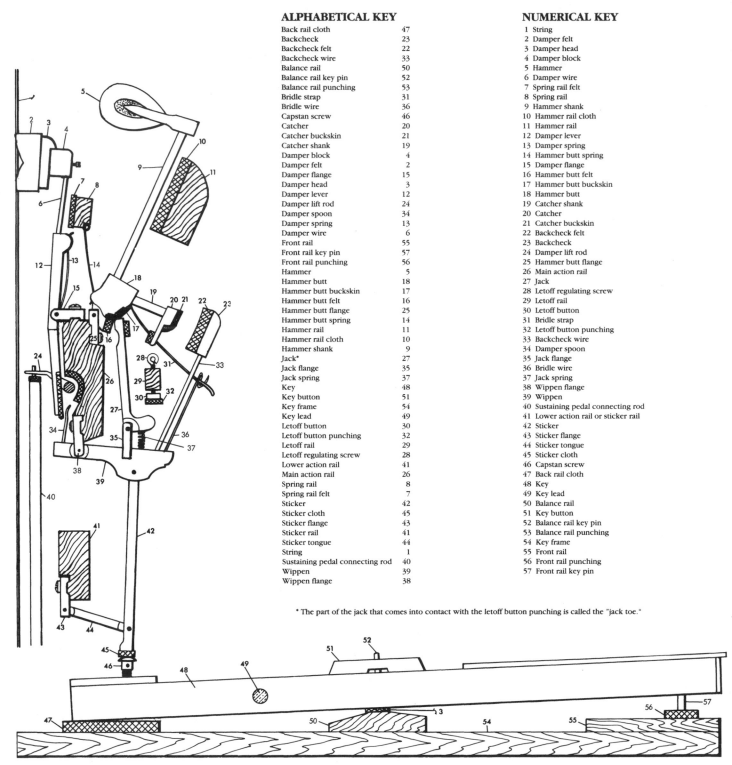

ALPHABETICAL KEY

Back rail cloth	47
Backcheck	23
Backcheck felt	22
Backcheck wire	33
Balance rail	50
Balance rail key pin	52
Balance rail punching	53
Bridle strap	31
Bridle wire	36
Capstan screw	46
Catcher	20
Catcher buckskin	21
Catcher shank	19
Damper block	4
Damper felt	2
Damper flange	15
Damper head	3
Damper lever	12
Damper lift rod	24
Damper spoon	34
Damper spring	13
Damper wire	6
Front rail	55
Front rail key pin	57
Front rail punching	56
Hammer	5
Hammer butt	18
Hammer butt buckskin	17
Hammer butt felt	16
Hammer butt flange	25
Hammer butt spring	14
Hammer rail	11
Hammer rail cloth	10
Hammer shank	9
Jack*	27
Jack flange	35
Jack spring	37
Key	48
Key button	51
Key frame	54
Key lead	49
Letoff button	30
Letoff button punching	32
Letoff rail	29
Letoff regulating screw	28
Lower action rail	41
Main action rail	26
Spring rail	8
Spring rail felt	7
Sticker	42
Sticker cloth	45
Sticker flange	43
Sticker rail	41
Sticker tongue	44
String	1
Sustaining pedal connecting rod	40
Wippen	39
Wippen flange	38

NUMERICAL KEY

1	String
2	Damper felt
3	Damper head
4	Damper block
5	Hammer
6	Damper wire
7	Spring rail felt
8	Spring rail
9	Hammer shank
10	Hammer rail cloth
11	Hammer rail
12	Damper lever
13	Damper spring
14	Hammer butt spring
15	Damper flange
16	Hammer butt felt
17	Hammer butt buckskin
18	Hammer butt
19	Catcher shank
20	Catcher
21	Catcher buckskin
22	Backcheck felt
23	Backcheck
24	Damper lift rod
25	Hammer butt flange
26	Main action rail
27	Jack
28	Letoff regulating screw
29	Letoff rail
30	Letoff button
31	Bridle strap
32	Letoff button punching
33	Backcheck wire
34	Damper spoon
35	Jack flange
36	Bridle wire
37	Jack spring
38	Wippen flange
39	Wippen
40	Sustaining pedal connecting rod
41	Lower action rail or sticker rail
42	Sticker
43	Sticker flange
44	Sticker tongue
45	Sticker cloth
46	Capstan screw
47	Back rail cloth
48	Key
49	Key lead
50	Balance rail
51	Key button
52	Balance rail key pin
53	Balance rail punching
54	Key frame
55	Front rail
56	Front rail punching
57	Front rail key pin

* The part of the jack that comes into contact with the letoff button punching is called the "jack toe."

2-47. The upright action.

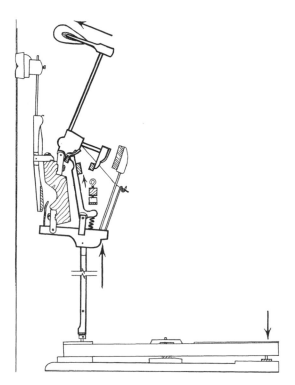

2-48 (above). Operation of the upright action: key begins moving down, raising sticker, wippen, jack and hammer butt.

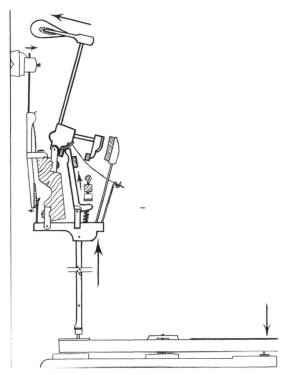

2-49 (above). Damper spoon begins to move damper lever, lifting damper off strings.

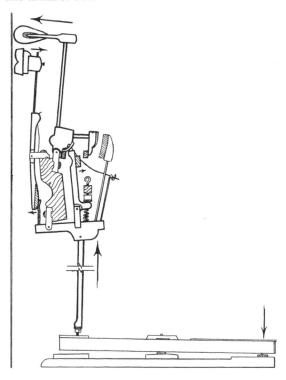

2-50. Jack disengages from hammer butt when jack toe engages letoff button.

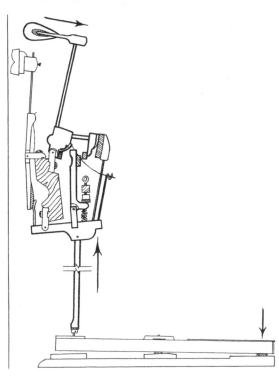

2-51. Hammer hits string and rebounds. Backcheck catches butt catcher. When key is released, all parts return to their positions in illus. 2-48.

41

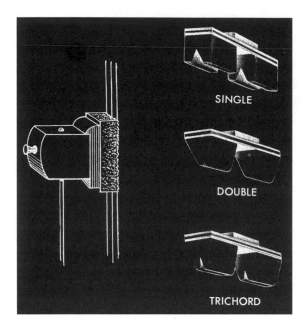

2-52. Various types of vertical piano dampers: treble damper, left; bass wedges, right.

The Dampers

The lower a note is, the more vigorously the wire moves when it vibrates, and the more dense the damper must be. Bass dampers usually have harder felt wedges, while treble dampers usually have very soft, fluffy felt pads, as illustrated. Treble dampers decrease in length (measured from top to bottom) from low tenor to high treble. The highest notes have no dampers, because the tone dies out so quickly in this range that none are necessary. Also, leaving the highest treble strings undamped permits them to ring sympathetically when you play lower notes, enhancing the brilliance of the piano somewhat.

In some verticals, including certain Steinway uprights, the lowest treble dampers have a wire extending upward and passing around the hammer, with a second damper or **overdamper** attached to the top. Here, where the treble dampers ought to be the longest, they must be cut off diagonally on

the bottom so they don't touch the bass strings that cross over in front of the treble strings in this area. The overdampers help to compensate. Another way of damping the longest tenor strings more effectively is to use trichord treble wedge felt instead of flat damper felt for the lowest six or eight tenor notes.

Upright Action Variations

Most upright piano actions are similar to the one shown in illus. 2-47, with minor variations in the size and shape of the parts. Some actions, however, have different types of hammer butt flanges, capstans, hammer butts, and other parts.

Common variations on the hammer butt flange include the **Billings flange, the brass flange rail, the Kimball brass flange rail,** and the **double flange.**

The Billings flange, made of brass, has two prongs that fit into a groove in the main rail to keep the flange in proper alignment. The flange grips the center pin tightly, and the center pin holes in the hammer butt contain the cloth bushings, just the opposite of a regular hammer butt flange, in which the butt grips the center pin and the flange contains the bushings.

The brass flange rail is a continuous piece of brass screwed to the main rail, with a tongue projecting upward for each hammer butt. A brass **butt plate** holds each center pin tightly in a small groove in the tongue. A small machine screw passes through an unthreaded hole in the rail into a threaded hole in the plate, to secure the plate to the rail. The Kimball brass flange rail is similar to the regular brass rail, but it has threaded holes in the rail instead of in the butt plates, so the screws go in from the opposite side.

The advantage of a metal flange or rail is that a center pin can't work its way loose, as it sometimes does when held by a wooden part that expands and contracts a little every time the humidity changes. Unfortunately, one property of brass is that it gets more brittle the more it flexes. Although a brass flange or rail doesn't appear to bend noticeably in normal use, the stress caused by many years of playing eventually makes it brittle. In this condition, it fractures or breaks easily. Most old Billings flanges are still intact, but it isn't uncommon to find an old piano action with a dozen or more Billings flanges each having a fracture line across the top, parallel to and immediately above the center pin, permitting the pin to slip out. It also isn't uncommon to

find a brass rail with several broken tongues. Manufacturers stopped using both systems sometime before the 1940's.

Another flange variation is the **double flange,** which holds the center pins for both damper lever and hammer butt in cloth-bushed holes. Manufacturers have used various types of double flanges in uprights since the late 1800's.

The capstan is another action part made in several different styles, including the **dowel capstan, rocker capstan,** and **regulating screw capstan.** The dowel capstan introduces a little more friction into the action than a regular capstan screw does,

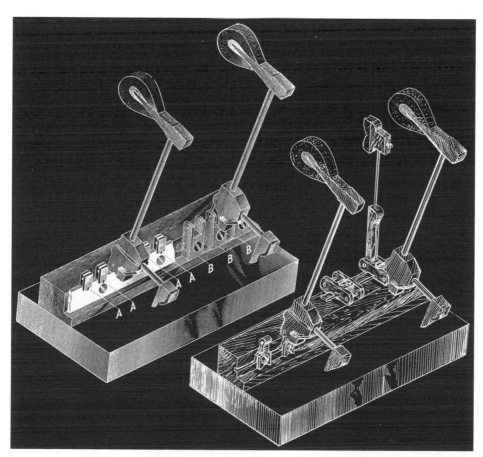

2-53. Left to right: brass flange rail, conventional flange, Billings flange, and double flange.

because the dowel has more of a rubbing movement against the cushion on the bottom of the wippen. Nonetheless, the dowel capstan is much cheaper to manufacture than a sticker and its many associated parts, so it has been a common feature of medium-sized uprights throughout the years.

The rocker capstan, obsolete by the early 1900's, added no extra friction to the action, but it was no better than the simple capstan screw, which is easier to regulate and much cheaper to make. The regulating screw capstan, also obsolete by the early 1900's, was exceptionally easy to regulate, but it added more friction than a simple capstan screw, cost more to manufacture, and tended to break because of the off-center thrust on the glue joint and regulating button.

In most American pianos, the traditional way of mounting the hammer butt return spring is to attach it to a spring rail, and the traditional jack has a flange glued to the wippen (see illus. 2-47). In contrast, the style of hammer butt found in many European pianos has a self-contained return spring, with a retaining cord glued to the flange. The jack has its two legs pinned directly to the wippen, without a flange, as shown in illus. 2-56.

The **touch rail**, found in some vertical pianos, provides a cushioned stop for the jacks. It takes the place of the more common felt pads glued to the front of the upper end of each jack and the back of each catcher (see illus. 2-47). The catchers in an action with a touch rail are shorter than those in an

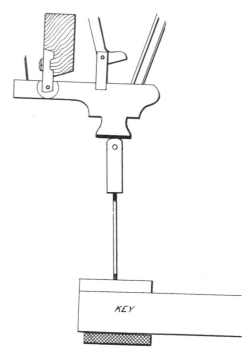

2-54. The dowel capstan, used in many studio uprights.

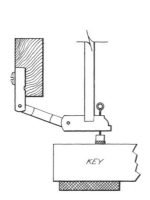 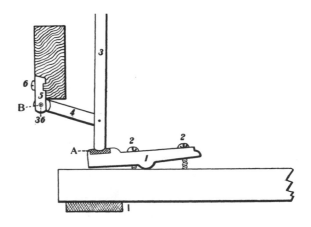

2-55. The regulating screw capstan, left, and the rocker capstan, right.

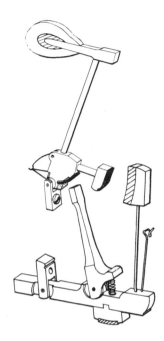

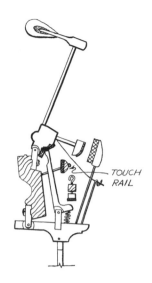

2-57. The touch rail, above, replaces the hammer catcher felts and jack felts to silence the operation of the jacks in some verticals.

2-56. A hammer butt and wippen used in many European, Japanese, Asian, and some American pianos. The main differences are the mounting of the hammer butt return spring and its retaining cord, and the mounting of the jack directly on the wippen without a separate flange.

ordinary action, so they don't need the usual holes for the bridle straps.

A deluxe feature found in some expensive uprights made in the early 1900's is the **lost motion compensator** mechanism. In an ordinary vertical action, when you depress the soft pedal, pushing the hammer rail and hammers halfway toward the strings, a gap or **lost motion** occurs between the top end of each jack and the buckskin cushion on the hammer butt. Lost motion reduces the pianist's control of fine nuance, because each key has to go part way down before it begins to do anything. Lost motion also accelerates wear of the buckskin, because each jack hammers on the buckskin instead of pressing on it. To eliminate lost motion and permit precise control of soft playing, some manufacturers of fine-quality uprights

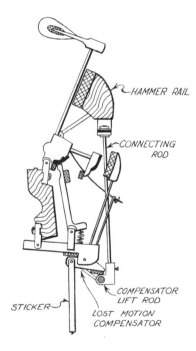

2-58. The lost motion compensator action, found in expensive uprights of the early 1900s.

installed various types of lost motion compensators. The compensator mechanism shown in illus. 2-57 incorporates an additional lever between each sticker and wip-

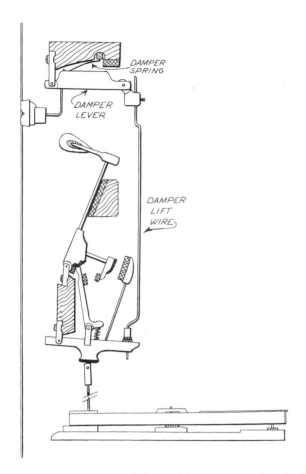

2-59. Cross-section of the troublesome, complex "bird cage" overdamper action installed in some Victorian pianos and universally dreaded by piano technicians ever since.

pen. As the soft pedal lifts the hammer rail and hammers, the connecting rod also lifts the compensator lift rod, rotating the intermediate lever to keep the jack close to the hammer butt without lifting the sticker off the back end of the key, thus preventing lost motion from occurring. In another type of mechanism, the compensator mechanism is close to the bottom of the stickers. Although the lost motion compensator greatly enhanced the soft playing capabilities of the vertical piano, it was more expensive than it was worth, and was obsolete by the 1920's.

Some very old uprights have a separate damper action mounted *above* the hammers

(see illus. 2-59). Technicians call the dampers **overdampers**, and the actions **bird cage** or **squirrel cage** actions, because viewed from the front, the damper lift wires resemble a cage. (Don't confuse this style of overdamper with the more common type described on p. 42.) At the time of their manufacture, someone must have thought these dampers had an advantage over ordinary ones. They're a real nuisance to anyone trying to service the piano, however, as they not only get in the way of regulating the action, but also interfere with tuning the piano. Fortunately for everyone connected with pianos and piano servicing, they were obsolete by the early 1900's.

The Console Action

A console piano, or studio upright, is a short upright without stickers. The action is identical to the full upright action, except the wippens have cloth pads instead of stickers, and rest directly on the capstans. Taller consoles and studio uprights have dowel capstans, while shorter consoles have regular capstans. Many medium-sized Victorian uprights and modern studio uprights have long dowel capstans instead of stickers.

2-60. The console action.

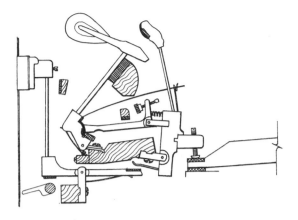

2-61. The Wood & Brooks 90° Inverted Direct Blow Action — just one example of the unusual actions built from time to time over the years.

Wood & Brooks, the action manufacturer, built this **90° Inverted Direct Blow** console action for piano companies in the 1940's and 1950's, just one example of the many odd action designs manufactured over the years. Just when you think you've seen everything in old pianos, you'll find another radically different mechanism. Knowledge of ordinary piano actions, coupled with common sense and mechanical aptitude, will always enable you to figure out how to service one of these unusual actions.

The Drop Action

In order for a piano to be built as short as possible, with the keyboard at a comfortable height above the floor, the piano must have a **drop action**, or an action located below the keyboard. The wippens in this action have **lifter elbows** and **inverted stickers** or **drop stickers** connecting them to the keys. The drop action works exactly like the upright action.

Some drop action brackets extend all the way to the piano plate at the top of the action, eliminating the need for upper action bracket bolts. This also eliminates the danger of bending or otherwise damaging the dampers when you remove or reinstall the action.

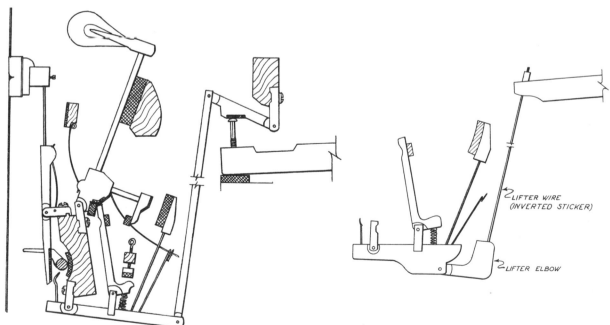

2-62. A spinet action with a wooden inverted sticker pinned to the end of the wippen.

2-63. Another common style of spinet action with a lifter elbow connecting the wippen to the lifter wire.

47

2-64 (left and below). Several styles of upright pedal trapwork.

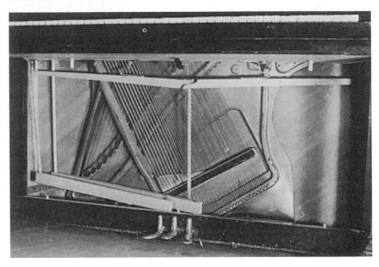

Vertical Piano Pedals

The pedals are usually made of cast iron or brass. They pivot on steel pins inserted crosswise through the center or toward the rear of their length. These pins are supported by wooden, metal, or plastic pivot blocks screwed to the bottom board of the piano. Many upright pedals have a vertical extension called the **horn** curving upward in front of the toe rail. Inside the case, various connecting wires, dowels, and pivoting levers known as **trapwork** connect the pedals to the action. Some pedal dowels fit into sockets in the trap levers, while others have steel pins that fit into holes in the trapwork and action parts.

The **soft pedal**, always on the left, operates the hammer rail. As it is depressed, it pushes the hammer rail and hammers about halfway to the strings. In this position, the hammers have less distance to travel, so not as much energy can be put into them when

the pianist plays, resulting in softer music.

The **sustaining pedal**, always on the right, operates the damper lift rod. When you depress the pedal, the damper lift rod engages with all damper levers, lifting all dampers away from the strings. Some pianos have a **dummy damper**, a regular damper lever having a spring but no wire or head, located at the end of one section of dampers. Its purpose is to help return the damper lift rod to the rest position away from the damper levers when you release the sustaining pedal. The dummy damper spring pushes the dummy lever against the lift rod, and thus acts as a lift rod return spring. In pianos having no dummy damper, the damper lift rod either returns to its rest position by its own weight, or rests gently against all the damper levers when you release the pedal.

The **sostenuto pedal**, found only in the most expensive uprights, works like its counterpart in a grand piano, holding preselected dampers off the strings. For further details, see the text under the heading "The Grand Pedals."

The **bass sustain pedal**, in the middle if present, operates a second damper lift rod, mounted above or below the full lift rod, which lifts only the bass dampers. In a few pianos, there is only one lift rod, split into two parts. The treble portion of the split rod, connected to the full sustaining pedal, has a tongue that also lifts the bass portion, but the bass portion, connected to the bass sustain pedal, *doesn't* lift the treble portion.

The **practice pedal**, in the middle if present, operates a wood or aluminum rail with a curtain of thick, soft felt hanging down about 1 1/2" (or 4 cm.). When this pedal is pushed down, it lowers the felt between the hammers and strings, muffling the tone. In some pianos, pushing the practice pedal down and to one side latches it into a notch in the toe rail, holding the muffler rail down and freeing your left foot.

In very rare instances, an old upright has a **mandolin attachment** consisting of a rail with a cloth or leather curtain slit into separate tabs. Each tab has a wood or metal piece attached to the end. When you lower the rail by depressing the middle pedal, the tabs hang between the hammers and strings. The hammers throw the tabs against the strings, causing a tinny "honky tonk" sound. Mandolin attachments were much more common in player pianos than ordinary hand played instruments.

Many inexpensive uprights, consoles, and spinets have a third pedal just for looks, not connected to anything, or connected to the same trap lever as the left-hand soft pedal. Sometimes, the useless middle pedal moves the hammer rail *only part of the distance* that the soft pedal moves it, providing an "intermediate" degree of softness. Considering that the ordinary soft pedal in a vertical has only a very subtle effect, piano makers might as well omit the third pedal instead of connecting it in this way.

In an ordinary upright, the pedal trapwork takes up a lot of space in the bottom of the cabinet (see illus. 2-64). In a player piano, the bottom compartment also contains the pumping bellows, fold-down pumping pedals, and other mechanisms. To allow room for all of this, steel rods running across the bottom of the piano connect the piano pedals to the pedal dowels in the back left corner. Usually, all the piano pedal hardware in a player lies below the level of the top of the toe rail, making more room for the player mechanisms.

2-65. Felt muffler rail lowered into place between hammers and strings.

Cross Section of The Grand Action

ALPHABETICAL KEY

Action Bracket	32	Damper wire	5	Key stop rail prop	53
Back rail	48	Damper wire screw	13	Letoff button	29
Back rail cloth	49	Drop screw	8	Letoff button punching	30
Backcheck	15	Front rail	56	Letoff rail	28
Backcheck wire	38	Front rail key pin	54	Letoff regulating screw	27
Balance rail	51	Front rail punching	55	Main action rail	10
Balance rail bearing***	52	Hammer	6	Repitition lever	19
Balance rail key pin	44	Hammer flange	9	Repitition lever button	21
Capstan screw	42	Hammer knuckle	20	Repitition lever flange	18
Damper felt	3	Hammer rest*	16	Repitition lever screw	17
Damper guide rail	4	Hammer shank	7	Repitition lever spring**	23
Damper head	2	Jack****	31	Sostenuto rod	14
Damper lever	36	Jack regulating button	25	Sostenuto tab or lip	35
Damper lever flange	33	Jack regulating screw	26	String	1
Damper lever key cushion	37	Jack spring**	23	Wippen	24
Damper lift rail	47	Key	45	Wippen cushion	41
Damper lift rail spring	34	Key button	43	Wippen flange	39
Damper wire block	12	Key frame	50	Wippen rail	40
Damper stop rail	11	Key stop rail	46	Wippen spoon	22

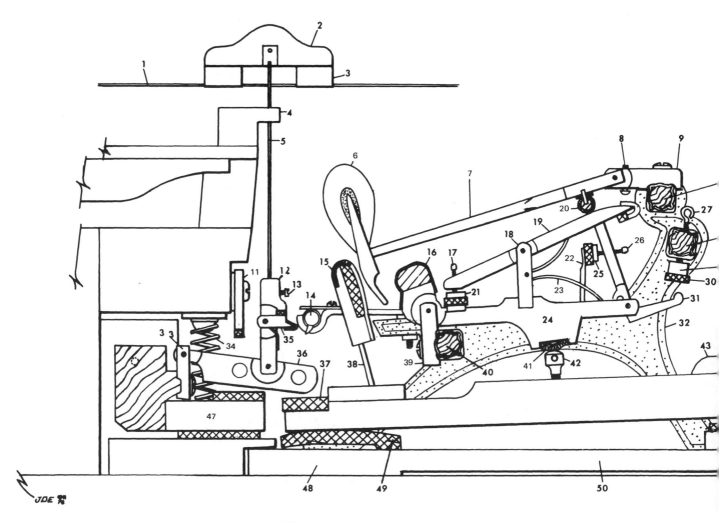

2-66. Cross section of the grand action.

NUMERICAL KEY

1	String	29	Letoff button
2	Damper head	30	Letoff button punching
3	Damper felt	31	Jack****
4	Damper guide rail	32	Action bracket
5	Damper wire	33	Damper lift flange
6	Hammer	34	Damper lift rail spring
7	Hammer shank	35	Sostenuto tab or lip
8	Drop screw	36	Damper lever
9	Hammer flange	37	Damper lever key cushion
10	Main action rail	38	Backcheck wire
11	Damper stop rail	39	Wippen flange
12	Damper wire block	40	Wippen rail
13	Damper wire screw	41	Wippen cushion
14	Sostenuto rod	42	Capstan screw
15	Backcheck	43	Key button
16	Hammer rest*	44	Balance rail key pin
17	Repetition lever screw	45	Key
18	Repetition lever flange	46	Key stop rail
19	Repetition lever	47	Damper lift rail
20	Hammer knuckle	48	Back rail
21	Repetition lever button	49	Back rail cloth
22	Wippen spoon	50	Key frame
23	Combination jack spring and repetition lever spring**	51	Balance rail
24	Wippen	52	Balance rail bearing***
25	Jack regulating button	53	Key stop rail prop
26	Jack regulating screw	54	Front rail key pin
27	Letoff regulating screw	55	Front rail punching
28	Letoff rail	56	Front rail

* The hammer rest is built into the Steinway-style wippen. Other actions have a separate hammer rail located in the same position.

** These are two separate springs in many actions.

*** The Steinway balance rail bearings take the place of the usual cloth punchings.

**** The part of the jack that comes into contact with the letoff button punching is called the "jack toe" or "jack tender."

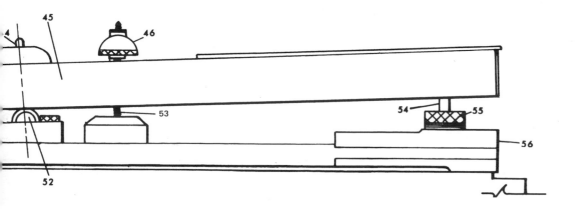

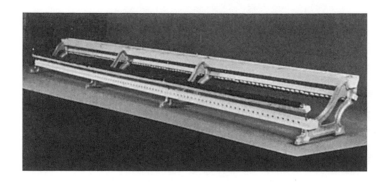

2-67. The action skeleton from a small Cable grand.

The Grand Action

Like the vertical action, the grand action has a framework of cast-iron or die cast action brackets — usually four or five — and several hardwood or aluminum rails, as illustrated. Two screws hold each grand action bracket to the key frame so the action, keys, and key frame all come out of the piano in one piece. The Steinway tubular metallic action has wooden rails encased in extruded metal tubing soldered to the brackets.

Some parts of the grand action have the same names as their counterparts in the vertical action, including the keys, capstans, wippens, jacks, hammer shanks, hammers, backchecks, dampers, and others. As in an upright, the key pushes on the wippen, the wippen on the jack, and the jack on the hammer. From here on, the resemblance ends, because the grand action has an additional assembly on each wippen called the **repetition lever.** This lever enables the grand action to repeat notes faster than the vertical can.

How the Grand Action Works

When you depress the key slowly, the capstan pushes on the wippen, which pushes on the jack, which pushes on the

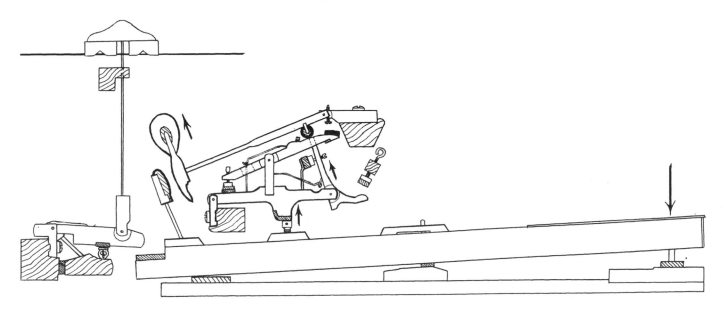

2-68. Operation of the grand action: the key starts moving down in front, raising the wippen, jack, hammer knuckle, shank, and hammer.

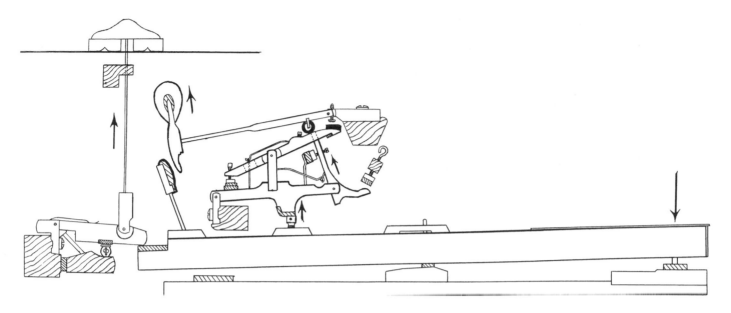

2-69. The key begins to lift the damper.

hammer knuckle and begins lifting the hammer. When the hammer is halfway to the strings, the back end of the key begins to raise the damper from the strings. As the key continues down, and the hammer is almost to the strings, the jack toe bumps into the letoff button, and the jack slips out

from under the knuckle. The hammer continues by inertia, hits the strings and rebounds. By the time the hammer rebounds, the jack is already tripped out from under the knuckle, so the knuckle lands on the repetition lever instead. The downward force of the hammer during

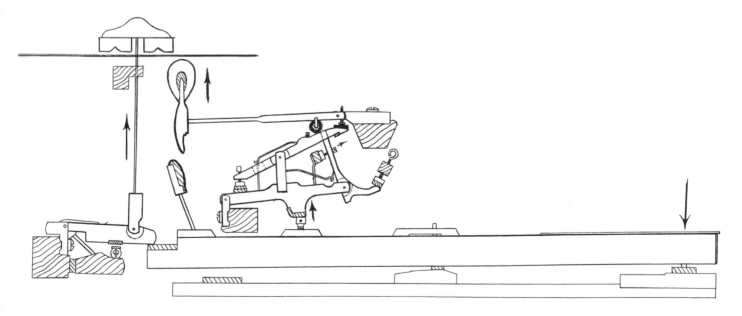

2-70. The jack disengages from the hammer knuckle when the jack toe engages with the letoff button.

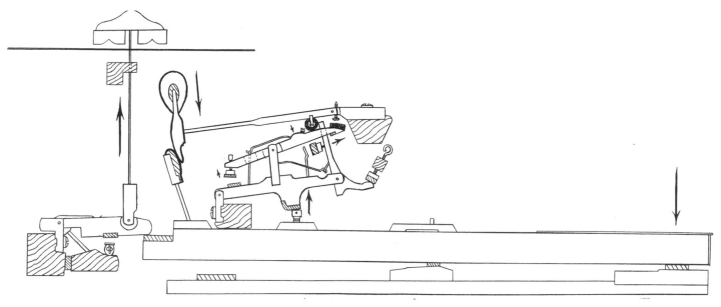

2-71. The key hits the bottom; the hammer simultaneously hits and rebounds from the strings. The hammer depresses the repetition lever, and the backcheck catches and holds the hammer tail.

medium or loud playing is stronger than the repetition lever spring, so the hammer knuckle pushes the repetition lever down, pivoting it on its flange. The downward motion continues until the hammer tail catches on the backcheck, and the hammer remains in this checked position as long as you hold down the key.

For a moment, pause to consider the positions of the various parts. You are holding the key down. The damper is off the strings. The hammer has bounced off the strings and is now being held in place by the backcheck. The jack is out from under the hammer knuckle, tripped by the letoff button. The repetition lever is down, in a "cocked" position. Its spring is strong enough for the lever to lift the shank and hammer, but it can't do this because the backcheck is holding the hammer tail.

When you release the key in slow motion, the backcheck releases the hammer tail, allowing the repetition lever to push the hammer upward until the repetition lever comes to a stop on the drop screw. As the

back end of the key continues to go down, the wippen follows, and as the jack drops, it pivots back under the knuckle when the jack toe clears the letoff button. Because the jack clears the letoff button when the front end of the key is less than halfway up, the action is ready for another complete cycle *without the key needing to return to its rest position*. When playing a vertical, you must release the key and let it come almost all the way up before the jack slips under the butt, allowing the cycle to be repeated. When playing a grand, you can repeat notes quickly without waiting for the keys to return all the way to their rest position. Because it takes less time and finger motion to reset the action, notes can be repeated on a grand more rapidly than on a vertical, particularly when playing softly.

When the key is fully released, it lowers the damper to the strings, muting the sound.

This sequence occurs much faster than the eye can follow, and in far less time than it takes to describe it in writing. From the above slow-motion description, it would

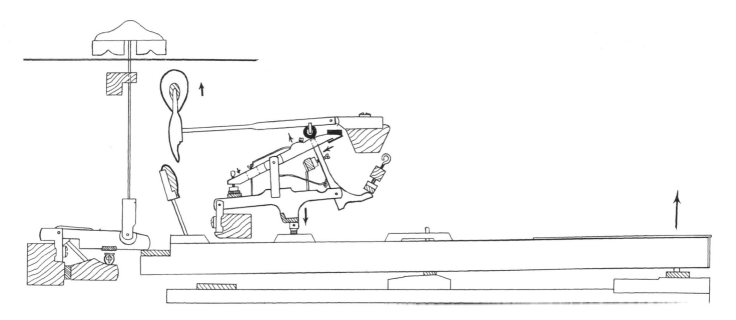

2-72. When the front of the key rises a little, the backcheck releases hammer, permitting the repetition lever to lift the hammer until the jack returns under knuckle. The action is ready for another cycle, although the key hasn't returned all the way to its rest position.

seem that the repetition lever always pushes the hammer upward to allow the jack to return under the knuckle. During louder playing, however, the pianist releases the key faster than in the above description, and the key and wippen drop as the lever supports the shank and hammer.

When you play a single sustained note *extremely softly*, the hammer may rebound from the strings with too little energy to cock the repetition lever or to be caught by the backcheck. In this state, the lever remains in its *rest* position and the hammer comes to rest very close to the strings. When the key is released, everything resets as described above.

For a perfectly clear demonstration of the effectiveness of the repetition lever, watch the hammers when a fine pianist plays a rapid trill, beginning very softly and then gradually trilling louder and louder. At first, the hammers will trill softly without dropping away from the strings very much at all.

As the pianist increases the key stroke and velocity to trill louder, the hammers will bounce farther and farther away from the strings. No matter *how soft or loud the trill, a properly regulated grand piano will always repeat.*

The Grand Hammer Rest or Rail

With the grand hammer knuckle normally supported by the repetition lever when the key is at rest, why is a hammer rest (part #16, illus. 2-66) or hammer rail necessary? When you play a loud staccato (very short) note once without repeating it, the hammer rebounds forcefully from the strings, but the backcheck is down because the key has been released. The entire returning force of the hammer would be too much for the jack and knuckle to support, so the hammer rest or rail does most of the job of stopping the hammer. The top surface of the rest rail cush-

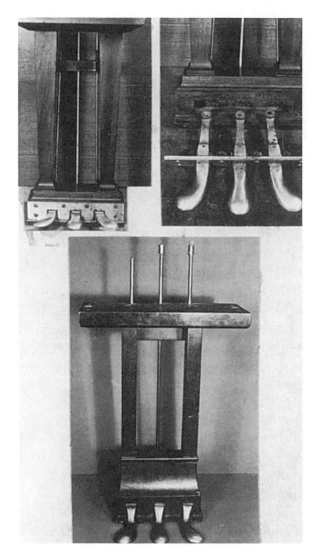

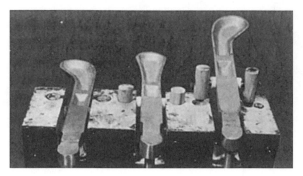

2-74 (above). A commonly used method of mounting the pedals in the pedal lyre, shown in an inverted view with the bottom cover board removed and each successive pedal pulled out a little farther, showing how the support dowels fit into sockets in the lyre, The bottom plate also contains thick felt or cloth cushions to keep the pedals from knocking on the wood.

2-73. Pedal lyre assemblies: Steinway (above) and Chickering (below).

ion is slightly below the line of the hammers at rest so it doesn't interfere with the repetition levers, but adds the extra needed cushion when the hammers rebound vigorously from the strings to their rest position.

Grand Pedals

Grand pedals are suspended from the bottom of the keybed by the **pedal lyre.** To withstand the heavy force exerted on the pedals, the lyre has large screws or bolts fastening it to the keybed, with diagonal braces helping to strengthen the entire assembly.

The grand soft pedal, to the left, is usually a shifter or **una corda** pedal. With a lever that fits into a notch in the bottom of the key frame, the pedal shifts the entire action to the right, just far enough so the treble hammers hit only two of their three strings, reducing the volume of sound and altering the tone quality. A large spring returns the action to its normal position when you release the pedal. (In some unusual grands, the pedal shifts the action to the left).

In some grands, the soft pedal lifts the hammer rail, moving the hammers closer to the strings and decreasing their striking distance, as in the upright. This type is not as desirable to the pianist, because it changes the feel of the action. Most grand reproducing pianos have this type of mechanism, because it takes much less power to move a hammer rail up and down rapidly than to shift the weight of the entire action from side to side. Also, reproducing rolls use it as an expression device far more often than a pianist ever uses the una corda pedal.

2-75. Details of grand damper action located directly behind the piano action: (A) lifter flange and damper wire screw, (B) sostenuto rod, (C) damper level and damper wire screw, and (D) damper lift rail or tray.

The sustaining pedal, to the right, uses the damper lift rail to lift all dampers at once.

The middle pedal in a good-quality grand operates the sostenuto mechanism. When you depress a key, and then the sostenuto pedal, the sostenuto rod lip engages with the lip on the damper assembly, holding the damper up off the strings after the key is released. This way, any notes played and held down while depressing the sostenuto pedal continue to be sustained after their keys are released, as long as the sostenuto pedal is held down. Any keys depressed *after* the sostenuto pedal is depressed aren't affected because their damper sostenuto lips remain under the lip on the rod, permitting the dampers to drop when their keys are released. The sostenuto allows you to play certain notes, sustain only those notes with the pedal, and then use both hands to play other notes that are sustained only as long as you hold down their keys.

In some grands, the middle pedal operates a bass sustain device with a separate lift rail or separated section of the main rail. This is an inexpensive substitute for the sostenuto pedal.

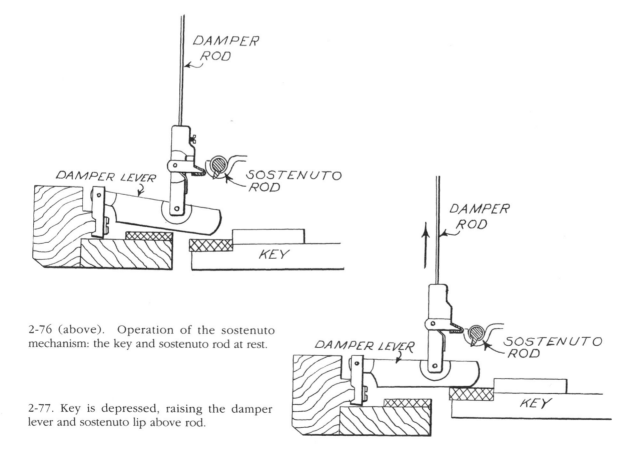

2-76 (above). Operation of the sostenuto mechanism: the key and sostenuto rod at rest.

2-77. Key is depressed, raising the damper lever and sostenuto lip above rod.

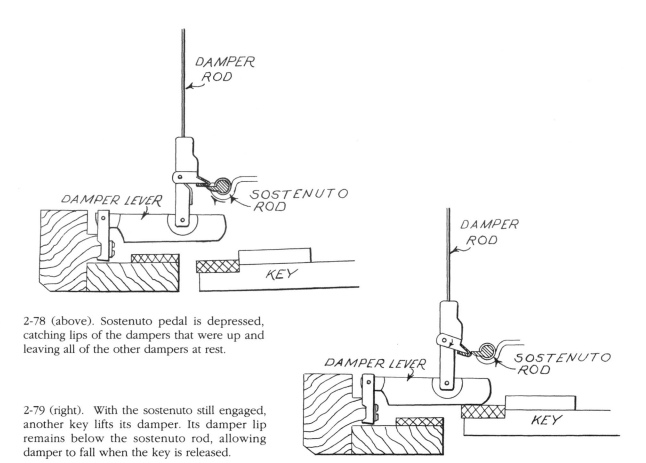

2-78 (above). Sostenuto pedal is depressed, catching lips of the dampers that were up and leaving all of the other dampers at rest.

2-79 (right). With the sostenuto still engaged, another key lifts its damper. Its damper lip remains below the sostenuto rod, allowing damper to fall when the key is released.

Grand Action Variations

Like vertical actions, grand actions have been made using many different design variations. All work according to the same principles but have parts of slightly different sizes and shapes. Illustrations 2-80, 2-81, and 2-82 show a few commonly encountered design variations. To get some idea of how many other variations exist, browse through the replacement parts section of any piano supply company catalog.

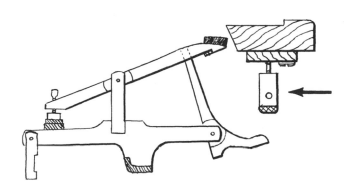

2-80 (right). The dowel letoff button.

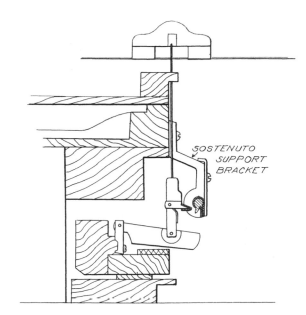

SOSTENUTO
SUPPORT
BRACKET

2-81. Two ways of mounting a sostenuto rod: left, suspending it from the body of the piano, as in a Baldwin; below, mounting it on the piano action, as in a Steinway.

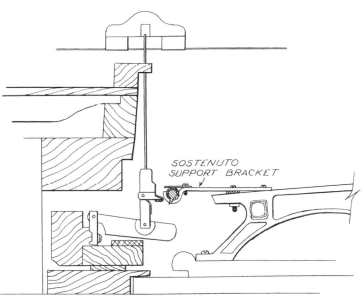

SOSTENUTO
SUPPORT BRACKET

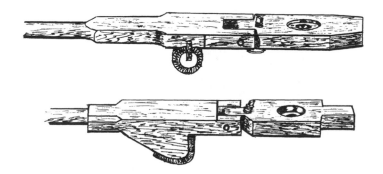

2-82 (left). Above: a grand hammer flange and shank with a true knuckle made of a thin strip of wood with a layer of buckskin wrapped tightly around an inner layer of compressed felt. Below: a cheap substitute.

59

2-83. Top view of a square piano with the lid open. Note the radial stringing pattern and the tuning pins located near the rear. Despite the massive size of the cabinet, the square piano soundboard is smaller than one in an average spinet.

The Square Piano

The **square piano**, also called the square grand, is a completely different type of piano. The strings form a fan-shaped pattern, with the pinblock and tuning pins toward the *back* of the cabinet. The soundboard is between the keybed and strings, with an opening for the hammers running parallel to the plate bridge toward the rear of the piano. Square piano keys are very long and every key is a different length, and the action parts and hammers form an arc corresponding to the pattern of the strings. The hammers are much smaller and lighter than in the modern piano, and there are no repetition levers or wippens. The jack flanges are attached directly to the keys. The dampers have long horizontal wooden levers lifted by damper lifter wires that rest on the back ends of the keys.

2-84. The square piano action. Note the curve of the hammer line.

How the Square Piano Action Works

The square piano action is even simpler than the vertical piano action, due to the absence of wippens. When you depress a key it raises the jack, lifting the hammer. When the hammer is halfway to the strings, the back end of the key begins to lift the damper. When the jack toe bumps into the letoff button and the jack slips out from under the hammer butt, the hammer continues toward the strings, rebounds from them, and the backcheck catches it. When you release the key, all parts fall back to their rest positions, and the jack spring returns the jack under the hammer butt. Because there are no repetition levers, the hammers rest on a hammer rail as in the upright. The sustaining pedal lifts all the damper levers. The soft pedal slides a felt strip between hammers and strings.

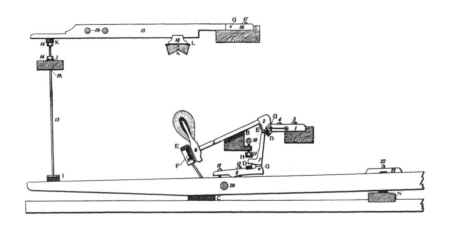

2-85. Cross-section of the square piano action, with no string drawn.

Chapter Three

Evaluating An Old Piano:
Is It Worth Buying or Repairing?

Factors to consider in selecting an old piano include its type and size, quality, brand name, age, and condition. Old pianos exist by the millions in every conceivable size, shape, style, and condition. Some are still in pristine condition, others are in such bad shape that someone should have hauled them to the dump years ago, but most pianos fall somewhere in the middle.

This chapter shows how to evaluate the quality and condition of an old piano so that you'll have some idea of what you're getting into before you buy it or begin fixing it. It doesn't include a discussion of brand names. The brand name is an indicator of the quality of an older piano, for it implies how expensive and how well-built the piano was when it was new. On the other hand, the brand says nothing about the state of preservation of an old instrument. A badly abused high-quality piano might be worth less than a well-preserved one of somewhat lower quality. Learn to recognize design and construction details that denote excellence, and the quality of a specific brand will be evident. For detailed information on many specific piano brands, see *The Piano Book* by Larry Fine, listed in the Bibliography.

If your goal is to find a piano to recondition for yourself so that you'll have a usable instrument to play, don't purchase one that will cost far more to fix than it will be worth after you finish repairing it. There are many pianos available in easily repairable condition. On the other hand, if your goal is to learn how to rebuild old pianos as a hobby,

sideline, or full-time business, then you should consider buying a few really dilapidated, cheap old clunkers, with the objective of completely rebuilding them. Whether or not you make any financial profit, you'll gain valuable rebuilding experience. You'll also learn whether or not you really want to keep doing this type of work, without damaging any valuable pianos in the process.

Selecting a Type and Size

The amount of money and space that you have available for a piano will affect the type and size you choose. The rule here is very simple: pianos with longer bass strings and larger soundboards usually have a better tone, so buy the largest piano you can afford.

If you only have room for a vertical, the taller the piano, the better. This means a large upright is better than a studio upright, which is better than a console, which is better than a spinet, *other factors, including the initial quality of the piano and its state of preservation, being equal.*

If you have room for a grand, consider both the overall length and the feel of the action. The action in a good-quality medium-sized or large grand feels and works better than a vertical action does. Also, the sound of a grand is brighter because the soundboard is more out in the open than it is in a vertical. In a tiny, inexpensive grand, however, the action and hammers are typically so light that the action doesn't feel as solid as in a large vertical, although the repetition is better.

The tone quality depends upon on the length of the bass strings and size of the soundboard, among other things. A vertical with longer strings has better tone in the bass than a grand with shorter ones. The bass strings in a large upright are about the same length as those in a 5'8" grand, so a grand shorter than this may not sound as good in the bass as a big upright. In a grand less than 5'8" long, the repetition is superior to that of any vertical, but the touch is sometimes inferior — particularly in a lower-quality piano — and the tone quality is markedly inferior to that of a large vertical.

Prioritizing these factors and choosing a cabinet style and finish can be complicated and involves personal preference and opinion. Most pianists and technicians generally agree that the various types and sizes of pianos can be rated in descending order of desirability as follows: large grand (longer than 6'4"), medium length grand (5'8" – 6'4"), fine-quality small grand (shorter than 5'8"), large upright, studio upright, fine-quality console or inexpensive grand, inexpensive console, and spinet.

Consider buying a square piano only for its looks, or if you're interested in recreating pre-1900 popular or salon music. If you want to play classical music on a historic piano, find a grand piano of the appropriate era, and if you're interested in playing ragtime, obtain a good-quality turn-of-the-century upright or grand.

Recognizing Quality

Although certain high quality piano brands have an almost mystical aura about them, there's nothing magic about what makes a high quality piano better than an inexpensive one. Some design and construction details and finishing touches that go into the making of a fine piano are hard to see in the completely assembled instrument, but certain earmarks are obvious when you know what to look for. A fine-quality piano is sturdier, with a stronger cabinet, plate, and frame or back structure. Compare expensive and inexpensive grand pianos, for example, and you'll see quite a difference in the thickness of the inner and outer rims. Fine grand pianos have a fan-shaped pattern of support posts; inexpensive grands have no support posts at all. The music desk in a fine-quality grand is stronger, with sturdier supporting hardware. Most fine-quality grands have a one-piece fallboard; lower priced grands have a folding fallboard like an old upright.

The back assembly of a fine-quality vertical piano is sturdy enough that the piano can be moved around a room without throwing it out of tune. The back of an inexpensive spinet or console is so flexible that you can throw the high treble somewhat out of tune simply by pushing upward on the treble end of the keybed with your knee, twisting the entire back structure. Some vertical pianos have no back posts, but have a plate that is substantial enough to provide the necessary support. A full-plate piano is sturdier than one with a three-quarter plate.

Fine grand piano cabinet hardware is solid brass, but cheaper piano hardware is brass plated; check the pedals and leg ferrules with a magnet. Fine older vertical piano hardware is often nickel-plated. Higher quality vertical pianos have full-length fallboard hinges; inexpensive ones have two or three small hinges. Fine piano cabinets have all parts made of solid or laminated wood covered on both sides with crossbanding and veneer. Less expensive ones made since the early 1970's have many parts made of veneered particle board. This can be hard to spot by eye, because many particle board panels have solid wood bands around the perimeter to make them look better and to help hold small hinge screws and other hardware. A telltale sign is that particle board is much heavier than solid or laminated wood.

Look inside and check the finishing details of the plate. In a good-quality piano, the visible surfaces of the plate are smooth, with high-quality finish and carefully formed and painted lettering. In an inexpensive piano, the plate casting is rough, the finish isn't as good, and the lettering molded into the casting is crude and carelessly painted.

In a grand piano, remove the fallboard and look with a mirror and flashlight at the back edge of the pinblock where it contacts the plate flange. In a fine-quality piano, the fit is perfect. Gaps, shims, and blobs of epoxy or other filler indicate carelessness in the manufacturing process, and a piano that could have unstable tuning.

The music wire coils should be wound neatly around the tuning pins. The end of each wire should be flush with the surface of the pin, not sticking out. Each pin should have the same number of windings. The bass strings should have copper windings (although some fine-quality pianos made before 1930 have steel windings). The windings on all strings for each unison should be the same length. Good-quality grand pianos have agraffes for all strings except in the high treble; lower-priced grands have no agraffes. Some very good vertical pianos have agraffes.

The best pianos have solid spruce soundboards; lower-priced instruments have laminated soundboards. You can tell whether a soundboard is solid or laminated by looking at the edge of the wood near the damper guide rails in a grand, or at a nose bolt hole. In a vertical, check the orientation of the grain. A solid spruce soundboard has the grain running at approximately a 45° to the

floor. The best soundboards have at least seven grain lines per inch.

Look at the back of the soundboard. In a good piano, the ends of the ribs extend all the way into notches in the back frame, helping to hold the crown in the board. In a lower priced piano, they stop short. Good-quality vertical pianos have a **sound trap**, or wood bar running diagonally across the upper bass corner and lower treble corner to dampen undesirable harmonics. Many fine pianos have these corners of the soundboard cut out, with openings that show from the back.

The bridges in a fine-quality piano have notches along both edges, for both the speaking length and hitch pin segments of each string. The notches are aligned very precisely along the centers of the bridge pins. In a grand piano, the plate struts should pass over the top of the treble bridge so the bridge doesn't need a large notch. In a vertical, the long curve of the treble bridge should have a jog in the area of the notch, so there isn't an abrupt change of string length between the notes on either side of the notch.

Everything in the piano action and keyboard should look perfectly neat. Compare the action in a fine-quality grand or upright with one in an inexpensive spinet of the 1970's. In the former, everything is in perfect alignment. The cloth and leather cushions are glued tightly to the wood, and the hammers are firm and neat. The general look of the action implies that it is possible to regulate each note to respond like its neighbors. In the latter, sloppy dribbles of glue are everywhere, hammers and other parts are misaligned, and cloth and leather cushions are crooked and coming loose. The hammers are lumpy or fuzzy, and the overall look is one that says none of the finishing touches were performed carefully and accurately. The knuckles in a high-quality grand action, and the jack contact area of the hammer butts, and catchers, in a vertical, should be covered with very smooth buckskin. Inexpensive pianos have very rough leather or even action cloth on some parts. Either material wears quickly and makes the action harder to play due to excessive friction. The stop and rest bumpers in a fine action are made of action cloth or buckskin, rather than neoprene.

The keys in better-quality pianos have lead weights located between the center rail and capstan screw. Good pianos have key buttons that hold the balance rail bushings; inexpensive pianos have no buttons, with the bushings located in the keys. Look under the keybed. Good pianos have expansion joints so humidity changes won't affect the regulation of the keys.

Most American pianos have three pedals, but only the finest have a true sostenuto. Many European pianos have only two pedals.

The ultimate test of the quality of a piano is in how it sounds and how the action feels. The only way to learn how pianos should sound and feel is to play many pianos. Anyone with any amount of musical ability can recognize the difference in sound and feel between a concert grand and a spinet sitting next to each other, but it takes experience to play an isolated piano and make valid comparisons with other instruments by memory, allowing for variations in room size and acoustics. It also takes experience to predict how a piano heard in one setting will sound in a larger or smaller one with harder or softer wall and floor coverings. Nonetheless, when you play up and down the scale loudly and softly, a good piano should have a smooth tonal transition from bass to treble, without sudden changes in tone quality from

one note to the next. The action should feel smooth and responsive, while providing uniform touch weight, for predictable control of expression and repetition. In short, a fine piano makes it easier for you to be a better pianist.

The Importance of Age

A brief discussion of age must necessarily contain generalizations to which there are many exceptions; but certain guidelines are useful. Although Victorian pianos are pretty to look at, pianos made after 1900 are better sounding, more durable musical instruments. The era from about 1905 to 1929 saw the production of many fine-quality pianos. The depression and war era from about 1930 to 1945 saw the arrival of small, inexpensive spinets and consoles, but production of fine-quality grands and larger verticals increased again after the mid-1940's. During the 1970's, the quality of some inexpensive American piano brands declined, and some manufacturers went out of business. The 1980's saw the simultaneous rise of both domestic quality and importation of medium- to fine-quality pianos.

How To Tell the Age of a Piano

Although a few piano owners can tell you the exact day, month, and year that grandma bought their piano, and a few others will proudly show you the original bill of sale written in 1921, many people have no idea how old their piano is. Some will admit their ignorance, but many others will exaggerate the age of a piano, in the mistaken belief that the older it is, the better it is. With other misconceptions (like "solid oak" cabinets, "upright grands," and "solid brass frames") many people think their pianos *must* date back to the 1800's. Many pianos contain elaborate decals inside the lid advertising the dates when their manufacturers won various awards and medals at world's fairs, expositions, or trade shows. At most of these events, every piano entered won some sort of award. Patent dates also frequently appear somewhere inside, often cast into the plate. These dates might have helped sales people to convince prospective buyers that the manufacturer was old and reliable, but *in no instance do they tell the actual age of a piano*. For example, Kimball was still using beautiful decals depicting medals won in 1857 inside the lids of pianos manufactured well over a hundred years later.

Actually, the vast majority of pianos extant today came out of the factory doors after 1900. The best way to date a piano, unless an original invoice or other paperwork exists, is to look up the serial number in factory production records. In most vertical pianos, you can find the number stamped in the front of the pinblock in a small "window" in the plate under the lid, rubber stamped on the plate under the lid, or stamped outside on one upper back corner. In a grand, you can find it stamped into the pinblock under the music desk, on the back of the keybed, or rubber stamped on the plate. The major reference work for piano dating, the *Pierce Piano Atlas*, listed in the Bibliography, contains serial number information for thousands of brands of pianos manufactured worldwide. This book is a valuable reference for dating most well-known pianos. Note, however, that some listings are inaccurate or incomplete, such as those for Knabe concert grands and Aeolian Co. reproducing pianos of various brands. Other listings are correct for ordinary pianos but not for players made by the same company. Also, many "stencil" pianos carry the name of a department store or music store instead of the name of their maker, and thus may not appear in the *Piano Atlas*. Another similar book published in Germany and containing mainly data on European pianos is the *Europe Piano Atlas*, also listed in the Bibliography.

In the absence of a piano atlas, or if you can't find a serial number in a particular piano, the following guidelines will help you figure out the age of an American vertical. Certain styles, veneers, sizes, and shapes of vertical piano cabinets had their specific periods of popularity in America just like furniture and automobile styles. By knowing when these styles were popular, it is possible to come up with an approximate estimate of age. These guidelines only apply to vertical pianos, because grand cabinets didn't undergo the constant evolution that vertical cabinets did. The dates are only approximate, and there was some overlap from one period to the next, but an experienced piano dealer or technician who has observed details of hundreds of pianos can usually date a vertical piano by its looks within about five years. Here are the basics:

- 1880-1895: Medium height cabinets, three-quarter plates, and dowel capstans were prevalent. Ornate "Victorian" style cabinets had fretwork and fancy veneer; rosewood, walnut, and ebony finish were popular.

- 1895-1905: Larger size, fancy cabinets, fluted columns, carved capitals, fancy walnut and mahogany veneer were popular. Quartered oak gained in popularity after 1900. Some of the prettiest fancy cases date from this era.

- 1905-1915: Quartered oak veneer was very popular. "Mission" style was in vogue, with rectangular shapes, square columns, sometimes with the front subdivided into two or three rectangular panels. Large round columns were also popular. Generally, the largest, heaviest pianos date from this period.

- 1915-1925: Simple rectangular mahogany-veneered cabinets, described by one collector as "Chicago Moderne Box" style, were popular; the size and weight gradually diminished through this period. Most pianos of this era were players.
- 1925-1935: Size continued to decrease, with walnut veneer gaining in popularity.
- 1935-1945: A few small, lighter-weight studio uprights, usually with walnut veneer, and the first consoles and spinets appeared, but few pianos sold during this period due first to economic depression and then to World War II.
- 1945-1950: Spinet and console pianos flourished, usually veneered in red or brown mahogany. Many cabinets were plain, but some of the prettiest fancy spinet and console designs came out of this era.
- 1950-1960: Plainer spinets, consoles, and studio uprights veneered with plain sliced oak, with white or blond finish became very popular. Some were covered with vinyl.
- 1960-1970: Brown walnut veneer became popular again, with both fancy and plain spinets and consoles popular.
- 1970-1980: Pecan and oak veneer became popular; knotty pine veneer was even popular for a few years after the USA Bicentennial. This era saw a general decline in quality of many inexpensive brands of American spinets and consoles. As quality deteriorated, many manufacturers of low-priced pianos went out of business.
- 1980-1990: Manufacturers marketed many styles for many tastes. More Japanese, European, and Asian consoles, studio uprights, and grands were sold in America,

these imported pianos being of higher quality than their poorly made American counterparts of the 1970's. "Survival of the fittest" saw the best American companies strengthened by the competition. Manufacturers bought and sold brand names so often that it was hard to keep up with who made what.

The above information is applicable to American pianos only; English, German, Japanese, and other pianos had their own popular cabinet styles through the years. For example, British piano companies made rosewood veneered "Victorian" pianos with brass candle holders for years after American manufacturers quit making this style.

Evaluating the Condition

The condition of a piano depends on the condition of its thousands of individual parts, many of which can't be seen without completely disassembling the piano. This section tells you how to diagnose the condition of the parts without complete disassembly, so you'll have a good idea of what repairs might be needed to put a piano into good playing condition.

First, check the piano from the outside. Pull a vertical piano away from the wall, or look under the bottom of a grand, to see if any glue joints of the back frame or cabinet are coming apart. This is less common in grands, but in verticals exposed to extremes of humidity and dryness, it isn't unusual for main glue joints in the back to come apart. In extreme cases, the pinblock of an upright piano comes unglued and the string tension pulls it forward from the back structure. If the frame is falling apart, the main structural portions of the piano will need complete disassembly, major woodworking, and regluing.

Never crawl under a grand piano unless you know that the legs are strong enough to hold it. The author knows of several instances in which a grand fell off its legs and came crashing to the floor. Also, never try to roll a grand piano across the floor with fewer than three people to lift some weight off the legs. It's surprising how slight an indentation in the floor it takes to snag a caster, causing a leg to break.

Have the owner remove all plants, piles of music, figurines, pencils, and coffee mugs. Then, *with the owner's permission*, remove the cabinet parts that come off, as described on p. 85 for vertical pianos and pp. 88-89 for grands. Plan in advance where you'll stand dirty cabinet parts so the dirt won't get all over the walls and rug, and so they won't fall over if a child or large dog bumps into them.

While removing cabinet parts, note their condition. Are panels badly warped? Is veneer or crossbanding unglued? Loose veneer and warped and cracked pieces suggest that a piano has been subjected to extremes of humidity and dryness. Is the bottom of a vertical piano still glued together, or do large cracks and loose screws let it bend downward when you use the pedals? Are the legs of a grand loose and wobbly? Are all casters supported solidly by their sockets, or are some of them leaning over, with the wheel dragging on the bottom of the case or leg? How much woodworking will it take to put the cabinet in good-looking, structurally sound condition? A few loose spots in the veneer aren't hard to fix, but if the veneer and underlying crossbanding are loose all over, it is literally easier to build a new cabinet than to repair the old one. Scrutinize the finish on the cabinet. Is it acceptable the way it is, or will it need to be refinished? A beautiful piano finish takes a lot more work than the type of finish that is acceptable on other furniture.

After checking the outside for structural and cabinet defects, turn your attention to the inside. First check the plate carefully for cracks. Common places for cracks to occur include the areas around the tuning pins or plate screws, under the pressure bar, in front of the capo bar or agraffe area in a grand, and across struts or beams. If you find any cracks, don't buy the piano.

Is the soundboard still glued to the liner all the way around the perimeter, and are all ribs glued tightly to the soundboard? Is the soundboard cracked? Small cracks aren't important, but large ones usually accompany sections of soundboard unglued from the ribs, making the piano sound like a bad loudspeaker. Is the soundboard buckled away from the ribs? This condition takes major work to repair properly.

If the piano has a bass bridge apron, is it in one piece? Are the bridge and apron glued together, or will they have to be repaired? Are the bridges in good condition, or do they have cracks and splits in the wood surrounding the bridge pins? Recapping or replacing a bridge is usually worthwhile only in a valuable piano.

Check the strings and tuning pins. Are the bass strings clean, or are they rusty and caked with dirt and corrosion? Are the treble strings, pressure bar, and tuning pins so rusty that the strings will break during tuning? A certain amount of tarnish isn't serious, but actual rust means the piano should be restrung. Are there any shiny new strings amidst a section of old rusty ones, indicating that more old strings are ready to break?

Is there any downbearing of the strings on the bridges? Check this with a downbearing gauge at several places along each bridge. Place the center foot of the gauge exactly halfway between the two rows of bridge pins for the string to be measured, and align the

3-1. A rocker bearing gauge used for checking the downbearing of the strings on the bridge.

outside feet over the same string. If there is downbearing, the gauge will rock on the middle foot. This is easy to do in a grand piano in someone's house. In a vertical, you won't be able to check the bearing on most of the treble bridge without removing the action. If the action is in poor condition, you'll risk damaging fragile parts by removing and replacing it, and then it will be your responsibility to repair them for the owner if you don't buy the piano.

Does the soundboard have any crown? Stretch a string along the back of the soundboard parallel to the longest rib. With the ends of the string touching the board, is there a gap between the middle of the board and the string? The presence of crown is desirable, because it helps to provide a better tone, and it implies that the piano has never been damaged by extreme humidity changes.

In what condition is the pinblock? In a grand piano, you can inspect the bottom layer after you remove the piano action. (*Be sure this is okay with the owner.*) To remove the action, slide it forward, being careful to avoid damaging the hammers (see illus. 4-15). The bottom lamination of the pinblock doesn't tell you how tight the tuning pins are, but it does tell you if the whole pinblock is falling apart. In some vertical pianos, you

can see part of the face and upper edge of the pinblock, but in others, you can't see any of it. In any piano, you can measure the tightness of the tuning pins with a torque wrench; refer to pp. 96 and 277 for further information. Has the pinblock been "doped" with pin tightener, indicated by dark stains on the pins or plate? Or has a previous technician driven the pins in until the music wire coils touch the pinblock or plate? These are signs that the piano will have to be restrung before it will stay in tune. If the pins are original and are somewhat loose, in many cases the problem can be solved with a "Dampp-Chaser Piano Humidity Control System" or equivalent installed in the piano. See pp. 146-148 for more information. If the pins are original and are too loose to hold, it is sometimes possible to restring the piano with larger pins. If someone has already restrung the piano and the oversize pins are loose or squeaky, the piano probably needs a new pinblock. This is a major job, particularly in a vertical piano.

Beware of Mason & Hamlin "screw stringer" pianos with threaded stringing hooks and tuning nuts instead of tuning pins. Although one of these in good condition isn't particularly hard to tune, the guide combs in some of these pianos deteriorate and are exceptionally difficult to duplicate, even for a highly-qualified machinist.

Next, check the condition of the keyboard and piano action. Are the keytops in good condition or will you want to replace them? How are the fronts of the keys? Are the keys warped, with the front leaning to one side and the back to the other? How are the hammers? Look down on the striking surfaces from above to see how much felt remains at the bottom of the deep grooves. Original hammers are usually uniformly dirty; carefully reshaped hammers are uniformly clean. Poorly reshaped hammers have irregular clean and dirty areas with flat spots and crooked surfaces that keep them from producing a good tone. How are the center pin bushings? The key bushings? Do hammer butts and other action parts wobble and click? Some clicks occur simply because of loose flange screws, but others are a consequence of worn bushings and other cloth and felt parts. How are the bridle straps? These are usually the first parts of a vertical piano to go bad, and they are the easiest to replace.

Was the piano ever wet inside? One giveaway is the presence of bright red streaks where the dye from red felts has run onto adjacent parts. If there is extensive water damage inside, don't buy the piano.

To check the general condition of the action, play all the way up and down the keyboard, playing each key first very softly several times and then very loudly several more times. This test will make obvious such things as hammers hitting the wrong strings, loose bass string windings that buzz, clicking action parts, broken, noisy, or loose keys, and unisons that play more than one note at a time, indicating very loose tuning pins.

If someone else repaired the piano previously, what is the quality of the repairs? Poorly shaped hammers and crooked keytops, for example, detract from a piano's value.

In summary, shiny metal and light-colored wood action parts usually indicate good condition; rusty metal and dark colored action parts imply moisture damage. If a piano has an unglued frame, unglued or cracked cabinet parts or veneer, a broken plate, rusty metal parts, large cracks in the soundboard and bridges, loose tuning pins, worn-out or moth-eaten hammers and action felts, severely warped keys, clicking action parts, or keys that play more than one note

at a time, look for another piano, or plan to do major repairs.

Player Pianos & Empty Player Pianos

Piano repair and restoration is a field of its own, requiring many additional techniques, tools, and materials not used in ordinary piano repair. The companion book to this one, *Player Piano Servicing and Rebuilding*, by the same author and publisher, covers this subject thoroughly.

Many old uprights had the player actions removed and discarded after they quit working in the 1940's and 1950's, so empty player pianos far outnumber the sets of extra parts in existence. If you run across an empty player piano, don't buy it in hopes of finding the correct action for it someday. Pianos and player actions had so many different shapes and sizes that trying to find the correct player action for an empty player piano is almost completely futile. On the other hand, if you run across a good restorable set of parts, keep them. You might find a piano in which they can be installed, among all the other empty players in which they won't fit. Gulbransen players are an exception to this rule, because the company standardized them to a greater extent than most other brands.

Of course, empty reproducing pianos, coin pianos, and orchestrions — and orphan parts for them — are worth preserving for collectors who specialize in restoring these rare and valuable instruments.

Mirror Pianos

During the 1940's and 50's, when console and spinet pianos became very popular and old uprights had little value, certain repair shops "restyled" large old uprights to make them look smaller. Restyling usually consisted of removing the original top of a worn-out upright, cutting the cabinet sides back to the front of the pinblock and just above the top of the hammers, and then modifying the front and top and adding a mirror in front of the pinblock to give the illusion of shorter height. Since these pianos almost invariably had the mirror installed in front of the pinblock, they became known as "mirror pianos." Many mirror pianos had their toes cut off, with or without spinet style legs added to the front corners. The final insult was a coat of white paint, or a covering of vinyl contact paper, sometimes secured around the edges with hundreds of "decorator" tacks. In the worst examples, the "restylist" shortened the height by cutting off part of the bottom, modifying the plate and rescaling the bass bridge, bass strings, and hitch pins.

Today, competent technicians consider the irreversible restyling of good old uprights to be butchery. Many mirror pianos were already in very sad shape before their restyling, and most people think they look pathetic, so today few of them are worth reconditioning. Now and then, however, a mirror piano turns up in perfectly good repairable condition; so if you find a good one and don't mind its looks, purchasing it might be a way to obtain an inexpensive but usable piano.

Where to Find a Used Piano

Finding a good unrestored piano isn't the easy job that it was in the 1950's, when a prospective buyer could find a good selection for under $100 each just by "asking around." Unfortunately, pianos continue to put out some kind of sound long after major repairs are necessary, leading the public to believe they're indestructible. Many old pianos have had minor repair work done, including new bridle straps (in verticals), new keytops, reshaping of the hammers, and poor-quality refinishing, so they work, but they don't look or sound very good. In the eyes of many owners these instruments have been "restored" and the owners believe them to be worth more than they really are, although the previous repairs usually must be redone. Occasionally, previous repairs will save you a little work, but it's far more common to have to spend a substantial amount of extra time undoing them. It is wise to consider a previously repaired instrument as worth no more, or little more, than one in good untouched condition, unless a fine technician made the repairs.

Good unrestored instruments do turn up now and then, so with diligence you can still find one. How? Study the local want ads, and let all your friends and acquaintances know that you're looking for a good used piano. Check all the used pianos for sale in local piano stores. If you want to buy one to repair yourself, you might find one that a piano shop hasn't yet repaired, and is willing to sell at a reasonable markup, saving you the time and trouble of shopping the want ads. Or you might want to run a "piano wanted" ad yourself in the local newspaper. Above all, be patient. Enough old pianos exist in restorable condition that you will find exactly what you want if you take your time looking.

Myths Versus Reality

Because a piano is so completely different from any other household item, it's no wonder that so many myths prevail among piano owners and even sales personnel. Here are a few common ones:

- *"This piano is an upright grand."* Translation: this is a big upright. Reality: many people apply the term "upright grand" to many old uprights, implying "fine-quality" or "having a large tone." The term, which actually originated as a sales gimmick with manufacturers who used the name "Upright Grand" on the fallboard, might accurately describe a very old vertical with a large curve built into the top, so the cabinet looks like a grand standing on end. But in no instance does it mean an upright has a grand piano action.

- *"This piano has a brass harp"* or a *"bell metal harp."* Translation: the plate has gold paint on it. Reality: the terms "brass harp," "brass plate" and "brass frame" are incorrect; piano plates are made of cast iron, with the rare exception of a few made of cast aluminum. Even in a piano with the wording "bell metal" cast into the plate, the plate is made of cast iron.

- *"This piano has a solid brass soundboard."* Reality: the plate has gold paint on it. Soundboards are made of wood, and plates are made of cast iron.

- *"This piano is worth a lot because it has ivory keys."* Reality: a keyboard with perfect ivories, or only a few chips, is a desirable thing to have on an old piano, but an ivory keyboard with chips from one end to the other doesn't enhance the value of a piano, and a poor-quality piano with good ivories is still just a poor-quality piano.

- *"This piano is very fine, because it is very old."* Reality: an older piano isn't necessarily better than a new one, although most people believe this because some older pianos are better than some new ones.

- *"This piano never needs tuning."* Translation: "I can't tell if a piano is in tune or not." Reality: despite what anyone thinks, when humidity goes up and down, it makes the soundboard expand and contract, throwing the piano out of tune.

- *"An upright player piano is inferior to a regular piano for hand playing, because the weight of the player mechanism makes the action stiff."* Reality: the player mechanism is separate from the piano action and has no effect on the touch.

- *"My piano tuner said this piano has a cracked soundboard, so it can't be tuned."* Translation: the tuner said the piano has a cracked pinblock, so it can't be tuned.

- *"This piano has a solid oak cabinet."* Translation: "I've heard antique dealers say that old round oak tables and other furniture are made of solid oak, so this piano must be made of solid oak too." Reality: crossbanded and veneered wood is much more resistant to warping and cracking than solid wood, and is much better for piano cabinets. Most old pianos — even most *inexpensive* old pianos — have crossbanding and veneer on the sides and other large panels.

Summary

Many old pianos are in somewhat poor condition contrasted to many newer ones, and a fine-quality smaller piano was better when new than a larger inexpensive one was, so you must weigh the size, quality, age, and condition against each other very carefully. After a fine restoration, a larger good-quality older piano will always sound better than a smaller good-quality newer one, but *don't assume that your first few repair attempts will bring an old piano back to brand new condition.*

When searching for a used piano, the more you know about what you're buying, the happier you'll be when you finally purchase one. Learn as much as possible about pianos by reading and by visiting with others who share your interest. Don't buy on impulse, don't underestimate the amount of time it takes to perform good-quality major repairs, and don't kid yourself about the imaginary value of many previous repairs. Reshaped hammers, new keytops and new bridle straps don't make a rebuilt piano, and they don't mean the piano will necessarily last for years of additional use.

Whether you buy an instrument in good condition or restore one yourself, you'll have a large investment of money or time in it; a musical instrument, especially one that has thousands of parts that are many years old, is not the place to be "cheap." A corner cut here and a dollar saved there will result in a disappointing instrument, but time and money taken to get the job done right will give you a piano that will provide many years of enjoyment.

Chapter Four

Cleaning and Minor Repairs: *Fixing Worn and Broken Parts*

This chapter begins with some information on tools, woodworking, and types of glue. It then discusses cleaning a piano and performing *minor* repairs that can be made on site, without moving the whole piano into a repair shop. Examples of minor repairs include replacing one broken string or a missing keytop, regluing a broken key or action part, easing a sluggish or binding mechanism, or fixing a damper that doesn't work. Most of these repairs can be made with portable tools carried to the location of the piano. Sometimes it might be easier to remove certain parts from the piano and take them to the shop for these repairs, but it isn't necessary to move the entire piano.

When a piano needs *major* repairs — repairs like replacing a pinblock, shimming and refinishing a soundboard, or restoring an entire action by installing new hammers, springs, felts, and other parts — it must be moved into a shop equipped with power tools. Major repairs fall under the category of "rebuilding," covered in Chapter 8. Rebuilding usually involves installing entire sets of new parts, or completely reconditioning the old parts.

Technicians use the terms "reconditioned," "renovated," "rebuilt," "restored," and even "remanufactured" to describe the results of various types of major repair jobs. Each term means something different to each rebuilder. In this book, to *repair* means "to fix a broken or worn part." To *rebuild* means "to do major work, usually including replac-

ing the pinblock, restringing, repairing the soundboard, and installing new hammers and all perishable action parts." To *restore* means "to return the piano as close as possible to what it was when it was new." To rebuild a Steinway, for example, you might use any good-quality brand of new hammers; to restore a Steinway would require Steinway hammers.

See Appendix for information on where to obtain repair parts and supplies.

Basics of Tools and Woodworking

Before learning about specific piano repairs, you should understand woodworking basics, the proper use of common tools, and how to prepare good glue joints. If you're sincerely interested in piano servicing, you should be willing to obtain and use the correct high-quality tool for each job. You can make some specialized piano tools easily in your workshop, and purchase the rest from a piano supply company. This chapter and the others illustrate appropriate tools for each job. Obviously, many volumes exist covering the proper use of hand and power tools, and the present book can't possibly go into any depth in covering these topics. If woodworking is new to you, spend as much time as possible studying books and magazines on the subject, as this will improve your proficiency in all areas of piano repair and rebuilding. Above all, keep tool safety and proper working conditions foremost in your mind at all times. Remember that any tool, from the simplest hand tool to the largest power tool, can be dangerous. Make a habit of following correct safety procedures for each and every tool.

The screwdriver is the most commonly abused tool. Screws come in many sizes and shapes, and the correct screwdriver should be used for each. The well-equipped piano technician should have at least a half dozen regular screwdrivers for cabinet screws — short and long blade screwdrivers for all commonly encountered screws, sizes 6 through 12, plus one or more huge ones for tightening plate screws — and a variety of specialized action regulating screwdrivers as described in Chapter 5. Some modern piano builders use Phillips screws of various sizes; the technician should have at least one medium and one large Phillips screwdriver. Offset and ratchet offset screwdrivers also come in handy for hard-to-reach screws. Using the wrong size screwdriver not only ruins the shape of the blade; it also leaves a trail of damaged screw heads wherever used. Disfigured screw heads are a sure indicator of a sloppy technician.

When you start a screw in an old hole, turn it backwards gently until you feel the threads aligning themselves with the old threads in the wood; then tighten it. This will help to prevent stripped screw holes.

Several pliers are useful: regular slip-joint, tongue and groove ("water pump"), long nose, locking pliers, diagonal-cutting or side-cutting (for cutting soft wire), music wire cutting (with compound action and hardened cutters), round nose (for making small springs), duck bill and bent nose (for hard-to-reach areas), and specialized pliers made for piano work, like key easing and wire bending ("smiling") pliers.

Other important hand tools include several sharp wood chisels, cold chisels, and a sharpening stone, small and medium size adjustable wrenches, a set of ignition wrenches, open end wrenches, a variety of small files, a cabinet scraper, paint scraper, utility knife, putty knife, single-edge razor blades, small pin punches, several hammers, steel and brass wire brushes, a sanding block, and many other miscellaneous small tools.

Important measuring tools include a variety of rulers from 6" to 36" long, a steel tape measure, gauges for measuring music wire, tuning pins, and center pins, and a good micrometer or dial caliper.

A hand-held electric drill is a necessity for many repairs, and if you don't already have one, consider buying a good-quality 1/2" variable speed reversible model. Drill bits come in a huge variety of sizes and types, including ordinary fluted bits, spade (or power woodboring), brad-point, multi-spur, and Forstner bits, all of which are handy for piano repair and rebuilding. At the very least, the beginning technician should have a set of fluted bits from 1/16" to 1/4" in 1/64" increments and 1/4" to 1/2" in 1/32" increments. The professional rebuilder should have a good-quality drill press, a complete set of numbered and fractional fluted bits from #60 to 1/2", and other specialized bits that are useful for making sophisticated cabinet repairs, drilling pinblocks, and other precise work.

Expendable supplies include various grits of garnet and aluminum oxide sandpaper, 4/0 steel wool, non-abrasive metal polish like "Simichrome™" or "Sea Power™," soft cotton polishing rags, ethyl alcohol, odorless paint thinner, and a variety of glues and adhesives described in detail later in this chapter.

Use each tool only for its designated purpose. Don't use a knife or chisel as a prying tool, nor a screwdriver as a chisel. Improper

4-1. A convenient vise for working on small action parts. It can be secured to any table with the built-in clamp, and turned on its ball and socket mount to any convenient working angle.

use eventually results in the tool breaking or the user receiving an injury. Keep tools sharp and properly shaped. A sharp knife, chisel, or screwdriver is dangerous enough, but a dull one is hazardous because it takes much more force on the handle to do its job. The more force that you use, the greater the chance of slipping and possible injury.

Always keep your hands behind the working end of a tool and aim the tool away from your body. Apply force to the tool with the strength of your arm, not the weight of your body. If a tool slips while you're leaning on it, you might fall into the sharp end of the tool or the work piece. Aim your strength at an angle oblique to the work, so if you do slip, your hand will run into thin air instead of something sharp.

When doing any work that requires putting force on a part — like cutting, scraping, or drilling — secure the part in a vise whenever possible. In a customer's home, use a small portable vise or some sort of clamp. This allows you to apply more carefully controlled pressure to the part with the tool, decreasing danger of slipping or injury. When holding a wooden part in a metal vise, insert thin wooden or fiber spacers between the vise jaws and the part to protect the part from jaw imprints.

Hold the part close to the place that will have force applied to it. This minimizes the chance of breakage. If you hold a long, slender wooden part by the opposite end, leverage multiplies your working force, and you might break the part next to where you clamped it.

When scraping glue or other materials from a strip of wood with a scraper or chisel, always work with the grain. Observe which way the grain runs from within the piece out to the surface. In one direction, the chisel will scrape over the surface, and in the other direction it will dig into the wood and gouge it.

To remove old felts from backchecks, damper heads, and other small action parts, secure the part in a small vise and scrape the felt off with short chisel strokes. It is sometimes possible to pull the felt from the wood with pliers. If necessary, soften the glue by dampening the felt with water or vinegar, let-

4-2. Always push a chisel in the same direction at which the wood grain rises to the surface, to avoid gouging the wood.

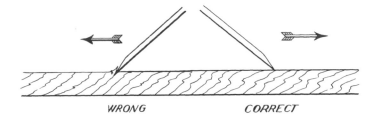

WRONG   CORRECT

4-3. A short version of a pickup tool or "grabber", useful for reaching where your fingers can't. A 12" or 18" long model is even better.

ting the water soak into the glue without soaking the wood.

Every technician should have a pickup tool (also known as a "grabber") and a magnet on a stick, for retrieving small screws and other parts dropped into hard-to-reach places.

Glue Joints

In a good glue joint, the wood surfaces just barely touch each other all across the surface of the joint. The glue soaks into the pores in both pieces, forming a solid bond. A good glue joint doesn't have a gap with a thick "sandwich" of glue between the two pieces. "Glue sandwiches" usually break apart somewhere in the layer of glue; tight glue joints with the wood fibers bonded together remain stuck together for a long time. (Glue joints requiring epoxy and contact cement are exceptions to this rule, as noted later in this section).

When repairing a broken glue joint — that is, two pieces of wood previously glued together — first remove as much of the old glue as possible. Secure each part in a vise, and scrape off the old glue with a cabinet

scraper blade, available from woodworking supply companies. Leave the wood surface intact; gouging the original wood is just as bad as leaving old lumps of glue in place. After removing the old glue from both parts, clamp them together temporarily to check the dry fit, using thin wood clamping blocks to protect the wooden parts from clamp marks. Apply a thin layer of glue to each part, instead of a thick layer to one part. Press the parts together in proper alignment until they begin to stick together, and the apply the clamps. Keep checking the alignment while tightening the clamps. When the clamps are tight and the alignment is perfect, remove any excess glue with a damp rag.

When clamping close-grained hard wood like maple, don't tighten the clamps so much that all the glue squeezes out of the joint. Leave the clamps in place until the glue dries. Finished glue joints should always be neat. A patch of dried glue on the surface of a part where there was none originally is a mark of a sloppy technician.

To repair a cracked piece of wood, open the crack as far as possible and apply a thin coat of glue with a small spatula or artist's palette knife, without disturbing any wood fibers. Align the parts and apply clamping blocks and clamps. When attaching two parts with both screws and glue, assemble them dry first, to test for correct fit.

Many types of clamps are useful for piano repairing, including C clamps, sliding bar clamps, spring clamps, pipe clamps, hand screws, and even rubber bands, string, and masking tape for small, delicate repairs.

Types of Glue Used in Piano Repair

When choosing the type of glue for a specific repair, consider the type of wood, the size of the glue joint, the amount of dry-

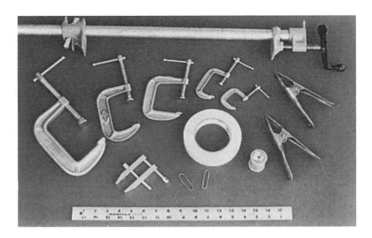

4-4. A few of the many types of clamps that are handy for various piano repairs.

ing time, whether it is practical to use clamps, and any other pertinent factors. The following section describes types of glue that are useful for a variety of piano repairs.

Hot glue (hide glue, or animal glue), the old standby for many piano gluing jobs, is a hydrolyzed collagen, a protein constituent of animal skins, connective tissue, and bones. Piano and woodworking supply companies sell it by the pound, in crystals or flakes. It sticks quickly, stays stuck, and is easy to sand. If applied correctly, it is very strong. It can be mixed thinner for gluing wood to wood, or thicker for gluing action cloth without having the glue soak all the way through the cloth.

Hot glue's superior stickiness and fast drying time make it the ideal glue for action cloth, felt, and leather. It is also the best choice for gluing cloth bushings in piano keys. When the bushings wear out again, hot glue will be easier to remove without damaging the wood than other types of glue.

Although any wood-to-wood glue joint, including one assembled with hot glue, can be stubborn to disassemble, the advantage of using hot glue is that when you separate the parts in the future, you can remove the old glue easily by sanding. This isn't the case with other common woodworking glues like white and aliphatic resin glue. The only real

disadvantages of using hot glue are the experience necessary to judge how thin or thick to make it, and the dexterity required to apply it neatly and assemble the glue joint in the short time before it begins to gel.

Hot glue doesn't stick to finished wood, nor to metal or plastic, so it is useless for these applications.

If you plan to do much piano repair and rebuilding work, obtain an automatic electric glue pot from a piano supply company. If you intend to repair or restore only one piano and want to avoid the expense of a "real" glue pot, construct a simple double boiler by placing a glass jar in a kettle of water on a stove or thermostatically controlled hot plate.

4-5. A thermostatically-controlled electric glue pot, available from piano and woodworking supply companies.

Whether you make your glue in a genuine glue pot or in a double boiler on the stove, use a candy thermometer to check the temperature, which should be kept between 135° and 145° Fahrenheit. Some commercially available glue pots have the thermostat set a little too high. If a check with the thermometer proves this to be the case, disassemble the glue pot and adjust the thermostat as necessary. It is normal for the temperature to swing approximately 10°F., but the thermostat should be adjusted so the highest temperature doesn't exceed 145°. If glue is heated beyond this temperature, it can harden in the pot after being heated for just a few hours.

Many commercial glue pots come with a wire insert for wiping the excess glue off the brush. This wire will accumulate large clumps of partially dried glue, and will gradually rust away, depositing particles of rust in the glue. Discard the wire and replace it with a wood dowel wedged in place. The wood rod will neither deteriorate nor accumulate stalactites of glue.

To make a batch of glue, fill the container of your glue pot about 1/3–1/2 full of dry glue crystals, with the pot turned off. This will produce plenty of glue for an average work session. If you make much less than a third of a pot, the glue will dry out quickly, making it necessary to add water frequently.

Slowly add cold water until there is about 1/4" of water on top of the glue. Don't stir yet; the water will mix in by itself, and if you stir it into the glue crystals, you might be tempted to add too much water. Cover the pot and let the glue dissolve overnight, or until the particles are 100% dissolved. Turn on the heat an hour before your work session, and when you're ready to start working, you'll have a batch of glue of approximately the right consistency for gluing wood to

wood. Each time you withdraw a brush full of glue, stir the glue well; this will ensure that the consistency will remain uniform. The consistency should be something like thick pancake syrup, thicker than water but thinner than molasses. You can judge this only when the glue is hot; after you apply it to a piece of wood, or even when you hold a brush full in mid air, it begins to cool and thicken.

Prior to applying the glue, preheat the surface of the wooden parts with a warm iron or heat lamp, to a temperature no hotter than that of the glue pot. Apply and spread the glue with a stiff brush as quickly as possible — within a few seconds after removing it from the pot. When you preheat two pieces of wood, stir the glue well and apply it to the wood, and assemble and clamp the parts together within five or ten seconds, the consistency of the glue is correct if just a little glue squeezes out of the joint, and if it is difficult or impossible to slide one piece against the other a few moments after assembly. If the two pieces of wood feel like they have a spongy cushion between them, either the glue was too thick in the pot, you didn't stir it well enough immediately before use, you applied too much to the wood, the parts were too cold, or you took too much time to assemble the parts. (Beginners often find all the above to be true.) On the other hand, if no glue squeezes out, it is too thin. In either case, quickly separate the parts, remove the glue, and begin again.

Make a cover for your glue pot and use it. A rubber disc sold as a polishing and sanding accessory for an electric drill makes a sturdy glue pot cover that won't slide around, but the plastic lid from a coffee can or margarine dish also works. It is important to keep the glue covered while the batch is initially dissolving and cooking, and as much as possible during actual use. If you leave the glue uncovered while it is mixing the night before, the top 1/2" or more will be composed of froth that will remain after the glue cooks for several hours. When you stir this mixture, the froth will permeate the glue with thousands of air bubbles that will gradually return to the surface as another layer of froth. A good batch of glue shouldn't be full of air bubbles. The more you leave the cover off the pot during actual work, the sooner the glue will have a hard crust on top, particularly in dry climates, requiring additional water, thorough stirring and more waiting for it to mix again. Keep your glue pot covered as much as possible, and add water as necessary to keep the consistency right for the job. If the glue soaks all the way through the material when gluing felt or action cloth, remove the cover from the pot and stir the glue once every few minutes until it thickens. Experience will show you just how thick to make it so it will grab action cloth or felt without soaking through. Clamping cloth to wood will exaggerate the problem, so it is usually better to keep pressing with your fingers until the glue sets.

Hot glue may be reheated often for jobs that don't require great strength, but clean your glue pot and make a new batch when gluing important wood to wood glue joints, or any time you see mold or mildew growing on the surface of the glue.

In summary, sticky hot glue is so much easier to use for appropriate jobs, and so much easier to remove from wood than white glue or aliphatic resin glue, that you're wasting time if you insist on using something else. The hardest part of using hot glue is *the process of learning how*; once you master this, you'll wonder how you ever got along without it.

Liquid hide glue is hide glue with a chemical like thiourea added as a drying retardant. It can be sanded off wood easily like hot glue, but it dries very slowly. In situations where slow drying time is desirable, as in gluing and clamping small pieces of veneer without a veneer press, liquid hide glue is useful. Some rebuilders feel that this glue is just as strong as many other types of woodworking glue, and use it for major structural glue joints, while others feel it isn't as strong as hot glue, aliphatic resin glue, and other types.

White glue was the most popular glue for piano and player piano repair during the 1950's when few rebuilders cared about how hard it would be to restore the player action again thirty years later. Now that over thirty years have elapsed, white glue's disadvantages have become painfully obvious. Its main disadvantage is the difficulty of removing it from wood, because it is too hard to remove by scraping, and sanding only turns it gummy and sticky, ruining the sandpaper. Because of the difficulty of removing it from wood, never use white glue for gluing anything that might have to be broken apart and reglued again in the future.

Aliphatic resin glue such as "Titebond™" (Franklin Chemical Industries) and "Elmer's Carpenter's Wood Glue™" (Borden, Inc.) is excellent wood glue, but it is almost as difficult to remove from large areas as white glue is, so its use should be confined to items that will never have to be disassembled, such as broken pieces of wood, large cabinet parts, etc. When using it for regluing veneer or broken cabinet parts in a piano that will be refinished, make all repairs prior to removing the old finish. This will help to keep the glue from soaking into bare wood and causing stains that will show through the new finish. If you use this type of glue for a wood joint that was originally hot glued, all traces of the old hot glue should be removed, or the two will mix, forming a soup that has little strength; the same thing applies to white glue mixed with hot glue.

Contact cement can be used for gluing most types of new white plastic keytops to the keys. Buy the best quality industrial-type contact cement available; inferior brands tend to dry out and become brittle with age. Follow the instructions on the can for safe usage. For gluing bits of felt to metal in modern pianos, automotive adhesive — supplied in squeeze tubes for gluing rubber weather-stripping around car doors — is superior to ordinary contact cement; you can obtain it from a good auto parts store.

Epoxy has great strength and gap-filling properties, and is the best glue for major structural glue joints that might not fit together perfectly. It comes in two parts that must be mixed and then used within a limited working time — usually from five to twenty minutes. One "professional" brand is "West System" ™ brand epoxy, manufactured by Gougeon Bros., Inc. (available through boat repair shops). The filler, or thickening agent, is packaged separately so you can prime the wood first with a very thin mixture that will soak into the wood, then add the filler to the mixture, and then coat the glue joint with the thickened mixture for good gap filling. Note that epoxy gives off toxic fumes that don't have a strong odor. Always follow the manufacturer's precautions; use proper ventilation and lung protection when using epoxy, even though it doesn't smell as bad as other materials that are less toxic.

PVC-E (plastic glue) is handy for gluing certain white plastic keytops to the keys, if the plastic is of a type that would be damaged by the solvent in contact cement. Don't confuse PVC-E with the thin, volatile, toxic PVC cement used for gluing PVC plastic pipe. PVC-E looks like white glue and smells completely different from PVC plastic pipe cement. It is available only from piano and organ supply companies, not hardware stores.

Super glue (cyanoacrylate ester) comes in several different types with different curing times and gap-filling or non-gap-filling properties. Especially convenient for technicians in the field, this modern product is handy for all varieties of "quick fixes," from gluing down little chips of veneer to regluing broken jack flanges and loose ivory keytops. In the shop, conventional woodworking glues should be used for major regluing jobs.

Burnt shellac, although not really glue, is useful for sticking felt to piano plates and other metal parts, where a layer of glue is undesirable and a stronger adhesive is unnecessary. Make this by mixing a small amount of alcohol with shellac flakes, or by burning alcohol out of premixed orange shellac until it's so thick after it cools that it doesn't run when applied to a vertical surface. If you burn the alcohol off, do it outside with the shellac in a metal container sitting on concrete where it won't spill or catch something else on fire. Thick burnt shellac takes a week or longer to dry, and it sticks to wood, metal, and other parts for years. It can be removed from wood by scraping it off or from metal by heating it without damaging the parts. Once you become accustomed to having a supply of thick burnt shellac on hand in an old white glue squeeze bottle, you'll wonder how you ever lived without it.

Repairing Loose Screw Holes

Stripped screw holes are a major bugaboo of the piano technician. Flange screws, capstan screws, regulating screws, leg screws, and all sorts of cabinet screws all get loose, and unless you know how to repair them properly, you'll never be competent at your work.

The simplest way to make a loose screw tight again is to replace it with a *longer* screw where practical. If the wooden piece holding the threads is thick enough, drill the hole deeper to accept a longer screw. To select the drill bit for the threaded portion of the hole, hold the bit beside the screw; the bit should be approximately the same as the small diameter of the threaded portion. If a longer screw can't be used, it might be possible to substitute a fatter one. This nearly always requires drilling out the holes in both pieces of wood — the larger one for the shank and the smaller one for the threads — to keep from cracking the wood when inserting the new screw.

In situations where neither a longer nor a fatter screw will help, or whenever any regulating screw is loose, you will have to repair or replace the threaded part of the wood. The old "toothpick and glue in the hole" trick might work sometimes, where little strength is necessary, but for a good-quality repair, drill out the wood and replace it with a dowel or plug (see illus. 4-6). Wherever possible, drill the hole *perpendicular* to the original screw hole. Use either a dowel or plug made with a small plug cutter as necessary so the grain of the new piece is parallel to that of the surrounding original wood. In the repair illustrated, for example, a plug would be better than a dowel, but if the hole entered the *end* of the piece of wood, then a dowel would be better. Cut the dowel or plug a little too long, knurl it for glue relief by rolling it between two large, coarse files, and test it for a snug but not tight dry fit. Coat it with glue and press it into the hole. After the glue is dry, cut the excess wood off with a coping saw or sharp chisel, and sand the area flush. Then drill the new screw

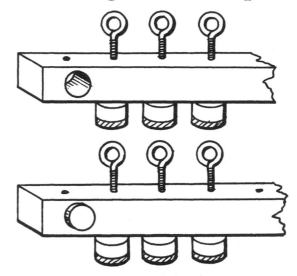

4-6. Whenever plugging a stripped screw hole, drill the hole for the plug perpendicular to the screw hole if possible.

hole. For a regulating screw, always drill a sample hole in a similar piece of scrap wood to find the best size bit. If the screw hole strips again in the future, you can insert another new plug with no further damage to the surrounding wood.

Sometimes it is impossible to drill a hole perpendicular to the length of the screw. Where the hole for the plug must be drilled parallel to the screw hole, drill with a Forstner bit from the side of the wood opposite from where the screw enters, and stop short of drilling all the way through the wood. (A Forstner bit drills a flat-bottom hole.) This way, the screw won't pull the plug out of the hole, like a cork out of a bottle, when you tighten it.

If the only way to drill for a plug is by drilling right into the screw hole, glue the plug in with epoxy and be sure the grain of the plug aligns with the grain of the wood, in hopes that some epoxy will lock the fibers of wood together.

Another alternative for repairing loose screw holes that don't need great strength is to "glue size" the holes, or swab them out with thin epoxy or gap filling super glue. When using epoxy, drill a pilot hole to make sure the screw isn't too tight. For additional information on stripped action rail screw holes, see pp. 125 and 307.

Removing Broken Screws

When a screw head breaks off, leaving a stump embedded in the wood, use a soldering gun to apply heat directly to the stump to loosen it. Then grasp the stump at an angle with side cutters to unscrew it. If this doesn't work, try chiseling out a little wood around the stump to provide a better hold for the side cutters. If you still can't remove it, one of the following methods will always work; consider which one will be the least destructive for the particular job. Drill a slightly oversized hole next to the stump, push the stump sideways into the new hole, and pull it out. Then plug both holes with one large plug, and redrill the screw hole. Or, file little pointed teeth into the end of a short piece of thin wall brass tubing just large enough to slip over the body of the screw. Chuck the tubing in a reversible electric drill, and set the drill to turn counterclockwise. Push the spinning tube down around the screw until the screw comes out of the wood as you withdraw the tube. Various sizes of straight thin wall brass tubing connectors (or "telescoping tubing") are available from piano supply companies and hobby shops.

Safety Precautions

When you spray any type of finish, or when you use noisy tools or tools that throw particles of metal or wood, protect yourself with the correct type of respirator, ear protectors, and eye protectors. Use the recommended safety guards on all power tools, and if you're inexperienced at using a particular power tool, obtain expert instruction in its safe use. Repairing the finest piano, or having the most enjoyable hobby imaginable isn't worth the loss of a finger, an eye, or serious injury or death by pieces of wood or metal thrown from a power tool at high speed.

Whenever you work with music wire, wear eye protection! Every time you cut the end off a piece of wire, there is a chance that a bit of wire might fly through the air into your eye.

When working with solvents, always use the least toxic product that will get the job done. Ethyl alcohol is somewhat less poisonous than methyl alcohol as shellac solvent; odorless paint thinner is less toxic than lacquer thinner for degreasing metal parts; and some types of paint stripper are safer to use than others. Search out the safest product and use adequate ventilation, skin protection, and common sense. If a little detergent, ammonia, or vinegar in water will work just as well as a more flammable or noxious substance, why take unnecessary risks?

Cleaning a Piano

Before repairing, regulating, or tuning an old piano, clean it thoroughly to remove dirt and objects that have accumulated inside over the years, such as old coins, pencils, small toys, mouse nests, and other miscellaneous debris. A thorough cleaning also will give you the opportunity to become familiar with your piano and possibly to find things in need of repair that you might otherwise overlook. Over a period of years, a piano collects an amazing amount of dust and dirt on the soundboard, among the tuning pins, and in other places where it's hard to get out. Cleaning not only enhances the appearance of a piano, but also helps to keep the old dirt from acting as an abrasive on moving parts. For a thorough cleaning job, first open the cabinet and remove the action.

Opening the Vertical Cabinet

The bottom front panel sits on two or three dowels or pins that fit into holes in the toe rail. A curved metal or wooden trap spring fastened to the bottom of the keybed holds the top of the panel in place. Push upward on the spring with one hand, and pull the top of the panel toward you with the other. Swing it forward, grasp it with one hand at each end, and lift it out of the piano. Be careful to keep the panel from slipping off the toe rail and damaging the finish or veneer, especially if there are missing dowels or damaged holes. In some small verticals, particularly those with fancy legs attached to the case at the bottom with toes or stretchers, you must slide the panel out at just the right angle to keep from scratching the finish.

Next, open the top; before doing this, check to make sure that the hinges are attached to both pieces and that the hinge pins are in place. If it has two pieces hinged together, swing the front portion all the way back until it rests on the back part. If it is one large panel, check the hinges to make sure they'll support its weight. Pull the piano away from the wall a few inches. Raise the lid and drape a dust rag over the edge of the top before leaning it against the wall. After opening the top, you'll see the fasteners that attach the upper front panel to the case. In some uprights, the front panel swings from metal or wood hangers attached to the back of the upper corners, and you can lift it off the support pins and out of the piano. In others, the bottom corners have hinged metal levers that keep it in position when you tilt it forward to hold sheet music, and you must slip these off their pins before you can remove the panel.

After removing the front panel, you can remove the support pillar at each side, usually by removing two large screws. This in turn will expose the two screws holding the music shelf in place. Remove it, and you'll see how to remove the fallboard. In some uprights, the fallboard has hinges attaching it to the nameboard strip, and large screws hold the ends of the nameboard strip to the key blocks. Remove these two screws and remove the fallboard and strip together, instead of unscrewing the fallboard hinges from the nameboard strip. In many consoles, the front panel, music shelf, and nameboard strip form one large piece that comes out after you remove two screws. Many spinets have a sliding keyboard cover supported by a large suspension rod, which must be disconnected before you remove the cover.

During disassembly, temporarily put each screw into its own hole. If all the screws are original, it usually isn't hard to figure out where they should go; but many old pianos have a mixture of correct and incorrect screws that will cause confusion during reassembly if you mix them together.

Removing the Vertical Action and Keys

Disconnect the top end of the hammer rail lift dowel from the rail and lean it out of the way or remove it from the piano. Then remove the four round nuts from the upper action bracket bolts. In small modern pianos, the action brackets and nuts fit so tightly that it often is difficult to remove the nuts. If a nut is so tight that you can't loosen it by hand, pad it with a small piece of leather before loosening it with pliers, to avoid scratching burrs into the edges. If you fail to do this, you'll wish the sharp little burrs weren't there when you try to tighten the nuts by hand again. Grasp the two outermost brackets and pull them forward just enough to come off the bolts. With your right hand, balance the action in place. With your left hand, disengage the sustaining pedal dowel from the damper lift rod. Grasp the end brackets again, and swing the top of the action out just far enough for the dampers to clear the #2 and #3 top action posts. Lift the action straight up and out of the piano. *Precaution: An action is heavy but has many fragile parts, so be careful when handling an action, removing it from the piano, and carrying it to and from the workbench. Pick up a vertical action only by the action brackets or hammer rail.*

To remove a spinet action with flanged drop sticker extensions, unscrew the sticker extension rail support brackets from the keybed. Leave this rail attached to the action brackets. Remove the whole action, stickers and all, following the instructions for the upright.

To remove a Baldwin or other action having a drop sticker guide rail attached to the keybed, lift each end sticker up to the guide rail and tie it to the rail. Unscrew the rail from the brackets, move it toward the ham-

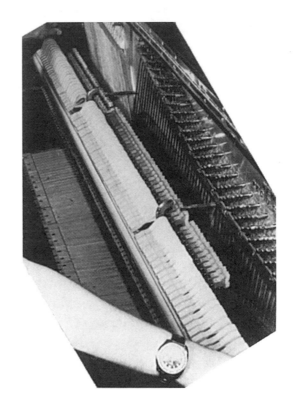

4-7 (above). Removing the upright action: Remove the nuts from the four upper action bracket bolts, disconnect the pedal dowels, and tilt the action forward. In this position, it is ready for you to lift it out of the piano.

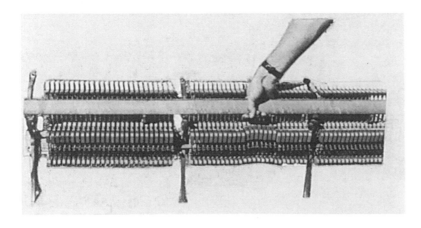

4-8. One way to carry an upright action. Be careful not to bend the hammer rail supports. The action in this photograph lacks stickers because the keys have dowel capstans. It is better to carry a large action by the end action brackets.

mer rail, and tie it to the action brackets. The action is then ready for removal.

In a spinet with the top ends of the stickers supported by the back ends of the keys, with no support rail, disengage all stickers from the keys and secure them to the action. Some spinets have a hook on each action bracket. Position a long metal rod, straightened coat hanger wire, or small-diameter dowel in the hooks to hold the stickers in place. A telescoping car antenna or small-diameter round curtain rod makes a handy tool for this purpose, as you can push it together and store it in a small tool box. If the brackets have no built-in hooks, tie the support rod to the brackets with mechanic's wire. After you secure the stickers, remove the action. It is very important to be careful that the dampers clear the action bracket bolts, as there is very little clearance in many spinets. Some spinets have long screws with

hollow spacers, or action brackets reaching all the way to the plate, eliminating the need for upper support bolts. This feature makes it much easier to remove the action, as there is nothing in the way to snag the dampers once you remove the screws.

Place the action on a sturdy table or bench. It's a good idea to support it in an **action cradle** or **Jaras upright action holder** to keep it from tipping over. The upright action holder is a handy little tool, both for use in the shop and to carry in the tool box for use "on location," while the cradle is more versatile when you want to support the action at an angle for shaping hammers.

Piano makers usually stamp little numbers on the keys, just behind the keytops, from #1 in the bass to #88 in the treble. These numbers are necessary because no two keys in a piano are exactly alike. Sorting

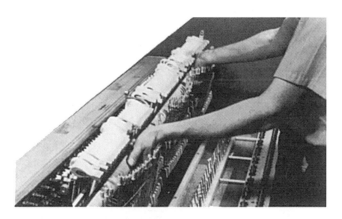

4-9 (right). Lifting the action out of a spinet piano.

4-10 (right). Securing drop stickers to a spinet action with coat hanger wire before removing the action from the piano. This action lacks hooks formed into the action brackets, so you have to tie the supporting wire to the brackets with mechanic's wire.

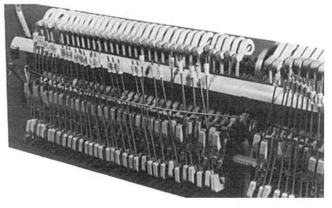

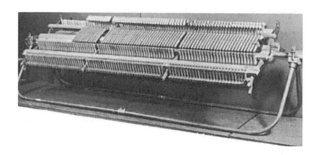

4-11. A portable action cradle provides sturdy support for the action at any angle.

a set of mixed up keys can be a very time-consuming job. Unfortunately, even if the numbers appear to be legible, when you remove them from the piano all the 6's, 8's, 9's, and 0's begin to look the same. So, any time you remove more than one key at a time, number them clearly, or draw diagonal lines across the keys before removing them, as illustrated, to serve as a guide when replacing them.

Remove the keys by lifting them straight up off their balance rail pins and out of the piano. Wiggle them a little if necessary to find the angle at which they slip off easily. With one hand slipped sideways under the front and the other under the back of a group of keys, you can lift a half dozen or so out at once.

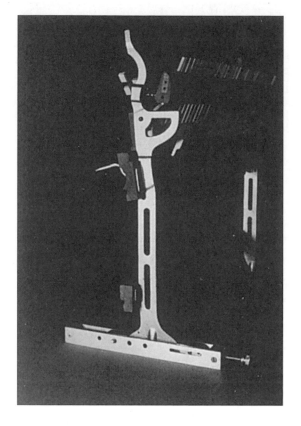

4-12. The Jaras upright action holder, available from certain piano supply companies, along with other handy Jaras tools.

Opening the Grand Cabinet

Check the lid hinges and hinge pins to make sure they are intact, so the lid won't go crashing to the floor. Then lift the lid and

4-13. Drawing several diagonal lines across the keys is a quick, easy way to index them.

4-14. Removing the fallboard and key blocks from a Steinway grand.

hold it up with its support prop; use the longer prop if there are two. Remove the music desk by sliding it all the way forward until it comes off its supports in some pianos, or by lifting gently and sliding from front to back until you find the notch that permits one end to be lifted clear in others.

Remove the key slip by unscrewing the three to five long screws from the bottom of the keybed. If there are no screws, as in many fine-quality grands, slip it straight up off its supports and set it aside.

If each hinged corner of the fallboard has a little machine screw showing, loosen the screws, tip the fallboard forward about 45°, and slip the fallboard up over the hinge pins and out of the piano. Be careful not to allow the fallboard to close all the way with the screws partially unscrewed; they might gouge the key blocks. If there is no visible hardware at the hinged corners of the fallboard, it will come out with the key blocks, as shown in illus. 4-14. In this case, remove the large screws at the bottom of the key bed that hold the key blocks down, and remove the blocks from the piano.

Removing the Grand Action

In fine-quality grands, the key frame has a **key frame shift pin** at each front corner,

and each key block holds the key frame in place with a metal **key block positioning guide** installed in the key block. These guides hold the key frame and action in the right place in the piano while permitting sideways movement when the una corda pedal is depressed. The treble positioning guide is usually adjustable forward and back, to permit regulation of the hammer striking line in the high treble. After you remove the key blocks, remove the action by sliding it straight out the front of the piano (see illus. 4-15). *Don't depress any of the keys, or you'll lift the hammers, which will catch on the pinblock and break off.*

In some medium quality grands, the key blocks are hollow, and separate little wooden blocks screwed to the keybed hold the key frame shift pins. These little blocks are accessible after you remove the key blocks. In this type of piano, mark the little wooden hold-down blocks so you can reinstall them in the correct orientation. In some inexpensive grands that have no una corda pedal, the action doesn't have to shift sideways, so the key frame front rail has several screws that fasten it to the key frame. There are no hold-down guides or blocks in these pianos.

Cleaning Out the Dirt and Debris

With the action removed, tighten all accessible plate and cabinet screws, except for the pressure bar screws in a vertical piano or the hex head plate perimeter bolts in a Baldwin or other grand having a threaded perimeter bolt plate suspension system. *If you try to tighten the plate perimeter bolts in one of these Baldwin grands, you will either strip the threads in the plate, break the head off the screw, or possibly even break the plate.* Then tighten all action bracket and flange screws, so you won't

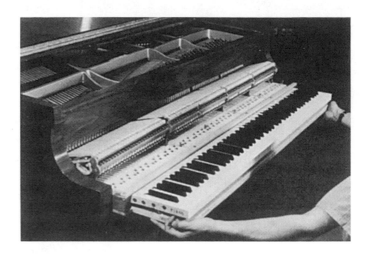

4-15 (right). Sliding the grand action out of the piano.

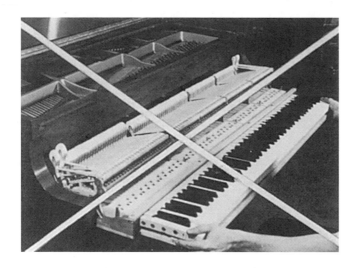

4-16 (left). Don't depress any of the keys while sliding the action out, or the hammers will break off.

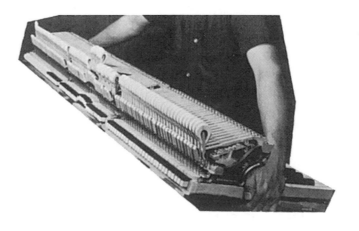

4-17 (right). Carrying the grand action by the ends of the key frame. Don't lift it by grasping an action bracket, a group of keys, or another part that won't carry the weight.

blow dirt under the flanges later in the cleaning process. Illus. 5-2 shows a handy flange screwdriver. If the piano has metal action rails, be very careful not to strip the screws.

By far the most effective way to clean a piano is to vacuum out the large quantities of dust and dirt, and then move the piano outside and blow it out with compressed air. If you don't have an air compressor, blow the dirt out with the pressure exhaust of a vacuum cleaner while brushing dirty areas with a toothbrush, razor cleaning brush, paint brush or whatever else it takes to get into the nooks and crannies. Clean the top of the beams in a grand, and between the bottom of the back posts in a vertical. When vacuuming the key frame, use a narrow crevice tool and hold it close to the wood so there is no chance of vacuuming up any of the punchings. When blowing the dirt off the key

frame with compressed air, stay far enough away from the punchings with the air stream to keep from damaging the paper punchings or blowing them out from under the cloth punchings.

Clean the tuning pins. Vacuum out loose dust while brushing around all sides of the pins and coils with a toothbrush or razor cleaning brush. If the pins are rusty, use a wire brush, but be careful not to scratch the finish on the plate. For a more thorough cleaning obtain a **tuning pin and coil cleaner kit**, shown in illus. 4-20, from a piano supply company. Chuck the holder in an electric drill and insert a rubber bushing in the holder. Apply a little cleaning compound (supplied with the kit) to the tip of each tuning pin. Press the bushing over the pin and spin the tool to clean the pin. You'll go through several rubber bushings to clean

4-18. Vacuuming loose dirt from the keybed. Be careful not to vacuum up any of the punchings.

4-19. Cleaning the bridge with a toothbrush.

a whole set of tuning pins, and the cleaning process will leave more dirt in the piano, which you'll have to blow out and vacuum again. This will leave the tuning pins cleaner but covered with very fine scratches that will quickly rust quickly again when exposed to high humidity. You might want to coat the pins with tuning pin bluing, also available from piano supply companies, to prevent this. This will look sloppy compared to smooth, shiny new blued tuning pins; but it will look better than heavy rust. Be careful not to slosh bluing onto the string coils and plate.

Clean the exposed areas of plain strings by rubbing lightly with 4/0 steel wool. Be careful to keep from snagging particles of steel wool around bridge pins and other parts of the piano. Also be careful that the steel wool isn't oily; if it is, clean it in lacquer thinner and let it dry before using it. You can also clean surface tarnish and rust off strings by rubbing them with a typewriter eraser. Like the cleaned tuning pins, the metal won't look as good as it did when new, but it will look better than it did when covered with rust. The accessible surfaces of the wound strings may be cleaned by brushing them lightly with a fine, flexible rotary brass brush in a variable speed electric drill. Don't apply much pressure to the ends of the string windings, or they might come loose, causing them to buzz. This won't help the sound of dead bass strings, however, because it will only clean the exposed surfaces of the strings, leaving enough dirt and corrosion embedded between the windings to deaden the tone. Clean the faces of the bridges by brushing vigorously with a toothbrush and vacuuming away the loose dirt. Again, vacuum or blow out the residue.

Clean the plate, including the area between the tuning pins, with a rag dampened in a solution of two tablespoons white vinegar to a gallon of warm water. To get between the tuning pins, wrap the rag around the end of a bluntly sharpened hammer shank or other slender tool and scrub until the paint looks cleaner. Don't scrub so hard that you rub through any of the paint and don't spill any liquid anywhere in the piano.

Clean the soundboard and edges of the bridges. Obtain a **soundboard steel** or flexible piece of spring steel with a hole punched in one or both ends. For better access in a grand, remove the lid. Dampen a rag in the water/vinegar solution. With one end of the

4-20. A tuning pin and coil cleaning kit.

4-21. Scrubbing away dirt with a damp rag. Don't rub so hard that you damage the paint.

rag attached to the soundboard steel and the other end tied to a piece of string, work the rag back and forth on the soundboard under the strings, as illustrated. Don't scrub too hard on the soundboard decal; it might begin to disintegrate if the finish covering it has deteriorated. A good job of cleaning the soundboard and plate might take several hours, but it can really improve the looks of a dirty old piano.

Clean the cabinet thoroughly with a rag dampened in the water/vinegar solution. Polish with furniture paste wax, which buffs up to a hard, glossy finish. Beware that the alcohol contained in some furniture polish might possibly damage lacquer or varnish.

Cleaning the Action

Next, turn your attention to the action. When vacuuming and blowing out the dirt, be careful not to exert too much pressure on fragile action parts. It is easy to break brittle old flanges by pushing on the ends of wippens, dampers, hammers, etc. Be careful also not to blow too hard on the soft treble damper felt with compressed air; this might deform the felt.

If the hammers have light grooves and have never been reshaped, reshape them now, as discussed on p. 138. If the grooves are so deep that it will be impossible to regulate the action properly after filing, replace the hammers, as discussed on pp. 300-305

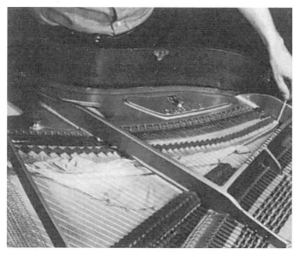

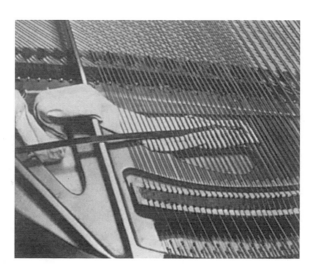

4-22 (above and right). Cleaning the soundboard with a "soundboard steel," rag, and string.

and 307-309 (If the hammers are that bad, the entire action probably needs to be rebuilt anyway.)

Cleaning the Keys

Clean the wooden bodies of the keys by blowing the loose dirt away with compressed air. If the piano has lived in a very humid environment, causing the wood to be darkened with a layer of dirt embedded in the surface, scrape the wood with a utility knife blade or scraper blade until it looks cleaner. Be careful not to remove any significant amount of wood — just the dirt from the surface. Most old piano keys have a thick smudge of greasy old dirt along the top edge of the sides from many years of use. Scraping this dirt away makes a big improvement in the way the keys look when you expose their sides by playing adjacent ones.

Clean the white keytops by rubbing vigorously with a damp rag; then clean the black keytops. Be careful not to wash away the original black stain under the years of accumulated grease and dirt that usually coats them. For further information on scraping and polishing discolored keys, see p. 123.

To clean grand piano keys thoroughly, remove the action from the key frame by removing the screws from the legs of the action brackets. Keep the screws in order— in many pianos, there are two different lengths for the front and back rows. Also, watch for shims under the bracket feet, and keep them in order.

Reinstalling the Keys and Action

Replace the cleaned keys on the key frame by holding each key in proper alignment and letting it drop gently onto the balance rail pin. Don't try to replace them by pressing down on the keys while rubbing them back and forth over the balance rail pins to find the holes, as this might damage the wood surrounding the holes in the bottom of the keys. Once you acquire the knack of helping the keys to find their positions, you can install groups of four or five keys at once without abusing them. In a grand, reattach the action to the key frame if you took this apart.

To reinstall the action in a vertical piano, reverse the procedure used in removing it, being careful again that the dampers clear the top action bracket bolts, and that the action brackets come to rest on the bottom ball bolts with the lower ends of the stickers

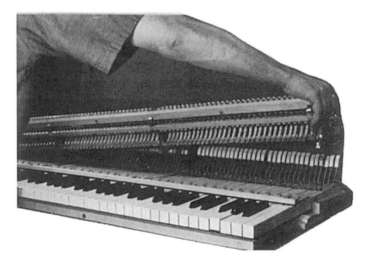

4-23. Removing the grand action from the key frame, after removing the action bracket screws.

resting on top of the capstans. If any of the stickers jam behind or in front of the capstans when you seat the action brackets on the bottom ball bolts, you might break the sticker tongues or flanges if you try to push the top of the action into place. This is particularly likely to happen if any bridle straps are broken, permitting the stickers to drop below their correct positions. If the bridle straps are bad, install a new set before you reinstall the action, as described on pp. 140-141.

Evaluating the Condition

Now that you've cleaned the piano, you're ready to determine what it needs in the way of repairs. If you encounter whole sections of the piano that need major repairs, read Chapter 8 — *Rebuilding* — to see if it might be wiser to rebuild the entire piano than to make an enormous number of "minor repairs." It will come as a rude shock, for example, to think that several days spent repairing and regulating the action will put a piano in good condition, and then find that the pinblock has to be replaced before the piano will stay in tune. After a thorough evaluation, you're ready to begin making repairs.

The Wooden Frame

Loose Glue Joints. If large parts are coming loose from each other, it is best to reglue them during complete rebuilding, when you have the piano completely disassembled.

Small Cracks. In many pianos, the back posts and other structural members have small cracks that have been there for many years, which don't cause any problems. If the wood inside the cracks looks dark, as though it has been dirty for a long time, if the cracks don't keep getting larger, and if the glue

joints are good, the cracks probably aren't a serious problem. If cracks continue to grow larger, or if major parts ultimately come loose from each other, the piano should be disassembled for the appropriate repairs.

Separated Pinblock/Back Structure in Vertical. See below, under the heading "The Pinblock and Tuning Pins."

The Plate

Broken Agraffe. If an agraffe breaks across the string holes, unscrew it with an agraffe remover, which fits in a combination tool handle available from a piano supply company. If it breaks at the threads, center punch the stump and drill a 7/64" hole down the middle. Remove the stump with a #2 "EZ Out" reverse thread extractor in a small tap handle. Renew the threads in the plate if necessary with an appropriate tap — common sizes are 7/32" x 36 or 1/4" x 36. Then screw in a new agraffe.

Broken Hitch Pin. On rare occasions, a hitch pin pulls out of the plate or breaks off. If a stump remains, and if the hole goes all the way through the plate, punch the stump out from the back. If the hole doesn't go all the way through, center punch the stump and drill it carefully without enlarging the hole. Obtain a new pin from a piano supply company, or make one out of an appropriate-sized piece of steel rod. Flatten one side a little with a hammer if necessary to make it fit tightly in the hole, and drive it into the hole with a pin punch and hammer. Reinstall the string.

4-24. An "EZ Out" screw extractor.

95

Cracked Plate. If the piano has a cracked or broken plate, it is unlikely that it is worth repairing unless it is a valuable grand, coin piano, or orchestrion. Refer to p. 242 in Chapter 8.

The Pinblock and Tuning Pins

If possible, make a visual inspection of the pinblock. Although the plate and other parts hide most of the pinblock in most pianos, here are some places to look: In a grand, the bottom of the pinblock is visible after you remove the fallboard and action. Check it for cracks or separated laminations. In a three-quarter plate upright, check the front of the pinblock for cracks. Tiny surface cracks in the face veneer might not matter, but any large cracks suggest that the piano needs a new pinblock. In a full plate upright, check the back. This is a separate piece of wood, but if you see major cracks and separation of glue joints, the pinblock is likely to be in equally poor condition.

Remove the lid. A separate piece of wood covers the top of the pinblock in many verticals, but in some pianos you can see the top edge. Check the top for cracks, including the ends of cracks which run down into the block. If you can't see the block, or if you can't tell anything about its condition by looking at it, check the tightness of the tuning pins by tuning the piano, and mark loose pins with chalk. If you have no experience tuning pianos, you can measure the tightness of the tuning pins with a torque wrench fitted with a ratchet lever star head, available from piano supply companies. If it takes less than fifty inch-pounds of torque to turn the pins counterclockwise, they are probably too loose to hold the piano in tune for a reasonable length of time. If some pins are so loose that their strings go out of tune immediately

after you remove the tuning lever, the pinblock probably has serious cracks. If so, there is no point in making any other repairs to the piano until you replace the pinblock, as an untunable piano will never make music. Chapter 8 covers pinblock replacement.

Loose Tuning Pins. If all tuning pins are just tight enough that the piano can be tuned, but not tight enough to hold it up to pitch for at least six months, the pinblock probably doesn't have any major cracks, but has loosened its grip on the pins. If so, there are several repairs that might make the piano tunable without replacing the pinblock: driving the original pins a little deeper into the pinblock, installing a Dampp-Chaser Piano Humidity Control System or equivalent, restringing with larger tuning pins, or applying a liquid called **tuning pin tightener**, which swells the wood.

Driving the tuning pins a little deeper helps in some pianos. Tuning pins usually have at least 3/16" (5 mm.) space between the

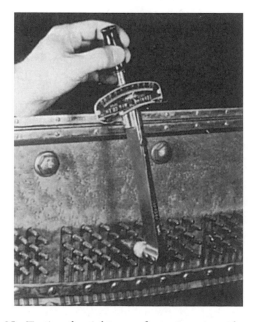

4-25. Testing the tightness of a tuning pin with a torque wrench.

4-26. A tuning pin setter, from a catalog illustration and in use.

string coil and the surface of the plate. By driving the pins in so the coils almost touch the plate, you can sometimes add enough friction between the bottom of the pin and new wood to make the piano tunable. Never drive the pins so far that the coils touch the plate. To drive pins you will need a large hammer, a tuning pin setter, and — for grands — a pinblock support jack. Use a hammer made specifically for driving steel objects; any other hammer might chip, sending fragments flying through the air.

Important note: Modern Bösendorfer pianos have tapered tuning pin holes in the pinblock, drilled with a 5.8–6.5 mm. tapered bit, with 7 mm. 1/0 tuning pins. Kimball International, Inc. recommends driving these pins 1 mm. deeper when they are loose. *Always use a pinblock support jack to avoid damaging the pinblock.*

If possible, lay a vertical piano on its back. Place the pin setter on the pin, and drive it in with the hammer, leaving a small space between the wire coil and plate. The pin setter prevents the pin from turning too much when struck with the hammer. If the strings come away from the bass tuning pins at a severe angle, don't drive the pins in so far that the strings break or the coils begin to overlap. Illus. 4-26 shows how to drive in a single loose pin, using a small hammer made for a combination handle, which is conve-

nient for carrying to the job in a tool box. When driving a whole set of pins, you'll have an easier time if you use a heavier hammer and lay the piano on its back.

When you drive pins in a grand, the pinblock must be supported with a pinblock support jack. In a vertical piano, the massive back structure supports the pinblock, but in a grand, there is no such back structure, so the plate has to do the entire job. There is always some chance that pounding on the tuning pins in a grand might crack the plate. Also, if the glue holding the laminations of the pinblock isn't very good, driving the pins deeper without supporting the block from underneath can cause them to break apart. Remove the action, insert the jack with one block of wood underneath and another on top, with as many support segments as necessary to build it up to the right height, and move it along to keep it under the work area. This transfers the hammer blow into the keybed, which is strong enough to withstand it.

If driving the pins deeper doesn't make them tight enough to hold a vertical piano in tune, a complete Dampp-Chaser Piano Humidity Control System might do the trick. See pp. 146-148 for further information.

If a piano is worth the expense, and if the pinblock isn't cracked, restringing the piano with larger tuning pins will add years

97

to the life of the piano without going to the greater expense of installing a new pinblock. If a piano has already been restrung with oversize pins, and they are loose even in the presence of a humidity control system, the piano will need a new pinblock. Chapter 8 describes restringing and pinblock installation.

If most of the pins are tight enough to hold their strings in tune but a few pins are too loose, tune the piano and mark the loose pins with chalk. Remove each loose pin by lowering the string tension enough to pry the wire out of its hole, slipping the coil up off the pin, and then unscrewing the pin the rest of the way out of the pinblock. Measure the diameter of the pin with a micrometer, dial caliper, or tuning pin gauge, and replace it with a pin two sizes larger in diameter. If you have to remove a "good" tuning pin — one that is reasonably tight — replace it with a pin one size larger. Piano manufacturers in the United States usually use 2/0 pins in their new pianos, but many pianos made outside of the U.S. have 1/0 or even smaller pins. When replacing a pin in a German or Asian piano, always measure the original pin to avoid installing a new one that is much too large.

If a larger pin isn't available, insert a shim made of maple veneer beside the old pin, or wrap one layer of 80 grit sandpaper around the bottom of the pin with the grit facing outward, and drive the pin back in. This will often cure random loose pins. Note, however, that if the pinblock is cracked and you drive in shims or oversize pins, you will only spread the crack apart further, making adjacent pins even looser.

If a piano isn't worth the expense of installing a humidity control system, restringing, or replacing the pinblock, the remedial measure of applying liquid tuning pin tightener might help. This is no cure-all, however. Much of the liquid is usually absorbed by the tuning pin bushings, and most of the excess runs onto the face of the pinblock between the pinblock and plate, where it forms big puddles and dries; little of the liquid actually soaks into the pinblock beyond the first layer of wood. In the experience of the author, when a pinblock has been "doped" with pin tightener and a technician later restrings the piano with oversize pins, the new pins sometimes stick to the wood after they've been in place for a time, becoming "jumpy," "creaky," or "mushy" and hard to tune. When deciding whether to try tuning pin tightener, consider the following guidelines: If a piano is in good general condition and if its value is such that it is worth restringing with oversize pins or installing a new pinblock, then do whatever

4-27 (above). A pinblock support jack.

4-28 (right). The support jack in use.

4-29 (left). Protecting the keybed before applying tuning pin tightener.

4-30 (right). Applying pin tightener with a "hypo-oiler" available from piano supply companies.

is necessary. If its potential value is questionable, and if restringing would cost more than the piano would be worth, then it might be worthwhile to try pin tightener. Once you use pin tightener, however, you might have to replace the pinblock if you decide to restring the piano.

One common type of pin tightener contains glycerin (which attracts moisture and swells the wood), a little rosin (which increases the friction between the wood and tuning pin), and alcohol (which acts as a medium to carry the solution down around the tuning pin into the wood and then evaporates). An easy way to apply it is with a

hypo-oiler available from piano supply companies.

In a grand, remove the action and cover the keybed with enough newspapers, paper towels, or rags to absorb any spilled liquid. Starting at either end of the pinblock and continuing to the other end, rest the needle on each tuning pin bushing or plate hole, slowly squeeze the bottle, and release it before any liquid runs onto the plate. If the bushings project up from the plate, surface tension will keep the pin tightener from spreading all the way around the pins immediately. Rather than spilling liquid on the plate, apply just a little the first time. By the time you're done applying it to all the pins once, it will have spread around the first pins, allowing the next application to soak in more quickly. Repeat the entire procedure until the piano doesn't soak up any more liquid, and then leave it overnight. If the pins were extremely loose, repeat the procedure several days in a row. When all traces of liquid have dried, remove the paper towels, replace the action, and tune the piano. If the block isn't cracked, the piano should stay in tune better than it did before.

When doping an upright pinblock, you must lay the piano on its back (see pp. 242-243). Follow the same application procedure as in a grand. Don't stand the piano up again until all traces of the liquid have dried; pin tightener that runs down the front of the pinblock can leave ugly stains on the soundboard and a sticky mess on the strings. Be very careful not to drip tightener on anything else in the piano, particularly action parts, which will swell and cease to function properly.

Jumping or Creaking Tuning Pins. If a tuning pin jumps or creaks instead of turning smoothly during tuning, the pinblock might be contaminated with oil or another foreign substance. Remove the pin, clean out the inside of the hole with lacquer thinner or naphtha on a swab, and install a new oversize pin. This repair may or may not work. A large number of creaky pins may be due to previous application of pin tightener, fiberglass resin, epoxy, or some other substance; the only cure will be to replace the pinblock.

Excessively Tight Tuning Pins. Sometimes, alternately rotating the pin counterclockwise and clockwise several times will loosen it satisfactorily. In other cases, loosening the pin enough to remove the string, unscrewing the pin several turns and driving it back in, and then reattaching the string will solve the problem. If the pin is still too

tight, remove it and ream the hole with an appropriate size spoon bit, as illustrated in Chapter 8.

Broken Tuning Pin. If a tuning pin breaks at the string hole, remove it by screwing a reverse thread tuning pin extractor over the stump. As you turn the extractor counterclockwise, it will tighten itself on the pin and then unscrew the pin from the block. If a pin breaks off flush with the plate in a grand piano in which the tuning pin holes go all the way through the pinblock, it may be driven out through the bottom with a machinist's pin punch of the appropriate size. Support the pinblock with a pinblock jack placed immediately next to the hole. If a pin breaks off flush with the plate in a vertical, it might be possible to drill an oversize hole all the way through the back of the piano behind the pin, and then punch it out into the hole. Whether or not this will work will depend upon your care in measuring and your aim with the drill. After removing the pin, plug the hole from the back with a plug made from a piece of pinblock, glued in place with epoxy. An easier repair — but one that requires removing all the other strings and tuning pins and the plate — is to drill an oversize hole into the front of the pinblock immediately next to the stump, work the stump into the adjacent hole and remove it. Plug both holes with pinblock stock plugs and epoxy, and redrill the tuning pin hole.

Separated Pinblock/Back Structure in Vertical. If parts of the back frame of a vertical piano have separated, and there is a way to work glue into the crack and clamp it back together, do so. Sometimes a glue joint along the top of the back separates, permitting the top of the pinblock to tip forward, bending the plate and stripping out the holes for the large lag screws in the top of the plate. If this has happened, and if the tuning pins still feel tight enough to hold the piano in tune, lower the string tension by turning each tuning pin counterclockwise one half turn, to reduce stress while gluing. For the simplest repair in an old piano that isn't worth a lot, remove the plate, temporarily clamp the parts together, and drill the lag screw holes all the way through the back of the piano. Clean out all sawdust and wood chips from the glue joint. Obtain bolts of the same diameter as the lag screws, just long enough to project out the back of the piano far enough to install a large washer and nut on each one. Spread aliphatic resin glue into the separation, and clamp the glue joint back together, being careful to pull the pinblock and plate back slowly and evenly to keep from breaking the plate. Install the bolts, washers, and nuts. After the glue dries and you remove the clamps, pull the strings up to pitch, or hire a piano rebuilder to do this if you're not yet familiar with stringing or tuning.

For a nicer looking job, drill the holes out and install carriage bolts from the back, with the nuts on the inside of the plate. This way, the back of the piano will have the gently rounded carriage bolt heads showing, instead of the threaded ends of the bolts, which might scratch the wall behind the piano.

A better repair for a good quality piano is to reglue the bad glue joint, bore in from the back with a 1" Forstner bit just through the threaded portion of each hole, and install a 1" diameter hardwood plug from the back. After gluing each plug in place, flush with the back surface of the piano, bore the hole for the threaded part of the screw into each plug from the front, and reinstall the screws.

Loose Pinblock in Grand. If one end of a grand piano goes out of tune as you tune the other end when you are not changing the pitch, and if the plate screws and tuning pins are tight, the pinblock might be fitted so poorly to the plate flange that the block rocks on a "high spot" near the middle as the string tension changes during tuning. When this condition exists, if it is undesirable to install a new pinblock, correct the problem by lowering the string tension and driving hardwood wedges between the back edge of the pinblock and the plate flange as necessary. Apply a little aliphatic resin glue to each wedge before driving it in, and pull the piano up to pitch. If a wedge sticks out so far that it interferes with installation of the action, trim the wedge with a coping saw, utility knife, or hacksaw blade.

The Soundboard

Cracked Soundboard. Cracks in the soundboard aren't inherently destructive to tone quality because the area of a crack is so tiny compared to the total surface area of the soundboard. The tone quality is hurt when the soundboard is not only cracked, but also separated from the ribs or unglued from the inner rim (in a grand) or the soundboard liner (in a vertical) around its perimeter.

Loose Glue Joint Between Soundboard and Ribs, Liner, or Rim. When the soundboard comes loose from a rib or the perimeter glue joint, one piece of wood can vibrate against another, causing an unpleasant tone reminiscent of a bad loudspeaker. If the piano is a high quality one, only the finest quality soundboard repairs should be made, as described in Chapter 8, leaving only tiny holes or none at all in the ribs. If the piano is an inexpensive old vertical or tiny grand, the following quick repairs will solve the problem without seriously damaging anything.

Visually inspect the back (or bottom) of the soundboard to see where it is loose. Then play each note loudly, from one end of the keyboard to the other. If a note produces an unnatural rattling or buzzing tone, have an assistant continue to play that note loudly. Press on the loose areas of the soundboard until the buzzing or rattling stops, and mark the spot. If the spot is in a location where you can use a soundboard gluing clamp (shown in illus. 8-16) without removing the plate, use this type of clamp, as the tiny hole drilled in the rib for the wire weakens the rib less than a larger hole would. If you can't use a soundboard clamp, drill a 3/16" hole through the rib and board. Clean as much of the dirt and old glue as possible out from between the board and rib with self-adhesive sandpaper stuck on an artist's palette knife. Insert liquid hide or aliphatic resin glue between the board and rib with the palette knife, and pull them together with an 8-32 machine screw and nut, using appropriate washers to keep the screw head or nut from marring the wood. Remove the excess glue. When dry, remove the machine screw, clean the glue out of the hole by running the 3/16" bit through it again, and plug the hole with a 3/16" dowel.

If the rattling area of the soundboard is behind the plate or strings, repair it from behind with a #8 flat head wood screw through the rib into the soundboard. Drill and countersink the hole, using a depth gauge on the drill bit to keep from breaking through the front of the soundboard. A rubber band, piece of masking tape, or dab of red fingernail polish on the bit makes a simple but effective depth gauge. Clean out the sawdust, insert glue, and screw together.

If the soundboard is loose around the perimeter, you'll need to use ingenuity to figure out how to apply clamping pressure to the front or top side while regluing it, without removing the plate. In some areas, you can insert a small temporary wedge between the plate and soundboard; in others, you can install a small screw. If it is necessary to

remove the plate, refer to Chapter 8 for other clamping methods.

The Bridges

Split or Cracked Bridge. A bridge often develops small cracks along the top where the side bearing of the strings pushes the bridge pins sideways. When the top of the bridge cracks, the pins are no longer held firmly in place. This causes ringing and buzzing noises and false beats, making the piano difficult or impossible to tune.

If the splits are so bad that they form one continuous crack, the bridge should be recapped or replaced, either of which is a rebuilding job. If the splits are small enough that they don't form one continuous crack, they can be filled with epoxy. Lower the tension on no more than six or eight strings at once, just enough to slip them off their hitch pins, leaving them attached to their tuning pins. Lift the strings out of the way and remove the loose bridge pins. If possible, obtain longer, pointed bridge pins of the same diameter, and drill the holes a little deeper to accept the additional length, to provide a new grip at least on the bottom end of the pins. Mix some epoxy and work it into each crack with a palette knife or small piece or wire until the crack is completely full, with no air bubbles in the epoxy. Insert each new bridge pin as close to its original position as possible, and clean off all epoxy that squeezes out. Repeat the procedure for each crack until you have installed all the pins. When the epoxy is completely dry, put the strings back around their hitch pins and bridge pins, pull them up to pitch, and continue with another section if necessary. When you're done, tune the piano.

Unglued Bass Bridge; Cracked Apron. In many old uprights that are in otherwise perfectly usable condition, the bass

4-31. A cracked treble bridge.

bridge apron shrinks and cracks, and the bridge comes unglued from the apron and slips out of the correct position. This situation produces a dead tone in the bass, particularly toward the top end of the bass bridge, even when the bass strings are obviously in good condition. Usually, the screws that are visible from the back of the soundboard still connect the broken pieces of the apron to the spacer strip. Always check for this condition before tuning an older piano. If the bridge has slipped downward, causing the speaking segments of the bass strings to be longer than they should be, you might break a bass string as you pull far too much tension on it in an attempt to bring it up to the correct pitch.

If the bass tuning pins are tight enough to withstand loosening the strings and then tightening them again, the following repair may be made. Loosen each bass string just enough to slip it off its hitch pin, and thread the hitch pin loop over a piece of wire to keep the strings in order. With all the strings strung on the wire, pull them aside and secure the wire to something in the piano to hold them out of the way. Remove the screws that hold the bass bridge apron to the spacer strip from the back of the soundboard. If necessary, bore a $1/2$" hole through a back post to reach an inaccessible screw with a slender screwdriver. Usually, when the bass bridge is loose from the apron, the apron is also loose from the strip, and it will

come off the board with no difficulty. Beware, though, of original factory nails or dowels holding the strip to the soundboard; *don't damage the soundboard when you break the glue joint apart.* Reglue the broken pieces of the apron back together, sand the glue off without removing any wood, and reattach the bridge to the apron with glue and several screws. Then reglue and screw the apron to the strip on the soundboard. If the apron has shrunk in length so much that the screws no longer line up, change the locations of the screws holding the bridge to the apron, but be careful not to drill into the bottom end of any bridge pins. Where the apron attaches to the soundboard, plug and redrill a hole in the apron if necessary for correct alignment with the original holes in the soundboard. Before gluing any of the parts together, always screw them together tightly in a "dry run" to make absolutely sure that the shanks of the screws don't bind in the holes, forcing the glue joint apart and cracking the apron, soundboard buttons, or other parts when tightened. After the glue is dry, twist each bass string one full turn in the direction of the winding to liven the tone (see pp. 115-117), and reattach it to the hitch pin. Thread it around its bridge pins and raise the tension. If necessary, drive the tuning pin in a little deeper (see p. 96–98). If the tuning pins are still tight enough to hold the bass strings in tune, this repair will dramatically improve the tone quality of the bass.

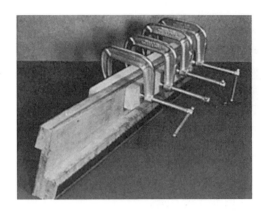

4-32. Regluing a bass bridge apron.

The Strings

It is easy to break rusty strings while raising their pitch unless you take certain precautions. When a string is rusty, there are usually tiny bonds of rust holding it to other metal parts such as the pressure bar, upper plate bridge (or nut), and bridge pins. If you try to raise the tension of a string in this condition, the added tension might be confined to the uppermost segment of the wire, causing it to break — usually at the tuning pin or pressure bar. To reduce the risk of this happening, let each rusty string down in pitch until you hear a soft "tick" as the rust breaks loose. Then raise the pitch and tune the string.

Broken Strings. If a two or three-string unison has one broken string, not only will the note sound bad, but the hammer for that note also will wear unevenly, eventually ruining the hammer. Also, the impact of the hammer will be absorbed by one side of the felt, putting a twisting strain on the hammer shank, butt, center pin, and bushings, making the hammer loose and causing it to wobble. If a string breaks in the low bass where there is only one string per note, the hammer will travel too far, putting strain on the shank and butt, and possibly the damper lever as

well. For these reasons, you should always replace broken strings promptly.

Fortunately for the piano technician, most strings break in the high treble and bass, where they are most easily accessible.

String Repair Tools:

- Safety goggles
- Tuning lever, T lever, or ratchet drive with tuning pin tip
- Long nose pliers, round nose pliers, and regular pliers
- Music wire cutter made for hard steel wire
- String lifter and spacer
- Stringing hook
- Several screwdrivers
- Music wire gauge, micrometer, or dial caliper
- Supply of music wire, sizes 12 through 20, including half sizes
- String looping machine or vise, for forming hitch pin loops on the end of single strings

Handling Music Wire Coils. Music wire is very stiff, but it doesn't have to be hard to control if you handle it properly. *When working with music wire, always wear safety goggles or other adequate eye protection!* If you have an "acid touch," or if your body chemistry tends to cause rust, always wear thin leather or cotton gloves when handling wire. To start a new one-pound coil, remove the wrapper and tighten the cross-shaped flat metal holder snugly around the wire to make sure it will hold the coil. Then cut off the wire retaining loops and discard them. Pull out the end of the wire with the metal or paper flag, and unwind as much wire as needed from *inside* the coil. Don't let the wire push itself through the windings of the coil when you cut the end off, or it will tangle. Leave the working end of the wire longer than the

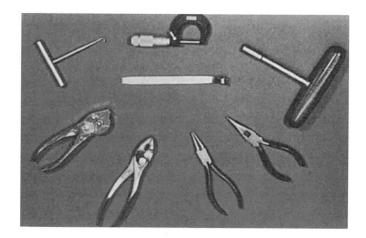

4-33. Some of the string repair tools discussed in the text.

diameter of the coil. Keep the retainer bent snugly around the coil at all times. When finished with the coil, replace the flag, insert the working end through the hole in the coil holder, and bend enough over to keep it from slipping out. Always use the same end of the wire.

The **reel and brake** type of dispenser is more expensive but somewhat easier to use. Bend the end of the brake arm almost straight to keep the wire from slipping through by itself (see illus. 4-34). Loosen the nut just enough to permit the reel to turn when you hold the brake with one hand and pull the wire through with the other. If the nut is too loose, or if you don't straighten the brake enough, the whole affair might unwind like a huge clock spring until it turns into a tangled mess. Another handy dispenser is the canister type, as illustrated.

Repairing Vs. Splicing. Replacing a broken string is easier than repairing it, but

this isn't always desirable. In old pianos, the bass strings lose their brilliant tone quality because of corrosion and dirt in the windings and become somewhat dead or "tubby" sounding. If you replace a broken bass string with a new one in a piano with dull sounding bass strings, that note will stick out like a sore thumb. It is usually more desirable for all the notes to sound alike than for one note to sound different from its neighbors, even if it sounds better. So, it is often better to splice a new leader onto a broken bass string when possible than to replace it with a new one, unless the original bass strings are still "live" enough to match the tone quality of a new string.

Old treble strings usually sound enough like new strings that if one breaks you should replace it instead of splicing it, since replacing is the easier procedure.

Splicing a String. Before attempting to splice a broken piano string, practice splic-

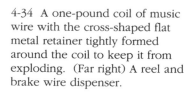

4-34 A one-pound coil of music wire with the cross-shaped flat metal retainer tightly formed around the coil to keep it from exploding. (Far right) A reel and brake wire dispenser.

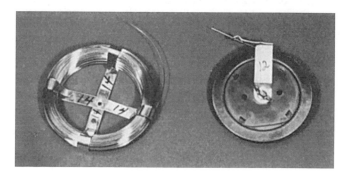

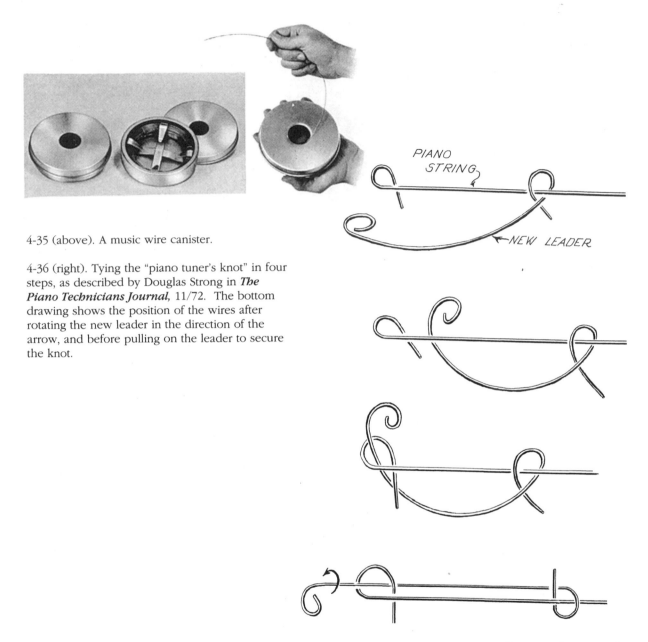

4-35 (above). A music wire canister.

4-36 (right). Tying the "piano tuner's knot" in four steps, as described by Douglas Strong in ***The Piano Technicians Journal,*** 11/72. The bottom drawing shows the position of the wires after rotating the new leader in the direction of the arrow, and before pulling on the leader to secure the knot.

ing scraps of music wire together. Begin with small wire, which is easier to handle, and work up to the larger sizes. Hold one piece of wire with regular pliers, and form a loop in the end with round nose pliers as illustrated. All bends should be rounded; kinking or bending the wire at a sharp angle will weaken it. Form a similar loop in the other piece. Face the loops in the proper direction

and assemble the knot, following the steps in the illustration.

Installing a New String. In a grand piano, there is no need to remove the action to repair or replace strings. In a vertical piano, remove the front panels and the action. An exception to this is when replacing a broken string in a spinet. It usually takes less time to replace the string with the action in place than it does to remove the spinet action with its drop lifters. The following instructions apply to both verticals and grands. The terms "up" and "down" in a vertical translate to "toward the keyboard" and "away from the keyboard" in a grand.

Broken Treble String. Find the two tuning pins for the broken string. Remove the broken wire from the pins, and unscrew each pin (counterclockwise) a total of four full turns. Leave each pin with the eye facing downward, ready to accept the new string. Don't unscrew a pin with a piece of wire still attached, or the wire might scratch the plate. If the wire breaks off at the pin, leaving a tight coil wound around it, pry the remaining coil out of the eye with a screwdriver and remove it with long nose pliers.

Measure the diameter of the old wire at a straight, clean spot with the wire gauge or micrometer. Measuring at a bent or rusty spot will give an inaccurate reading.

When measuring old treble strings, you will often find that the diameter consistently falls between two wire sizes, such as .0345".

It is usually safe to assume that the wire was originally a half thousandth *larger* and that it became thinner as it stretched in length over the years, so replace it with the next larger size — in this example, .035" or size 15. An exception to this rule is if the piano has the original stringing scale stamped on the plate or pinblock, and it shows another size.

Pick out a new coil of the correct size wire, and cut off a piece long enough for both strings, including enough for the tuning pin coils. Insert one end of the new piece of wire up through the agraffe or pressure bar, and guide it through the eye of the tuning pin with the stringing hook. In a vertical, start with the right-hand pin, and in a grand, the left-hand pin, so the first new coil won't be in the way of the second.

Slowly turn the tuning pin clockwise with a tuning lever, T handle, or ratchet drive, maintaining firm pressure on the string with the hook. While you turn the pin, guide the wire so it forms neat coils that don't cross each other, until there are about two and a half coils on the pin. Then feed the

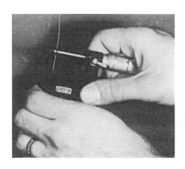 

4-37. Above left: Measuring the diameter of a broken string with a micrometer. Above right: A music wire gauge. Don't confuse music wire sizes with any other standard.

4-38 (right). A convenient memory aid for the wire sizes in this table is that doubling the gauge size and adding five gives the wire diameter in thousandths of an inch. For sizes smaller than 12 and larger than 23, this rule doesn't apply.

PIANO WIRE SIZES

Size	Dia.	Feet per lb. (approx.)
12	.029	445
12½	.030	414
13	.031	384
13½	.032	366
14	.033	330
14½	.034	300
15	.035	295
15½	.036	290
16	.037	275
16½	.038	260
17	.039	248
17½	.040	234
18	.041	223
18½	.042	212
19	.043	200
19½	.044	190
20	.045	182
21	.047	165
22	.049	156
23	.051	140

wire down across the appropriate bridge pins, pull it as tight as possible by hand, and bend it around the hitch pin. If you initially bend it a little more than 180° around the pin and then pull it straight, you'll reduce the need to squeeze it with pliers as described below. Hold the remaining part of the wire next to its tuning pin, and cut it off about 3" (7.5 cm.) — or approximately the width of four fingers — above the pin. This is the right amount for three coils around the pin. If your wire cutter is the type that is held parallel to the wire when cutting, mark the handle 3" from the blade, and use that for a guide.

Feed the wire up through the agraffe or pressure bar, guiding it into the eye of the pin with the stringing hook, and turn about two neat coils onto the pin. When the string is tight enough to stay in place, position it in the right place on the bridge. Snug the coil on the tuning pin with the stringing hook, string lifter, or screwdriver, and tighten the pin just enough to keep the coil in place. Then snug the coil on the other end of the wire, and tighten its pin just enough to hold the coil in place. Examine both tuning pins. Each should have almost three coils of wire, snug against each other. The end of the wire should be flush with the outside surface of the pin. Loose or uneven coils, coils of two or four turns, coils that cross each other, wire that sticks out of the pin, and scratches on the plate or pinblock are all signs of

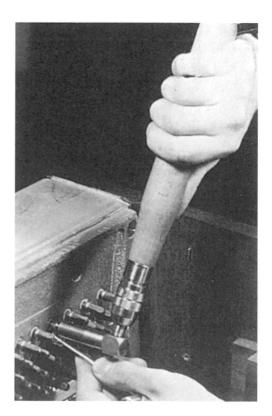

4-39 (top left). Guiding the end of the new string into the tuning pin eye with a stringing hook.
4-40 (above). Winding two and a half neat coils. You will add the last half coil when you pull the string up to pitch and tune it.
4-41 (above right). Some technicians prefer to use a tuning lever instead of a T handle. A ratchet drive with a tuning pin tip is also handy for this job.

4-42. Securing the first half of the new string.

4-43. Measuring the length of the second half.

4-44. Using a string lifter to tighten a loose coil.

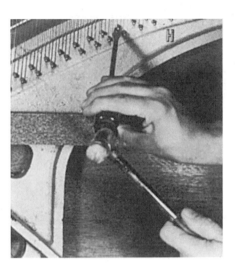

4-45 (above). Seating the string on the plate. Hold the screwdriver blade parallel to the wire to keep from marring the wire. A 3/16" brass rod makes a better seating tool.

sloppy work. If necessary, loosen the pin just enough to rearrange the coil and then tighten it again. Then, with a hammer and 3/16" diameter brass rod, tap the wire where it goes around the hitch pin to seat it firmly on the plate. If you use a screwdriver for this, hold the screwdriver blade parallel to the wire to keep from marring the wire. If you didn't bend the wire far enough around the hitch pin when installing it, the wires will now spread out too far just above the pin; squeeze them with pliers to make them parallel (see illus. 4-46). Check the spacing of the new strings in relation to their neighbors, and with grooves in the hammer, and slide them sideways with a string spacer if necessary. Raise the pitch, drive the tuning pins for the replaced strings down even with their neighbors with a hammer and tuning pin setter, and tune the new strings.

The above method for replacing a broken string is relatively simple, but it involves unscrewing the tuning pins three turns so

4-46. Pinching the wires parallel as they leave the hitch pin, in the event that you didn't bend the wire far enough around the pin during installation. This dramatically improves tuning stability.

they'll be the right height after you turn the three coils of new wire onto them. If the tuning pins are somewhat loose to begin with, turning them out and then back in three turns will make them even looser. A better method for replacing a string in a piano in which the tuning pins aren't very tight is to form the hitch pin loop in the new piece of wire, temporarily install the string and cut each end of it to the right length, measuring it against its tuning pin. Then remove the string and turn the new coils onto dummy tuning pins, out of the piano. Bend the beckets out just enough to remove the coils from the new pins, reposition the string in the piano, and push the coils over their tuning pins. Using needle nose pliers, guide each becket into the hole in its pin. Add tension, snug the coils, and tune the strings. If one of the pins is very close to the pressure bar this method is more difficult; but if it results in the tuning pins being tighter and holding their strings in tune longer, it is worth the inconvenience.

The string lifter is a handy tool when there is room to use it. But be sure to use it only for lifting the wire; if you pry with it, the end will break off.

Broken Tied Treble String. Some treble strings are tied individually to their hitch pins, like wound bass strings. The best way to make a hitch pin loop on a new string is by hand, as illustrated.

Clamp a twelve-penny nail in a vise, with the head sticking up about 1/2" (13 mm.). Bring three or four inches (eight or ten cm.) of wire around the nail, and then about a half inch from the nail, wrap the wire around itself three times at a right angle. Wind the coils as tightly as possible. Snip the end off, leaving about 1/8" (3 mm.) of wire sticking out. Remove the nail from the vise, and slip the loop off the nail.

Crank-operated string looping machines turn a spiral twist on the wire instead of the loop shown here. The forming process tends to weaken the wire, causing it to be more vulnerable to breaking.

Missing Treble String. To find the size of a missing treble string, look carefully at the plate or pinblock. Some pianos have the wire sizes written or stamped in this area. If only one string of a three string unison is missing, use the same size wire for it as the remaining strings. All strings of a unison are always the same size. If several strings in a row are missing, gauge the strings on either side of the gap. If they are the same size, use that size wire. If not, gauge six or eight strings on each side of the gap and decide by interpolation where the wire size should change.

Broken Bass String. When a bass string breaks at the becket (the bend where the wire enters the eye of the tuning pin), enough of the original string usually remains that you can tie it to a new leader. Remove the old wire from the tuning pin and unscrew the pin four full turns, leaving the eye facing downward, ready to accept the repaired string.

Find a straight spot in the original string and measure the core wire. Cut a 14" (40

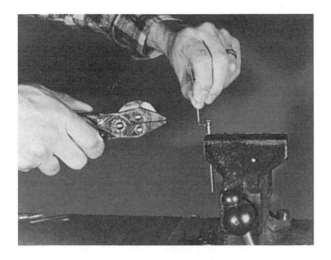

4-47. Forming a hitch pin loop by hand.

cm.) piece of new wire of the same diameter, and lay it aside. Hold the original string in position in the piano, and locate the exact place where the splice can be made without interfering with the upper plate bridge (nut) or tuning pins. Add just enough to the measurement to allow for the knot, and cut off the rest of the old string. When you tune the string it will stretch a little, moving the knot closer to the tuning pin.

Tie the new leader to the old string (see illus. 4-36). Hitch the string to its hitch pin, position it on the bridge and upper plate bridge, and hold it against the plate. Cut the new leader off 3" (7.5 cm.) above the tuning pin, and wind it onto the tuning pin. After putting about two turns of wire on the pin, stop and unhitch the string from the hitch pin. Insert a small screwdriver or awl in the

loop, and twist the string one full turn in the direction of the winding, to help ensure that the winding will be tight on the core. Grasp the twisted string just above the loop with pliers, remove the screwdriver or awl from the loop, and hitch the string over the hitch pin again. Check the position of the string on the bridge; then snug the coil and pull the string almost up to pitch. Seat the loop on the plate at the hitch pin by tapping with a screwdriver and hammer. Drive the tuning pin down flush with its neighbors, and tune the string.

If a bass string breaks near the hitch pin, it can be repaired as long as there is enough wire left beyond the winding to tie to a new leader. Tie a loop on one end of the leader first, and then splice it to the old string (see illus. 4-36). This repair can be very challeng-

4-48. A successfully spliced bass string, with the neat knot midway between the tuning pin and v-bar, where it doesn't interfere with tuning.

ing due to the stiffness of the wire; but with strength, persistence, and great care taken not to cut your fingers, it can be done.

If a bass string breaks near the winding, it must be replaced. The best replacement is a custom made duplicate from a piano supply company that specializes in making bass strings. If possible, send the original string as a sample, specifying the number of the *note* in the scale, and how many strings there are for that note. For example, if you send the second B from the bottom, state: "This string is for note 15 (B), and there are two strings per note."

Piano supply companies also make sets of "universal bass strings," which contain enough different sizes that one of them will come close to any broken original string. These are handy in situations where there is no time to wait for a replacement to be ordered through the mail, but an exact replacement is always better than a universal bass string that is only approximately the right size. The catalogs of most supply companies include instructions for installing universal bass strings.

Missing Bass String. The piano manufacturer, if still in business, might supply you with a correct replacement bass string, given the following information: the serial number of the piano, the name and number of the note as it lies in the scale, and the number of strings per note.

If a new bass string is unavailable as a stock item from the manufacturer, measure the plate and adjacent strings to find the following dimensions: the diameter of the core wire, the length of the winding, the length of the core wire from the hitch pin to the beginning of the winding, the name and number of the note as it lies in the scale, and the number of strings per note. Send this information with the brand name, serial num-

ber, and model of the piano (if known) to a bass string maker, to obtain a replacement string.

Broken Strings in Baldwin Pianos with "Acu-Just" Hitch Pins. Each string in this type of piano may be moved up or down its hitch pin to adjust the amount of down-bearing on the bridge. To replace a broken string, follow the usual procedure, but adjust the string on its hitch pin just a little higher than the neighboring strings. Pull it up to pitch, and then tap it down gently with a brass rod or special tool, as illustrated. Measure the downbearing on the bridge with a bearing gauge, inserting a feeler gauge under one leg, and tap the string down a few thousandths of an inch at a time until the bearing is the same as for neighboring strings. If a whole section of strings must be replaced in a Baldwin of this type, contact the Baldwin Company for detailed instructions.

Broken Spinet String. To replace a broken treble string in a spinet, remove the top action bracket screws or nuts and tip the action forward as far as possible. Remove the broken pieces of wire, and turn the tuning pins out a total of four turns each. Cut the new wire a little longer than necessary, form the hitch pin loop, and insert the string into a straight section of ordinary curtain rod. Push the string into place with the curtain rod, and hook the loop over the hitch pin. Place a small spring clamp over the hitch pin, or have an assistant hold the string in place by hand or with a long screwdriver if there is no room for a clamp, and withdraw the curtain rod. Then attach the string to the tuning pins as usual. Turn enough wire onto each tuning pin to hold the string on the hitch pin, and then lay each string in the correct place on the bridge. Raise the pitch, drive the tuning pins down flush with their neighbors, and tune the strings. To thread a bass

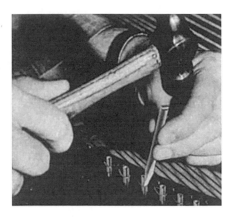

4-49. Tapping a string down on a Baldwin "Acu-just" hitch pin to increase downbearing on the bridge.

4-51. Measuring downbearing in a Baldwin with a simple bearing gauge and feeler gauge.

string down into a spinet without removing the action, thread a paper clip through the hitch pin loop of the new string and around the adjacent bass string, and let the adjacent string guide the new one down into place.

Broken String Under Overstrung Section. If there is no room behind the bass strings for a curtain rod, cut a groove in the end of a small dowel and use it to guide the string into place.

Tuning Repaired or Replaced Strings. All new strings gradually stretch and go out of tune. When confronted with a broken or missing string, replace it before tuning the piano, so it can stretch for the hour or two that you spend with the piano, giving

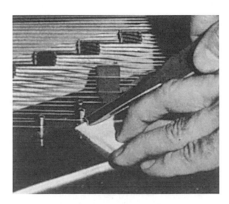

4-50. Lifting the string slightly by prying it with an appropriate tool resting on a small block, if the downbearing is too great.

you the chance to raise its pitch several times. After repairing or replacing a string in a customer's piano that won't be tuned again for several months, leave the string tuned as sharp as possible without making it sound too objectionable, so it won't fall as flat as it would if you had tuned it perfectly. If it is one string of a two or three string unison, mute it with a tuning mute, folded piece of action cloth, or front rail punching, and leave it muted until the next time you tune the piano, if the customer prefers this to having a bad sounding unison.

Dead Treble String. If the tone of a treble string dies away too quickly, this is usually due to problems with downbearing, soundboard crown, hammer shape, or striking point. If the wire is so rusty that it doesn't sound good, the piano should be restrung, and the other possible causes for poor tone can be checked simultaneously and repairs made as necessary.

Ringing, Jangling, or False Beats in Treble Strings. **Beats** are pulsations in the loudness of the tone that occur when two strings are out of tune with each other, as described in Chapter 6. **False beats** are pulsations in the loudness of *one string* that can't be eliminated by tuning. Most false beats in treble strings arise from improper contact between the string and one of its bearing points due to grooves in the capo bar, inadequate bearing on an agraffe, loose bridge pins, a poorly notched bridge, or a faulty or damaged wire.

In many grands, the treble strings form small grooves in the capo bar at the contact point, causing faulty termination of the vibrating part of the strings, and resulting in false beats and metallic ringing noises, which make the strings difficult or impossible to fine tune. In vertical pianos, the same condition sometimes exists where the strings cross over the v-bar. The contact surface of either the capo or v-bar should be slightly rounded, so there is just enough friction between it and the strings to hold them in place but allow them to be tuned. If the bar is too sharp, the strings will break, and if it is too blunt, they will slip sideways and go out of tune more easily. If a string has a metallic ringing noise, try pushing it sideways slightly at the capo bar. If this improves the tone temporarily, you must reshape the bar for permanent results. The best opportunity to do this is during rebuilding, when the plate is out of the piano, but sometimes you can make an improvement by removing the action, loosening the string tension, pulling the strings aside, and surfacing the capo or v-bar with a file and sandpaper. In a grand, lay a mirror on the keybed, and use a low wattage work light that won't get too hot. After removing the burrs with a medium file, sand with 320 aluminum oxide paper, then 400, and finish with 600. Raise the string tension and realign the strings with the hammers.

Where a string passes through an agraffe, the agraffe should always pull the string downward for firm contact between the two. If the string passes straight through the hole with no deflection, there is a good possibility

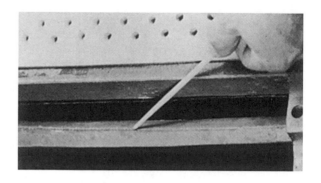

4-52. The bottom of this capo bar has tiny grooves where the strings rest against it, causing troublesome noises and poor tone quality.

that it will vibrate against the agraffe, producing a metallic jangling noise. If this occurs, try pressing down hard on the non-speaking portion of the string just in front of the agraffe to see if this cures the problem. If so, loosen the string enough to insert a shim made of action cloth, or a narrow strip of veneer covered with action cloth, or other suitable material between the plate and the string in front of the agraffe, to raise the string a little and increase its bearing against the agraffe.

A common cause of false beats is sloppy notching and pinning of the bridge, particularly in the highest two or three octaves. The length of the vibrating portion of a string is terminated by the agraffe, capo bar, or v-bar at one end, and by the bridge notch and pin at the other end. The notch determines the length of the *bottom* surface of a string in a grand, or the back surface in a vertical, while the bridge pin determines the length of the *side* of the string. After a hammer strikes a string, the plane in which the string vibrates changes rapidly — up and down, from side to side, and in all other planes. As the string vibrates in one plane, its length is influenced primarily by the notch in the wood. When the vibrational plane rotates 90°, the length is influenced to a greater extent by the bridge pin. If the bridge notch coincides perfectly with the center line of each pin, then the notch and the pin both terminate the vibrating portion of the string at the same length, and the string has a pure tone with no false beats (if there are no other problems). As the vibrational plane of the string changes, the length and pitch remain constant. If the bridge notch doesn't coincide with the center line of the pins, pronounced false beats occur because the string has two different effective vibrational lengths: one along the side of the string from agraffe to bridge pin, and the other along the bottom of the string from agraffe to bridge notch. To correct this cause of false beats, loosen the strings enough to pull them aside, pull the pins out of the bridge, and remove wood with a sharp chisel so the edge of the notch coincides with the center line of the pins. In

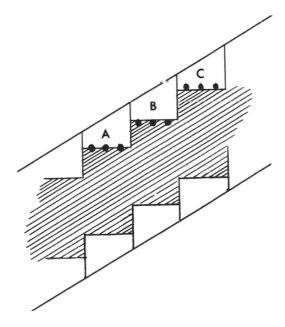

4-53. In this drawing, the center line of bridge pins "A" aligns with the notch in the wooden bridge. A string in position "A" will have a clear tone, other factors being ideal. Notches "B" and "C" don't align, and each of their strings will have false beats. In many pianos it is common to find conditions "A", "B", and "C" for the three strings of one unison due to crooked placement of the chisel during hasty notching.

a fine-quality grand — some of which do have this problem — the repair is well worth the time involved. In an inexpensive grand or vertical with dozens of carelessly placed notches, attempting to correct this problem is worthwhile only during rebuilding.

If false beats occur in a piano with adequate downbearing, a good v-bar or capo bar, and careful bridge notching, check the bridge for small cracks or loose pins. If one of these conditions exists, refer to "Split or Cracked Bridge" on p. 102 and the section on bridges in Chapter 8.

If the downbearing is inadequate, the string might ride up the bridge pin away from the top of the bridge, causing false beats. Sometimes you can correct this problem temporarily by tapping the string down gently to the bridge. If you use a screwdriver for this as shown in the illustration, hold the blade parallel to the wire and tap gently to avoid nicking the wire. Or, use a $3/16"$ diameter brass rod. Any improvement gained in this way will be temporary. For a permanent repair, increase the downbearing or recap the bridge during rebuilding, and restring the piano.

Other possible causes of false beats, ringing, or jangling noises in treble strings are twists, bends, kinks, heavy rust spots, or raising the string too far above the correct pitch during tuning, which causes the wire to stretch so far that it becomes deformed. If none of the above repairs seems to work, try replacing the string in case the wire is defective.

Dead Bass Strings. First, check to see if the bass bridge is has come unglued from its apron; if so, refer to "Unglued Bass Bridge; Cracked Apron" on pp. 102-103. If the bass bridge is in good condition, muffled or "dead" tone in dirty or corroded bass strings can sometimes be improved by the following

4-54. Gently tapping a string down to the bridge.

method. Pick a string near the middle of the bass section, where any improvement will be the most obvious. Loosen the tuning pin enough to slip the string off its hitch pin. Note the number of turns that it untwists itself as you unhook it. Put a 6" (or 15 cm.) loop in the string and run it up and down from one end to the other to flex the wire and loosen the dirt, as in illus. 4-55. Remove the loop, twist the string as many turns as it untwisted when you removed it, plus a half twist more. Small vise grip pliers work well for this job, and make it easy to count the turns. Replace the string on the hitch pin, add tension, seat the hitch pin loop on the plate, and tune. If there is a noticeable improvement in the tone quality, repeat the

process for each string in the bass, one at a time. If this procedure makes the tuning pins loose, drive them in a little more or replace them with one size larger pins.

Buzzing or Rattling Bass Strings. A rattling or vibrating noise in the bass usually occurs because of a loose or split bass bridge or an unglued soundboard rib.

A metallic buzzing in a bass string is often caused by a loose winding. To correct this, loosen the tuning pin enough to slip the string off the hitch pin, add an extra twist in the direction of the winding, reinstall the string, and tune it. If the winding still buzzes, gently crimp the end of the winding with a rotating motion of long nose pliers. Be careful; too much pressure with the pliers will

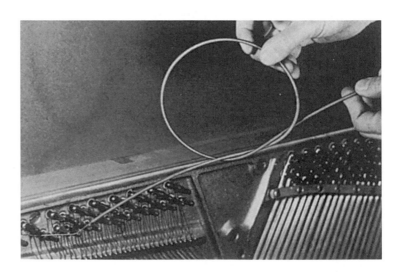

4-55. Loosening dirt and corrosion in a bass string sometimes improves its tone. Leave the string attached to the tuning pin throughout the procedure.

make the problem worse. If the string still buzzes, apply a small drop of white glue to the offending end of the winding with a toothpick. If that doesn't help, or if it noticeably deadens the tone, replace the string.

Dirty Strings. Refer to the section on cleaning strings on p. 92.

The Key Frame

Decayed Punchings. If the front and balance rail punchings and back rail cloth are in bad condition, replace them (see p. 290) and level the keys (see pp. 162-166 and 180).

Loose Balance Rail or Front Rail Pins. Remove the keys in the area of any loose pins, remove each loose pin, and apply a small amount of epoxy inside the hole. Reinsert the pin and align it with its neighbors. Wipe off all excess glue. After the epoxy is completely dry, bend the pin if necessary to realign the key.

Tarnished or Rusty Key Pins. Polish the pins with metal polish on a soft rag, being careful not to let the polish soak into the wood surrounding the pin. If the nickel plating is only oxidized, this will return the pins to a smooth, shiny condition.

If the plating is bad and the steel is rusty, this treatment will only provide temporary results, and the pins should be replaced for a permanent repair. If they're still tight in the holes, replace them with the same size new pins. If they're loose, use oversize pins and drill the holes out as necessary, a few thousandths of an inch under the size of the new pins. (Before doing this, be sure the oversize pins will fit in the keys.)

The Keys

As discussed earlier in this chapter, keys have little numbers embossed in the top surface, but if you mix them up, the 6's, 8's, 9's, and 0's all tend to look the same, particularly if the keys are dirty. Draw several diagonal lines across the keys before removing them, to make it easy to put them back in the right order (see illus. 4-13).

Sticking or Sluggish Keys. Push down on the back end of the key, near the capstan. If both ends of the key go down at once, the key is broken. See "Repairing a Broken Key" on pp. 120-121. If the back end of the key won't go down, a foreign object has probably fallen under it.

If the back end of the key goes down when you push on it, and the front comes up, you must determine whether the key or the action is sticking. Hold the key down in the back with one hand, raise the wippen with the other, and then release the wippen. If the wippen drops to its rest position properly, the problem is in the key. If the wippen stays up, or is slow to fall to the rest position, the problem is in the action.

If the front of a white key rubs on the key slip — probably the number one cause of sluggish keys — remove the key slip and insert shims made of index card stock or key frame punchings in front of each key block, and in line with each key slip screw, to hold the key slip a little less than 1/16" (or 1 mm.) away from the front ends of the keys when you tighten the screws. After determining the correct thickness for the shims, attach them to the key frame with a small dot of glue, so they won't fall out every time someone removes the key slip. Some pianos have little flat head screws located in the front of the key frame, which may be turned in or out to adjust the position of the key slip. If you prefer to install screws instead of cardboard shims, drill and countersink holes in the key frame for 1/2" x #6 flat head screws.

If a key binds on an adjacent key, there is either a bent balance rail pin or a warped key. See if the front of the key is square with

117

4-56 (left). Placing cardboard shims between the key frame and key slip to prevent the keys from rubbing on the key slip.

4-57 (right). Key easing pliers. The jaws stay parallel while you squeeze the wood.

its neighbors and the capstan is centered under the wippen or sticker. If the front and back of the key both lean in the same direction, the balance rail pin is bent. Square the key by tapping the top of the pin lightly with the palm of the hand on a screwdriver, being careful not to slip onto the key itself.

If the front of the key leans to one side and the back leans to the other, the key is warped or twisted. Bend the balance rail pin sideways to center the front and back of the key as well as possible, and sand the side of the key if it still rubs.

To straighten a badly warped key, secure the back 2" of the key between two wooden clamping pads in a vise. Lay a small damp cloth on the side of the key, and steam the wood by applying a very hot iron, keeping the cloth damp. Steam the wood alternately on each side while twisting the front end of the key gently with your other hand, *until you feel the wood becoming flexible.* Keep applying gentle pressure until you can twist the key a little farther than necessary. Remove the damp cloth, turn down the iron a little, and heat the key with the iron to dry the wood while continuing to twist it. As the wood stiffens, it might want to return part

way to its old twisted position, so by twisting it a little too far initially, you can let it return to exactly the right place. This can be a very slow process. Take your time; if you twist too hard, you'll break the key, but if you proceed slowly and gently, you can shape the key just the way you want it. If the key button or bushings come loose, reglue them after the wood is completely dry. Be careful not to loosen the keytop.

If a key sticks without rubbing on the key slip or an adjacent key, one or more

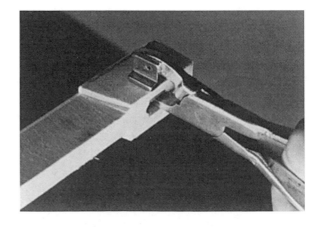

4-58. Easing a key by squeezing the wood on either side of the bushing. Be careful not to enlarge the hole so much that the key wobbles or knocks.

118

4-59. Left: Easing a tight balance rail hole with a balance rail hole easing tool. IMPORTANT: Insert the tool with the flat sides facing the ends of the key, to keep from enlarging the hole from front to back. Below: Closeup of the tool.

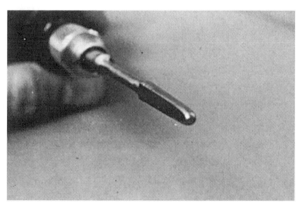

bushings are binding on their pins. Clean the pins if necessary, and if the key still sticks, gently squeeze, or "ease" the key with key easing pliers, as illustrated. Ease the bushing just enough to provide free movement of the key without excess side play.

If the key is still sluggish after you have eased the bushings, the balance rail hole in the bottom of the key might be a little too tight. Lift the front end of the key above its normal rest position, and see if it falls back to the balance rail of its own accord. If not, ease the sides of the balance rail hole with a balance rail hole easing tool as shown in illustration 4-59. Insert the tool with the flat sides facing the ends of the key, to keep from enlarging the hole from front to back.

If nothing else seems to help a spinet key that is slow in returning to the rest position, the drop lifter wire or dowel might be binding in the hole in the back end of the key. If so, bend the wire as necessary. In spinet pianos having **dog leg keys** (see illustration), one side of the balance rail bushing supports more weight than the other when you depress the key. When the bushing becomes worn, it develops an indentation on the side that receives the weight, and this indentation prevents the key from returning properly when released. To correct the problem, replace the worn bushings.

If a key won't go down, determine whether the problem is in the key or the action. Try to lift the wippen by hand. If it won't go up, the problem is in the action. If it will go up but the key won't go down, either the key is binding or a foreign object has fallen under the front end.

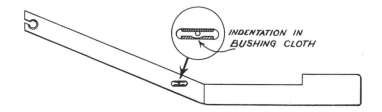

INDENTATION IN
BUSHING CLOTH

4-60. A compacted balance rail bushing in a "dog leg key" will cause the key to return to the rest position sluggishly or not at all. To correct this, replace the bushing.

Many old player pianos have a **key lock**, consisting of a rail mounted under the front of the keys. When a small lever under the keybed is moved, the rail moves up and prevents the keys from moving. Occasionally, a customer accidentally locks the keys on an old player piano and, being unaware of the existence of the key lock, calls a technician thinking the piano has a serious problem.

Rattling or Loose Keys. The purpose of the cloth bushings is to allow the keys to work properly without being noisy. If the bushings are worn, compressed, or missing, the keys will knock and rattle as they're played.

If there is only a slight amount of excess side play, you can correct the problem by needling the bottom of the key with a fine sewing needle, and applying a drop of water, which will swell the wood a little, tightening the bushing.

If a bushing is badly worn or missing, obtain a piece of bushing cloth of the proper thickness. With a sharp, slender knife, clean as much of the old cloth and glue out of the key as possible without disrupting the wood fibers. Glue the new bushing in place using hide glue and a bushing clamp, as illustrated on p. 291.

If a key has end play because the balance rail hole has become elongated, needle the wood surrounding the hole, and apply a drop of water. While the water is drying, clean the pin with metal polish. When the surface of the wood feels dry, apply a drop of aliphatic resin glue to the wood, which will soak in and strengthen the wood. Wipe off excess glue, and put the key on the pin without pushing it down against the punchings. After the glue is dry, ease the key just a little if necessary.

Never turn a front rail pin to take up side play in the bushing. If you turn it, the corner will wear the bushing away even faster, aggravating the condition. If the bushing is bad, replace it.

Repairing a Broken Key. Breaks usually occur near the middle of a key where the wood is the thinnest. Separate the broken parts, make appropriate wooden clamping blocks, and assemble and clamp the parts without glue to check the fit and alignment. Coat the broken surface with aliphatic resin glue and reassemble the parts, leaving them clamped until the glue is thoroughly dry. If the repaired key looks like it might be weak, sand the side of the key down a little, and glue a piece of veneer in place, using appropriate clamps and clamping blocks. When dry, sand the veneer down so the key will fit between its neighbors.

White Key Covering Materials. Four types of white keytops have been popular over the years: ivory, celluloid, pyralin, and molded plastic. Ivory is the covering on most old upright and grand keys; elephant ivory has a grain pattern resembling a fingerprint or very fine wood grain, while walrus ivory has a coarser, larger grain pattern. Piano makers used celluloid on medium priced and inexpensive pianos made until the 1940's; it is sometimes a little more yellow or gray than

120

4-61. A typical broken key.

4-62 (right). Clamping the glue joint after aligning the parts very carefully.

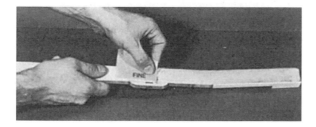

4-63 (above). Sanding away the excess glue.

4-64 (above). A veneer patch, ready for gluing.

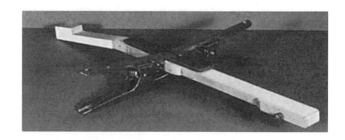

4-65 (above). Gluing and clamping the patch.

4-66 (left). The complete patch after sanding.

121

ivory, and it usually has a fine "grain" of thin parallel lines running through it lengthwise. Pyralin is a thin plastic supplied in sheets or blanks, and it must be trimmed and shaped after being glued to the keys. Manufacturers installed it on many new pianos during the 1950's, and many repair shops used it over the years. Molded plastic keytops are thicker than pyralin and have the rounded edges and corners preshaped, requiring little additional shaping after being glued to the keys. Almost all pianos made since the late 1960's have molded plastic keytops. Since ivory and celluloid tops are difficult to obtain, the technician should save an assortment of old keytops of various materials, colors, and thicknesses from junk pianos, for replacement purposes.

Replacing a Broken or Missing White Keytop. If a broken part of the old keytop is still attached to the key, remove it by heating it for a minute with an iron set on medium, or with judicious use of a heat gun, and then slipping a 1" wide putty knife under it. Sometimes dry heat works the best, and sometimes it helps to use a damp cloth between the iron and key. Some old plastic keys may be removed by applying a solvent like lacquer thinner under a loose spot with a palette knife or other thin blade, and gradually prying as the adhesive lets loose. Be extremely careful if you decide to apply heat

to a plastic keytop, to avoid melting or burning it. If you begin lifting a splinter of wood from the key while prying the old keytop up, start over at the other end. If a piece of wood does come off with the old keytop, slice it off the keytop with a new single edge razor blade and reglue it to the body of the key.

After removing the keytop, remove old glue by dampening it with water or an appropriate solvent and then scraping the wood clean, to avoid removing any wood. Use water to dissolve hot glue, ammonia for white glue, or lacquer thinner for contact cement. If it is necessary to sand the top of the key, obtain self-adhesive 320 aluminum oxide sandpaper made for a high speed orbital sander. Stick it to a piece of plate glass, apply even pressure to the key body as illustrated, and keep checking the front end of the key for squareness as you proceed.

Choose a replacement keytop that matches the adjacent keys, and glue it in place, using the best quality professional contact cement for molded plastic, pyralin glue for pyralin, and ivory cement or an ivory wafer (a glue-impregnated piece of cloth available from piano supply companies) for ivory. Clamp the keytop (unless using contact cement) with ivory clamps and clamping plates obtained from a piano supply company, as shown. If the new clamps have blunt ends on the tightening screws, grind the end

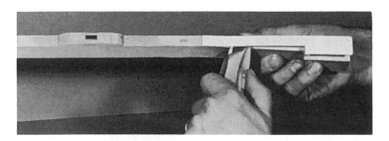

4-67. Cut the old plastic keytop off the key with a sharp knife, if you can do this without removing any wood.

122

4-68 (left). Sanding the key as described above. In this illustration, a piece of sandpaper is taped to a bench, but self-adhesive sandpaper stuck to a piece of plate glass is better.

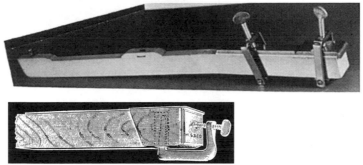

4-69. Clamping the new white keytop or front.

of each screw to a point so it doesn't push the brass clamping plate sideways as you tighten it.

To use an ivory wafer, heat the clamping plate in boiling water. Wet the wafer in room-temperature water, apply it to the key, position the ivory on top of it, and apply the hot clamping plate and clamp. After the glue is dry, remove the excess glue and trim the edges of the new keytop with a fine file and sandpaper if necessary. If the thickness of a new ivory head is a little different from an old tail, sand the whole keytop again as shown in 4-68 with successively finer and finer sandpaper. Then buff the key with the finest buffing compound on an unstitched buffing wheel to bring its surface to the same gloss as the adjacent keys. To recover an entire keyboard, see Chapter 8.

Replacing a Missing Black Keytop. Black keytops are made of ebony or other hard wood or plastic. Obtain a new one of the correct type from a piano supply company, or find an appropriate used one. Scrape or sand the old key smooth to remove old glue, and attach the new sharp with aliphatic resin glue. Clamp until dry. When gluing a plastic sharp, apply enough glue that it will squeeze up into the hollow area inside the sharp, helping to strengthen the glue joint. If the hole for the front bushing goes all the way through the wooden part of the key, don't let any glue run down into the front bushing.

Discolored Keys. Ivory keys may be lightened in color somewhat by scraping the surface with an ivory scraper and then buffing to restore the surface finish. Little can be done to enhance keytops with ink or crayon stains or cigarette burns. Usually these must be replaced. Worn sharps may be sprayed with several coats of gloss black lacquer. To

123

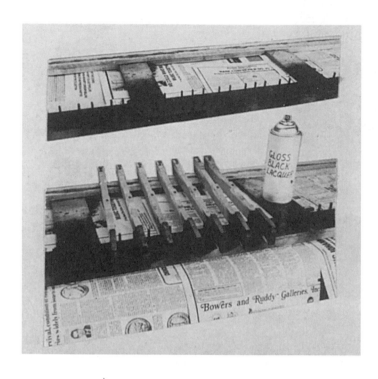

4-70. A sharp-spraying rack made from a junk upright key frame.

hold the keys upright while spraying, make a spraying rack out of an old key frame, or with finishing nails and a piece of 3/4" plywood, as shown.

The Action

The action — the mechanism linking the keys to the hammers — is the most complicated major component of a piano, with the largest number of parts and the greatest chance for many different things to go wrong. The following discussion breaks the action into several major groups of parts: **action rails and screws**; **flanges**; **the wippen assembly** (including the wippen, sticker, jack, jack spring, backcheck, and bridle wire in a vertical, and the wippen, repetition lever, and jack assembly in a grand); **the hammer assembly** (including the hammer, butt, spring rail and butt spring, catcher, and bridle strap in a vertical and the hammer,

shank, knuckle, and flange in a grand); and **the damper assembly** (including the damper lever, spring, and damper in a vertical, and all parts related to the damper including the sostenuto mechanism in a grand). Since flange bushings that are too tight or too loose cause many problems, and most of the moving parts of an action have flanges, the section on flanges is pertinent to all the other parts of the action.

Before you remove a set of parts from an action, always number them starting with #1 in the bass. Number wippens on the back end, stickers and damper levers on the back side, and hammer butts on the side.

Action Rails and Screws

Stripped Flange Screw Holes. When a wooden action rail has a stripped screw hole, try substituting an oversize flange screw, available from piano supply companies. If an oversize screw doesn't help, plug the screw hole, as discussed on pp. 83-84.

If a Steinway "Tubular Metallic Action Rail" has a few stripped holes, it might be possible to make the screws hold by the following method: Cut a piece of thin buckskin about $^3/16$" wide by $1^1/4$" long (5 mm. x 3 cm.). Fold the buckskin in half, work hot hide glue or liquid hide glue into the hole with a pipe cleaner, and push the middle of the buckskin strip into the hole with a small pointed tool. While holding the ends of the buckskin in place, thread the screw into the hole without the flange, being careful to center the screw in the hole, and trim off the excess buckskin with a sharp knife. After the glue sets, but before it dries, remove the screw and carefully screw the flange in place, holding it in line with its neighbors as you tighten the screw.

An alternative repair is to "glue size" the hole, or swab it with aliphatic resin glue or thin epoxy, and then insert the screw before the glue dries completely. If a Steinway action has most of the screw holes stripped, see p. 307.

Manufacturers of modern pianos with metal action rails typically have oversize screws available, or can recommend the ideal size for replacing original screws in stripped holes. If you can't use an oversize screw,

attach a 6-32 nut to the back side of the rail with super glue, and attach the flange with a standard 6-32 machine screw threaded all the way through the nut. Use an appropriate washer under the screw head if necessary.

Rusty Regulating Screws. When a regulating screw rail absorbs so much humidity that the regulating screws rust, the screws become bonded to the wood and might break off if you try to turn them. Badly rusted regulating screws should be replaced. Take the regulating rail out of the action and heat the end of each screw with a soldering pencil or iron, without scorching the wood. When the screw is hot, rotate it back and forth with a regulating screwdriver; this should loosen it in the wood and enable it to be removed. If both ends break off, drill a slightly oversize hole immediately next to the stump, work it sideways into the new hole, and remove it. Cross plug and redrill the hole, and insert a new regulating screw.

Flanges

Wood flanges with their cloth center pin bushings may be the source of two opposite problems: loose, wobbly parts due to worn bushings and excessive dryness, and sluggish parts due to swollen or dirty bushings.

When a flanged part is loose or wobbly, it is necessary to replace the bushings. Remove

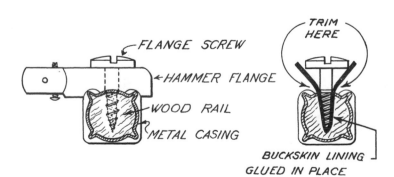

4-71. A remedial repair for a stripped Steinway flange screw hole.

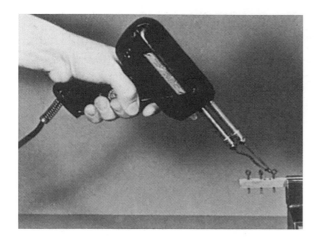

4-72. Heating a rusty regulating screw to free it. Don't scorch the wood.

the part with its flange from the action, and remove the center pin with a center pin punch or special pliers, as illustrated.

Measure the diameter of the old center pin, and select a new one of the same size. Push the pointed end into the non-bushed hole in the wooden action part to make sure it is tight in the wood; if not, select a larger pin. The wood should grip the pin tightly enough so it will never slip out by itself, but the pin shouldn't be so tight that there is any risk of cracking the wood.

When you find a pin that fits tightly in the wooden part, remove it and check its fit in each side of the bushed flange. Test each bushing separately, because they sometimes wear unevenly. If the pin is loose in either bushing, you should rebush the flange.

Remove the old bushings with a hand-held flange bushing drill or drill press. Carefully select the correct size drill bit to remove

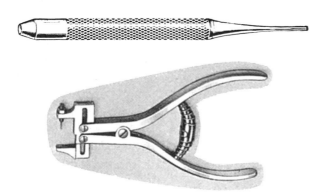

CENTER PINS
(Diameters Given In Inches)

Size	Diameter	Size	Diameter
18	.046	22	.054
18¹/₂	.047	22¹/₂	.055
19	.048	23	.056
19¹/₂	.049	23¹/₂	.0575
20	.050	24	.059
20¹/₂	.051	24¹/₂	.061
21	.052	25	.063
21¹/₂	.053		

4-74. Above: Center pin sizes.
Below: A handy holder for commonly used sizes of pins, and a combination center pin and tuning pin gauge.

4-73 (above). Punch and special pliers for removing center pins, available from piano supply companies. A lever operated press is also available for production work in the shop.

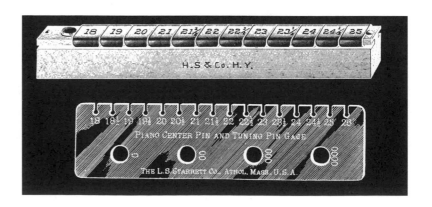

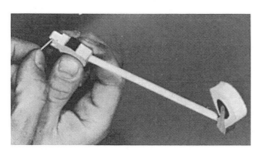

4-75. Testing the fit of a new center pin in the hammer butt.

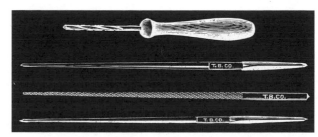

4-76. Flange repinning tools. Top to bottom: Bushing drill, cornered reamer, rat tail file, and round burnisher.

the old cloth and glue without removing any wood from the hole. Tear a piece of thin flange bushing cloth, to a width equal to the circumference of the hole, and cut a long tapered point on one end. It will take some experimentation to find the right width, so tear the strip a little too wide, and then make it narrower — one thread at a time if necessary — until the cloth forms a neat bushing with neither a gap nor an overlap at the seam. Tearing the cloth instead of cutting it produces a strip of more uniform width, and the rough edge helps the cloth to merge at the seam.

Pull the cloth through both sides of the flange, as illustrated. Apply a little hide glue with a toothpick around the cloth next to each hole in the flange, and pull the cloth through a little farther to drag the glue into the hole. Cut the end of the strip away, leaving a little excess cloth on both sides of the flange, and insert a center pin .001" larger than the size of the actual pin that will be used, to press the bushing tightly in place until the glue sets. After the glue turns hard enough that it won't smear, but before it turns brittle, remove the pin and trim away the excess cloth and glue with a new razor blade or very sharp knife, starting at the seam side of the bushing. If you trim the cloth before the glue sets, you'll pull the bushing out of the wood or drag glue into the hole and onto the working surface of the

cloth. If you wait too long, the glue will be so hard that it will be difficult to cut it off without cutting into the wood.

When you need to rebush several flanges, pull the strip of cloth almost all the way through the first flange. Glue it, cut it off, and keep using it until it runs out.

After the glue is dry, mix a solution of nine parts ethanol (denatured alcohol) to one part water, and apply a drop of this to each bushing with the center pin still in place. This will help to compact the fibers of the cloth, making the bushing less spongy. If the alcohol mixture dissolves the red dye in the cloth, be careful not to apply so much that it runs all over the wood. Let it dry — the drying time will vary, depending upon the relative humidity in the surrounding air — and remove the oversize pin.

Test the fit of the correct center pin — not the oversize one used for pressing the bushing during gluing — in each new bushing. The fit should be snug, but loose enough that you can rotate the pin in the bushing with your fingers. If the pin is too tight, you must ream the bushing. Attach a tapered bushing reamer to a little wooden handle as used for the drill bit in 4-77, carefully insert it into one side of the flange, and spin it, removing as little cloth as possible. Then press the burnisher into the hole and spin it to pack the cloth a little, remove it, and try the fit of the center pin again. Keep doing

127

4-77. Drilling the old cloth bushings out of the flange with an appropriate drill bit held in a small wooden handle.

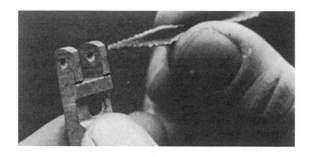

4-78. Inserting the pointed end of a torn strip of bushing cloth into the hole in the flange.

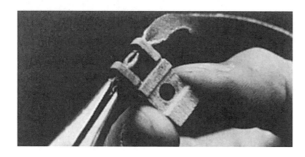

4-79. Pulling the cloth through the flange with long-nose pliers. After starting it, grasp it with your fingers to pull it almost to the end of the strip. Apply glue around the cloth next to each tongue of the flange, and pull it into the wood.

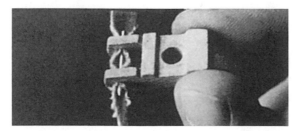

4-80. Clamping the cloth in place with a new center pin, until the glue begins to dry.

this until the fit of the pin is just right. It is far better to ream the bushing several times in tiny amounts than to ream too much and have to rebush the flange, although the latter is likely to occur frequently until you become proficient at judging the correct tightness. Since the reamer and burnisher are both tapered, treat each side of the flange separately for uniform results. The farther you insert the reamer, the more material you will remove. When the fit is correct, you'll feel the bushing gently "pinch" the end of the pin as it passes through the bushing. Then as you continue to push it in farther, it should have a snug but smooth feel.

Before pinning the two parts together, examine their fit. If a bushing sticks out of the side of the wood and rubs on the other part, trim the bushing. If the two wooden parts rub on each other, correct this by filing, sanding, or trimming as necessary, without creating any noticeable side play between the two parts. After you're sure that there is a good fit between the parts, pin them together and check the fit of the pin in the bushings. A hammer flange (or hammer butt flange, in a vertical) shouldn't drop under its own weight, but should move under the weight of the flange screw.

Another way to test this is to hold the flange in one hand with the hammer (or butt and hammer) hanging down, lift the hammer to one side with the other hand, release it, and count how often it swings to and fro — counting "to" as one, "fro" as two, etc.; the hammer should swing five or six times before coming to rest. A jack, with the spring removed, should move under its own weight as you tip the wippen gently back and forth. A wippen flange should be a little tighter, and should just barely hold up the weight of the flange screw until you tap the wippen on the side, causing the flange to move a little

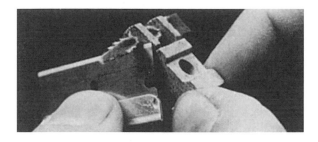

4-81. Trimming the cloth and little donut of glue off the wood before the glue turns brittle and too hard to cut. After trimming, insert the pin again until the glue has dried thoroughly. Although the razor blade is shown under the cupped part of the bushing for clarity in this picture, you should always start cutting at the seam in the cloth for a neater trim..

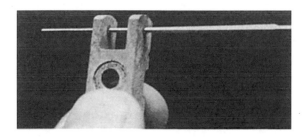

4-82. Enlarging the hole in the bushing slightly with a tapered reamer.

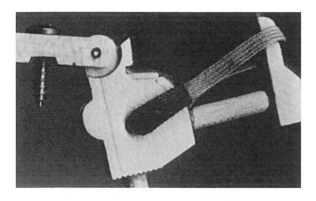

4-83. Testing the tightness of the pin in the bushings; a vertical hammer butt flange shouldn't drop under its own weight, but should move under the weight of the screw.

with each tap. A grand repetition lever with the spring removed should move under the weight of a nickel placed on the drop screw

cushion. A grand damper underlever should move easily under its own weight, and an upright damper flange with the spring removed should fall under the weight of the flange screw.

The above tests are valid only if both flange bushings are equally tight. If one bushing is too tight and the other is too loose, the total friction or resistance will be correct, but the action part will wobble anyway, which is obviously wrong.

If your first few attempts produce a new bushing that is just as loose as the old one was, remove the bushing and try again until you get it right. It's better to learn by doing one flange two or three times than by having to redo a whole set.

If you insert and remove the same pin several times while testing its fit, either push it out carefully with the punch, special pliers, or press, being careful not to damage the new bushing, or pull it out by gently grasping the pointed end with pliers. If you don't nick the working area of the pin you may reuse it, but if your pliers nick the pin, throw it away. After the fit is just right, push a new pin all the way in so the flat end is flush with the bushing, and cut the other end off with center pin nippers — special flush-cutting side cutters available from piano supply companies. Remove the burr with a small file, and reinstall the part in the action.

If you have to rebush a whole set of flanges and have access to a drill press, you can make a parallel-sided (non-tapered) bushing reamer for uniform results from one bushing to the next, without having to judge precisely how far to insert the tapered reamer. Take two center pins of the same size that you will use to repin the parts, and knurl them by rolling them between two files. By using two pins simultaneously, a few inches apart from each other on the files, you

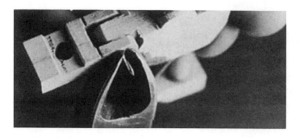

4-84. Clipping the pointed end of the pin with center pin nippers.

will avoid damaging the files by scraping one against the other. Insert one of the pins in the drill press, and set the press on a medium high speed. Use this to ream a trial bushing, and test the tightness of the bushing with a new center pin. Depending on how coarse your files are and how hard you press, you might need to use a slightly smaller or larger pin to get the desired results. If your reamer wears down and doesn't remove as much material after reaming dozens of bushings, make another one. After you gain experience using this method, you should be able to prepare a whole set of bushings in the time it takes to do ten or twenty with a tapered reamer.

If an action has previously been repaired, there is a good chance that it has a variety of different size center pins in the action parts; if you think this might be the case, measure and custom-fit each pin as you go.

When a note is sluggish, test each action part separately to find which flange or flanges are contributing to the problem. For example, in a grand, first lift the hammer to see if it drops promptly when released. Then swing the hammer up out of the way, hold the back of the key down, and lift the wippen to see if it moves freely. Then hold the wippen up and check the key. This process of elimination is useful for isolating any action problem.

When an action part is sluggish, either one or both of the center pin bushings are too tight or are rubbing on the side of the part, or the parts are rubbing against each other. Remove the sluggish part with its flange from the action, separate the two parts, and correct the problem by the same methods described above for easing new bushings. If an old bushing has swollen from high humidity, try to shrink it by applying a little of the alcohol/water mixture. You'll have to wait twenty-four hours to see if this does the trick. If not, apply a drop of center pin lubricant, available from piano supply companies. If that doesn't help either, ream the bushing.

Some technicians advocate the use of a "zapper," which heats the center pin by applying low voltage electric current from a small transformer with two narrow electrodes, without removing the part from the action, to dry the water out of the bushing or to "iron" the cloth. Unfortunately, this tool tends to scorch the cloth in the flange and the wood in the other part, so it won't hold the pin tightly any more.

In many old actions, the combination of the bushing cloth, center pins, and sometimes a lubricant used by the manufacturer causes a chemical reaction that results in an accumulation of a waxy greenish substance that causes the center pins to stick to the bushings, resulting in very sluggish action parts. In many old Steinway grands, for example, you can depress the entire top octave of keys at once, release them, and then watch the hammers fall back to rest over a period of several seconds or even longer, because of this condition. While some technicians feel that flushing out the bushings with naphtha or another solvent will clean them well enough for at least a temporary cure, in the author's experience, dissembling the parts and carefully reaming out the accumulation of waxy matter without removing any significant amount of cloth is more effective. The best solution to the problem, of course, is to rebush all the parts.

Teflon Bushings. In an attempt to improve on cloth bushings, Steinway began using solid Teflon center pin bushings in their American piano actions in about 1963. These new bushings had their advantages, but training technicians to service them properly remained a problem, so Steinway quit using them around 1983.

Teflon bushings don't change size with humidity changes, but wooden action parts do. Holes in wooden parts change dimension across the grain, shrinking when they dry and expanding when they gain moisture. This causes some Teflon bushings to squeeze their center pins a little too tightly, and others to get loose in the wood. A conventional tapered reamer will ruin Teflon bushings, so it is necessary to use parallel-sided reamers instead. Obtain a set of reamers from .049" to .053" graduated in .0005" steps, and a Teflon center pin repair kit from Steinway or a piano supply company. This kit includes several sizes of center pins with both ends rounded slightly so they may be reused.

A loose center pin is usually looser in the bushing in one side of the flange than in the other. Remove the original center pin, and find a new one that has the proper fit in the looser of the two bushings. To test the fit, insert the pin in the looser bushing, hold the pin in one hand, and allow the flange to hang by that bushing. When you rotate the pin, the flange should rise almost to the horizontal position and then drop under its own weight almost vertically. After you find the correct pin for the looser bushing, ream the

tighter bushing until it fits too. Start with the reamer the same size as the pin, and test the fit of the pin again. Ream the bushing with increasingly larger reamers, one size at a time, until the pin fits perfectly.

If a bushing clicks in the wood or comes loose during the pin fitting process, replace it with a slightly oversize bushing if available, or size the wood surrounding the hole with glue. After the glue dries, press the bushing back into place, and ream it for proper fit.

Broken Flanges. When a flange breaks, it invariably breaks across either the screw hole or the center pin hole, usually leaving the wood somewhat deformed or with small pieces of wood missing, making it difficult to reglue properly. If both pieces of wood are intact, try repairing the flange with aliphatic resin glue or a good-quality super glue made for wood and other porous materials. If this doesn't work, replace the flange. If the flanges are so brittle that they seem to keep breaking as fast as you can fix them, replace all the flanges in the action with new ones having the right size mortise and the correct distance from the center of the screw hole to the center of the pin. If the exact style isn't available from a piano supply company, try one of the custom action parts suppliers that advertise in the *Piano Technicians Journal*.

Broken Brass Flanges and Rails. Repair a broken brass flange rail with one of several types of brass flange rail repair clips available from piano supply companies, as illustrated. Use type A when the rail breaks at the groove, and type B when the rail breaks at the screw hole. See if the flange rail is of the regular or Kimball type. The regular type

4-85. Steinway Teflon ™ flange bushings and inserting tool.

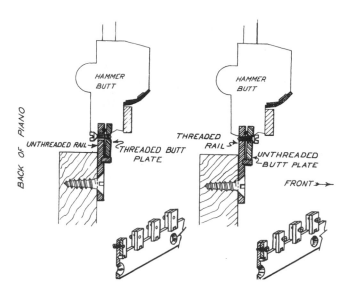

4-86 (above). Regular (left) and Kimball (right) brass flange rails, showing opposite mounting of flange screw and butt plate.

REPAIR CLIPS

Type A   Type B   Type KA   Type KB

Type A is used when the tongue is broken at the groove. One half of the old groove is used and the broken part replaced by the repair clip.

Type B is necessary when the tongue has broken at the screw hole.

Type KA is special for Kimball pianos.

Type KB is special for Kimball pianos when the tongue has broken at the screw hole.

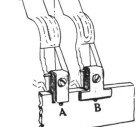

4-87 (right). Repair clips.

has a threaded hole in the butt plate, with the screw entering through an unthreaded hole in the rail. The Kimball type has a threaded hole in the rail, with the screw entering through an unthreaded hole in the butt plate. *The two types are not interchangeable.* A butt plate inserter is handy for holding the plate while tightening the screw.

Supply companies stock Billings flanges intermittently. If a new replacement isn't available, replace a broken Billings flange with one from a junk piano action. In an emergency, take a flange from a less frequently played note at the extreme end of the action.

The Wippen Assembly

Unglued Jack Flanges. It is common in old vertical pianos for jack flanges to come unglued from the wippens. When this happens, the jack often tips sideways just enough to miss the hammer butt, and the result is a "dead note," or a note that won't play. Remove the action from the piano, unhook the appropriate bridle strap from its bridle wire, and remove the wippen flange with a flange screwdriver. Remove the wippen, pull the jack and flange loose, scrape the old glue off both parts, and reglue with hot hide or aliphatic resin glue. Be sure to

132

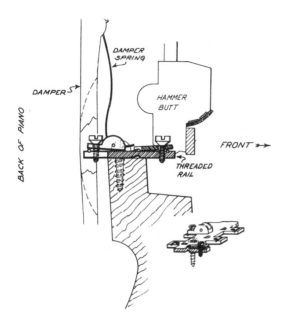

4-88. A butt plate inserter.

4-89 (left). The Kimball double flange rail holds both the hammers and the dampers.

4-90 (below). A Billings brass flange.

seat the flange tightly against the wippen so the jack will aim in the right direction. Usually in old uprights, when you align a jack properly, the top end of the jack is centered on the backcheck, so you might be able to use this as a guide. After the glue dries, replace the jack spring under the jack and replace the wippen in the action. Before installing the action, observe the jack from the front, loosen the wippen flange screw, tip the wippen left or right to align the top of the jack with the bottom of the hammer butt if necessary, and tighten the screw. Recon-

nect the bridle strap and install the action in the piano.

If several jack flanges are loose in an older action, all the rest of them probably are ready to come loose too. It is a good idea to disassemble the action, break all the jack flanges loose from the wippens and reglue them, to avoid having to make another repair every time another one comes loose.

Broken, Missing, or Weak Jack Spring. This is a common occurrence in older vertical pianos. If the spring is defective or missing, the jack won't reset itself

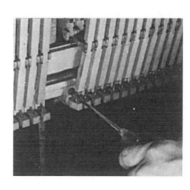

4-91. Left: Removing a wippen screw with a flange screwdriver. Right: A jack flange unglued from its wippen.

133

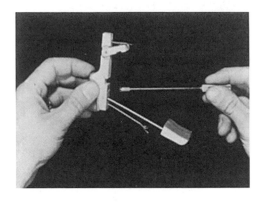

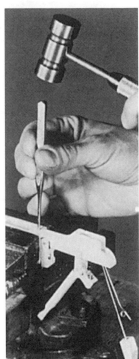

4-92 (above). A jack spring hole reamer, for cleaning the old glue out of the hole in the wippen.
4-93 (right). Punching out a broken damper spoon. Many spoons have serrations instead of threads like the one in the picture.

under the hammer butt, causing a dead note. Remove the wippen and clean the old glue and broken spring out of the hole in the wippen with a jack spring hole reamer. Barely fill the hole in the wippen with new hot glue without smearing it onto the top of the wippen, and press the larger end of the new spring in place. If you use too little glue, the spring might come loose, and if you use too much, the glue will smear onto the working part of the spring. After the glue sets, insert the top end of the spring in the hole in the jack, and replace the wippen in the action. Jack springs come in two sizes, longer for uprights and shorter for spinets.

Loose or Broken Bridle Wire, Backcheck Wire, or Damper Spoon. If one of these is loose, remove it from the wood, insert super glue or epoxy into the hole, and reinsert the wire or spoon. Note whether the wire or spoon has threads

requiring unscrewing, or serrations requiring pulling it straight out. If one is broken, replace it with a new one or an appropriate part taken from a junk piano action.

Broken Wippen. A vertical piano wippen occasionally breaks where the center pin connects it to the sticker. If you are unable to reglue the thin piece of wood successfully, repair the wippen with a Peniston wippen repair pin, as illustrated.

Broken Spinet Lifter Elbows. Many spinets built in the 1940's and 1950's have plastic lifter elbows connecting the drop sticker wires to the wippens. The plastic in most of these elbows eventually degenerates into a crumbling, sticky mess. Two types of replacements are available: Vagias snap-in plastic elbows and wood elbows. Snap-in elbows are made of high quality plastic that doesn't deteriorate like the old plastic did, and they are very convenient to use, because

134

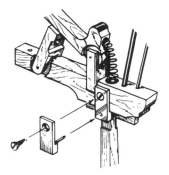

4-94. The Peniston wippen repair pin, available from piano supply companies.

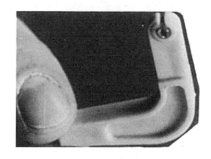

4-95. The easy-to-install Vagias replacement elbow.

they may be slipped into place on the wippens without removing the action from the piano. Pick all remains of the old plastic elbows from the wippens and lifter wires, crushing obstinate bits with needle nose pliers if necessary. Screw the lifter wires into the new elbows, snap the elbows in place in the wippens, insert the lifter wires into the keys, and regulate lost motion.

To install a set of wood elbows, remove the action and number and remove the wippens. Punch out the old center pins with a center pin punch or extractor, as shown in illus. 4-73. Screw the wires into the new elbows. Pin the elbows to the wippens with new center pins the same size as the old ones, clip the ends of the pins with a side cutter, reassemble the action, install it in the piano, and regulate lost motion.

The Hammer Assembly

Broken Hammer Shanks. Hammer shanks usually break near the middle, as illustrated on the following page. To repair, remove the butt (or flange, in a grand) from the action with a flange screwdriver. In an upright, be careful not to apply excessive pressure to the jack with the screwdriver. This might bend the jack center pin, break

the jack flange loose from the wippen, or break the wippen flange.

Apply aliphatic resin glue, align the parts, and press together. Remove excess glue and wrap the joint with heavy carpet thread. You can remove the thread and sand the shank clean after the glue is dry.

You also can splice broken shanks with shank repair sleeves, which come in two styles. The short sleeve is continuous, while the longer one is slit so it may be drawn tight around the broken shank. When using either type, apply glue to the broken wood joint before assembly. Don't use repair sleeves in a fine quality piano; the added weight of the sleeve changes the touch of the repaired note.

To replace an irreparable grand shank, remove the old stump from the hammer head with a grand shank press, as illustrated. Because the grand shank goes completely through the hammer, the press merely pushes it back out. Select a new shank identical to the original, to ensure that the knuckle will be the correct distance from the center pin or axis of rotation. If an exact replacement is is not available, obtain a universal replacement shank that can be adjusted to the correct position, as illustrated.

To replace a broken vertical shank, remove the old stump from the hammer and

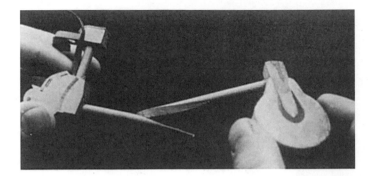

4-96 (left). A typical broken hammer shank.

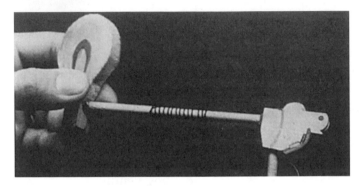

4-97 (right). Wrapping the neatly aligned glue joint with strong thread.

butt with an upright hammer extractor. Because the vertical shank doesn't go completely through the hammer head, the vertical shank extractor requires a clamp on the shank, as illustrated. Before using this tool, chip the old glue away from around the shank to weaken the joint.

If a shank breaks off at the surface of the butt or hammer head, mark the exact center with an awl and bore the remaining shank out with a hammer head and butt borer, as illustrated. Adjust the drill guide carefully before boring.

Cut a new shank to the correct length, and knurl each end with a shank knurler, or by rolling it under the edge of a large, coarse file, or by squeezing it gently with ordinary pliers held perpendicular to the shank, to provide for glue relief. Screw the hammer butt to the action and test the shank and

4-98 (above). Cutaway view of one style of hammer shank repair sleeve.

4-99 (right). A grand hammer shank press.

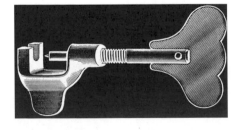

4-100 (above). An adjustable replacement grand hammer shank.

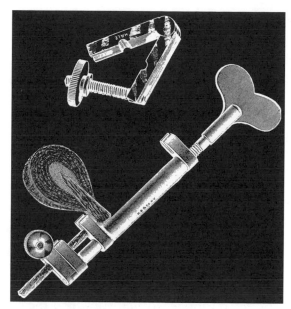

4-101. Removing an upright hammer with an upright hammer extractor and clamp.

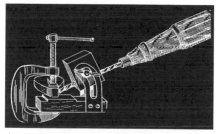

4-102. A hammer head and butt borer.

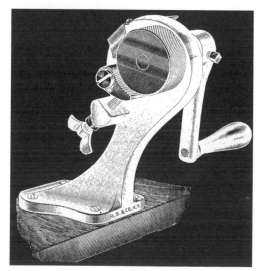

4-103 (above) A hammer shank knurler.
(Right) Knurling with the edge of a large file.

hammer head for proper fit. Then glue the shank to the butt, and the hammer to the shank, aligning the hammer with its neighbors.

Missing Hammer. If a hammer is missing, inspect the inside of the piano thoroughly; you often can find missing hammers lying somewhere in the bottom of the piano. If not, replace with a similar hammer from a junk action, usually available from any technician who has replaced the hammers in several pianos and has kept a few old ones.

"Jumping" Hammers. If the buckskin on the butt or knuckle has an indentation where the jack pushes on it, the hammer will jump when the jack rubs across the high spot. The best repair is to replace the buckskin, and the cloth if necessary, but if the buckskin still has enough thickness to be usable, its shape may be restored temporarily by sewing yarn between the buckskin and under cloth, as illustrated.

Broken Hammer Butt Springs. If a hammer butt spring breaks off at the spring rail, install a repair spring, as illustrated. Make a small hole in the wood with a very sharp, slender awl, and then screw the repair spring in place, starting it with a screw holding tool. If many springs are broken, remove the rail from the action and replace the entire set of springs, as described in Chapter 8.

Reshaping Worn Hammers. Illustration 4-107 shows the shapes of new and typically worn hammers. To restore a flat ham-

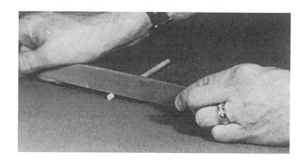

4-104. A hammer shank reducing tool, for use in any situation where it is necessary to remove old glue from a shank or reduce its diameter. Adjust the inside diameter of the jaws by turning the knurled nut.

mer to its original shape, draw a line centered down each side and across the worn face with a sharp pencil to locate the striking point, as illustrated. (If the correct shape is obvious and the hammers need only minor reshaping, the pencil lines aren't necessary). Then sand the hammer in the direction shown until you eliminate the grooves and restore the shape. Support the hammer firmly with your other hand during filing to prevent damage to the center pin, flange, or bushings. Use a flat stick with 80 grit garnet sandpaper glued to it, or a commercially available sanding stick with replaceable sandpaper. When you're done, smooth the surface of the hammers with 150 grit garnet paper.

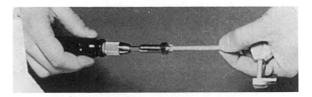

Sand carefully to keep from rounding the surface of the hammer from one side to the other. Never sand extreme treble hammers if doing so will expose the wood or will weaken the felt so the strings will rapidly cut through it to the wood. Flat treble hammer felt is better than wood striking the strings.

It is important to sand the hammers accurately, maintaining the striking points in their correct positions, to help produce the best possible tone quality. If you reshape hammers carelessly, with one striking point out of line with the next, the tone quality will vary from one note to the next. Remove an equal amount of felt from both shoulders of the hammer so the crown will have symmetrical support. If you remove significantly more felt from the top than from the bottom, continued playing will gradually pound the felt into the wrong shape, distorting the crown and the striking point. For further discussion about the importance of the correct striking point, see pp. 297-298.

INDENTATION IN BUCKSKIN

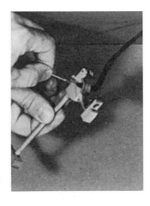

4-105. Temporarily eliminating the indentation in buckskin by padding underneath with yarn, drawn by a 2" fine steel yarn needle.

4-106. Installing a hammer butt repair spring without removing the spring rail from the action.

138

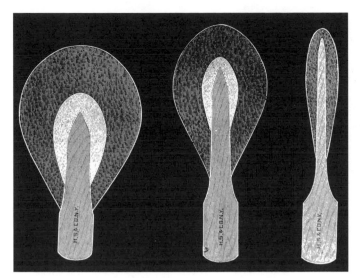

4-107 (left and above). New and worn hammers.

To check the accuracy of filing, keep inspecting each hammer from different angles. The overall shape should be like that of new hammers, as shown in illustration 4-107. The top and bottom of each hammer should be perpendicular to the sides. The striking point on each hammer should be parallel to the strings when you look down on it. Feel the crown of each hammer with one finger, to make sure the striking point feels like it is where it should be, directly in line with the end of the wood molding. As a final test after you have shaped all the hammers, install the action in the piano, and hold the hammer for each multiple string unison gently against its strings. With the other hand, pluck each string separately; the hammer should dampen all the strings equally. If one string rings, the hammer isn't hitting all the strings and should be reshaped as necessary.

Another tool for reshaping hammers is the hand-held motorized tool fitted with a drum sanding attachment and guide, available from piano supply companies. Using a motorized sander can be much faster than sanding by hand, but it increases the risk of nicking the felt or filing the hammers crooked. Confine its use to pianos in which tone quality is relatively unimportant, and

reshape the hammers in any fine-quality piano only by hand.

If treble hammers are worn all the way to the wood, replace them with a new partial set, or replace the whole set. For more information on how to judge when to install a new set of hammers, refer to pp.150-151.

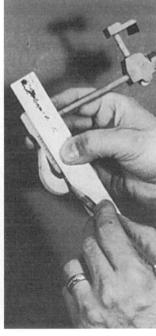

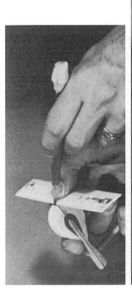

4-108 (above). Locating the striking point on a badly worn hammer by extending lines centered down the length of the hammer across the worn area.

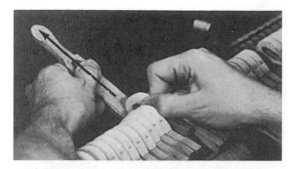

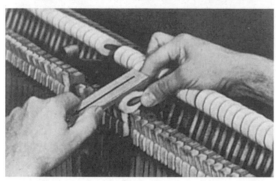

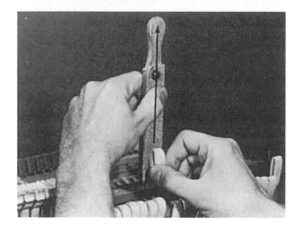

4-109 (three photos above). Sanding hammers toward the striking point, as shown by the arrows. Move the sanding stick in an arc as you pull it, to recreate the correct shape of the hammers.

4-110 (above). Careless reshaping is worse than none at all.

Broken Bridle Straps. If a few bridle straps are broken, the rest of them are also ready to break, so replace the whole set. The best replacement tapes are new ones glued to the catcher shanks, like the original ones. This allows the tape to be flexible where it passes through the hole in the catcher.

Cork-tipped bridle straps are very popular and easy to install, but in many pianos they interfere with the backchecks because the tapes are stiffer where they come out of the catchers than the original tapes were, making precise regulation of hammer checking difficult. Save this type of bridle strap for inexpensive old pianos; use the original glued-in type in fine quality pianos and any piano that you rebuild.

Cork tapes come with small, medium, and large corks to fit various size catcher holes. Push the cork into the hole with an inserter, as illustrated. Be careful when work-

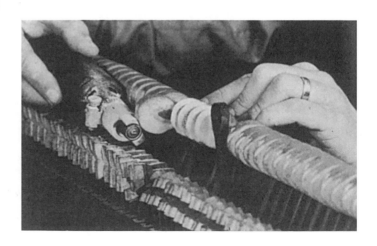

4-111 (right). Shaping hammers with a motorized tool.

140

ing with a brittle old action to avoid breaking the catchers.

In actions with catchers that don't have holes, spring-clip bridle straps may be used.

The Damper Assembly

Ringing Strings. In order for dampers to work properly, the levers must work freely, the springs in a vertical must be good, the wires in a grand must be free in their guide rail holes, and the felt must meet the strings squarely.

If a vertical damper spring breaks, replace it with an original style spring or with a damper repair spring. To use the original type of spring, obtain new springs of each available strength and a length of damper flange cord from a piano supply company, and select a spring that is closest to the original. Remove the flange center pin to disassemble the flange and damper lever, and remove the old cord and broken spring from the flange. Push the cloth back from the end of the new cord, cut off about an inch of the core, pull the cloth out to a point and size it with glue to stiffen it in the pointed shape. After the glue dries, insert the new spring in the damper flange, and pull the cord through the hole. If the original cord wasn't glued, trim the excess cord, repin the flange to the lever, and install it in the piano. (If the cord was glued originally, glue the end into the thinner side of the flange, as in gluing new flange bushings. See pp. 127-128.)

An easy alternative to installing an original style damper spring is to use a damper repair spring, as shown in illus. 4-113.

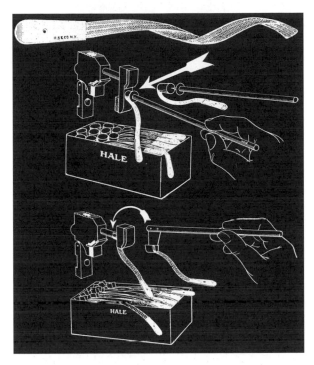

4-112. Top to bottom: glued-in, cork-tipped, and spring-clip bridle straps.

In one otherwise fine-quality upright piano restored by the author, the manufacturer had designed the damper flanges badly, with the flange screw heads rubbing on the coils of the damper springs, eventually causing most of the springs to break. The action rail tenon, damper flange mortises, and screw holes were spaced so that new flanges couldn't be used or adapted, and in this piano damper, repair springs were actually an improvement over the original style of springs. This isn't to say that it is common for the technician to be able to improve on the original design of a piano action by installing remedial repair parts, but it is cited as just one example of the odd, unanticipated problems that a technician encounters in old pianos.

141

4-113. A damper repair spring for a vertical piano.

If a grand damper stays up when you release the key, check the action to see that it isn't too far back in the piano, causing the keys to bind on the damper levers, or other parts to bind on the sostenuto mechanism. If that isn't the problem, remove the action and decide whether the damper wire is binding in its bushed guide rail hole or whether the lever is sluggish. To correct a binding damper wire, ease the bushing in the guide rail by inserting a grand damper wire easer to compact the cloth a little. If the damper wire is bent, causing binding in the bushing, straighten it as necessary and then reseat the damper head on the strings. If the lifter lever is sluggish, apply a center pin lubricant (available from a piano supply company) to the bushings; if that doesn't help, remove the lever from the piano and ream the flange bushings. In some pianos it is possible to remove the offending lever simply by removing its damper, but in others it is necessary to remove all the dampers and the entire damper lever rail to get at the flange screws. Number all parts as you remove them, and put them back in the right order.

If a properly regulated damper works freely but fails to damp, it isn't seating on the strings. Allow the damper to seat itself, and pluck each string separately. Double check the contact visually, and bend the damper on its wire until the felt lies in firm contact with the strings.

If a string twangs when the damper makes contact, the felt is probably hard or crusty from being wet or very damp. To soften the felt, needle it with a hammer voicing tool. If the damper still won't work, replace the felt.

If the sostenuto mechanism in a grand doesn't work right, regulate it, as described on pp. 191-192. If you can't regulate it to work right, check the bushings for the rod and associated linkages for excess play, and replace them if necessary, making sure the mounting screws are all tight.

Sluggish Action Parts

The most common cause of sluggish action parts is sluggish center pin bushings, as described above. Other causes include corroded capstans (clean with metal polish or by buffing), swollen key bushings (ease as necessary), rusty or broken vertical hammer springs (clean or repair), or lack of lubricating graphite on dowel capstans, jack tips, hammer butts and knuckles, etc. (apply a paste of powdered graphite and a little denatured ethyl alcohol).

Clicks, Buzzes, Rattles, and Other Foreign Noises

If a note has a click, try to isolate which part is causing it by a process of elimination, as when locating sluggish parts.

See that all cloth and felt is present on all the parts. Replace missing felt or cloth with material of the proper thickness and texture.

Tighten all action screws. Loose wippen, hammer, sticker, and damper underlever screws are common causes of clicking. Don't overlook the screws that hold the letoff rail in place. If this rail is loose, the clicks it produces are particularly hard to locate.

Check the bridle and backcheck wires, which sometimes click against each other. Bend the offending wire sideways to correct the problem. If the bridle strap tips are brittle and the holes are enlarged, they will click against the bridle wires. Replace the bridle straps, or apply a drop of PVC-E glue to each tip at the hole. This glue remains rubbery enough after it dries that it will silence the clicking.

Unglued hammer heads and catcher shanks are common offenders. If either part wobbles, it will click. Remove and reglue. Some clicking hammer heads have come unglued from the shank but are still tight enough that this problem isn't immediately obvious. Put one finger under the hammer tail and the others under the head, with your thumb clamping down on the opposite side, and try to rock the hammer. If it is loose, and if you rock it persistently and carefully, you will succeed in removing it for regluing. A small heat gun can be helpful here, but *be careful not to apply too much heat.*

In a grand, clicking or thumping noises may occur if the key frame doesn't make firm contact with the keybed. See p. 179.

The most obvious source of rattling and vibrating noises is loose cabinet parts—a cracked soundboard vibrating against a rib, etc. Less obvious sources include such things as a caster vibrating against the floor, a foreign object lying on a grand soundboard, a grand bass string buzzing against a damper wire, nuts loose on vertical action bolts, or sympathetic vibration of another object in the room. One fine technician once related the story of spending over an hour searching through a piano and the room trying to find the source of a particularly annoying vibrating sound, only to find a loose piece of glass in a stained glass window in a room divider located about five feet behind the piano.

Squeaks of all sorts

If a pedal squeaks, operate the action mechanism (damper lift rod, grand shifting lever, hammer rail, etc.) to find whether the squeak is in the action or the pedal. If two metal parts squeak against each other, such as a pedal squeaking on its metal pivot screw, lubricate with a drop of oil. If two wooden parts, as in wooden pedal trapwork, squeak against each other, lubricate with graphite mixed with alcohol and rubbed into the wood.

Corroded damper springs are a common source of squeaks in vertical pianos. If you hear the same squeak when you depress the sustaining pedal and when you play individual notes, the damper springs are probably the culprits. Remove the action and polish any offending springs with metal polish. Rub all squeaky damper spring felts with the end of a hammer shank sharpened in a pencil sharpener and dipped in the powdered graphite and alcohol mixture. Pure graphite applied this way is better than rubbing with a pencil or graphite stick, which leaves a residue of clay or other binding material, and might become sticky.

Jacks sometimes squeak when they slide out from under their hammer knuckles or hammer butts. If graphite applied to the buckskin doesn't cure the squeak, clean the buckskin. Fill a hypo-oiler (from a piano supply company) with a solution of eight parts naphtha and one part mineral oil, and insert it into the cloth under the buckskin. Apply enough to flush the old dirt and graphite out of the pores of the buckskin. Apply new graphite, and the squeaks should be gone.

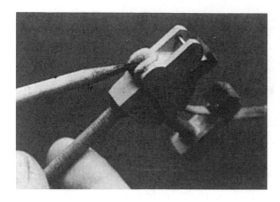

4-114. Burnishing a squeaky hammer spring slot with a sharpened hammer shank dipped in a mixture of powdered graphite and alcohol.

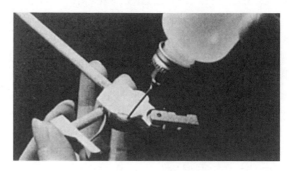

4-115. Flushing the dirt out of the buckskin with naptha-mineral oil solution. Following this treatment, burnish the buckskin with new graphite.

For a summary of action problems and their remedies, refer to the "Action Problem Checklist for Quick Reference" on pp. 195-196.

The Pedals

Any time you disassemble any of the parts associated with the pedals, mark their position and orientation so you can reassemble them correctly. A particularly perplexing situation can arise if you fail to mark and number the six blocks holding the three pedals to the bottom of a player piano. These blocks look alike, but they're not, and pedals won't work right if you put the blocks back in the wrong order.

If a pedal breaks, remove the parts and have them welded in perfect alignment by a welder capable of doing very precise work. Then have all three pedals replated. If done properly, the repair job will be invisible. If a pedal is missing and you can't find a matching one in the junk box of a piano shop or another technician, buy a new set that closely matches the original pedals, from a piano supply company.

To repair a rickety grand pedal lyre, remove it, plug and redrill the screw holes as necessary, and reglue all loose glue joints.

Install longer screws holding the lyre to the keybed, but make sure the new screws don't go all the way through the keybed into the key frame. When removing a grand lyre for repairs, keep the rods and braces in order. If the bottom of the lyre box has symmetrically located screws, mark its orientation for correct reassembly. If you remove dowels from pedal pins, keep them numbered and oriented correctly. Making note of these details will save you time during reassembly. If the buckskin or hard leather has deep indentations or if the material is rotten, replace it with material as close as possible to the original. Hard leather like that used on shoe soles is available from shoe repair shops and large leather shops. When gluing hard leather to wood, roughen the surface with coarse garnet sandpaper and clamp the leather while the glue dries, for better adhesion.

If the bottom board of a vertical piano is broken so it provides inadequate support for the pedals, remove the pedal dowels, tilt the piano on its back and remove the bottom with the pedals and trap levers still attached. Glue and clamp the bottom as illustrated; remove the pedals and trap levers as necessary to make room for the clamps and temporary braces. If the bottom looks warped

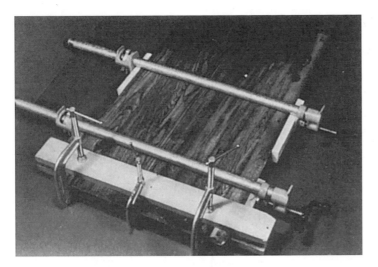

4-116. Gluing and clamping the cracked bottom board from a vertical piano.

when you remove the clamps, the screws should pull it flat when you reattach it to the bottom of the piano. Use longer screws, or move their positions as necessary.

If a bottom board has so much damage that regluing it is impractical, but the value of the piano doesn't warrant making a new one, and if the bottom is high enough over the surface of the floor to allow room for installation of mending plates from the hardware store, install several of these as illustrated.

If depressing a pedal causes a squeak, refer to the above section "Squeaks of All Sorts."

The Cabinet

Regluing structural glue joints and loose veneer requires common sense and ingenuity to figure out how to use the appropriate clamps and clamping blocks so the repairs won't pop apart again in the future. Refer to the section on plugging stripped screw holes on p. 83, and to the books and magazines on woodworking and refinishing recommended in the Bibliography.

Taking Care of A Piano

The best possible environment for a piano is a dry climate, if the piano lives there all its life. Manufacturers build pianos for an

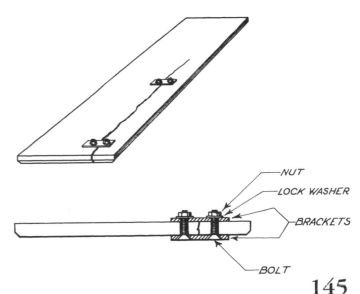

4-117. Reinforcing a cracked bottom board with mending plates from the hardware store. Use the correct size flathead bolts or machine screws so the heads are flush.

145

"average" climate with relative humidity of 40-45%; but technicians from other parts of the country have a hard time believing their eyes when they first encounter Victorian and early-twentieth-century pianos that have lived all their lives in dry parts of Colorado, New Mexico, Utah, Arizona, and other areas where rust doesn't occur under normal circumstances. Wood remains as white as in a new piano, metal remains shiny, soundboards don't come unglued from the ribs, bass strings still sound good, and tuning pins even stay tight.

The next best climate is one that stays somewhat humid all year. An average relative humidity of 60% all year long is better than a humidity level that swings up and down with the seasons.

The worst possible environment for a piano is one that alternates from high humidity in the summer to very low humidity in the winter — such as a humid location with inadequate air conditioning or dehumidification in the summer, and dry heat in the winter — causing the wood and felt in a piano to expand and contract. Expansion and contraction from seasonal humidity variations are a major cause of many piano problems, including loose glue joints, checked varnish or lacquer, loose tuning pins, a cracked soundboard, etc.

The very worst thing that can be done to a piano is to keep it in a very humid climate for years and then move it to an extremely dry climate, where it will fall apart.

Protecting A Piano From Environmental Changes. Never place a piano over a hot air register or next to a radiator. Never place a piano in front of a window. When possible, locate a piano against an inside wall. This will minimize the effect of temperature changes and condensation when the outside and inside temperatures are different. Avoid placing a piano on a damp concrete floor. Never place a piano in direct sunlight, which can bleach the finish, warp the keys and keybed, loosen the tuning pins, crack the soundboard, and cause many other problems.

To preserve a piano in the best condition for the longest possible time, control the climate — particularly the humidity — surrounding the piano. If an effective building or room humidification/dehumidification system is out of the question, the piano may be protected somewhat by installing a moisture control system such as "Dampp-Chaser™," available from piano supply companies.

The Dampp-Chaser™ system includes a dehumidifier, humidifier, and humidistat control, as illustrated. The dehumidifier is a slen-

4-118. This location has three counts against it: the radiator, the window, and the outside wall.

4-119. The complete Dampp-Chaser™ moisture control system installed in a vertical piano (top) and a grand (bottom).

der metal tube containing a low wattage heating element. The humidifier consists of another low wattage heating element submerged in a bucket with evaporator pads, with a plastic shield mounted overhead to help disperse the moisture more evenly throughout the inside of a vertical, or the bottom cavity of a grand. The "brain" of the system is a humidistat that switches the dehumidifier and humidifier on and off as necessary. The complete system also includes a filler tube and coupling for a convenient plastic funnel, making it easy to refill, and a low water warning light. In damp climates (over 42% relative humidity) having moderate seasonal humidity change (20%

change or less) the dehumidifier and control might provide adequate protection. In climates having more extreme changes, use the entire system. If you use a humidifier, refill it with water faithfully. It is better not to use a humidifier at all than to forget to fill it some of the time, as the resulting humidity fluctuations could cause more damage than would probably have occurred in the course of nature.

Unfortunately, most player pianos, reproducing pianos, and orchestrions which might benefit by the installation of a humidity control system have no space available inside the cabinet. So it is especially important to have an effective humidity control system in the room or building where these instruments are housed.

Many people place a small jar or pan of water in the bottom of a vertical piano, or a plant on the floor under a grand, in the mistaken belief that this will significantly help to stabilize the humidity in the piano. Neither of these adds enough water to the surrounding air to be of much help. In addition, jars of water placed in vertical pianos often get spilled, causing far more damage than bene-

fit. A steam or cold water mist vaporizer placed close to a piano is even worse; the moisture from one of these is so concentrated that it will ruin the finish, swell and buckle veneer and other wooden parts, and cause glue joints to come loose, among other problems.

Controlling Insect Damage. Moths like to lay their eggs in piano action felts. When the eggs hatch, the larvae eat the felt, leaving it riddled with holes and sometimes completely ruining every piece of felt in a piano. Powder post beetles and termites destroy wooden parts of pianos left in damp or unheated buildings in some regions. Some pest control chemicals that were considered safe for consumer use in the past have been removed from the market and are no longer available. Follow whatever practices are considered safe for keeping pests out of the house, and don't store a piano in a damp, unheated building. If you have a specific problem, consult a pest control specialist. If fumigation is recommended, find out whether the fumigant will harm the leather parts of the piano, and be prepared to replace them if necessary.

Chapter Five

Regulating:
Adjusting the Action, Keyboard, and Pedals to Work Correctly

Basic Regulating Concepts

The correct operation of any piano action depends on a specific ratio of key travel to hammer travel, or the distance the key moves from its rest position to its stopping point relative to the distance the hammer moves from its rest position to the point at which it hits the strings. For the action to work right, the travel of each key must be a certain specified amount — usually 3/8" (9.5 mm.), while the travel of each hammer must be another specified amount — usually 1 3/4" (44.5 mm.). (Some literature specifies that the hammer travel in old uprights should be 1 7/8", but in most pianos the action will work better if regulated to 1 3/4", so this dimension is used throughout this book.)

Each time you depress a key, a whole chain of events must take place as described in Chapter 2, with the damper lifting when the hammer has moved to a certain specified distance from the strings, the jack tripping out from under the hammer butt or knuckle at another specified distance, and the hammer rebounding and being caught by the backcheck at yet another specified distance. If the key travel is inadequate, relative to the hammer travel, the action won't go through its complete cycle. The backcheck (and repetition lever, in a grand) won't work right, permitting the hammer to "double-strike," or bounce against the string several times, and

the action will feel weak and uncontrollable. Conversely, if the key travel is too great relative to the hammer travel, the action parts will be forced to move farther than they should, causing other problems. During each key/hammer cycle, each intermediate action part — the damper, jack, repetition lever, and backcheck — must come into play at precisely the right time and move just the right distance. Additionally, each pedal must do its job correctly.

All of the various dimensions and movements in the piano are adjustable, by turning regulating screws, bending wires, changing spring tension and changing the thickness of felt and cloth cushions and paper shims, so that the piano action can be made to work correctly. **Regulating** a piano involves the careful adjustment of these parts so each does exactly what it should at exactly the right time.

Because there are so many adjustable parts that interact with each other, thorough regulating requires very careful attention to many precise details. Once a piano is regulated correctly, why is further regulation necessary later? Because felt, cloth, and buckskin cushions become packed down, and hammers become worn. Wooden parts warp a little, altering the relationship of one part to another. These factors all diminish the piano's ability to play softly, loudly, and with good repetition. This book uses the terms

regulating and **action regulating** interchangeably; both refer to the adjustment of all moving parts, including the action, keys, and pedals.

The term **tone regulating** refers to the altering of tone quality, achieved primarily through the adjustment of hammer shape and hardness, of the positions where the hammers hit the strings, and of certain details of stringing. Loosely, tone regulating encompasses any procedure that improves the sound of a piano, and in that sense it includes tuning, action regulating, adjustment of touch weight, attending to soundboard problems, etc. This book treats these other topics separately. Tone regulating — discussed on pp. 196-201 — refers here to hammer voicing and associated procedures that should be performed only after you put a piano into the finest possible mechanical condition, regulate it thoroughly, and tune it carefully.

Deciding What to Do with Worn Hammers

As hammer felts become packed down as a result of heavy use, the striking points become grooved. As the grooves get deeper and deeper, the hammers are effectively shorter and shorter, so they have to move farther before striking the strings. The hammer travel increases, relative to the key travel, and the action must be regulated.

Normal maintenance of a concert piano by a fine technician includes frequent light filing of the hammers to maintain the correct shape of their striking points, and correspondingly frequent *minor* regulating to compensate for the filing and other effects of wear. When the hammers have been reshaped so much that they no longer produce a good tone and are so light that the touch weight of the action is incorrect, the concert technician replaces them and regulates the action back to its original specifications.

Normal maintenance of an average home piano (which receives only moderate use) by an average technician includes no filing of the hammers for many years, so that most five- to ten-year-old pianos have grooves at least $1/16$" (approx. 1.5 mm.) deep, and most thirty-year-old pianos have grooves $1/8$" (approx. 3 mm.) deep. In this condition, a piano can have its hammers reshaped, and the action usually can be brought into regulation within the limits of the built-in adjustments.

Many fifty- to eighty-year-old pianos have grooves nearly $1/4$" (over 5 mm.) deep, or the hammers have been sanded back more than $1/8$" (c. 3 mm.) and there are new grooves over $1/16$" (1 or 2 mm.) deep, resulting in much greater hammer travel than the standard $13/4$" (44.5 mm.). If you raise the hammer rail or repetition lever rest position to bring the hammers back to their correct distance from the strings, everything else in the action and keyboard will require major reregulation to compensate for the change. In extreme cases, changes must be so drastic that the whole geometry of the action is thrown off. Parts of the action will be out of their normal range of adjustment, making it necessary to add thick shims, change the back rail cloth, turn regulating screws until they run out of threads, and other problems that will result in the action not working properly. Also, when you sand grand hammers down too far, they become so light that the repetition spring tension has to be altered beyond its intended adjustable range. In this condition, it is always better to replace the hammers before regulating the action. To summarize, if the hammers have only light to moderate grooves — up to $1/8"$ deep (or 3 mm.) — they may be reshaped, and the action may be regulated to work properly. If the hammers have grooves $1/4"$ (or over 5 mm.) deep, or if the total of previous filing and new grooves makes them $1/4"$ shorter than they were when new, replace them. If the wear is in the "gray area" between $3/16"$ and $1/4"$, you should replace the hammers in a fine quality piano, but an inexpensive old upright might get by with major regulation. Chapter 4 covers hammer filing and reshaping; Chapter 8 covers installation of new hammers.

Regulating Tools

This chapter illustrates several specialized tools. Some of these may be made by modifying regular tools, and others should be purchased. Many of these tools fit into a standard combination handle, to eliminate the bulk and expense of having a separate handle for each tool. Each has a special purpose. Whether you purchase action regulating tools or make them yourself, always use the right tool for each job, to keep from damaging delicate parts with a tool that is too big, too small, or the wrong shape.

Preparation for Regulating

Before you regulate an action, remove it from the piano for a thorough cleaning and inspection. Tighten all screws in the piano except for the pressure bar screws, and the hex head plate perimeter bolts and nose bolts in a Baldwin or other grand having the threaded perimeter bolt plate suspension system. Repair all broken and malfunctioning parts, and replace deteriorated or missing felt, cloth, and leather. Decide whether to

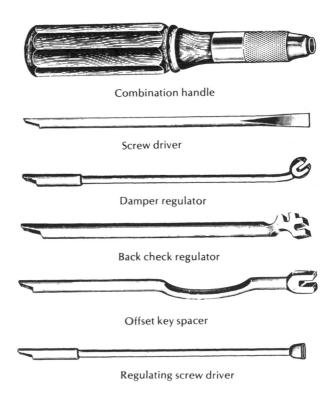

Combination handle

Screw driver

Damper regulator

Back check regulator

Offset key spacer

Regulating screw driver

5-1. A combination handle and some tools that may be inserted in it, making it easier to fit everything into a compact tool roll or case.

5-2. The shape of the flange screwdriver enables you to insert it between action parts and turn it without damaging them.

reshape the hammers, replace them, or leave them alone. Everything must work freely, with moving parts neither too tight so they bind, nor too loose so they wobble or knock. If you encounter missing, broken, binding, or knocking parts, now or during regulating, refer to the chapters on repairing and restoring to learn how to remedy these problems. *Before you disassemble an action, number all sets of parts — wippens, dampers, hammer butts, stickers, etc. — from #1 to #88, starting in the bass. Identical-looking parts aren't necessarily interchangeable.*

Complete regulating also includes leveling the keys, and this can be done only if the cloth balance rail punchings and front rail punchings are in good condition. If they are packed with dirt, moth damaged, or otherwise deteriorated, replace them with new punchings of the same diameter and thickness, as discussed on p. 290. When removing the keys from a piano, be sure to number them or mark their order with a diagonal line, as discussed on p. 88. In a vertical, leave the key frame in the piano. In a grand, remove the action/key frame assembly from the piano, and then remove the action from the key frame to remove the keys.

Many otherwise healthy-looking actions have parts that are slow to return to their rest position due to tight center pin bushings. Never increase the tension of a spring before checking to see if its associated part is sluggish. Sluggishness is caused by binding and excessive friction far more often than by a spring becoming too weak; tightening a spring excessively won't solve the problem.

Although certain regulating procedures are applicable to both vertical and grand pianos, this chapter treats the two separately to make it easier to follow the entire procedure from beginning to end for each type of piano, with a minimum of cross referencing in the text.

Vertical Action Regulating

With all the parts clean and in good repair, with all action centers working freely with no binding or wobbling parts, with the cloth balance rail and front rail punchings in good condition, and with all accessible screws in the piano tightened (except the pressure bar screws, which you ordinarily don't adjust unless you restring a piano), the action is ready to be regulated. The author has developed the following sequence as the most efficient after having regulated thousands of pianos. By following it, you'll get the most accomplished with the least amount of backtracking if you're careful to pay close attention to detail during every step.

Before performing each step, read all information associated with that step, to avoid getting ahead of yourself. If an action is so far out of regulation that major changes are necessary, it might be necessary to go back and reregulate certain parts that you already regulated, due to the interaction of one adjustment with another.

1. Check the position of the letoff rail before reinstalling the action in the piano. Adjust it in or out if necessary so the jack toes are centered on the regulating button cushions when the jacks bump into them and swing out from under the hammers. Tighten the screws.

2. Turn the action around and check the damper lift rod to see that both ends swing out simultaneously when the dowel lifts it. If not, look for bent hangers, and straighten them if necessary. At this point, with the action on the bench, don't worry about whether all the dampers appear to lift simultaneously.

3. Check the travel of the hammer butts to see if the hammers move in a line perpendicular to the hammer rail, as shown in illus. 5-3. Check each hammer by swinging it and its neighbors slowly toward the dampers and back several times, by lifting the catchers with the ends of your fingers. This is always necessary when you have installed new hammer butts, or when you have removed the original butts and some traveling papers have fallen out. Observe the hammer first from above and then from the front of the action. If you have a hard time spotting problems, swing five hammers at once. This way, even if several hammers in a row travel off to the same side, you'll be able

to spot them by comparing them to their neighbors.

For the thinnest shim, cut a strip of newspaper and wet it lightly with your tongue before pressing the strip to the flange. The right combination of moisture and pressure will cause the paper to stick to the flange long enough to screw it into place. For a thicker shim, use gummed paper tape — the type that has to be wetted to make it stick. The adhesive on this tape is fish glue, which makes it possible to scrape the paper and glue off the flange with a razor blade if this becomes necessary in the future. Don't use masking tape, cellophane tape, electrical tape, or other products that turn gummy after a short time.

If the old butts have never been removed, chances are that the hammers will travel as straight as they did when the piano was new. If you find a hammer that is parallel to its neighbors when at rest, but travels off to one side a little, the factory didn't travel the butt properly when the piano was new. If the hammer strikes all its strings, leave it alone. If not, remove the hammer from its shank as described on p. 136, travel the butt,

5-3. The paper-shim method of correcting hammer travel. If papering the flange corrects the travel but makes the hammer crooked, remove the hammer from its shank and reglue it.

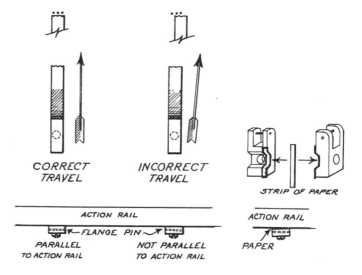

CORRECT TRAVEL   INCORRECT TRAVEL   STRIP OF PAPER

ACTION RAIL   ACTION RAIL

FLANGE PIN

PARALLEL TO ACTION RAIL   NOT PARALLEL TO ACTION RAIL   PAPER

and then reinstall the hammer. If you travel the butt without removing the hammer, you'll have a crooked hammer that travels in a straight line and still doesn't hit all the strings evenly.

To travel a hammer in a Steinway upright with **double flanges** (flanges that hold the hammer butt on the front end and the damper lever on the back end), insert a paper shim under one corner or diagonally opposite corners of the flange; this will rotate the flange a little, correcting travel. Readjust the damper as necessary.

INSTALL THE KEYS AND ACTION IN THE PIANO.

4. Align the hammers to the strings. Move each hammer all the way to the strings by pushing on the catcher, and check the alignment of the hammer to the strings. If a hammer is off to one side, and if the action has wood flanges, loosen the flange screw. Insert a small thin screwdriver between that flange and the adjacent one, and twist *gently* in the desired direction. Hold the hammer butt so the head is in the correct alignment while tightening the flange screw. Apply a lit-

tle sideward pressure to the hammer butt to counteract the tendency of the screw to rotate the flange clockwise just as it becomes tight. If there is no room to insert a screwdriver between the flanges, push the hammer butt to the side by hand. The advantage of using a screwdriver is that in some pianos, the hole in the flange is a little larger than the shank of the screw, permitting you to move the flange a little to the left or right by prying against one side. Sometimes this sideways movement is enough, without rotating the flange as well. If the action has an aluminum action rail, be careful not to strip the screw holes. If you find any hammers that are loose on their shanks while completing this step, reglue them now.

Aligning the bass hammers to the strings can be tricky when the hammers lean sideways at a different angle from that of the bass strings. If a hammer seems centered on its strings when viewed only from the top, the bottom will be off to the left; if the hammer seems centered when viewed only from the bottom, the top will be off to the right. For greater accuracy, see that the *top left* and *bottom right* edges of the hammer felt appear to be equidistant from the corre-

5-4. Aligning a hammer to the strings. Position the hammer or butt with one hand and tighten the screw with the other. It is usually necessary to hold the butt instead of the hammer head to keep from moving the hammer to the right when you tighten the screw.

sponding edges of the strings, and the hammer will be centered.

If the hammers have any trace of old grooves, be careful to align the grooves to the strings, even if the old grooves are off center on the striking point of the hammer. If you misalign the old grooves with the strings, they will try to mate with the strings anyway, springing the hammer sideways at the moment of contact, putting a strain on the shank and butt, and eventually loosening the flanges or bushings.

If a hammer is still out of line after you rotate the flange as far as possible, or in a piano with a brass flange rail, apply gentle heat to the shank with a small alcohol lamp or electric shank bender, and gently bend

the shank in the required direction. This is a tricky process, as it's easy to scorch the shank by overheating it, and it's even easier to break the shank by pressing too hard. If necessary, apply a few drops of water to the shank with your index finger to help the shank bender do its job. Take your time and be gentle, and you'll align the hammer correctly.

In an action with Billings flanges, it is usually possible to slide a flange sideways a little to align a hammer. If more adjustment is necessary, a flange may be rotated a little by bending the little prongs that fit into the slot in the wooden rail. Work slowly, bending one prong up and the other down equally. If you bend them too quickly, you'll increase

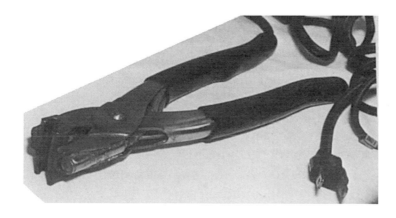

5-5. An electric hammer-shank bender is easier to use than an alcohol lamp, but it too must be used gently to avoid scorching or breaking the shanks.

5-6. Using the shank bender. The hammer rail was removed for this illustration.

the chance of breaking the brass. If you bend only one prong, you'll change the height of the hammer, throwing it out of line with its neighbors.

In the treble of a vertical piano that has a pressure bar instead of agraffes, it's sometimes possible to correct hammer/string misalignment somewhat by moving the strings sideways, as shown in illus. 8-55. This is acceptable if the strings appear to be spaced unevenly among their neighbors and if you don't push them out of the imaginary straight line running from the left side of the tuning pin to the upper bridge pin. If you do this in an older piano, be prepared to spend a lot of time fussing with the damper to realign the grooves in the old damper felt with the strings so the damper still works.

In a Steinway upright with double flanges, adjust hammer-to-string alignment by papering under the entire left or right side of the flange. This also will move the damper off to the side, so you'll have to readjust it. (Spacing the hammers involves *tipping* the entire flange to one side or the other. Traveling the hammers involves *rotating* the flange one way or the other, as described previously.)

Align the height of individual hammers if necessary. If possible, remove a misaligned hammer from its shank, and reglue it in the correct position. If the shank looks warped, heat the shank and apply gentle pressure to the hammer head until the shank cools.

REMOVE THE ACTION FROM THE PIANO.

5. Align the jacks to the hammer butts. After aligning the hammers with the strings in step 4, check the position of each jack under its hammer butt. If the top end of a jack is off to one side, loosen the wippen

flange screw and tilt the wippen sideways to center the jack under the butt; then retighten the screw.

In extreme cases, it may be necessary to paper one side of a wippen flange to bring the jack into alignment, but this also moves the front end of the wippen off to one side, which may be undesirable.

REINSTALL THE ACTION IN THE PIANO.

6. Space and square the backchecks from side to side, so they meet the catchers squarely. At this point in the regulating procedure, you will align the backchecks with the catchers laterally by bending the stiff backcheck wires sideways if necessary, but you won't regulate hammer checking, which involves bending the backcheck wires forward or back.

First, space the backcheck by bending the lower end of the wire just above where it enters the wippen. Then, square the backcheck if necessary by bending the wire just below where it enters the backcheck. Never bend the wire in the middle. It is easiest to bend the wire using the type of wire bending pliers shown in illus. 5-7. Because the backcheck wire is so much larger in diameter than the bridle wire, it is usually possible to put the pliers around both wires just above where they enter the wippen, and bend only the backcheck wire, without bending the bridle wire. If the pliers cause a bridle wire to bend a little, it's easy to bend it back to where it was by hand after the backcheck wire is where you want it. The advantage of this tool is that you can apply bending force to the wire without applying undue force to the delicate wippen flange.

Supply companies sell another type of wire-bending pliers that have parallel sliding

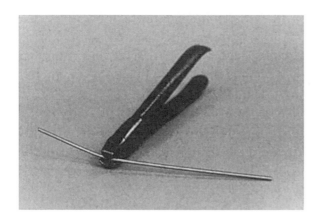

5-7. The handiest wire-bending pliers, also known as "smiling pliers," or "frowning pliers", depending on your disposition.

jaws with a curved slot. In those owned by the author, the curved slot isn't broad enough to fit a backcheck wire, and even if the slot were big enough, the bridle wire would be in the way of the jaws.

If you don't have "smiling pliers," use a backcheck regulating tool in a combination handle. Hold the wippen firmly with your other hand, or hold the stationary part of the wire with needle nose pliers, as shown in illus. 5-8, to keep from damaging the wippen or flange.

When you're done with this step, all backchecks should be aligned with their catchers and in alignment with each other straight up and down, as viewed from the front of the action. They won't necessarily be in a straight line with each other as viewed from the top; you'll regulate this in step 15.

7. *Square and space the keys.* If the front end of a key leans to one side, bend the balance rail pin by holding a broad screwdriver against the top of the pin and tapping it with your palm, as shown in illus. 5-9. Use a large screwdriver with a blade that is broad and blunt enough that it won't scratch the top of the balance rail pin. If the crookedness was due to the balance rail pin being bent a little, bending it back will solve the problem. The front of the key will be square when the key button is centered between the two adjacent keys, with the capstan directly under the center of the sticker. If the key button or capstan is off to one side when the front of the key is straight, then the key is warped or twisted; repair it as described on p. 118.

The front end of each white key or sharp should be centered between its neighbors. If a key is off center, lift the front end of the key up off the front rail pin, lift the punchings, and grasp the pin just where it comes out of the rail with an offset key spacing tool in a combination handle. The offset makes it possible to get the tool around the white key pins to bend the sharp front rail pins. Bend

5-8. Spacing and squaring a backcheck without a "smiling pliers," by using the backcheck regulating tool and needle nose pliers.

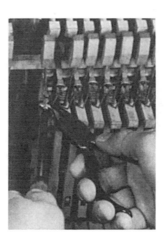

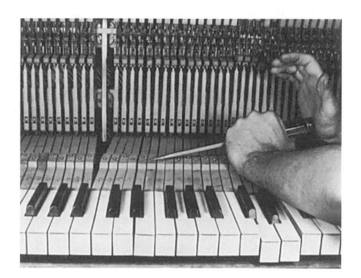

5-9. Squaring a crooked key by bending the balance rail pin. Tap gently with your palm; too much force or too sudden an impact will damage the hole where the pin enters the balance rail.

the pin sideways a little to center the key. It usually takes only the smallest amount of bend to center a key between its neighbors. Insert the tool just above the front rail under the punchings to avoid nicking the pin, which will cause the key bushings to fail prematurely. Never turn a front rail pin in its hole; the flat sides should be parallel to the cloth bushings to maximize the life of the bushings.

Ease any binding keys and replace any missing bushings, if necessary, as described on pp. 118-119 and 290-291.

8. *Set the hammer stroke*, or the distance between the hammers at rest and the

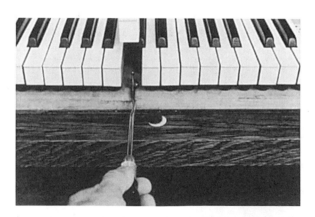

5-10. Spacing a key by bending the front rail pin gently with an **offset key spacer** inserted in the combination handle.

strings. Hammer stroke should be 1³/4" (44.5 mm.) in most old uprights, and it varies from 1¹/2" to 1³/4" (38 – 44.5 mm.) in spinets and consoles. (As mentioned at the beginning of this chapter, some literature specifies that the hammer stroke in old uprights should be 1⁷/8", but in most old uprights the action will work better if regulated to 1³/4", so this dimension is used throughout this book). For measurements recommended by specific manufacturers, consult the *Piano Action Handbook*, listed in the Bibliography. If the hammers are worn, and the action has not been regulated to compensate for the wear, the stroke will be too much. Measure this by inserting a thin steel ruler between hammers to get an accurate reading from the striking point to the front surface of the strings, as shown in illus. 5-11. Look down at the ruler either from straight above or directly from one side, so an angular view doesn't cause an incorrect reading. Correct the stroke by building up the thickness of the hard felt cushions glued to the bottom of the hammer rail over each action bracket, using action cloth or hard felt attached with hot glue or liquid hide glue. Add material to all the cushions, not just one or two of them, so they all touch the action brackets when the rail is at

5-11. Measuring the hammer stroke.

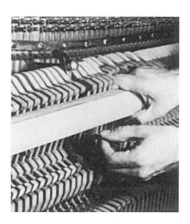

5-12. Gluing action cloth under the existing hammer rail cushion to correct excessive hammer stroke.

rest; if only one or two cushions touch their brackets, the hammer rail will have more tendency to bounce if you release the soft pedal quickly.

In many pianos, the hammer stroke in the bass section is different from that in the treble/tenor section. Sometimes this is due to the length of the bass hammers not precisely compensating for the overlap of the bass strings over the treble strings, and sometimes it's due to the treble hammers being worn or sanded more than the bass hammers. To bring all sections of hammers to the same striking distance from the strings, glue a thin strip of cardboard, name board felt, or thin action cloth along the back of the hammer rail near the top, to shim the hammer rail cloth back a little in the section where the hammer stroke is too great. This is one reason why the hammer rail cloth is never glued along its top edge; the other reason is to provide the softest possible cushion for the hammer shanks, in order to minimize any noise as the hammers return to the rail. Don't glue the hammer rail cloth to your insert.

If the hammer rail is crooked due to previous careless handling of the piano action,

this will cause a gradual tapering of the hammer stroke, from one end of the action to the other. To correct this, grasp the hammer rail firmly in both hands, with one hand near each inner action bracket, and carefully but firmly twist the entire rail in the desired direction. Apply pressure slowly to avoid breaking any of the hammer rail support hooks.

9. Regulate lost motion, or the gap between the top end of each jack and the buckskin glued to the underside of the hammer butt, by turning the capstan at the back end of each key. (By turning the capstan counterclockwise, you'll raise the sticker, wippen, and jack. By turning it clockwise, you'll lower them). The top end of the jack should almost touch the buckskin when the key and hammer shank are at rest. If the jack is too high, with no lost motion at all, the hammer butt will rest on the jack, instead of the shank resting on the hammer rail as it should. This will prevent the jack from slipping back under the butt when you release the key, causing the note to strike softly or not at all the next time you play it. If the jack is too low, with more lost motion than necessary, the key must move too far before the jack begins pushing on the hammer butt, resulting in poor dynamic control and rapid wear of the buckskin on the butt.

Alternately press and release each key just enough to feel for lost motion — usually this is 1/32" or less (or .5 mm.) as measured at the front end of the key. Eliminate any play between the top of the jack and the buckskin on the butt by turning the capstan counter-clockwise with a capstan wrench, until you can just barely move or "wink" the key before the butt begins to move. In most large uprights, the capstan wrench fits the capstan screws without removing the keys from the piano, except for several keys on either side of each action bracket. In many spinets and some consoles, you have to remove the keys to fit the wrench onto the screws. To regulate rocker capstans, loosen one screw and tighten the other to raise or lower the working end. In pianos having regulating screws mounted on the stickers, carefully turn each screw down with a regulating screwdriver to reduce lost motion, holding the surrounding wood with the other hand if necessary to keep from cracking any wooden parts.

Important note: Most American player pianos and some ordinary verticals have the keys weighted toward the front, so they go down under their own weight when the player mechanism plays, or when you lift the wippens by hand. In a piano with front-heavy keys, you must gently add enough weight to the back end of the key with one finger to make the key back-heavy, while you test for lost motion by winking the front end with your other hand. If you fail to do this, the weight of the key will take up the lost motion, making it impossible to regulate the capstans correctly.

The technique for precise adjustment of lost motion is very difficult for some beginners to master. To make it easier to see what you're doing, keep your eye on the top of the backcheck and the butt or catcher; these parts are close enough to each other that you

5-13. Universal capstan wrench, which fits common types of capstan screws.

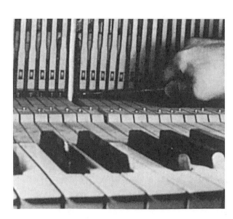

5-14. Regulating a capstan to eliminate excess lost motion between the top end of the jack and the buckskin on the hammer butt.

5-15. Testing for excess lost motion; there should be minimal movement of the key and backcheck before the hammer begins to move.

160

5-16. Two methods of testing for correct regulation of the capstan screws. Left: Pulling the hammer rail gently toward the front of the piano; all hammers should follow. Right: Tripping each jack by pushing the toe down with a small screwdriver; the jack should return under its butt when released.

can watch them both simultaneously. As you gently wink the front end of the key, you should see the top of the backcheck move approximately 1/64" (or about .5 mm.) before the catcher begins to move. Another test is to pull gently on the hammer rail, forcing it about 1/16" (or 2 mm.) toward the front of the piano, while scanning all the hammer heads. If any hammers don't follow the movement of the rail, those notes have inadequate lost motion. As a final check, trip each jack out from under the butt with a small screwdriver and make sure it slips back in by itself. This lengthy test won't be necessary after you get proficient at regulating lost motion, but it might save you from having to go back and reregulate the capstans in the first few pianos that you service.

When you shim the hammer rail up far enough to provide the correct hammer stroke in a piano with badly worn hammers, you introduce a lot of lost motion between the jacks and hammer butts. In this situation, if you unscrew the capstans far enough to eliminate lost motion, they sometimes get so loose in the keys that they ruin the threaded holes in the wood. The best solution to this problem is to replace the hammers, which will permit the hammer rail to be adjusted back down to where it belongs. If you don't want to replace the hammers, use the following procedure instead: insert card stock or veneer shims under the back rail, or nameboard felt under the back rail cloth, to eliminate most of the lost motion, and then regulate the capstans. This will have the side-effect of reducing the key dip so much that you'll have to shim the balance rail up to bring the front ends of the keys back to where they were. If this is necessary, perform step 10 at this time, and then recheck it again after you finish step 9.

10. Regulate the average key height.
The bottom of the front end of each white key should be about 1/8" (or about 3 mm.) below the top edge of the key slip. At this height, the top surface of low A and high C (or the first and last white keys, in a piano with fewer than 88 keys) should be a little below the top surface of the key blocks. If the keys are too high, you'll be able to see under their front ends, and they might bump on the bottom of the fallboard or name board strip. If they're too low, the white key-tops will come too close to touching the top of the key slip when you depress the keys. In many pianos, each key front has a shadow showing how much of the front has been behind the top of the key slip during the life of the piano, and this shadow is often a valid guide to setting the key height.

Since you won't adjust the precise height of each individual key until step 11 below, for now adjust the average height of all white keys relative to the key slip, key blocks, and fallboard. This adjustment is usually necessary only under the following circumstances: when the balance rail punchings are so com-

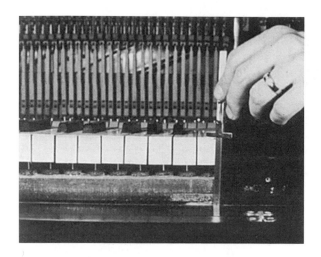

5-17. Checking to see if the average height of the white keys is uniform, as measured down to the keybed after comparing the height to the key blocks, key slip, and name board strip or fallboard.

5-18. Adjusting the average height of the keys by inserting shims cut from an index card or business card. If you must use something as thick as veneer, cut the shims narrow enough to fit between the balance rail pins.

pressed that all keys are too low, when you install new felts in the action, or when you increase the thickness of the back rail cloth or the height of the back rail to compensate for filing the hammers extremely short, without unscrewing the capstans so far that they would be loose in the keys.

To adjust all keys at once, add or subtract paper, card stock, or veneer shims under the balance rail. Remove several keys at each end of the key frame and over each cross slat, to expose the flat head screws holding the rail to the keybed. Loosen each screw several turns, lift the rail, and add or subtract shims between the balance rail and slats. The old shims often have indentations where balance rail pins have pressed into them, so you'll have to loosen the screws to lift the rail far enough to insert the new shims under the protruding ends of the pins. When you tighten the screws again, the pins should push their way down through new paper or card stock shims, but if you use something as thick and stiff as veneer ($1/32$" or 1 mm., or thicker), you'll have to make the shims nar-

row enough to fit between the pins, or the new shims will push the pins up when you tighten the screws.

To change the average height of the entire rail, insert identical shims under it on both sides of each screw. If you sight down the line of the front ends of the keys from one end of the keyboard to the other, and see a general curve in the key height, you can flatten this curve by shimming only on one side of certain screws. Adding shims under the rail from the front all the way to the back will change the height of all keys; shimming the front more will have a greater effect on the white keys than the sharps; and shimming the back more will have a greater effect on the sharps.

11. Level the white keys. After adjusting the average key height in step 10 above, adjust the precise height of each individual key by adding or subtracting paper or cardboard punchings *under* each cloth balance rail punching. These punchings are available in thicknesses ranging from .001" to .045" and from .05 mm. to 1 mm., from American and German piano supply companies, respectively. During this procedure, you'll have to remove and reinstall many cloth punchings several times. If you belatedly discover that the original punchings are in worse condition than you had thought, and are too fragile to be removed and reinstalled, replace the entire set now with new punchings of the same thickness and diameter, as recommended on p. 152 earlier in this chapter. Make sure the tops of the key buttons are at least 1/16" (approx. 2 mm.) below the tips of the balance rail pins. If the pins are below the buttons, reduce the thickness of all balance rail punchings. Either remove paper or cardboard punchings, or replace the cloth punchings with thinner ones, as necessary. Go back and recheck step 10, and then proceed.

The easiest way to level the keys is to use a **Davis key leveling tool** or equivalent, which has a floating brass button that rides on the keytops as you slide the tool across the keybed with the key slip removed. This tool is very accurate if the keybed is flat. First, slide the tool from one end of the keybed to the other, to see if any keys are a lot higher than the average. If so, lower these keys to the average level by removing paper or cardboard punchings, or replacing cloth punchings with thinner ones — even if this means removing all cardboard and paper punchings, and using the thinnest possible cloth punching.

Next, check the whole keyboard again, and adjust the height of the leveler so when you position the button over the center of *each remaining highest key*, the top of the brass button is perfectly flush with the top of the tool. Temporarily place the key slip and fallboard in position again, to verify that these highest keys represent the desired height, as all the rest of the keys will be lev-

eled to these. Change the shims under the balance rail if necessary. Remove the key slip.

Finally, position the tool over the center of each white key, with the back of the tool touching the front of the key frame, and see how far below the top surface of the tool the brass button is. Add cardboard and paper punchings under the cloth punching until the tool shows that the key height is exactly right. To verify this after inserting or removing punchings and replacing the cloth punching and key on the pin, hold the back end of the key down with one hand and give the key button several heavy taps with the other index finger, to seat the punchings. Then play several staccato notes on the key, and again put the tool in place to see that the height is still correct after the punchings have assumed their natural state of compression. If you bend a punching while handling it, throw it away; a bent punching will ultimately settle or warp, throwing the key out of level again.

When you shim a key up with a thicker balance rail punching, the front end of the key naturally moves up farther than the thickness of the additional punching — roughly twice as far if the balance rail is centered under the length of the key, for example. You'll learn by experience to judge approximately how many punchings each key will need, by observing how far below the top of the leveling tool the brass button is. While many beginners regulate each key individually, removing and installing it until the height is just right, most experienced technicians graduate to one of the following methods:

• Go from one end of the keyboard to the other, finding all keys that need the thickest punching and inserting the punchings as you proceed. Go over the entire key-

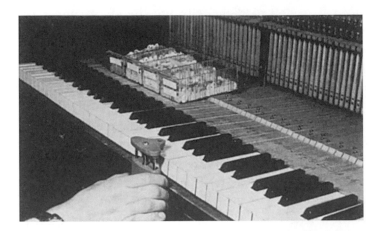

5-19. Using the Davis white key leveling tool.

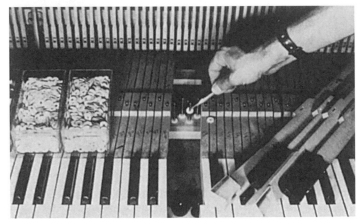

5-20. Adjusting individual key height by changing paper punchings under the cloth balance rail punchings.

board again, inserting the next thinner punching where needed. Keep doing this until you're down to the thinnest tissue paper punchings. This method provides instant feedback, and you'll learn quickly to recognize exactly what effect each thickness of punching has on key height. By the time you're half done leveling your first keyboard, you'll probably have memorized the thickness of your various punchings, and you'll recognize what combinations you need, you can insert several punchings at a time instead of going all the way back and forth for every individual thickness. — OR —

• Center the tool over each key, guess how many punchings you need, and lay them in a little pile in order of thickness — with the thinnest ones on top — on top of that key. Proceed like this all the way up the keyboard, and then go back and insert all punchings in one operation. Go over the entire keyboard again for fine regulation. An experienced technician can usually do all but the very finest regulation in one pass, and then make the final adjustments with tissue paper punchings the second time.

Whichever method you use, always arrange the punchings in order of thickness, with the thickest ones on the bottom. As you proceed through the leveling job, you'll be making smaller and smaller changes, and when you need to remove a punching because it's just a little too thick, the thinnest one will be available for removal at the top of the stack. Some technicians make all adjustments with the paper and cardboard punchings on top of the cloth ones, and then turn the stack over after everything is right. If you use this method, the keys might not be perfectly level after you invert the punchings, and you might have to remove a tissue paper punching from the bottom of a stack here and there. In any event, always finish with the cloth punchings on top of the paper ones, because the cloth ones will withstand repeated movement of the key. If you leave paper punchings on top, they'll wear through and fall apart.

If the keybed is warped so badly that the Davis leveler can't be used — or if the piano is a player piano with control levers, buttons, and escutcheon plates protruding from the keybed — level the lowest and highest keys, and one in the middle of the keyboard, and insert a stack of glued-together cardboard punchings on the front rail pins to hold them up in their level position. (If they're not glued together, they will be too spongy to hold the keys consistently at the correct height). Obtain an aluminum yardstick or a long straightedge sold by piano supply companies for leveling keys, and rest it on edge on the two or three sample keys. A three-or four-foot-long 3/4" x 3/4" x 1/8" angle also makes a good straightedge for this purpose. Visually check the space between the straightedge and keytop, and use one of the above methods to choose and install the paper and cardboard punchings. Experienced technicians can level a keyboard just as fast with a straightedge as with a leveling tool, but the tool permits you to sit on a chair or stool while doing the job, while the ruler requires you to kneel or crouch to look under it. Be sure to hold the ruler straight up and down; if you tip it backward or forward a little, it might flex, giving you false readings.

12. Level the sharp keys with a **Jaras combination sharp leveler and key dip tool** or equivalent, as shown in illus. 5-21. This is similar to the Davis device, but the two legs straddle the sharp, resting on the adjacent white keys, which you already leveled in step 11. Level a few sample sharps so the top of the wooden body of each sharp key is level with the top of the wooden body of the neighboring white keys. In other words, if you were to strip the keytops off the keys, the unfinished tops of the keys would all be level with each other. The one exception to this rule is when a previous technician has installed new white keytops thicker than the originals without cutting down the thickness of the key bodies. In this case, the sharp key bodies must be leveled a little higher to make up the difference. If you do this, temporarily install the fallboard again to make sure the sharps don't touch the name board felt, and make further adjustments if necessary.

5-21. The Jaras leveling device. Adjust the tube by turning it up or down in the base. The plunger has a slot exactly 3/8" from the top, so you can use the tool both for leveling sharps and adjusting key dip. If necessary, stick a small piece of masking tape across the tube and base to keep the tube from inadvertently rotating during use.

Adjust the sharp leveling tool to the sample keys, so the button is flush with the top of the tube. Then level the rest of the sharps with the tool, adding or subtracting punchings until the floating button is flush for each sharp key. If you don't have a leveling tool, you can use a straightedge, as in leveling the white keys.

Important Note: After leveling the keys, check the lost motion again. In a heavily-used piano, the cloth cushions on the bottoms of the stickers (or the wippens, in a piano with dowel capstans) usually have indentations where the capstans have pushed on them over the years. If you've changed the key height drastically, the capstans might be pivoted forward or back a little, causing them to push on uncompressed cloth, and altering the regulation of the lost motion. If this has happened, reregulate the capstans as necessary.

13. Regulate hammer letoff. When you depress each key slowly, the hammer should move to within $1/8$" (or 3 mm.) of the strings and then fall back when the jack slips out from under the butt. To decrease the letoff distance so the hammer will move closer to the strings before the jack trips, raise the letoff regulating screw by turning it counterclockwise. To increase the letoff distance, lower the screw.

At this time, the keys may or may not have sufficient dip (or travel) to move the action through its entire cycle and trip the jack when you regulate letoff to $1/8$". If not, regulate letoff by lifting the wippen instead of pressing on the key. If you lift too far, or if the backcheck is regulated too close, the backcheck will push on the hammer when it should let off, preventing you from regulating letoff correctly. If this is the case, simply bend the backcheck toward the front of the

5-22. Left: regulating letoff with a regulating screwdriver. Right: using a thin wood letoff strip as explained in the text.

piano just far enough so it doesn't interfere. You'll regulate the backchecks later, in step 15.

Regulating an action so each hammer lets off at precisely the same distance from the strings is another technique that some beginning technicians have a hard time learning. One problem is that it is sometimes hard to view the letoff gap between every hammer and its strings from either straight above or straight from one side; viewing different hammers from different angles makes it hard to guess what the exact letoff distance is. If you have trouble with this, make a strip of wood or metal exactly 1/8" (3 mm.) thick, about 3/4" (or 2 cm.) wide and 12" (or 30 cm.) long. Hold it in place against the strings, in line with the hammer striking points, by wedging one hammer against each end of the strip with thick felt wedges inserted between the hammer shanks and hammer rail cloth. Turn each regulating screw high enough so the jack doesn't trip when you depress the key. Hold each key down, gently pressing the hammer against the letoff strip, and slowly turn the regulating screw down until the jack slips out from under the butt and the hammer lets off. Use the same pressure on each key for uniform letoff. If you press a key too hard, the jack will compress the buckskin and cloth cushions, causing the letoff to be incorrect.

A strip of of flexible magnetic stripping exactly 1/8" thick — the type used on the back of refrigerator magnets — is handier to use, as it will stick itself to the strings, eliminating the need for wedging two hammers against the strip to hold it in place.

Ordinary letoff regulating screwdrivers have a small cup attached to the end of the shank, which fits over the eye of the regulating screw. This works well if you hold the tool straight above the screw, but it has a ten-dency to break screw heads if you hold it at an angle, which often is necessary to get around the hammer rail. A more expensive version of the tool has a slotted socket with the slot cut wide enough for the tool to act more like a universal joint, permitting it to turn the screws without breaking the heads off while held at an angle.

Most old pianos have pockets formed into the hammer butt buckskins where the jacks have pushed on them for many years, causing an apparent "double letoff." As you depress the key slowly, the jack toe touches the regulating button and begins to trip. As the jack trips, it slides out from the pocket, pushing the butt a little farther and then releasing it. In pianos where this condition exists, it is frequently necessary to adjust letoff to more than 1/8", or the hammers will block against the strings when you play the piano loudly.

Another problem that makes it difficult for the beginner to regulate letoff accurately is that the cloth cushions on the letoff buttons in a heavily-used piano are always compressed unevenly, due to the jack toes bumping against them repeatedly. When this is the case, the slightest rotation of the regulating screw will cause a dramatic difference in letoff distance — far more than it does in a new piano with new regulating button cushions. Simply being aware of this will make it easier for you to understand how to adjust letoff accurately.

If the piano has a thick felt practice muffler or curtain-type mandolin attachment, lower it into the playing position, and regulate the letoff so there is 1/8" between the hammer striking point and the muffler felt or mandolin curtain. This means the total letoff distance with the rail raised out of the way will be 1/8" plus the thickness of the muffler felt or mandolin curtain. Regulating the letoff

5-23. Measuring white key dip with a 3/8" (or 10 mm.) key dip block. The Jaras leveling tool shown in illus. 5-21 makes the job easier.

to 1/8" from the strings as in a piano with no mandolin will cause the hammers to block against the mandolin tabs or clips when lowered into the playing position. A Coinola or Cremona coin piano or orchestrion with a plunger-type mandolin attachment has no curtain to get in the way, so in one of these pianos you can regulate letoff to the usual 1/8".

14. Regulate white key dip. Key dip is the distance the key moves down until it stops on the front rail punching, usually 3/8" (about 10 mm.). Regulate this by adding or subtracting paper punchings under the cloth front rail punchings. The simplest regulating tool is a 3/8" thick **key dip block**. Place the block on top of each key as shown in illus. 5-23, and change punchings so when you depress the key, the top of the block is flush with the tops of the adjacent keys. An easier method is to use the Jaras leveling and key dip tool shown in illus. 5-21. Place the tool with its legs straddling the key to be regulated, and adjust the tube until the bottom of the groove in the plunger is flush with the top of the tube. When you depress the key, the top of the plunger will be flush with the top of the tube when the key dip is 3/8".

Each key must have enough dip to go down a little beyond the point at which the jack trips and the hammer lets off. This additional travel of the key in the vertical piano is called **after touch**, and it is necessary in order for the backchecks to work properly. Despite the fact that most vertical piano actions require 3/8" (or 10 mm.) key dip and 1 3/4" (44.5 mm.) hammer stroke, many actions will have insufficient after touch and won't work right if regulated to these dimensions. You can be sure that the action will work properly under all playing conditions — loud, soft, staccato, legato — if when you press each key firmly down into its front rail cushion, the top of the jack trips forward far enough so the back edge of the top of the jack is just clear of the area where it pushes on the buckskin. If the top back edge of the jack is still under the pushing area of the buckskin, the jack isn't tripping out far enough. If the jack swings far out to the front, with over 1/16" gap between it and the buckskin, then it's usually tripping too far. In many old uprights, key dip must be regulated to 7/16" (11 mm.) instead of 3/8" to have enough after touch, and this amount of dip doesn't feel unnatural. To regulate key dip to 7/16", glue a 1/16" shim to your dip block, or adjust your Jaras tool accordingly. If 7/16" dip still isn't enough for the jacks to trip properly, then shim the hammer rail to decrease the hammer stroke a little more, and reregulate the lost motion. Since the correct mechanical functioning of the action depends upon the ratio of key dip to hammer stroke, decreasing the hammer stroke has the same effect as increasing the key dip. Excessive key dip — more than $7/16"$ or 11 mm. — makes the action feel very awkward; decreased hammer stroke reduces the maximum playing volume a little, but it doesn't make the action feel strange.

15. Regulate hammer checking by bending the backcheck wires forward or backward to put them in a straight line. Adjust the backchecks for the end white keys in each section of hammers so that when you play the key moderately hard, its

hammer will check, or come to rest, $5/8"$ (or 16 mm.) from the strings. The closer the backcheck is to the catcher at rest, the closer to the strings the hammer will be when it checks. Set the checking distance by bending the wire just above where it enters the wippen. Then set the angle for good contact with the hammer catcher if necessary, by bending just under where the wire enters the backcheck. Never bend the wire in the middle. After you regulate the end backchecks in each section, align all the intermediate backchecks with them — including the ones for the sharp keys — with a straightedge.

If the backcheck felt is worn into a concave shape, as viewed from the side, it will

5-24 (right, top). Regulating the backcheck to a sample white key hammer catcher so the hammer checks $5/8"$ (or 16 mm.) from the strings. If you use a backcheck regulating tool, hold the wippen with the other hand. A "smiling pliers," shown in illus. 5-7, makes the job easier.

5-25 (right). Regulating the backcheck angle for optimum contact between backcheck felt and catcher buckskin.

5-26 (below). Bend at the lower arrow for regulation of checking distance, and at the upper one for good contact with the catcher. Here, the tool is held parallel to the piano keys, and the handle is swung up or down. In illus. 5-24 and 5-25 pictured above, the tool is held parallel to the hammer rail and the handle is *rotated* to bend the wire in the right direction. Use whichever method works the best.

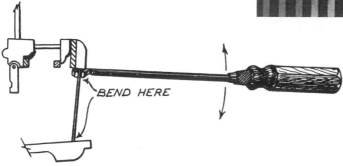

BEND HERE

5-27. Checking the alignment of the backchecks with a straightedge. Push gently on the fronts of all backchecks in each section simultaneously to see which ones need adjustment. Or, an alternative method: hold the straightedge on top of the backchecks, with the back edge of the straightedge aligned along the back edge of the top of the wood of each sample backcheck, and align the rest of the backchecks to this reference line. With a little patience, it's possible to put them all in a perfectly straight line.

be hard to adjust the backchecks to work properly. As an expedient in an old piano, regulate the backchecks to catch the hammers too far from the strings if necessary, instead of letting the hammers bounce or block against the strings. Of course, the correct remedy is to replace the backcheck felts.

16. Regulate the sharp key dip to 3/8" or 7/16" (10 or 11 mm.), whichever was dimension used for the white keys, using the

Jaras leveling and key dip tool. You have already regulated all the backchecks, so when the sharp key dip is correct, the hammers should check at an average of 5/8" (or 16 mm.) from the strings, if the backcheck felt and other parts are in good condition.

The hammer checking distance is determined by the regulation of the backchecks and the key dip. In a new, fine-quality action, the hammers will all check at the same distance from the strings when the key dip is perfectly uniform and backchecks are in a straight line. In many old pianos, the backcheck felts and other parts are worn unevenly, and in many inexpensive pianos, the action parts are not all precisely uniform. In either case, if the key dip is uniform and the backchecks are in a straight line, the hammers won't all check at the same distance from the strings. Since it is always more important to have uniform key dip and uniform hammer checking distance than it is to have the backchecks in a straight line, regulate the backchecks wherever they have to be, to make the hammers check correctly, *even if this means putting the backchecks out of alignment with each other.* As a final test of key dip and backcheck regulation, play up and down the keyboard, first softly and then loudly. Each time, all hammers should check at the same distance from the strings.

5-28. Regulating sharp key dip by changing the front rail punchings until the key goes down the same distance as the white keys.

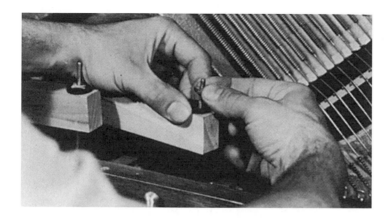

5-29. Regulating the sustaining pedal to the lift rod by adjusting the trap lever linkage.

17. Regulate the sustaining pedal to the damper lift rod. Note: Before making this adjustment, check to see if the damper spoons are interfering due to their being out of regulation. Slowly depress the keys. If the dampers begin to lift before the hammers are halfway to the strings, *REMOVE THE KEYS FROM THE PIANO UNTIL STEPS 17 AND 18 ARE COMPLETED.* This is usually necessary in a piano in which the hammers have been sanded and the hammer rail has been shimmed up to decrease excessive hammer stroke. Leaving the keys in the piano at this point will prevent you from regulating the dampers correctly.

Depress the pedal slowly while watching the dampers lift away from the strings. Adjust the connecting linkage so the dampers begin to move after the tip of the pedal has moved about 1/4" (about 6 mm.). In a piano with a threaded rod connecting the pedal to the wooden trap lever, pull the trap lever down and hold the wire up with the same hand, and turn the nut up or down as necessary. In a piano with the pedal secured to a long round metal rod with a large machine screw or a square- or hex-head set screw, loosen the screw, adjust the pedal, and tighten the screw securely, making sure that the screw doesn't push itself back into

the old position in the rod. At this point, the dampers in most pianos will lift erratically, some lifting early, some barely lifting at all, and some whole sections lifting in a long diagonal sweep. Regulate the pedal to the average of all dampers, so the largest possible number of dampers begin to lift when you press the pedal down about 1/4". If the piano has a bass sustaining pedal, regulate it the same way.

18. Regulate the dampers to the damper lift rod, so all dampers lift at precisely the same moment when you depress the sustaining pedal slowly. This is a very time-consuming procedure, but you must do it as carefully as the easier steps, or the dampers will be unsatisfactory.

In American pianos, adjust the dampers to the lift rod by bending the damper wires, as shown in illus. 5-30. If a damper lifts earlier than it should, bend the wire back a little just above where it enters the damper lever. If it lifts late, bend the wire forward a little. If the damper felt then fails to seat on the strings, bend the wire just under where it enters the head. To see if the damper is seating properly, pull the neighboring damper away from the strings so you can view the entire side of the damper head that you are regulating, from top to bottom. Gently lift

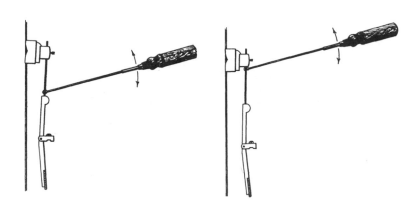

5-30. Left: Regulating a damper to the lift rod by bending the wire just above where it enters the damper lever. Right: Seating a damper on the strings by bending the wire just under where it enters the damper head.

and release the one you are regulating just a little, to see if the felt compresses more toward the bottom or toward the top when the damper presses on the strings. Bend the wire just under the head so the top and bottom of the damper felt touch the string simultaneously when you allow the damper lever spring to push the damper head gently against the strings. (One Steinway manual recommends that the top of the felt should touch the string very slightly ahead of the bottom.)

To simplify this job, make a block of wood just the right thickness so that when you insert it under the sustaining pedal, the pedal will only go down to the point where the largest number of dampers barely begin to lift from the strings. Fasten the block to the floor with masking tape or duct tape, so it won't scoot out from under the pedal. With the block in place, you can repeatedly

press the pedal down until it stops against the block, as you regulate each damper, until every damper just barely "winks" when you depress the pedal. Take your time. If your back begins to ache from the awkward stance required to push the pedal and simultaneously peer along the side of the damper and manipulate the regulating tool, take a short break.

When you bend the damper wire to make the damper lift earlier or later, you'll then have to adjust the head to make the felt seat properly on the strings, diminishing the effect of the first bend. With experience, you'll learn to overshoot the desired position with the first bend, so the second bend brings the regulation back to where you want it.

Illus. 5-30 makes the procedure look easier than it is, because in the drawing there are no hammers, shanks, and hammer rail in

5-31. Inserting the damper-regulating tool between the hammers to grasp the damper wire just under the head.

the way of the regulating tool. If you're installing a new set of hammers, or restoring a piano from the ground up, it saves time to install and regulate the dampers before installing the hammer butts, shanks, or hammers. In a completely assembled piano action, it is necessary to use a damper regulating tool with the slotted head at a 45° angle, as shown in illus. 5-1. Insert the tool at a 45° angle from above the hammer rail, and hook it around the wire. You can achieve any effect you want by rotating the handle of the tool on its own axis, lifting the handle straight up and down, moving it from side to side, moving it in an arc while twisting it one way or the other, or performing any of these movements in various combinations. Until you become experienced at upright damper regulating, nearly every movement will have some undesired side effect, which you will then have to correct. Not only will bending the wire just above the lever cause the damper head to seat poorly, but it often will cause the damper to become misaligned from side to side. Until you learn how to manipulate the tool effectively, you'll often find yourself correcting an undesired side effect only to find the damper back where it was before you started. Ignoring the minute results of each movement of the tool will lead to frustration, but if you methodically study what happens when you make each adjustment, you'll gain valuable experience rapidly, and after regulating several sets of dampers you'll be proficient at the job.

Many fine-quality vertical pianos made in Germany and other countries outside America have convenient little regulating screws in the damper levers for adjusting each lever individually to the damper lift rod. The damper heads have soft, flexible felt cushions where they attach to their mounting blocks. By adjusting the regulating screw in the damper lever, you can regulate the moment of damper lift without bending the wire; the felt cushion provides enough flexibility for the damper head to seat on the strings without any adjustment at that end of the wire. Typically, the action brackets have a ball and socket connection where they rest on the bottom support bolts, so the action may be tilted outward quickly for regulation of the damper lever screws.

When you have regulated the dampers so they all lift precisely at the same moment when you depress the pedal slowly, you may congratulate yourself for finishing one of the most difficult parts of piano regulating. This detail is one of several that the author always inspects when evaluating a piano serviced by someone else, for it says a lot about that individual's patience and attention to small but important details.

REINSTALL THE KEYS, IF YOU REMOVED THEM AT THE BEGINNING OF STEP 17.

19. Regulate the damper spoons so each damper lifts as you push its key down to the point where the hammer has moved halfway to the strings. This job is also difficult, but not nearly as awkward as step 18. Regulate the spoons by bending them with a spoon bender, with the action in the piano. Insert the bender between the wippen to be regulated and the one to its left, and hook the end of the tool over the spoon, as shown in illus. 5-32. Hold the wippen with one hand, and raise or lower the handle of the tool with the other to bend the spoon. Bending the spoon toward the keyboard by lowering the handle will cause the damper to lift later in the hammer stroke; bending the spoon toward the back of the piano by raising the handle will cause the damper to lift

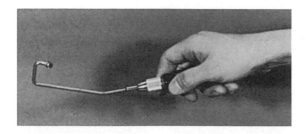

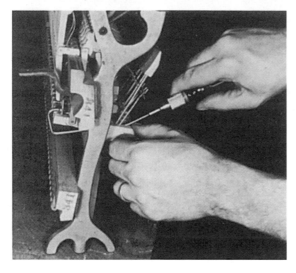

5-32. Top: The damper spoon bender in the combination handle. Bottom: Using the spoon bender.

earlier. After bending the spoon, remove the tool, test the key, and repeat the procedure until the damper lifts at the right time.

To learn to find the spoon and grasp it with the tool, remove the action and place it on a bench. Rest the end of the spoon bender on the bottom of the wippen, and slide it backward all the way to the end of the wippen. At that point, note what it feels like to drag the end of the tool upward along the back end of the wippen, and then forward along the top until the notch in the tool engages with the spoon. Feel each part of the motion while watching what you're doing, and soon you'll be able to do it entirely by feel. When you can do this consistently, put the action back into the piano and regulate the spoons.

One thing that can make spoon bending unduly difficult is the shape of most modern spoon benders, which have a slotted portion that is much too fat. Grind the sides of the slotted piece down until there is just barely enough metal left to provide the necessary strength to grasp and bend the spoon without breaking the tool. This will remove a major obstacle in the way of learning to bend spoons efficiently.

Another problem that you'll encounter is the plate strut that lies parallel to, and to the right of, the highest bass string. In many pianos, this gets in the way of regulating the lowest three or four tenor damper spoons, so these must be regulated with the action tipped forward. When you tip the action back onto the top action bracket bolts, be sure none of the stickers have slipped behind the capstans, or they will jam or break.

Many technicians have spent far more time trying to figure out short cuts to spoon regulating than it takes to learn how to do the job right. In talking with other technicians, you'll constantly hear of yet another way of doing this with the action on the bench. Trust the author: if you spend one hour paying attention to what you're doing while learning to find the spoons by feel with the action on the bench, you'll learn to regulate a whole set of spoons in the piano in less time than it takes most technicians to explain their short cuts to you.

20. Regulate the soft pedal the same way you adjusted the sustaining pedal, as shown in illus. 5-29. When you press the soft pedal all the way down, the hammer rail should move the hammers halfway to the strings.

21. Regulate bridle straps by bending their wires so each bridle strap is taut, but doesn't pull on its wippen, when you depress the soft pedal all the way. In other

174

words, pushing the soft pedal down should remove all the slack from the bridle straps, but it shouldn't cause any of the keys to wink. Bend each bridle wire sideways so it doesn't touch the backcheck wire or the head of a regulating screw, to prevent clicking noises.

Special Procedures for Spinet Pianos

Regulating a spinet is the same as regulating an upright or console, with the following exceptions:

• *Regulating the lost motion.* Some spinets have capstans at the rear ends of the keys, but drop sticker supporting levers cover them, making it impossible to insert the capstan wrench. These keys must be removed to regulate the capstans. Other spinets have short dowels screwed onto the top ends of the lifter wires, and held in sockets drilled into the keys. Turn the dowels up or down to regulate lost motion, and reseat them firmly in their sockets after adjusting them. Some spinets have hex-head screws that you turn with a small open-end wrench. Remove the tool from the adjustment screw when you test the accuracy of regulation.

• *Regulating the backchecks.* After you regulate the rest of the action, bend the backchecks so the hammers check correctly; there isn't enough room in a spinet to use a straightedge for this job.

• *Regulating the damper spoons.* Use a spoon bender made specifically for spinets. Grind the slotted head down just like your upright spoon bender, and insert the tool from under the keybed.

Vertical Regulating Check List for Quick Reference

Thoroughly clean the piano and action, and make all necessary repairs. Ease sluggish bushings, fix wobbly and loose parts, and repair broken parts. Polish rusty and corroded parts, reshape or replace the hammers, and tighten all the screws. Then regulate the piano as follows:

1. Position the letoff rail.
2. Straighten the damper lift rod.
3. Travel the hammer butts.
4. Align the hammers to the strings; align their height.
5. Align the jacks to the hammer butts.
6. Space and square the backchecks.
7. Square and space the keys.
8. Set the hammer stroke.
9. Regulate lost motion.
10. Regulate the key height.
11. Level the white keys.
12. Level the sharp keys.
13. Regulate hammer letoff.
14. Regulate white key dip.
15. Regulate hammer checking.
16. Regulate sharp key dip.
17. Regulate the sustaining pedal.
18. Regulate the dampers to the lift rod.
19. Regulate the damper spoons.
20. Regulate the soft pedal.
21. Regulate the bridle straps.

Remember that the further out of regulation a piano is, and the more the hammers have been sanded, the more adjustment is necessary, and the greater the chance is that one step will throw a previously completed one out of regulation again. After you've completely finished regulating the action, go back to the beginning of the list and check everything again. While each step makes only a small difference in the performance of a piano, the entire regulating procedure makes a tremendous improvement.

Partial Vertical Regulating

When a piano has had moderate but not extremely heavy use, the felts usually are somewhat compressed and the hammers have shallow grooves. There is a little too much lost motion, and hammer letoff is too great. If all parts are in good condition, no moving parts are sluggish, the keys are level and have enough dip, and the dampers all lift simultaneously when you depress the sustaining pedal, it is often possible to improve the operation of the action by performing a partial regulating job. First, remove the action, clean it and tighten the screws, and reinstall it in the piano. Then do the following steps from the above check list: 8, 9, 10, 13, 15, 17, 19, and 20.

Changing the Touch Weight of a Vertical Piano

If the touch of a vertical piano seems too light or heavy, refer to p. 193 for information about measuring and adjusting the touch weight. You can also strengthen the hammer butt springs, or regulate the damper spoons to engage with the dampers earlier in the hammer stroke to make the action heavier.

Preparation for Regulating the Grand Action

There are several important differences between regulating grand and vertical actions. One is that the grand action has many parts that can't be reached for adjustment when the action is in the piano, so you have to remove it to make these adjustments. Another is that the grand action is fastened to the key frame, and the two slide in and out of the piano in one large assembly. During the process of regulation, you will remove

the action temporarily from the key frame for some steps, and then reassemble them for the final steps.

The flatter your workbench top is, the more accurately you'll be able to regulate the action. Even if the keybed of the piano isn't perfectly flat, a warped or uneven bench top will only make regulating more difficult. If you only plan to regulate a few pianos, you can improvise a bench by laying a thick sheet of particle board on any available table. If you intend to continue to service pianos as a hobby or vocation, make a bench something like the one shown in illus. 5-33. Many regulating procedures are dependent upon the precise height of the strings in the grand piano, so it's handy to have overhead **letoff rails** — one for each section of strings — built into the back of the bench to take the place of the strings. Since each piano is different, the height of each section of the letoff rail can be adjusted individually. If you install large compression springs on the support bolts between the rails and the support rail, with wing nuts and washers above the support rail, the letoff rails will withstand the blows of the hammers without moving as

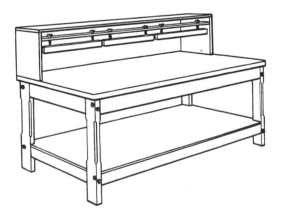

5-33. A sturdy, flat bench is essential for grand action regulating. This one has adjustable letoff rails, which take the place of the strings in the piano, and a shelf beneath for storing an action.

you simulate playing the action during regulation.

Read the section "Preparation for Regulating" on pp.151-152, if you haven't already done so. After removing the action, tightening the screws (except for hex-head plate perimeter screws in a Baldwin or other grand), cleaning the piano, attending to the hammers, repairing broken parts, correcting loose or binding parts, etc., a few more steps are necessary in a grand before you can regulate the action.

The damper action is mounted in the piano, separate from the rest of the action, and you'll need to check the tightness of the screws that hold the damper wires in the damper wire blocks. You'll adjust these parts later in the regulating procedure. For now, check to see that the screws are tight enough to keep the damper wire blocks from slipping down under their own weight. The damper wires are soft, and it's easy to bend the wires or put burrs on them by tightening the screws too much. If you encounter loose screws, tighten them just barely enough to keep the blocks from slipping up or down on the wires.

Remove the action from the key frame to check for action parts and keys needing repair. Action centers should be free but not loose. Each jack should be centered from side to side in the hole in the repetition lever, so the side of the jack doesn't rub on the lever. If a jack is off center, remove the wippen from the action. Gently heat the repetition lever support flange with an alcohol lamp or other clean heat source to soften the glue, and press it in the right position until cool. Reglue it, if necessary. If the jack can't be centered by this method, support underneath the wippen and tap on one side of the top of the jack to bend the center pin until you center the jack. This is the only place in a piano action where bending a center pin is acceptable.

If the repetition lever springs ride in slots in the levers, clean the slots. Neglecting to do this will make it impossible to adjust the repetition spring tension correctly later in the regulating procedure. To clean the slots, number and remove the wippens from the action frame. Release the springs from the slots, and clean each slot by rubbing the wood with a hammer shank sharpened in a pencil sharpener. Apply a little graphite-alcohol mixture to the slots with another pointed hammer shank. This is especially important if the slots have any residue of gummy old graphite grease or any other sticky substance. Clean the rubbing end of each spring with silver polish on a rag, carefully reposition the springs in their slots, and reattach the wippens to the action.

In most good quality grand pianos, the capstans are solid brass. If the piano hasn't been used much for a long time and the tops of the capstans are dirty or tarnished, polish them with non-abrasive metal polish — like "Sea Power," "Simichrome," or an equivalent — on a soft rag, being careful not to get the polish on the wooden parts of the keys.

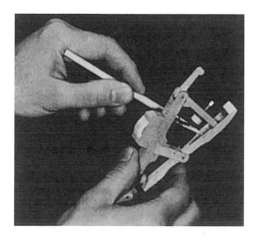

5-34. Cleaning the repetition spring slot with a sharpened hammer shank.

5-35. Sanding the key frame with 220-grit sandpaper, abrasive side up, to mate it to the keybed. This will eliminate any knocks caused by high spots.

Never use sandpaper, steel wool, or other abrasive pads, which will scratch the surface of the brass. If the capstans are brass–plated steel, as they are in many medium priced and inexpensive verticals, leave them alone. Heavy polishing might wear all the brass away, exposing the steel to the moisture in the air and in the wippen cushions, thus permitting rust to form, which is worse than smooth tarnish on brass plating.

Grand Action Regulating

With all parts clean and working properly, you're ready to regulate the action. Because each note in the grand piano has so many parts, and the adjustment of one part often affects something that you adjusted previously, it is often necessary to go back to recheck a previous step more frequently in grand than in vertical regulation. Don't expect to fine regulate a grand piano by going through it "once over lightly." The uni-

5-36. This Cable grand has adjustable front rail key frame glides built into the keybed, thus eliminating the need for sanding. Tap on the front rail and turn the glides a little at a time, until you eliminate any knocks.

178

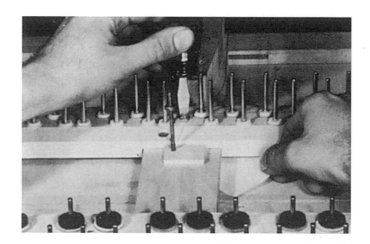

5-37 (above). Tugging gently on the newspaper with one hand while turning the screw slowly with the other, to adjust the key frame glides. When the glides are adjusted correctly, the paper will slip out without tearing.

form response necessary for fine control, and for the pianist's satisfaction with the piano, are directly proportional to the amount of care taken to regulate the action with fine precision. By adhering to the following sequence, you'll complete the job with the least possible amount of backtracking. After reading each step below, refer to the equivalent step in the vertical regulating section for additional pertinent information.

1. Bed the key frame. In a grand piano having an action-shifting (una corda) soft pedal, the key frame slides sideways on the keybed, and it must fit the keybed as closely as possible with no high or low spots. If the front rail of the key frame doesn't make good contact from one end to the other, it will knock when you play keys located above the high spots.

REMOVE THE ACTION FROM THE KEY FRAME, NUMBER AND REMOVE THE KEYS. REATTACH THE ACTION TO THE KEY FRAME, AND INSTALL THE KEY FRAME AND KEY BLOCKS. INSTALL AND TIGHTEN THE KEY BLOCK SCREWS.

Turn all the key frame glides in the balance rail up so they don't hold the key frame up off the keybed. Tap the top of the front rail from one end to the other, listening for the knocking of wood against wood. Mark the front of the key frame with chalk wherever it knocks. Remove the key blocks. Insert a piece of 220 grit sandpaper face up between the key frame and keybed wherever there was no knock, and sand the bottom of the key frame lightly. Repeat this procedure wherever there was no knock. Vacuum out the powdered wood, replace the key blocks, and test again. Repeat the procedure until you have eliminated all knocks. Don't sand the keybed, and don't insert shims between the key frame and keybed to eliminate a knock. In a grand in which the key frame is screwed to the keybed, this step isn't necessary.

Check the hold down blocks for the back of the key frame; make sure the key frame doesn't bind or knock against them.

2. Regulate the key frame glides. In step 1, above, you turned all the glides in the balance rail up so they weren't touching the keybed. Now insert a strip of newspaper under each glide and turn the glide down (clockwise) just far enough so you can pull the paper out without tearing. If a glide is too high, the keys might bounce. If it is too low and too tight against the keybed, the action will be thrown out of regulation and will be hard to shift sideways with the soft pedal.

5-38 (right). The top ends of some key frame glides are shaped like tuning pins, for easy adjustment with a tuning lever.

REMOVE THE ACTION FROM THE KEY FRAME, INSTALL THE KEYS, AND INSTALL THE KEY FRAME IN THE PIANO WITH THE KEY BLOCKS, WITH KEYS BUT NO ACTION.

3. Square and space the keys. See #7, vertical regulating.

4. Level the keys. Block the damper lift rail as high as it will go, to keep the damper levers from resting on the back ends of the keys. Attach a set of clip-on lead weights which you can obtain from a piano supply company, to the back ends of the keys or the backchecks, to hold down the back ends of the keys. Regulate the height of the lowest white key in the bass and the highest one in the treble, so the front end of each is $1/8$" (about 3 mm.) below the top of the key slip, by adding or subtracting paper balance rail punchings. Set middle E $1/32$" (or 1 mm.) higher, so the leveled keyboard will have a slight crown in the middle. After leveling these three keys, block them to this height by inserting a stack of cardboard and paper front rail punchings on each of their front rail pins so they won't go down. Lay a straightedge from the lowest white key to middle E, and level the keys between them by adding or subtracting paper punchings under the cloth balance rail punchings; then do the same thing from middle E up to the highest white key. Repeat the procedure for the sharp keys.

5. Regulate key dip. Using a $3/8$" (10 mm.) dip block or Jaras leveling tool as shown in vertical action regulating, #14, regulate first white and then sharp key dip by adding or subtracting paper balance rail punchings.

6. Travel the hammers. With the action on the bench, check the stroke of each hammer. This should be a line exactly perpendicular to the top of the bench (or key bed). Lift each hammer with its neighbors to see if it moves sideways as it rises. Correct hammer travel to eliminate sideways movement by inserting a thin paper shim

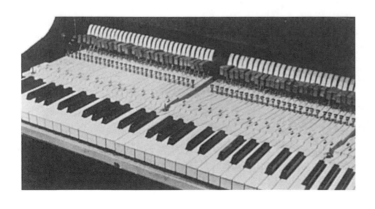

5-39. Weighting the back ends of the keys with inexpensive lead key weights during leveling. Clip-on weights, which slip over the backchecks, are better.

5-40. While raising the hammer by pressing up on the jack with one finger, look straight down into the piano to check the alignment of the hammer with the strings.

under one side of the hammer shank flange, to change the angle of the center pin. Refer to vertical action regulating, #3 for more details.

REMOVE THE KEY FRAME FROM THE PIANO, INSTALL THE ACTION ON THE KEY FRAME, AND INSTALL THE ACTION AND KEY FRAME IN THE PIANO WITH THE KEY BLOCKS. FROM HERE ON IN THE TEXT, THE ASSEMBLED KEY FRAME AND ACTION WILL BE CALLED "THE ACTION."

7. *Align the hammers to the strings.* Lift each hammer as close as possible to the strings by pressing the jack upward slowly with one finger. Look straight down at the hammer to see if it needs to be adjusted to the left or right. With the action at rest, each hammer should be centered on its strings. Slide the action out, loosen the hammer flange screw, adjust the hammer, tighten the screw, and slide the action in again. With practice, you'll know just how far to adjust each hammer so it will be centered when you slide the action back in.

8. *Regulate the una corda pedal* so the action shifts sideways just enough so the treble hammers hit only two of their three strings. In most pianos, you can adjust this by turning a capstan located somewhere on the pedal linkage. If the action has an adjustable stop — often located somewhere near the right hand key block — regulate it too. If the capstan has a lock nut, tighten it after making the adjustment.

In a piano having a hammer rail lift instead of an action shifting soft pedal, regulate this later, in step 23.

5-41. Regulating the back edge of the jack to the back edge of the wood core of the hammer knuckle, by turning the jack regulating screw. The black line drawn on the photo represents a straight line extended down the back of the wood core of the knuckle.

REMOVE THE ACTION FROM THE PIANO.

9. *Align the wippens to the hammers.* Place the action on the bench with the hammers facing you. Tip or shim each wippen flange as necessary to bring each jack and repetition lever cradle into alignment (from side to side) under the hammer knuckle. If tipping the flange brings the jack into alignment but causes the bottom of the wippen to become misaligned with the capstan, then shim instead.

10. *Regulate the jacks to the knuckles.* Adjust each jack regulating screw so the back edge of the jack is directly under the back edge of the wood core of the knuckle, as shown in illus. 5-41. If the jack is too far back under the knuckle at rest, there will be excessive friction when the jack trips out from under the knuckle. If the jack is too far forward at rest, it will slip out from under the knuckle prematurely — before the letoff point — when you play the key loudly, causing the hammer to lose most of its power. To be sure you've regulated the jack correctly, push the repetition lever down, as shown in illus. 5-42 and view it straight on from one side, not at an angle.

11. *Regulate the height of the repetition levers* by turning the repetition lever screws. The top end of each lever must be just a little higher than the top end of the jack, so the lever — not the jack — supports the hammer knuckle. There should be about .003" (or about .1 mm.) space between the top of the jack and the buckskin where the jack presses on it, when the key is at rest. This space is hard to see, because in any piano other than a brand new one, the buckskin is compressed where the jack pushes on it, making it impossible to see the gap by looking at the side of the knuckle. Theoretically, in a piano with new knuckles, the top of the lever straddling the jack should be .003" above the top of the jack. If the buckskin has an indentation of .015" however, then the top of the lever should actually be .012" below the top of the jack, in order for there to be a .003" gap.

Important: Before adjusting the repetition lever height, check the strength of each repetition spring to make sure it's strong enough to support the weight of the hammer. If a spring is too weak, as is often the case when new hammers have been installed, the hammer will push the repetition lever down until the knuckle comes to rest on the jack no matter how you regulate the repetition lever screw. Step 17 describes how to adjust the strength of the springs. You'll regulate the precise strength during that step, but for now, it's only necessary to make sure the springs support the hammers.

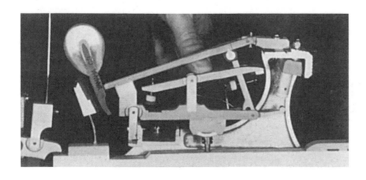

5-42. Checking the alignment of the back edge of the jack with the back edge of the wood core of the knuckle by pushing down on the repetition lever.

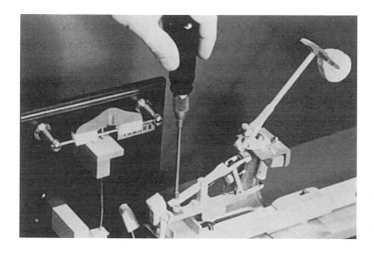

5-43. Regulating the height of the repetition lever with a drop screw regulating tool. This tool has a narrow slot to fit the small spade head.

The easiest way to adjust the repetition lever is to turn the repetition lever screw, remove the regulating tool from the screw, and then trip and release the jack with your other hand. Turn the screw downward (clockwise) until you can feel the jack rubbing on the knuckle. Then turn the screw upward, about a quarter turn at a time, until the jack slips positively under the knuckle by itself. If you don't remove the tool from the screw each time you trip and release the jack, the weight of the tool will compress the cushion on the regulating button, pushing the top end of the repetition lever a little higher than it is after you remove the tool. When you have just the right gap between the jack tip and knuckle, you will be able to

push the top end of the repetition lever downward just a little, and the hammer will just barely wink before the knuckle comes to rest on the jack.

If the lever is too high, with too much lost motion between the jack and knuckle, there will be a noticeable "thump" when you play the note loudly, at the moment that the quick movement of the key takes up the lost motion. If the lever is too low, the jack won't slip back under the knuckle reliably when the key returns to the rest position, and the note won't play the next time you try to play it.

12. *Regulate the hammer height* to 1³/₄" (44.5 mm.) below the bottom surface of the strings, by adjusting the capstans. If you

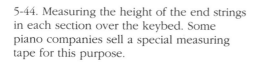

5-44. Measuring the height of the end strings in each section over the keybed. Some piano companies sell a special measuring tape for this purpose.

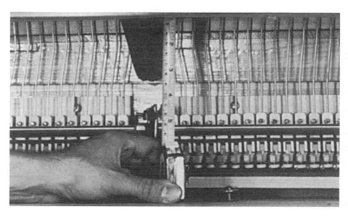

183

5-45. Regulating a capstan screw to adjust hammer height.

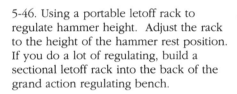

5-46. Using a portable letoff rack to regulate hammer height. Adjust the rack to the height of the hammer rest position. If you do a lot of regulating, build a sectional letoff rack into the back of the grand action regulating bench.

have a letoff rack, position the action so the keys face the front of the bench. With a tape rule, measure the distance from the keybed to the bottom of the strings at each end of the bass section, and set the letoff rack on your bench — or a portable letoff rack — to 1³/4" (or 44.5 mm.) below this height, or to the dimension specified by the manufacturer of the piano if it is different. Note that the string height over the keybed is often different from one end of a section to the other, requiring one end of the letoff rack to be a little higher than the other. Turn all the capstans down a little so all the hammers rest a little below the height of the letoff rack, slide the action so the hammers are directly under

the rack, and then turn each capstan up so the hammer just touches the rack. If you measured and adjusted the rack carefully, the hammer height should be correct when you slide the action back into the piano. Repeat this procedure for each section of hammers. If the action has an adjustable hammer rail, lower it if necessary so it doesn't interfere with the hammer height. You'll regulate it in step 13.

If you don't have a letoff rack, install the action in the piano, and set the height of each end hammer in each section to 1³/4" (44.5 mm.) by turning the capstan while measuring from the top of the hammer to the bottom of its string(s). Remove the

5-47. Checking the height of the hammers with a straightedge, in the absence of a letoff rack.

action from the piano, and regulate all the intermediate hammers to the samples with a straightedge. This method works just as well as using a letoff rack, as long as you're careful to measure the exact distance from the hammer to the bottom of the strings. A narrow pocket ruler with sliding crosspiece simplifies this measurement. Or, bend a piece of wire into a square question mark shape, with the offset portion exactly 1 3/4" long; use it as a gauge by inserting it between the strings and hammer.

13. *Regulate the height of the hammer rail,* if present, so there is 1/8" (or 3 mm.) space between it and the bottom side of the hammer shanks. In a grand action, the shanks should not rest on the hammer rail.

5-48. Regulating letoff with the letoff rack adjusted to 1/16" below the bottom surface of the strings.

Its purpose is to help to cushion the hammer rebound impact during loud staccato playing.

14. *Regulate letoff.* The hammers should let off when their striking points are 1/16" below the bottom surface of the strings. If you have a letoff rack, set it exactly 1/16" (1.5 mm.) below the string height (as previously measured with your tape rule), and slide the action under it with the hammer striking point directly under the rack. Turn each letoff screw or dowel up, until the hammer blocks against the rack when you depress the key. Then, holding the key down gently with the hammer blocking against the rack, turn the letoff screw down slowly until the hammer lets off. Repeat the procedure for each key, using the same finger pressure on each, for uniform letoff. Replace the action in the piano, and recheck the letoff of each key, making corrections as necessary. If you set the letoff rack carefully and press on each key uniformly, the letoff will be close, but it's important to do the final regulation with the action in the piano. If you don't have a letoff rack, do this step with the action in the piano.

If you have trouble adjusting the letoff, the drop screws might be adjusted too high. If necessary, go back and forth between steps 14 and 15 until the drop screws don't interfere with the correct regulation of letoff.

15. *Regulate the depth of the hammer drop*, by turning the drop screws (#8 on illus. 2-67). When you play a sustained note very softly, the key pushes the wippen up, the jack trips out from under the knuckle, the hammer hits the strings and rebounds gently without being caught by the backcheck, and the front of the key is held-down against the front rail punching. In this state, the repetition lever, not the jack or backcheck, supports the hammer. With the key down, the wippen up, and the jack out from under the knuckle, the repetition lever is pushed down from its rest position by the drop screw pressing on its top (front) end, and the hammer rests on the repetition lever in a position slightly below the point at which the hammer lets off. The amount that the lever pivots away from its rest position, and therefore the height of the hammer as it rests on the lever, is determined by the adjustment of the drop screw. This regulation is called **hammer drop** because it is always a little lower than the letoff point.

Before attempting to regulate hammer drop, recheck to make sure each repetition spring is strong enough to support the weight of the hammer and shank when the jack trips out from under the knuckle. You

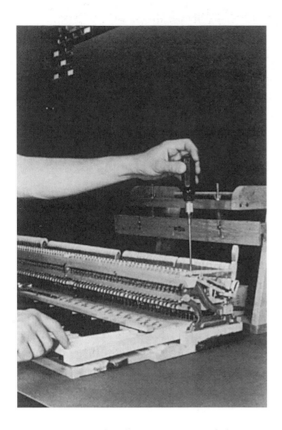

5-49. Regulating the drop screw so each hammer drops and comes to rest on the repetition lever 1/16" below the point of letoff.

5-50. Checking hammer drop. With the letoff rack height adjusted to the point of hammer letoff, insert a 1/16" thick gauge between each hammer and the rack to check drop height. Alternately, set the letoff rack to string height and see that each hammer lets off 1/16" below the rack, and drops an additional 1/16" for a total of 1/8" below the rack.

186

5-51. Measuring hammer checking with a ⁵/₈" (16 mm.) gauge, with the letoff rack adjusted to string height.

already checked the springs in step 11 above, but recheck all of them now, just in case any of them are still too weak. If you have to strengthen any weak springs at this point, you'll probably have to go back and do steps 11 and 12 over, which is why you were supposed to check the springs in step #11.

To regulate the amount of hammer drop, place the action on the bench. Press each key slowly until it hits bottom, and the hammer lets off and comes to rest on the repetition lever. While continuing to hold the key down, turn the drop screw so the hammer comes to rest ¹/₁₆" (or 1.5 mm.) below the point at which it lets off. If you have a letoff rack, leave it adjusted at the letoff point, as in step 14 above, and regulate the drop screws so the hammers drop ¹/₁₆" (1.5 mm.) below the rack. Since you previously adjusted the rack to ¹/₁₆" below the string line, this will provide a drop height of ¹/₈" below the string line (¹/₁₆" letoff + ¹/₁₆" drop).

If you have no letoff rack and if you regulated letoff very carefully in step 14, you can regulate the drop of each hammer by comparing it to the letoff of the hammer next to it. To do this, hold the key down for the note you're regulating, while gently playing the adjacent note repeatedly with

another finger, watching where the adjacent hammer lets off, while turning the drop screw for the note that you are regulating.

Whether you regulate drop by using a letoff rack or by comparing the drop of each hammer to the letoff of the adjacent hammer, put the action in the piano and recheck drop regulation. Each hammer should now let off ¹/₁₆" below the strings, and come to rest ¹/₁₆" lower, or a total of ¹/₈" (a little over 3 mm.) below the strings.

16. *Regulate the backchecks.* First, space and square them to the hammer tails, as described in vertical regulating, step 6. Then, with the action on the bench and the letoff rack adjusted exactly to string height, play each key with a moderate blow. Each hammer should check exactly ⁵/₈" (16 mm.) from the strings (rack). Measure the space with a ⁵/₈" gauge, and bend the backcheck forward or backward to change checking distance from the strings. After bending the backcheck wire, play the key with several hard blows in case the wire springs a little toward its previous position.

All previous regulating steps up to this point have required that the repetition springs be strong enough to support the hammers, but it hasn't mattered if the

187

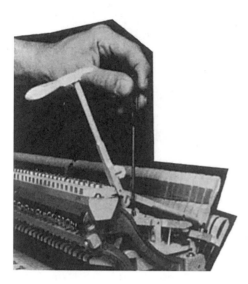

5-52. Many grand actions have adjusting screws for regulating the tension of the repetition springs.

springs are too strong. If some hammers won't check properly, but jump upward against the letoff rack even when you play loudly, regulate the backchecks as closely as possible, do step 17, and then come back for fine regulation of the backchecks. If neces-

sary, adjust the angle of the backcheck for maximum contact with the hammer tail. If the backcheck angle is too steep, or too far toward the horizontal, the end of the hammer tail will hit the buckskin, and the hammer will rebound upward again, even if the repetition spring is regulated correctly. If the backcheck angle is too shallow, or too close to the vertical, the hammer will slip down too far.

17. *Regulate the repetition spring tension.* Play each key so the hammer checks. Then let the key come up just a little, and immediately push it all the way down again, releasing the hammer from the backcheck and permitting the hammer to rise slowly but positively to the drop position $1/8"$ below the string line. If the spring is too weak, the hammer won't rise or will rise only part way. If the spring is too strong, the hammer will jump up suddenly when the backcheck releases the tail. Some pianos have regulating screws for adjusting the spring tension; others, including the Steinway, have no regulating screws, and you must adjust the springs by bending them, as shown in illus. 5-53.

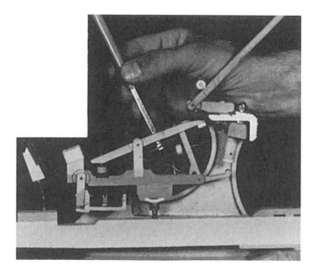

5-53. Regulating a Steinway-style repetition spring with a special spring-bending tool. First unhook the spring from its slot. Then "massage" the spring in the desired direction with the tool, rather than introducing a sharp bend or kink. Then position the spring back in the slot.

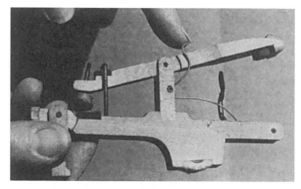

5-54. Repetition springs have the distressing habit of popping out from under the levers unless you are very careful to relocate them in their slots after regulating.

If you didn't clean gummy repetition spring slots before regulating the action, as shown in illus. 5-34, you won't be able to complete step 17 because the hammers will never do the same thing twice in a row. If you didn't clean the slots because it looked like too much work, and you muddled through steps 11 through 16 wondering why it was so hard to adjust things right, the result of your hurrying will be painfully obvious right now. You will need to go back to the beginning of the grand action regulating section, clean the slots, and start over.

18. *Regulate the height of the key stop rail.* Loosen the lock nuts on top of the rail. Regulate the support nuts under the rail so the front end of each white key may be lifted barely 1/8" (or 2 mm.), and the front end of each black key a little less than this, with the rail in place. Tighten the lock nuts when regulation is correct. If the rail is too low, it might push the keys down if it swells during periods of high humidity.

19. *Regulate the dampers* to the damper lift rail and the keys. In many grands, the damper lift rail and the back ends of the keys have felt glued to the top surface where they lift the damper levers, as shown in illus. 2-67. The damper lift rail should lift all dampers at precisely the same moment when you depress the sustaining pedal slowly, and each damper should begin to lift individually when you push its key down to the point where its hammer is halfway to the strings.

First, regulate a few sample dampers in each section so they begin to lift when their hammers are halfway to the strings, by loosening the screw in each damper wire block, sliding the block up or down the wire as necessary, and tightening the screw gently into the soft wire. Tightening the screw too much will indent the wire or cause a burr, making it difficult to make fine adjustments later.

Install the action in the piano and check the samples to make sure they all lift when the hammers are halfway to the strings. Remove the action and make corrections as necessary. The lever for each type of sample damper — monochord, bichord and trichord wedges, and flat treble felt if present — might have to be at a slightly different height over the keybed, due to the depth to which that type of damper felt descends around or between the strings. In some pianos, the felt on the lift tray and back ends of the keys might be of slightly different thickness from one section to the next, to compensate for the different types of felt. In others, everything is set to one average thickness.

For each section, make a jig out of a small block of wood whose thickness equals the space between the keybed and the bottom of the sample damper levers. Slide the block under each remaining damper lever in that section. Loosen the screw, make sure the damper felt rests on the strings with the lever resting on the block, and gently tighten the screw. After going through the entire set of dampers, you will have all the levers in each section suspended the same distance over the keybed. Install the action temporarily to see that all the keys begin lifting their levers when the hammers are halfway to the strings. If they don't, adjust the thickness of the jig and the setting of the dampers as necessary. Remove the action, and watch the damper heads as you slowly depress the sustaining pedal. Typically, the dampers will now all lift at approximately the same time, but most of them will be a little early or late, and many will tip or rotate a little one way or the other.

You are now about to embark upon one of the most difficult procedures in the world of piano regulating. As when regulat-

ing a vertical piano, make a block of wood just the right thickness so that when you insert it under the sustaining pedal, the pedal will only go down to the point where the largest number of dampers barely begin to lift from the strings.

Depress the sustaining pedal until it stops on the block. Watch damper head #1, and see if it lifts before or after the average. If it does either, loosen the screw, slide the wire up or down in the block just a tiny amount, gently tighten the screw, and test it again. If one end of the damper head lifts before the other, or if the head tips to one side as it lifts, bend the wire a little by tilting the head as necessary. When the timing is perfect, check to see if the damper head rotates at the moment it lifts off the strings. If so, grasp the wire just above the damper wire block with pliers, and twist the wire a little. The gently-tightened screw should be loose enough to permit the wire to be turned without bending it. When you have regulated the damper just right, tighten the screw just a little more to lock the wire in place. If this causes the head to rotate again, twist the wire again as necessary. When the regulation is perfect, both ends of the damper head will come to rest on the strings without turning or twisting sideways. Repeat this procedure for every damper; when you're done, the dampers should rise uniformly and with a minimum of twisting as you slowly depress the pedal.

Now it's time to get really finicky. At this point, many technicians say "well, that's good enough," even though the dampers aren't perfect. If necessary, go to a music store and observe how perfectly the dampers lift in a fine-quality new grand piano when you slowly press the pedal. Then go back to your piano and make fine adjustments so your dampers work just as well as they do in

the new piano. One of the best signs of the amount of care put into the repair and regulation of a grand piano is how uniformly the dampers work, and it's one of the easiest things to check when evaluating the quality of a technician's regulating.

Put the action in the piano. Presumably, if you set the height of the sample dampers carefully, and if you checked your progress from time to time as you went along, all the dampers will now lift when their hammers are halfway to the strings. If necessary, regulate the individual dampers to their keys by adding or subtracting paper shims from the back end of each key under the damper lever lift felt where the felt isn't glued to the wood.

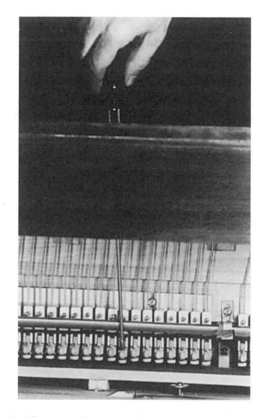

5-55. This piano has a regulating screw and button for each damper lift lever, greatly simplifying the fine-regulation of damper lift. Either use an extremely short regulating tool or insert a long tool between the strings.

Some pianos have the luxurious feature of individual regulating screws for each damper lever, mounted either on the lift tray or the damper levers, as shown in illus. 5-55. In this case, most of the regulation can be done by turning the regulating screws, although it is still necessary to adjust the damper wires if any of the dampers rotate as they lift away from the strings.

After you regulate the dampers to lift perfectly, some of the wedge dampers will no longer dampen all their strings. With the dampers at rest, pluck the strings of each unison to find which ones are leaking through. Carefully analyze the shape of the wedge felt to see why it isn't muting all strings equally. In a section of the piano having a capo bar, check the spacing of the strings, and move one of them sideways just a little so they all touch the wedges. In a section having agraffes, if one string is lower than the others, bend it up a little by lifting with a stringing hook near the agraffe. If the wedge felt is hard and dense, it might be possible to file it with a sandpaper stick until it seats properly. If it is soft, try pressing or squeezing the part that is too thick. If none of these remedies is appropriate, tilt the head to the left or right by bending the wire a little so the damper mutes all strings.

20. *Regulate the height of the damper stop rail.* This simple but important adjustment has a lot to do with how the action feels to the pianist. Adjust the height of each section of the rail to prevent the dampers from going up more than about 1/16" (or 1.5 mm.) higher than the keys lift them. After adjusting each part of the rail and tightening the screws, hold a sample key down under each end of the stop rail, and see that the damper can be lifted by hand just a little higher. If a stop rail is too low, it will limit the travel of the keys during very

loud playing. If it is too high, the dampers will bounce, giving the action an extremely distracting and annoying feeling. It isn't uncommon for one or more of the stop rail screw holes to be stripped, permitting the damper levers to bump part of the rail upward. If any of the screws can't be tightened, fix the screw holes or insert longer screws now.

21. *Regulate the sustaining pedal.* Adjust the pedal rod by turning its capstan, or by shimming at an appropriate place in the trap linkage. Adjust it so there is about 1/16" (1.5 mm.) space between the damper lift rail felt and damper levers at rest, or so the pedal goes down about 1/4" (about 6 mm.) at the front tip before it begins to lift the dampers. If the piano has a damper pedal stop capstan, regulate it so the pedal stops just before the damper levers touch the stop rail.

If the piano has a bass sustaining pedal, regulate it the same way.

22. Regulate the sostenuto mechanism and pedal, if present. All sostenuto lever tabs should form a straight line, as viewed from the top. Regulate their alignment forward or back by bending each damper wire in or out directly above the damper lever, and reseat the dampers on the strings if necessary. The sostenuto rod should be 1/16" (1.5 mm.) above the sostenuto lever tabs when at rest. Adjust its position by repositioning or bending the support brackets for the rod. The sostenuto rod lip should overlap the lever tabs by 1/16" (1.5 mm.) when you depress the pedal.

To check if the sostenuto mechanism works right, play each note, depress the pedal, then release the note to make sure the pedal holds up the damper. While sustaining the note with the pedal, repeat the note several times to see if this causes the tab to slip off the rod. Next try clusters of notes, in case the increased weight of a group of adjacent dampers deflects the rod a little, causing any tabs with marginal overlap to fall. For another test, depress the pedal and then play all the keys one after the other, to make sure that the rod doesn't trap any tabs above it when it shouldn't. If the overlap of the rod lip with the tabs is insufficient or misaligned, it might be possible for the tabs to jam against the rod when you play certain notes. If the overlap is too much, you might feel the rod lip rubbing on the tabs when you push down the pedal. When the overlap is just right, every damper will work as it should.

For a final test, press the sustaining pedal, press the sostenuto pedal, and then release the sustaining pedal, to see that the sostenuto holds all dampers up simultaneously. Then release the sostenuto, press it again, and press and release the sustaining pedal, to see that no dampers stay up.

23. Regulate the hammer rail lift, if there is one, to the soft pedal. Adjust the linkage or trap work so the hammers move a little less than halfway to the strings when you depress the pedal fully. The keys may "wink" or dip down a little. This is in contrast to the vertical piano, in which depressing the hammer rail pedal shouldn't cause them to move at all. If the pedal lifts the grand hammer rail too far, the back ends of the keys will touch the damper levers, possibly lifting the dampers off the strings.

24. Regulate the hammer striking line in the treble. Many fine-quality grands have hold down screws or plates in the key blocks, which can be adjusted to the front or back to fine-regulate the striking line of the hammers. Remove the key blocks, and slide the treble end of the action in and out a little, shifting the position of the hammer striking point along the length of the strings. Listen for an improvement in the tone as you do

this. If you can distinctly hear the tone become brighter and clearer in the treble when you move the action in or out, adjust the key block screw or plate accordingly. If you can't hear any improvement, leave the adjustment alone.

Grand Regulating Check List for Quick Reference

1. Bed the key frame.
2. Regulate the key frame glides.
3. Square and space the keys.
4. Level the keys.
5. Regulate key dip.
6. Travel the hammers.
7. Align the hammers to the strings.
8. Regulate the una corda pedal.
9. Align the wippens to the hammers.
10. Regulate the jacks to the knuckles.
11. Regulate the height of the repetition levers.
12. Regulate the hammer height.
13. Regulate the height of the hammer rail.
14. Regulate letoff.
15. Regulate hammer drop.
16. Regulate the backchecks.
17. Regulate the repetition spring tension.
18. Regulate the height of the key stop rail.
19. Regulate the dampers.
20. Regulate the height of the damper stop rail.
21. Regulate the sustaining pedal (and bass sustaining pedal).
22. Regulate the sostenuto mechanism and pedal.
23. Regulate the hammer rail lift, if present.
24. Regulate the hammer striking line, if adjustable.

(Note that steps 11, 12, 14, 15 and 16 are all dependent upon step 17 being approximately correct, but you can't regulate 17 precisely until you have finished the previous steps.)

Changing the Touch Weight of a Grand Piano

Touch weight refers to the amount of weight that it takes to depress the key. **Down weight** is the specific amount of weight, measured in grams, that it takes to push the key down to the point of the beginning of letoff (or to the point where the jack first makes contact with its regulating button), with the damper lifted off the back of the key. **Up weight** is the amount of weight that the key will lift from this position back to the rest position. Piano supply companies sell gram weight sets for measuring touch weight. The ideal down weight is between 50 and 55 (usually 53 or 54) grams. Place a 53-gram weight on the front end of the key, centered over the balance rail pin, and bump the action with your hand. The key should slowly descend to the point of letoff, at which point the added resistance of the jack will stop the key. With the key in this position, if you remove the 53-gram weight and place a 20-gram weight on the front of the key, the key ideally should return to the rest position by itself.

There are several ways to change touch weight. To increase it, you can install heavier hammers, or add lead weights to the keys behind the balance rail, or subtract lead-weights from the keys in front of the balance rail. To decrease it, you can file the hammers, or replace them with lighter hammers, or add lead weights to the keys in front of the balance rail, or rarely, remove leads from the keys behind the balance rail.

The simplest way to alter touch weight is to add a **Jiffy Key Lead** to the top of the key. Slide the weight forward or back as necessary to adjust the balance so the key falls to the letoff point under approximately 53 grams and returns to rest under approximately 20 grams. Then screw the weight in place. This method is easy to reverse in case the results aren't what you expect.

If the piano action is equipped with auxiliary wippen springs, you can increase or decrease the touch weight by weakening or strengthening the springs. Adjust the tension by bending the loop in the spring farther open or shut, as you would to change the strength of a safety pin. Don't bend or kink the spring with a wire bending tool. Adjust these springs only by using gram weights, after consulting with an experienced technician or manufacturer's service representative.

Before experimenting with touch weight, find an accurate scale to verify the weights of your gram weight set. In one case, an expert piano technician couldn't regulate a new fine-quality grand to specifications. After much investigation, including a visit by the manufacturer's service representative, it was found that the technician's gram weights were marked incorrectly.

Adding weights to the keys, moving or removing original weights, and changing the size of the hammers all alter the inertia of the action as well as altering the touch weight. Before you attempt to change the touch weight of a fine piano, consult with an expert concert grand technician so you don't damage anything.

Square Piano Action Regulating

Tighten all screws, clean the piano and action, check for proper operation of all working parts, space and level the keys,

193

space the hammers to the strings, etc., as in any other piano. Then regulate the action to the following specifications, referring to illus. 2-85. Set the key dip to 3/8" (or 10 mm.). The hammer shanks should rest on the rest rail cloth as in a vertical piano, not hover above it as in a grand with repetition levers. Regulate the jacks with a small offset screwdriver or homemade tool that will fit between all the other parts. Adjust the rocker capstans so there is just enough lost motion between jacks and hammer butts for the jacks to slip back under the hammer butts without rubbing, as in a vertical piano. Set the hammer letoff to 3/16" (5mm.) for the wound strings, and 1/8" (3 mm.) for the plain strings. Regulate the hammers to check as close to the strings as possible without having the tails rub against the backchecks on the upstroke.

Regulating a square piano can be very challenging, due to the extremely fragile action parts and the difficulty of sliding the action in and out in some instruments. The hammers are so light that they won't fall back to the rest rail if any of the hammer flanges are at all sluggish. Make absolutely certain that all hammers are resting on the rail before sliding the action out, every time you remove it from the piano, or you'll break hammers and shanks. It is also very difficult to regulate the rocker capstans in many square pianos using conventional tools, because the hammer rest rail and backchecks are in the way. You might be able to turn the screws with a modified ratchet screwdriver, with one blade and part of the handle cut off, or you might have to reach under the other action parts with a special homemade offset screwdriver.

Action Regulation Problems: Their Symptoms and Cures

If a hammer bounces on the string twice in rapid succession when you play a key, it is **double-striking.** In a vertical piano, this is usually caused by inadequate key dip in proportion to hammer stroke. When a piano gets old and worn, the hammers become shorter, lost motion between the jack and hammer butt increases, and the backchecks wear thinner, but the key dip doesn't increase proportionately. So, the key reaches the bottom of its stroke before the action finishes its cycle, and the backcheck can't do its job. To correct this situation, regulate the hammer stroke, lost motion, letoff, and backchecks.

If grand hammers double-strike during very soft playing, the repetition lever springs might be too strong, or the hammer drop might be set too high. Regulate accordingly. If the hammers double-strike during louder playing, the backchecks aren't catching them properly, and should be regulated or releathered. Badly worn key bushings sometimes permit the keys to wobble from side to side, and this can cause the backchecks to malfunction in a grand.

If a hammer travels all the way to the strings and stays against them, damping out all tone, it is **blocking.** Blocking can be caused by a jack not letting off, by too much key dip in proportion to hammer stroke, or by a backcheck pushing the hammer against the strings. Regulate letoff, key dip, and the backchecks if necessary.

If a hammer begins to let off and then accelerates toward the strings again just at the last moment, the buckskin on the butt or knuckle has a depression or pocket where the jack pushes on it. When the letoff button trips the jack, the jack has to ride out of the pocket over the resulting ridge in the buck-skin, making precise letoff regulation impossible. To correct this, replace the buckskin, the butt, or the knuckle.

If a note sounds odd at the moment when the hammer strikes the strings, but the sustained portion of the tone sounds good, the hammer might be hitting the adjacent string. Since the adjacent damper instantly dampens the vibration of the neighboring string, the problem is noticeable only for a moment. Hold the sustaining pedal down while playing the note in question; if the hammer is hitting a neighboring string, it will ring too, revealing the source of the problem. Correct this by aligning the hammer to the string. If the hammer has grooves, reshape it before attempting to align it, or the old grooves will force it back into its old position. The author has seen many old uprights with poorly installed new hammers, in which every bass hammer grazed the adjacent string, causing the entire bass section to sound peculiar.

If a customer complains that a key won't play or won't repeat, but it works fine every time *you* play it, try playing it with the soft pedal, sustaining pedal, and both pedals on. Sometimes a sluggish wippen will return to its rest position when the damper spring helps it, but won't return when you raise the damper with the sustaining pedal. If you still can't get the piano to malfunction when you play it, ask the customer to show you what's wrong, and you might find the problem.

If an action is too light or heavy to the touch, refer to the discussion on touch weight on p. 193.

To eliminate clicks, buzzes, rattles, and other annoying sounds, refer to pp. 142-143.

Action Problem Check List for Quick Reference

Note Doesn't Play (Dead Note).

- Key bushings are too tight, or key is warped and rubbing on adjacent key, preventing key from returning to the rest position and jack from resetting.
- Foreign object has rolled under back end of key.
- Key is broken.
- Sticker or associated part is broken, so capstan doesn't push sticker up.
- Spinet lifter elbow is broken, or drop sticker has come loose from key.
- Jack flange bushings are too tight, preventing jack from resetting.
- Jack spring is broken.
- Jack flange is unglued from wippen, and jack isn't pushing on hammer butt.
- Hammer is missing.
- Capstan is regulated too high, preventing jack from resetting under butt.
- Repetition spring is too weak, keeping repetition lever from lifting hammer high enough to let jack reset.

Note Plays Weakly.

- Hammer letoff is regulated too far away from the strings, or grand jack rest position isn't under knuckle far enough.
- Hammer shank is cracked or broken.
- Repetition lever spring is too weak, keeping lever from lifting hammer high enough to let jack reset.
- Hammer butt spring is broken, or hammer is sluggish and doesn't return all the way to rest position.
- Hammer rail is stuck in the up position, limiting hammer stroke.

195

Note Double Strikes.
- Backcheck is worn badly or is out of regulation; buckskin on catcher is worn..
- Hammer letoff is regulated too close to strings.
- Butt or knuckle has deep indentation or pocket where jack presses on it.
- Hammer butt spring is broken.
- Key has insufficient dip.

Hammer Blocks Against Strings.
- Backcheck is regulated too close.
- Key dip is excessive.
- Letoff is regulated too close to strings.
- Jack is broken.
- Letoff rail has become displaced, causing all notes to malfunction.

Sluggish Note.
- Key bushings are too tight, or key is warped and rubbing on adjacent key.
- Bushing in "dogleg" key has indentation.
- Any action bushing is too tight.

Damper Doesn't Damp.
- Damper is misaligned with strings.
- Felt is damaged.
- One string of a two- or three-string unison is bent, holding damper off the other strings.
- Spoon or underlever needs to be regulated; damper spring is broken.
- Sustaining, bass sustain, or sostenuto pedal is out of regulation, holding dampers off strings.

Note Has Clicking Noise.
- Flange screw is loose, or bushing is worn. Teflon bushing is loose.
- Hammer head, hammer shank, catcher shank, or catcher is loose.
- Small object like paper clip is sitting on front rail punching.

- Key lead is loose.
- Damper lift lever is hitting damper stop rail in grand.
- Hole in end of bridle strap is enlarged, and hardened tip is clicking on bridle wire.
- Bridle wire is striking neighboring backcheck wire.

Tone Regulating

Tone regulating is the fine art of adjusting the tone quality of a piano so that each note has the desired amount of brilliance or mellowness. It may involve anything from changing the tone of a few notes that are brighter than their neighbors, to revoicing an entire piano. Although some technicians consider tone regulating to be synonymous with hammer voicing, or changing the resilience of the hammer felt, it also encompasses anything that may be done to a piano that affects tone quality, including hammer reshaping (which changes the harmonic structure of the tone), action regulating (which affects the amount of muscular power required to produce a tone of a given volume), tuning, replacing dead strings, adjusting string bearing, etc. For a complete tone regulating job, the piano must first be brought into optimum mechanical condition. All mechanical problems such as sluggish or loose action parts, buzzing strings, loose bridge pins, etc. must be corrected. Only after you repair, regulate, and tune the piano as well as possible are you ready to voice the hammers.

Before attempting to regulate the tone of a valuable piano, you should be able to reshape a set of hammers so accurately that they look as neat and uniform as a new fine-quality set, as described on pp. 137-139. If your reshaped hammers look like they've been reshaped, with crooked surfaces anywhere, practice on inexpensive old pianos until you perfect this technique. You also should have the experience of fine tuning hundreds of pianos, and then should practice voicing many inexpensive vertical pianos before attempting to voice the hammers in a fine quality grand.

Preparation for Hammer Voicing

Lightly sand the hammers. The striking point of each hammer must be just the right shape, and it must hit all three strings squarely and equally. For each unison having more than one string, gently press the hammer against the strings and pluck them one by one. If you have shaped the hammer correctly, it will dampen the sound of all the strings evenly. If not, reshape it as necessary. Sometimes a perfectly shaped hammer might not hit all three strings because the strings aren't all level with each other. To make a minor correction, use a string hook to bend the string near the agraffe or capo or v-bar a *tiny amount* in the desired direction, so the hammer hits all three strings at once.

Fine tune the piano. Recheck the hammer striking line in the treble; adjust for the

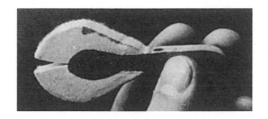

5-56. A good-quality hammer will spring apart when you slice the striking point open, showing the compression and tension in the felt.

brightest, clearest possible tone.

Check the agraffes, if present, to see that they're perpendicular to the length of the strings. Rotate them slightly with an agraffe removing tool, if necessary, so all three strings of each unison are precisely the same length, so their harmonic series will all be the same. Be careful not to break any agraffes. Ideally, the shoulder of each agraffe should come to rest snugly against the plate just as the agraffe is facing in the right direction. Many agraffes are already tight, and forcing one, especially in the clockwise direction, will break it.

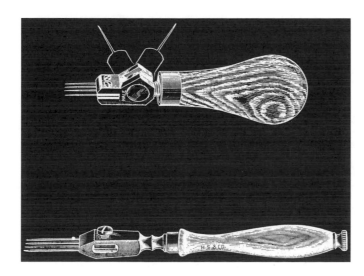

5-57. Two types of voicing tools. The swivel-head model is handy for voicing hammers in vertical pianos.

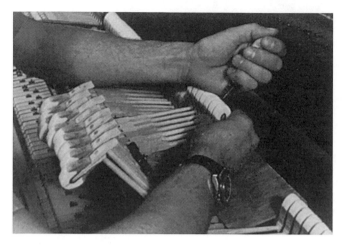

5-58. Supporting the hammers during needling with a small, thin board.

Hammer Voicing

Hammer manufacturers glue the felt around the wood molding under tremendous pressure, creating a state of compression on the inside and tension around the outside of the hammers. The tension and compression provide the resilience necessary for good tone quality, and help to keep the striking point from flattening out prematurely under heavy use. The tension around the outside of a good quality hammer may be shown by cutting the striking point open with a sharp knife, as illustrated.

New hammers, and reshaped old hammers, often produce a tone that is too brilliant, and you must soften them to make their tone more mellow. You do this by carefully needling the felt, to separate some of the fibers and soften the cushion supporting the striking point. Voicing requires sensitive hearing, experience in judging the most subtle differences of loudness and tone quality, and much patience.

You will voice hammers for loud, then medium, and finally soft playing in separate operations; voicing for each loudness requires needling a different part of the hammer. Of course, there is a certain amount of overlap between the areas, but voicing a set of hammers for uniform tone quality at a loud playing level doesn't necessarily make them uniform at a softer level.

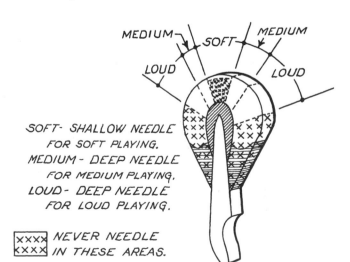

SOFT - SHALLOW NEEDLE FOR SOFT PLAYING.
MEDIUM - DEEP NEEDLE FOR MEDIUM PLAYING.
LOUD - DEEP NEEDLE FOR LOUD PLAYING.

XXXX NEVER NEEDLE
XXXX IN THESE AREAS.

5-59. Needling for loud, medium, and soft playing.

Tools Required

- Hammer voicing tool with adjustable head
- Supply of #6 sharp needles
- Hammer support board 1/4" thick, 4" x 10" (or 5 mm. x 10 cm. x 25 cm.)

Procedure

Use the small board to support the hammer that you are needling, as illustrated. Hold the hammer very steady in one hand, and hold the voicing tool in the other. Some technicians favor jabbing the hammer with short, firm strokes, and others favor pressing the needle into the felt with slower, more controlled pressure. If you decide to try the jabbing method, use great care not to slice the edge of the hammer — or your thumb — apart, and be sure to support the hammer firmly so you don't break it or its shank, or damage the center pin or bushings.

To voice the hammers at a loud playing level, insert one #6 sharp needle in the voicing tool so it sticks out about 3/4" (or 20 mm.). Play up and down the keys within an octave near the middle of the keyboard with strong, uniform finger pressure. Listen carefully for any notes that sound brighter than the others. If you're not sure, keep playing loudly up and down the scale repeatedly, until it becomes obvious which notes, if any, are too bright or "tinny." Pull the action out of the piano, and deep needle the areas marked loud on illus. 5-59. To begin, deep needle each shoulder five times. Put the action back in the piano and play up and down the scale again. If you notice no difference, deep needle the hammer a few more times on each shoulder, and listen again. Repeat the procedure until all notes within the octave sound uniform. Move up half an

octave and repeat the procedure. By overlapping sections of notes, you'll be able to do a smoother job. As you proceed toward the high treble, the tone quality will change gradually to a very bright, clear ring, and in the highest two octaves you won't do any deep needling at all. Go back to the middle of the keyboard and work your way down to the bass. The lowest two or three tenor notes on the treble bridge are often the most difficult to voice, due to scale design; if you can feel with your finger that the hammer felt is becoming soft, and they still sound tinny, stop. Further needling will ruin the hammers.

To voice for medium-loud playing, deep needle the areas marked *medium* on the drawing. Repeat the procedure used for loud voicing, but play at a uniform medium loudness. As in loud voicing, needle the hammer the same number of times on each shoulder.

To voice for soft playing, insert three needles in the voicing tool so they protrude only 1/16" (or 1.5 mm.). Using very precise touch, play up and down the notes of one octave as softly as you can, and again pick out any notes that are brighter sounding than their neighbors. Check to make sure that the regulation is uniform and that none of the notes have excess friction, too much or too little hammer travel or letoff distance, or any other condition that might make them sound different. After ascertaining that the regulation is perfect, shallow needle any hammers that are still too bright, in the area marked soft on the drawing. Begin by inserting the voicing tool with its three short needles five times, distributing the needling uniformly over the entire "soft" area on the drawing, and play up and down the scale again. Repeat this procedure until no notes stand out as you play all the way up and down the scale.

Needling a set of hammers can be strenuous work, particularly if the entire low and middle sections are too bright because of extremely hard, dense felt. If a needle breaks off in a hard hammer, try to grasp the stump with fine needle nose pliers whose jaws mate perfectly. If you can't get it out, leave it in the hammer instead of risking cutting the hammer or otherwise spoiling it. You should never deep needle the striking point, so there should be no risk of breaking a needle off in an area where it will hit the strings.

Every time you put the action back in, put the retaining blocks in place, so the hammers always hit the strings at the ideal striking point. In a fine-quality piano, the retainers are always built into the key blocks, which have large locating dowels, enabling them to hold the action in place without requiring the hold-down screws to be inserted each time. In an inexpensive grand with tiny screwed-down blocks located inside cavities in the key blocks, do your best to locate the action without tightening the small screws, or you'll wear out the screw holes long before you finish voicing.

Never needle the shaded areas on the drawing. The underfelt glued to the wood molding must provide a firm, hard foundation for the thicker outer felt, so you should never needle it. Never deep needle the crown, or striking point; to do so is to risk cutting the hammer and ruining it. Never over-needle. It is better to pull the action a dozen times, needling a little each time, than to soften a hammer too much. With a lot of experience, you'll learn whether a hammer needs five more needlings, or just one or two, to bring it to the desired tone quality. Once you've broken down a hammer by excessive needling, there is no way to regain the desirable tension and compression. Fine concert voicing involves needling techniques that go beyond the procedures presented here. These skills are the result of years of experience, and should be learned under the personal supervision of an expert who can monitor the student's progress and provide immediate feedback.

Making Hammers More Brilliant

So far, the discussion of voicing has focused on making bright hammers more mellow, but there are some instances in which hammers must be made brighter, particularly in the high treble. A dull tone in the highest two octaves of a piano with good strings, termination points, bridges, soundboard, correct downbearing, and **optimum striking line** is caused by hammers that are too thick, or have too much felt on them. Before filing them thinner, check again to make sure that you have regulated the striking line of the hammers to the position where they produce the best possible tone. If they are still dull sounding, thin them by sanding away a little felt from the shoulders without removing any from the striking point. Smooth and pack the felt by sanding with fine paper, as described on p. 138, and the tone should be brighter.

If thinning the high treble hammers doesn't brighten them enough, apply several coats of nitrocellulose lacquer — not acrylic lacquer — thinned with four parts lacquer thinner; this can be obtained from any professional refinishing supply company. The thinned lacquer will soak into the outer layers of felt, stiffening the felt a little. Let the lacquer dry overnight, and check the results. In some pianos, the hammers will sound better. In others, they might sound brighter but "woody," in which case it will be necessary

5-60. The hammer ironer.

to needle them a little again. Learn the effects of lacquering hammers by experimenting on many old pianos of little value, before applying it to a fine piano.

To pack down and harden soft, spongy felt — temporarily, at least — use a hammer ironer as shown in illus. 5-60. This tool can also be useful for temporarily drying the moisture out of hammers in a damp environment. Gently heat the head to a moderately hot temperature with a clean heat source such as a propane torch or electric stove; wipe it with a clean rag in case any carbon or other residue is present, and stroke the hammers with it, rubbing from the shoulder toward the striking point. With experience you'll learn just how hot to make it, so it packs the felt down without scorching it. Learn the proper use by practicing on worn hammers in an old upright before taking a chance on hurting fine-quality hammers. If you inadvertently harden the felt too much, needle the hammers as necessary to soften them.

Chapter Six

Tuning Theory and Terminology

A piano sounds **in tune** when its strings vibrate at certain frequencies determined by musical and acoustical rules. This chapter explains enough about musical and acoustical theory for you to understand how and why tuning works. The next chapter explains actual tuning procedures and techniques, and how to master them. The music theory presented in this chapter will seem elementary to a trained musician, as will the acoustic theory to anyone trained in physics. Read it anyway. Even if you already understand certain portions of the material, you'll need to know exactly how the music and science fit together, and you'll need to memorize piano tuners' terminology to understand the next chapter.

Musical Tone Versus Noise

When something vibrates, it causes the surrounding air to imitate its movement. For example, when the surf pounds on the shore, the movement of the water transmits its scrambled collection of vibrations to the surrounding air. In turn, the air makes your eardrums vibrate and creates the sensation of **noise**. You hear any unorganized collection of vibrations as noise. On the other hand, when an object vibrates at a certain speed and causes your eardrums to vibrate at the same speed, you hear **musical tone**, if the vibration is within the range of human hearing. If the vibration is too slow, you hear each cycle individually like the clicks of a ratchet or the pounding of a jackhammer. If the rate is too fast, you can't hear it at all.

The speed at which the object vibrates is its **frequency**, measured in **cycles per second**, or **hertz (hz)**. As the object vibrates faster, its frequency is higher, and you hear a higher tone. The frequency of vibration in hz is also called **pitch**. The faster the vibration, the higher the pitch.

The Vibration of Wire

Three factors influence the pitch of a vibrating wire:

1. The length: other factors being the same, the shorter the wire, the higher its pitch.

2. The thickness: other factors being the same, the thinner the wire, the higher its pitch.

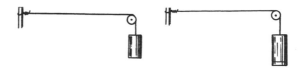

3. The tension: other factors being the same, the tighter the wire, the higher its pitch.

6-1. In each of the three illustrations above, the string on the right will have the higher pitch.

203

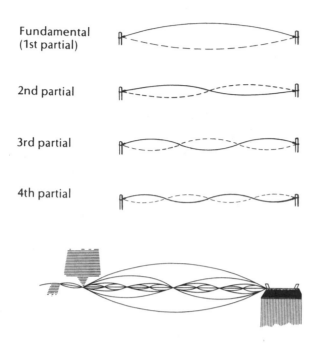

Fundamental
(1st partial)

2nd partial

3rd partial

4th partial

6-2. A vibrating wire subdivides itself into many simultaneously vibrating fractions. Each fraction produces an audible pitch of its own, called a partial.

Another factor, the wire's **stiffness**, is a result of a combination of the other factors. If two wires of different lengths — made of the same material — have the same thickness, the shorter wire is shorter in proportion to its thickness than the longer wire, so the shorter wire is stiffer. Other factors being the same, the stiffer a wire, the higher its pitch.

Wire vibrates in a complex way. Not only does an entire string vibrate, producing the **fundamental pitch**, it also divides itself into two vibrating halves, three thirds, four quarters, and so on, all simultaneously. Each portion produces its own pitch called a **partial**. Whenever a string vibrates, it produces a whole series of partials (or **partial series**) together with the fundamental pitch.

The partials are usually much softer than the fundamental, but it is possible to force a partial to predominate by touching the string lightly at a half, third, or other fraction of its length, and then playing it. The partial produced by the isolated segment will then sound louder than the fundamental.

Musicians have used the words **partial**, **harmonic**, and **overtone** interchangeably to describe vibrating string segments, but each term has its own specific meaning. A **partial** is the pitch produced by the whole vibrating string, or any vibrating string segment. The fundamental is the **first partial**, the two halves each produce the **second partial**, the three thirds the **third partial**, and so on.

A **harmonic** is a theoretical frequency that is an exact multiple of the fundamental. The second and higher partials of a piano string don't necessarily vibrate at frequencies that are exact mathematical multiples of the fundamental or first partial. Thus, not every partial is a true harmonic. In this book, partial refers to any vibrating string segment, while harmonic refers only to a partial that is a multiple of the fundamental pitch. Wire stiffness causes the vibrating segments to produce partials that are not true harmonics.

6-3. Touching a string lightly at its midpoint and then playing it forces the second partial to predominate. Touching it at various fractions of its length allows a listener to hear other partials easily.

204

The deviation of partials from the harmonic series is called **inharmonicity**.

An **overtone** is like a partial, but overtones are numbered differently. The first partial is the fundamental, but the first overtone is second partial. To avoid confusion, the term "overtone" is not used in this book.

Simultaneously Vibrating Wires

If you strike two wires that have their tension adjusted, or **tuned**, to the same pitch, the sound produced by one reinforces the other, and the two produce a louder combined tone by **constructive interference**. If one wire vibrates out of synchronization with the other, they subtract from each other and produce a softer tone, by **destructive interference**.

If you tune one string to 440 hz and the other to 442 hz, the vibration of the faster string will catch up to and overtake the slower string twice per second. Likewise, the tone will grow louder and then softer twice per second. Each time the tone gets louder and softer is called one **beat**. Two strings vibrating at 440 produce no beats; two strings vibrating at 442 produce no beats. Strings tuned to 440 and 441 beat once per second; strings tuned to 440 and 445 beat five times per second. If strings beat much faster than fifteen times per second, the beats are too fast to be heard. Instead of sounding like one tone with beats, the tone sounds like two pitches played at once.

Partials and fundamental pitches can each cause beats. Thus, if one vibrating string has a fundamental or partial in its series vibrating at 100 hz, and another has a fundamental or partial vibrating at 102 hz, two beats per second will be heard.

What Pitches Form the Musical Scale?

The musical scale, or tuning scale, of a piano is the assortment of pitches to which the strings are tuned, which can be played by playing the keys in order, one after the other. The word **scale** has several meanings. Don't confuse the musical scale discussed in this chapter with the stringing scale discussed elsewhere in this book. The latter refers to the physical dimensions of the plate, bridges, and strings.

Of the infinite number of possible pitches, only certain ones sound good when played simultaneously, and these pitches are the ones that make up our musical scale. They are related to each other according to certain rules of music theory, including the following:

1. One pitch, or a **unison**, sounds more pure than anything clsc. This is logical, since a single vibrating string theoretically produces no beats.

2. The most pure sounding combination of two pitches is produced when one is twice the frequency of the other. If you compare the partial series of two theoretically perfect strings, one tuned to 220 and the other to 440, none of the partials will beat, because no two of them are close enough together. These two pitches sound more pure than any other combination. In fact, two pitches, one of which is twice the frequency of the other, sound so much alike that they have the same letter name in the scale.

Every so often on illustration 6-5 another "A" comes along, and each A is twice the frequency of the previous one. If the scale consisted of only one basic pitch and those pitches obtained by doubling its frequency repeatedly, these pitches sound so much

SIXTH PARTIAL	1320	2640
FIFTH PARTIAL	1100	2200
FOURTH PARTIAL	880	1760
THIRD PARTIAL	660	1320
SECOND PARTIAL	440	880
FUNDAMENTAL		
(1st Partial)	220	440

6-4. The partial series of two theoretically perfect strings, one tuned to 220 and the other to 440, produce no audible beats because all partials either coincideor are too far apart.

alike that there wouldn't be enough variety to play melodies. This leads to the next rule:

3. Going up the scale, there are twelve pitches between any two notes of the same name, or between a pitch of a given frequency and the pitch of double or half that frequency. Look at the keyboard again, and count the keys between one A and the next. Every time the frequency doubles, twelve steps have gone by.

To review, random vibrations produce **noise** while organized vibrations produce **musical tone**. A vibrating wire produces a whole series of **partials** by subdividing itself into many vibrating parts, besides its **fundamental tone**. Pitches of nearly **coincident** frequencies produce **beats**, or pulsations in the loudness of the tone. The mathematical difference between the two pitches determines the speed of the beats. From these principles, some logical conclusions may be drawn, to arrive at the basis for the Western tuning scale.

A vibrating string has a fundamental and a series of partials. This theoretical string produces no beats. A single vibrating string is the most pure sound in a piano. Therefore, a beatless tone is the most pure, and the more beats that a combination of pitches produces, the less pure the sound. The most pure combination of two pitches occurs when one has double the hz of the other, because theoretically these two pitches produce no beats. Since the musicians who developed our scale decided on twelve steps every time the frequency doubles, then the twelve basic pitches should be those that produce the fewest beats when played together in any combination. This, indeed, is the basis of the tuning system.

Musical Terminology

Before you can have a complete understanding of the tuning system, you need to learn the names of the pitches as represented by the keyboard, and the names of certain combinations of pitches, or **intervals**. An interval is the distance between any two keys on the keyboard. The distance between any two adjacent keys is a **half step**, or **semitone**, and the distance between any key and the key two half steps away is a **whole step**. Two white keys having a black key between them are not adjacent, so the distance between them is a whole step.

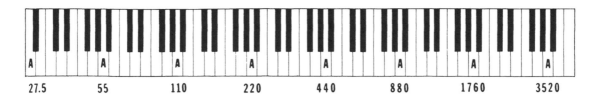

6-5. A piano keyboard with the theoretical hz of all A's identified.

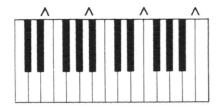

6-6. The smallest interval on the keyboard is the half step. Any two adjacent notes form a half step. The two legs of each carat point to notes which are a half step apart.

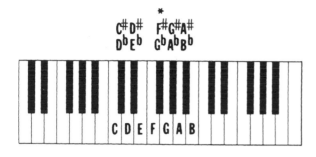

6-7. Names of all the white and black keys.

Each white key has its own letter name. *Memorize them.* Each black key borrows the name of *either* adjacent white key and therefore has two names. The **sharp symbol (#)** indicates the pitch a half step higher than the letter name. The **flat symbol (b)** indicates the pitch a half step lower. For example, the key marked with the asterisk in illustration 6-7 is a half step higher than F and a half step lower than G, so it can be called either F# or Gb. In music, the adjacent white keys also borrow each others' names, such as Cb or B#, but tuners don't use these names. The interchangeable names are necessary for musicians to be logical about music theory; as a tuner, you only need to memorize what the names are. There are twelve different notes, but only seven different letter names. The remaining five notes are the sharps (or flats), which borrow their names from the white keys.

Another symbol, the **natural symbol (♮)**, indicates that a note is neither flat nor sharp. When a note previously had a flat or sharp in a discussion, the natural sign tells you that the flat or sharp is no longer in effect.

To go *up* the musical scale means to go higher in pitch, to the right on the keyboard. To go *down* is to go lower in pitch, farther to the left. A note above another is higher in pitch and farther to the right; a note below another is lower in pitch and farther to the left.

In the following discussion, the first letter is always the lower pitch in an interval. The interval C-G refers to C and the next higher G. G-F# refers to G and the next higher F#. G-G is G and the next higher G.

The half step consists of any two adjacent notes. The names of larger intervals tell how many letter names the two notes are apart. To identify an interval, count the letter of the starting note as "one," and keep count-

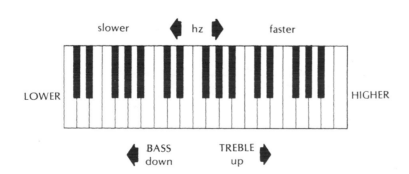

6-8. The higher the pitch, the farther to the right the note is on the keyboard.

ing each letter, until you reach the desired note. Counting C as "one," and going up the scale, C-D is a **second**, C-E a **third**, C-F a **fourth**, C-G a **fifth**, and so on up to C-C, the **octave**. The octave is a very important interval because it identifies a given note and the next higher or lower note of the same letter name, which is double or half its frequency. To identify intervals larger than an octave, you can either continue the same sequence (ninth, tenth, etc.) or break the interval into two parts (octave and a second, octave and a third, etc.). Don't count sharps and flats when figuring the size of an interval. C-Eb, C-E, and C#-E are all thirds.

A fourth having five half steps (C-F, for example), a fifth having seven half steps (C-G), and an octave are **perfect intervals**. A second having two half steps (C-D), a third having four half steps (C-E), a sixth having

Musical Interval	No. of Half Steps	Examples	Tuning Terminology
Unison	0	**Any Single note**	**Unison**
Minor second	1	C-Db, C#-D	
Major second	2	**C-D, C#-D#**	**Second (2nd)**
Augmented second	3	C-D#, Cb-D	
Minor third	3	**C-Eb, C#-E**	**Minor third (m3rd)**
Major third	4	**C-E, Cb-Eb**	**Major third (M3rd)**
Augmented third	5	C-E#, Cb-E	
Diminished fourth	4	C-Fb, C#-F	
Perfect fourth	5	**C-F, C#-F#**	**Fourth (4th)**
Augmented fourth	6	C-F#, Cb-F	
Dimished fifth	6	C-Gb, C#-G	
Perfect fifth	7	**C-G, C#-G#**	**Fifth (5th)**
Augmented fifth	8	C-G#, Cb-G	
Minor sixth	8	C-Ab, C#-A	
Major sixth	9	**C-A, C#-A#**	**Sixth (6th)**
Augmented sixth	10	C-A#	
Minor seventh	10	C-Bb, C#-B	
Major seventh	11	C-B, Cb-Bb	
Augmented seventh	12	C-B#, Cb-B	
Perfect octave	13	**C-C, C#-C#**	**Octave (8ve)**

6-9. Musical intervals. Those commonly used in piano tuning are used in bold face, and the right hand column lists their tuning name and abbreviation.

nine half steps (C-A), and a seventh having eleven half steps (C-B) are **major (M) intervals**.

If you increase any perfect or major interval by a half step, it becomes **augmented**. Thus, C-F# and Cb-F are both augmented fourths, and C-A# and Cb-A are augmented sixths.

If you reduce any perfect interval by a half step, it becomes **diminished**. If you reduce any major interval by a half step, it becomes **minor (m)**. Thus, C-Fb and C#-F are diminished fourths, while C-Eb and C#-E are minor thirds. ("M" and "m" are the abbreviations for major and minor, respectively.)

Another term used when discussing tuning is the unison. A unison is any single pitch. The term is necessary because in the treble or upper range of a piano there are two or three strings per note to augment the loudness. Tuning these strings to each other — so they reinforce each other to produce one loud pitch — is called **tuning the unisons**. Of all the intervals contained within an octave, tuners commonly use only the ones listed in the right-hand column of illus. 6-9, as explained later in the text. Tuners also use larger intervals, including the

tenth (octave and a third), twelfth (octave and a fifth), double octave, and seventeenth (two octaves and a third). Unless otherwise specified, each larger interval is always major or perfect.

Two like intervals which are next to each other chromatically in the scale, such as the major thirds B-D# and C-E, are called **adjacent** or **successive intervals**. Two like intervals in which the top note of one is the same as the bottom note of the other, such as the two major thirds C-E and E-G#, are called **contiguous intervals**. Tuners refer to three or more contiguous intervals as being **stacked**. C-E, E-G#, and G#-B# (or G#-C) are an example of stacked major thirds.

Piano tuners ordinarily use sharps exclusively in their discussion of tuning, and never use flats. This means most piano tuning literature calls C-D# and C#-F "minor thirds," for example. These names are correct insofar as the way the intervals sound, but technically incorrect according to music theory. This book calls intervals by their correct musical names wherever possible. In the instructions for tuning the temperament, however, the text uses tuners' terminology, because this is what you will use when communicating with other tuners. In tuners' language, B-D# and D#-G are contiguous major thirds. In musical language, D#-G is a diminished fourth. The musically correct spelling for the contiguous thirds in this example is B-D# and Eb-G, with D# and Eb being two different "enharmonic" spellings of the same note.

The author feels that it isn't asking too much for you to learn the names of five flats so you can communicate with musicians in musically correct language. Remember this idiosyncrasy, though, when you read other literature in the field and discuss tuning with other technicians.

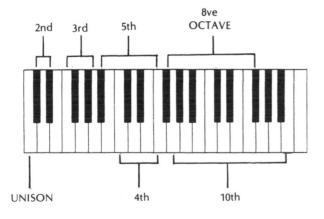

6-10. Various intervals on the keyboard.

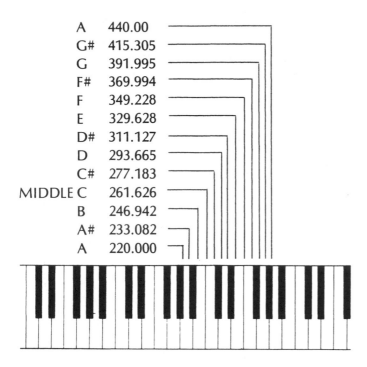

A	440.00
G#	415.305
G	391.995
F#	369.994
F	349.228
E	329.628
D#	311.127
D	293.665
C#	277.183
MIDDLE C	261.626
B	246.942
A#	233.082
A	220.000

6-11. Theoretical pitches of the twelve basic notes near the middle of the keyboard. The frequency of each pitch is found by multiplying the adjacent lower pitch by the twelfth root of 2, which is 1.0594631.

Mathematics of the Theoretical Scale

The octave interval consists of two notes of the same name. One pitch is double the frequency of the other, and there are twelve pitches between.

Given the pitch of the middle A on the keyboard (A440, or key number 49), you can find the theoretical pitches of all the higher A's by doubling 440 repeatedly, and the theoretical pitches of all the lower A's by halving 440 repeatedly. See illustration 6-5. Given the theoretical pitches in hz of all A's, how do you find the frequencies of the remaining pitches? The frequencies of all twelve pitches are related according to a mathematical law. This law states that starting with any pitch (say A37, or A220, for example), and multiplying it by a *constant number* twelve times in a row, the result is double the frequency of the starting pitch (or A440). The constant number is 1.0594631, which is the twelfth root of two. In 1925, musicians decided that

the **international pitch standard,** or **tuning standard,** would be A440. Starting with A an octave lower (A220) and multiplying it by 1.0594631 twelve times in a row gives the theoretical frequencies for the twelve pitches near the middle of the keyboard, ending on A440. Given these twelve pitches, it is a simple matter to find the theoretical frequencies of the remaining keys on the piano, by halving each basic pitch repeatedly for the lower octaves, and doubling each repeatedly for the higher octaves. Illustration 6-12 contains the results.

The **octave numbers** across the top of illustration 6-12 start with the lowest A on the keyboard as "A1" and end with the highest C as "C8." Most European and Asian piano makers, and the Yamaha electronic tuning device, use this system for numbering the octaves of a piano. Some American piano technicians, and the Conn, Peterson, and Sanderson Accu-Tuner electronic tuning devices made up to the time that this is being written, call the lowest three notes "A0,"

"A#0" and "B0". The #1 octave runs from C1 up twelve notes through B1, throwing the numbers of all A's, A#'s, and B's off by one octave. For example, in the European system, A-440 is "A5," as in illustration 6-12. In the American system, A-440 is "A4." To eliminate confusion in this book, all notes are called by their key numbers, from A1 through C88. If you have a piano with fewer keys in the bass, translate all key numbers into the standard 88-key format.

Another important concept in piano tuning is the division of half steps into **cents**. One cent equals one hundreth of a half step; there are 100 cents in any half step. As you go up the keyboard, each higher half step has a greater change in hz than the previous one, but every half step always has 100 cents. In other words, if any note is 100 cents flat, it is a half step flat. This is a very handy way of measuring how sharp or flat a note is, without having to know its vibration in hz.

At this point, don't proceed until you master everything discussed so far, including how wire vibrates, partials, harmonics, beats, cents, the names of all notes, the definition of an interval, sharps and flats, determining the size of an interval given the names of the two notes, and how to find the frequencies of all pitches, given the standard pitch of A440.

Tuning Theory

To tune a piano, you must listen, compare and adjust the tension of the strings so they sound pleasant when played in combinations. When comparing one pitch to another, you listen for beats, and either eliminate them or adjust their speed.

To begin, you tune A440 (A49) to a reference pitch such as a tuning fork, tuning bar, or electronic device. From A49, you tune an octave encompassing twelve notes near the middle of the keyboard. The initial tuning octave is called the **temperament octave**, or simply the **temperament** because when tuning this section of the piano you adjust, or temper, the various intervals. An alternate

OCTAVE

PITCH	1	2	3	4	5	6	7	8
G#	51.913	103.826	207.652	415.305	830.609	1661.219	3322.437	
G	48.999	97.999	195.998	391.995	783.991	1567.982	3135.963	
F#	46.249	92.499	184.997	369.994	739.989	1479.978	2959.955	
F	43.654	87.307	174.614	349.228	698.456	1396.913	2793.826	
E	41.203	82.407	164.814	329.628	659.255	1318.510	2637.020	
D#	38.891	77.782	155.563	311.127	622.254	1244.508	2489.016	
D	36.708	73.416	146.832	293.665	587.330	1174.659	2349.318	
C#	34.648	69.296	138.591	277.183	554.365	1108.731	2217.461	
C	32.703	65.406	130.813	261.626	523.251	1046.502	2093.004	4186.009
B	30.868	61.735	123.471	246.942	493.883	987.767	1975.533	3951.066
A#	29.135	58.270	116.541	233.082	466.164	932.328	1864.655	3729.310
A	27.500	55.000	110.000	220.000	440.000	880.000	1760.000	3520.000

6-12. Theoretical fundamental pitches of all 88 notes. The box includes the twelve theoretical pitches of the temperment octave. The author computed this table with an electronic calculator by multiplying each successive half step by 1.0594631 (the twelfth root of 2). Although this illustration rounds off the numbers to three places, computations were carried out to six places (five places from C64 up).

HARMONICS
(THEORETICALLY PERFECT PARTIALS)

	Fundamental or 1st	2nd	3rd	4th	5th	6th
F	349.228	698.456	1047.684	1396.912	1746.140	2095.368
E	329.628	659.256	988.884	1318.512	1648.140	1977.768
D#	311.127	622.254	933.381	1244.508	1555.635	1866.762
D	293.665	587.330	880.995	1174.660	1468.325	1761.990
C#	277.183	554.366	831.549	1108.732	1385.915	1663.098
C	261.626	523.252	784.878	1046.504	1308.13	1569.756
B	246.942	493.884	740.826	987.768	1234.710	1481.652
A#	233.082	466.164	699.246	932.328	1165.410	1398.492
A	220.000	440.000	660.000	880.000	1100.000	1320.000
G#	207.652	415.304	622.956	830.608	1038.260	1245.912
G	195.998	391.996	587.994	783.992	979.990	1175.988
F#	184.997	369.994	554.991	739.988	924.985	1109.982
F	174.614	349.228	523.842	698.456	873.070	1047.684

6-13. Theoretical frequencies of the first six partials of each note in the temperament octave. The fundamental is the first partial.

tuning system, as described in Chapter Seven, uses an extended temperament section larger than an octave. For the present chapter, however, the temperament will be confined to an octave for ease of understanding the theory. Prior to the adoption of the equally tempered scale, the scale had certain intervals that were beatless, and others with such rapid beats that they were unusable for music. In our theoretical equally tempered scale, all intervals within the temperament, except for the octave, are tuned with a slow beat. No other interval is pure (beatless), but none is so bad that it is unusable in music.

Tuning the temperament involves setting each interval within the temperament to the correct beat rate. Refer to illustration 6-11 showing the theoretical fundamental pitches of each note within the temperament octave. The difference in hz between the fundamental pitches of any two notes is so large that there are no beats. Each pitch, however, also has a series of partials. To tune the temperament, you compare **nearly coincident partials** between each two notes. That is, in any temperament tuning interval, each pitch has

a partial somewhere in its series that nearly coincides with a partial of the other pitch, and the partials are mathematically close enough to produce beats. Illustration 6-13 lists the first six theoretical partials of each theoretical pitch within the temperament octave, showing some of the coincident partials.

To find the theoretical beat rate between any two notes in the temperament octave, find the partials that are closest. For example, find the theoretical beat rate between C and G. The third partial of C (784.878) is closest to the fourth partial of G (783.992). Subtracting gives the theoretical beat rate for C-G in the temperament octave: .886 per second, or 4.43 beats per 5 seconds.

Illustration 6-14 gives the theoretical **beat rates per second (bps)** of all intervals within the temperament octave, as derived from illustration 6-13. To find the theoretical beat rate of a certain interval, follow the line of numbers to the right of the *lower* note over to the column below the *upper* note. That number is the correct rate. For example, find the beat rate between G and C. G is

	F#/Gb	G	G#/Ab	A	A#/Bb	B	C	C#/Db	D	D#/Eb	E	F
E												*
D#/Eb											*	*
D										*	*	15.850
C#/Db									*	*	14.958	10.997
C								*	*	14.121	10.382	1.180
B							*	*	13.327	9.798	1.116	*
A#/Bb						*	*	12.577	9.250	1.053	*	.790
A					*	*	11.870	8.732	.995	*	.744	*
G#/Ab				*	*	11.202	8.244	.941	*	.702	*	9.424
G			*	*	10.578	7.778	.886	*	.664	*	8.894	*
F#/Gb		*	*	9.982	7.343	.838	*	.625	*	8.396	*	*
F	*	*	9.424	6.930	.790	*	.590	*	7.925	*	*	0

* The beat rates of these intervals are too fast to be useful.

6-14. Theoretical beat rates per second of all temperament octave intervals.

the lower note. Following the line to the right of G over to the C column, you will find that the theoretical beat rate is .886. Intervals marked with asterisks on the chart have beat rates too fast to be useful in tuning.

Illustration 6-15 lists all useful tuning intervals from illus. 6-14 in order of theoretical speed of beat rate. The left portion includes the fast beating intervals, including major thirds, minor thirds and sixths. The

Test Interval	Theoretical Beat Rate Per Second			Rounded Off Beat Rate
	Maj. Thirds (4 Half Steps)	Sixths	Min. Thirds (3 Half Steps)	
F-A	6.93			7 −
F#-A#	7.34			7 +
G-B	7.78			8 −
F-D		7.93		8
Ab-C	8.24			8 +
F#-D#		8.40		8.5 −
A-C#	8.73			8.5 +
G-E		8.89		9 −
Bb-D	9.25			9 +
Ab-F		9.42		9.5 −
F-Ab			9.42	9.5 −
B-D#	9.80			10 −
F#-A			9.98	10
C-E	10.38			10 +
G-Bb			10.58	10.5 +
Db-F	11.00			11
G#-B			11.20	11 +
A-C			11.87	12 −
A#-C#			12.58	12.5
B-D			13.33	13 +
C-Eb			14.12	14 +
C#-E			14.96	15
D-F			15.85	16

	Tuning Interval	Theoretical Beat Rate Per Five Seconds	Rounded Off Beat Rate
Fifths	F-C	2.95	3 −
	F#-C#	3.125	3 +
	G-D	3.32	3.5 −
	G#-D#	3.51	3.5
	A-E	3.72	3.5 +
	Bb-F	3.95	4 −
Fourths	F-Bb	3.95	4 −
	F#-B	4.19	4 +
	G-C	4.43	4.5 −
	G#-C#	4.71	4.5 +
	A-D	4.98	5
	A#-D#	5.27	5.5 −
	B-E	5.58	5.5 +
	C-F	5.90	6

6-15. Beat rates of tuning and test intervals in order of speed, including the fast-beating thirds and sixths (left) and slow-beating fourths and fifths (right).

right portion includes the slow beating intervals, including perfect fourths and fifths. Because it is impossible to count beats in hundredths or tenths of a second, all beat rates are rounded off to the nearest half beat per second (bps).

If you examine the theoretical frequencies in illustration 6-13 and the theoretical beat rates in 6-14 and 6-15, you'll see that all fifths are **narrow**, and all major thirds, fourths, and sixths are **wide**. The top note of any fifth is a little flat of the bottom note, or conversely, the bottom note is a little sharp of the top one. The top note of any major third, fourth, or sixth is a little sharp of the bottom one, or the bottom one is a little flat of the top one. Memorize this, so you'll always know which way to tune an interval.

You will tune the temperament octave from the F below middle C to the F above (F33 to F45) by adjusting the intervals to certain beat rates in a certain sequence, explained in the "Defebaugh F-F Temperament" in the next chapter. After you tune the temperament, you'll use it as your reference for tuning the rest of the piano. (As men-

tioned earlier, the next chapter also includes the "Potter F-A Temperament," expanded from an octave to a tenth.

Theory vs. Reality

The above discussion treats strings as if they vibrate according to theory, which they don't. In reality, wire stiffness causes the partials of strings struck by piano hammers to be sharp of their theoretical harmonics, so all numbers in the charts and tables are incorrect by a small amount. The sharpness, or distortion of the partials from the true harmonic series, is called **inharmonicity**.

Despite inharmonicity, a string sounds in tune with itself — if it has no false beats — because the partials within the range of human hearing are far enough apart that they don't create beats. When you tune an octave, you compare the entire partial series of both strings, with the second partial of the lower note and the fundamental of the upper note predominating. If you tune these coincident partials to be beatless, the octave is stretched to whatever extent the second partial of the lower note is sharp of its fundamental.

In cases where two strings share more than one set of coincident partials, as in the octave interval, tuners refer to specific partials by their numbers. For example, to tune a "4:2 octave," you tune the 4th partial of the lower note to the 2nd partial of the upper one. To tune a "6:3 octave," you tune the 6th partial of the lower note to the 3rd partial of the upper one. It is important to be able to identify a specific harmonic when you tune strings that have high inharmonicity, in order to describe the correct way to tune them.

The strings for F below middle C have inharmonicity like all other strings, and the F33-F45 temperament octave is stretched to the extent of this inharmonicity. Therefore, all intervals within the temperament must be

6th Partial	196.218	198.435
5th Partial	163.515	164.779
4th Partial	130.812	131.434
3rd Partial	98.109	98.401
2nd Partial	65.406	65.523
Fundamental Pitch	32.703	32.703
	Theoretically perfect harmonic series of low C.	Actual series of partials.

6-16. Because of the stiffness of piano strings, among other factors, the actual series of partials deviates from the theoretical harmonic series. This table illustrates the inharmonicity in hz of a low C bass string in a fine-quality upright piano, as measured in a laboratory.

a little wider than their theoretical counterparts, in order for the temperament to come out right. (Fourths and fifths are still narrow, but not quite as narrow as the tables suggest; thirds and sixths are just a little wider than in the table.) Every note in the temperament octave has its own particular inharmonicity, depending on the design of the stringing scale, causing the coincident partials to vary from one piano to the next. Because of this, no two pianos with different stringing scales have the fundamental pitches of the notes within the temperament octave — or any of the other notes except A440 — tuned precisely the same.

In a piano, then, equal temperament can't be defined as a table of frequencies or specific beat rates. Equal temperament in piano tuning can only mean "the tuning of the temperament octave so it sounds as smooth and even as possible, given the inharmonicity peculiar to the particular piano."

Chapter Seven

Tuning Procedure

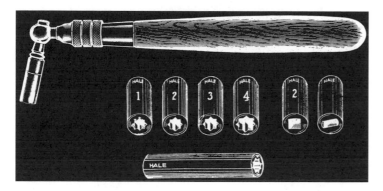

7-1. An extension tuning lever with interchangeable heads and tips. The long head is for tuning grands; the short, for tuning most verticals. The tips fit various sizes of tuning pins, including the oblong pins used in some Victorian pianos.

Tools

To tune a piano, you'll need a **tuning lever, tuning fork** or **bar, felt temperament strip,** and **some wedge mutes.** Buy the best tuning lever that you can afford, preferably an extension lever. Few professional tuners ever extend the handle, but most prefer the extension lever over a smaller, lighter one because the extension lever is sturdier and it flexes less.

For the most efficient tuning, you should have a **tuning lever tip** for each size tuning pin. To begin, order #2 and #3 tips, and short and medium length heads. Use the tip that fits the best on your piano. Ideally, the tip should fit over the pin snugly when the end of the tip almost touches the coil of wire on the pin. If the tip won't go on the pin far enough, use a larger tip; if the end of the tip touches the music wire coil, use a smaller tip. If you progress into professional tuning, purchase as many tips and heads as necessary so you don't have to change tips frequently. It is easier to change the head on the lever than to change the tip on the head.

The **impact hammer** is a tuning lever that has a little slack between the handle and tip. With the tip firmly placed on the tuning pin, you can bump the pin in small increments by wagging the handle, instead of turning it smoothly as you do a tuning lever. Some tuners prefer an impact hammer, but you should learn to tune with a regular tuning lever first.

The best tuning fork is a plated steel one. Large aluminum forks and bars look impressive, but a steel fork is better because it remains more stable when the temperature changes. Obtain an A-440 fork for all conventional tuning. If you plan to tune orchestrions containing organ pipes, xylophones, or bells tuned to A-435, get an A-435 fork too.

You'll also need a felt temperament strip and some wedge mutes. There are three strings per note in the treble of most pianos. Some tuners favor muting all bichord and trichord unisons throughout the piano at once.

7-2. A tuning fork.

7-3. A felt temperament strip and rubber wedge mutes.

7-4. Mechanical and electric metronomes.

If you choose this method of tuning, you'll need two or three temperament strips. Get a dozen long slender rubber wedge mutes, and a dozen shorter wider ones, for muting strings where a temperament strip is inconvenient to use.

One other tool is handy for learning to judge the speed of beats: a **metronome**. This is a mechanical, electric, or electronic device that is set to tick at a certain speed by adjusting a dial or sliding scale. You can purchase a metronome from a piano supply company or most music stores where musical instruments are sold.

Tuning Exercises

It is very difficult to learn to tune by practicing on a piano that has hammers that click, wobble, and miss some strings, an action that is so badly regulated that the hammers don't have enough power to produce good solid tones, strings so rusty that they break, single strings that produce beats, tuning pins that jump or are so loose that they don't stay in place, and so forth. Repair any such defects before attempting to learn to tune.

If you haven't had any previous musical experience, or if you're unsure of what a beat sounds like, obtain and study one of the good videotapes on tuning. (See the Appendix.) You might also find it helpful to locate a good piano tuner and have your piano tuned professionally. Watch your tuner's posture and grip on the tuning lever. Listen very carefully. When the tuning is complete, you might not understand everything the tuner did, but your piano should be in tune, giving you an example of what it should sound like.

Using the Tuning Lever

The first skill to learn is the correct use of the tuning lever. Above all, you must learn the feel of applying the right amount of force to the lever. Without this feel, it will be impossible for you to control the way the pins turn and make them stay in the right position. Unless a piano is drastically out of tune, you will move the lever only a tiny amount at a time, so learning this feel is very important. Using the most rigid lever possible and the right size tip for the best fit on the tuning pin is a big help.

Steel (of which tuning pins are made) is a very elastic material. Though the pins are embedded as deep as $1^1/4"$ in the pinblock and have some support from the plate bushings, they can bend enough to affect the pitch of a string, and the torsion (which could be termed "internal wind-up") can also affect the pitch. You must learn to *rotate* the pin, feeling the amount of twisting and bending as you manipulate the lever. Any twisting or bending is only temporary, and a string that you tune by flexing the pin will go out of tune as soon as the pin springs back to its natural position. Because of the tight grip of the pinblock and the slight flexing of the pins, you must first turn each pin a little too far and then ease it back to the position where it will stay. Tuners call this procedure **setting the pins**.

Visualize an extra long tuning pin coming out the bottom of the pinblock in a hypothetical grand piano, and imagine a pointer extending out perpendicular from the bottom of the pin. As you begin twisting the top of the pin with your tuning lever, at first the pointer doesn't move. As you apply more force to the lever, the whole pin finally rotates, and the pointer moves. When you release the tuning lever, the top of the pin springs back a little, but the pointer stays put. This has actually been demonstrated at a Piano Technicians' Guild convention, proving the importance of setting the pins when tuning.

You must also learn how to set the same amount of tension along the entire length of the string. Each string passes from the tuning pin across several bearing points. There is friction at each bearing point. As you raise the pitch of a string, you add tension to one end. Imagine stretching a rubber band over a small box and pulling on one end. That end has much more tension than the center section, because of the friction at the bearing point at the edge of the box. The friction in the rubber band example is greatly exaggerated, but the same effect does occur to a lesser extent in a piano. If you raise the pitch of a string by turning the tuning pin in a single motion, the string segment nearest the tuning pin will have more tension than the speaking segment. When you play the string loudly, the hammer blow will equalize the tension a little, causing the string to go sharp. Conversely, if you lower the string tension by turning the pin in one motion, the segment nearest the tuning pin will have less tension, and the string will go flat. Therefore, you must play each note loudly during each movement of the lever, to try to equalize the string tension. Tune and play, with increasingly smaller movements of the lever, until the string remains in tune after you play it loudly. Tuners call this procedure **setting the strings**.

The tuning lever tip has a star-shaped hole, although the tuning pins are square. This allows you to place the lever on each pin with the handle pointing in the correct direction, no matter which way the pin is oriented. You will bend the pins the least if you keep the handle of the tuning lever approximately parallel to the strings, extending away from them. As you look at the tuning pins in a vertical piano, orient the lever in a position around one o'clock if you are right handed, or eleven o'clock if you're a lefty. Looking down on the tuning pins while sitting directly in front of a grand, orient the lever somewhere around five o'clock. In these positions, you'll have the least tendency to bend the pins as you tune. In the early stages of learning, try using the lever in several different positions; once you find the most comfortable position for you, stay with it. An exception to this rule is when you replace a broken string or restring a piano. Then, you should place the tuning lever or ratchet wrench at right angles to the string, on the string side of the tuning pin, so you pull against the string tension as you turn the pin.

Good tuning posture is very important. To remain comfortable and at the same time maintain a good grip on the tuning lever, keep your back straight as you tune. Lean into the piano as necessary, but don't slump or round your back. If you are right-handed, you'll push on the lever to raise the pitch in a grand, and pull on it in a vertical. Most tuners favor using the same hand for tuning both types of pianos, even though the motions are opposite.

For best control of the lever, rest your elbow firmly on the pinblock, cabinet, or other convenient part of the piano. With your elbow resting on the piano, your wrist and elbow are the pivot points for your hand. With your elbow hanging in midair, your shoulder is also a pivot point, decreasing control.

In the following exercises, the directions apply to a right-handed tuner tuning a grand, or a lefty tuning a vertical. If you are the opposite, exchange the words "push" and "pull" wherever they occur.

All notes in the following exercises are identified by their key numbers, from low A1 to high C88. If the numbering system is confusing while you are learning to tune, neatly write each key number in pencil near the back of each key. By the time you learn how to tune, you'll know the sequence by memory, and you won't need to refer to the numbers any more.

Tuning Exercise #1

PURPOSE: To gain a feel for the tuning lever, and to learn to hear beats.

Play A above middle C, or A49 and find the three strings for this note. Mute the right string with a wedge mute, leaving the center and left strings unmuted. To do this, insert the mute about halfway between the hammer and the string termination point — the v-bar in a vertical, or the agraffe or capo bar in a grand. In a grand, lift the dampers with the sustaining pedal while inserting the mute to avoid deforming the damper felt. Put the tuning lever on the pin for the left string, in the correct position. Double check to be sure that the lever is on the *unmuted* string. Many strings are broken by beginning tuners who are "tuning" a *muted* string, can't hear any difference in the sound, and keep turning the pin until the string breaks.

Grasp the lever, and play A49 firmly, once every two or three seconds, listening carefully for pulsations in loudness. Gradually pull the lever in a counterclockwise direction, to feel the grip of the pinblock on the pin. With just a little force, you won't rotate the pin, but you will twist it enough to change the sound. Keep playing and listening. As you pull harder, you will turn the pin, and you will hear beats. As you keep turning the and lowering the pitch, the beats will get faster and faster. Finally, the note will be so out of tune that the beats become inaudible as the two strings begin to sound more like two different notes. Now, gradually push the lever clockwise, as slowly as possible, until the strings are almost in tune and you can hear beats again. As you keep pushing on the lever, listen for the beats to get slower and slower until they disappear and the note is in tune. If you make the unison beatless and release your push on the lever, the note will go slightly out of tune again. If the string you are tuning is flat, you have to raise it slowly until it is slightly above beatless, and as you relax your push, the pin will settle back in tune. If the pin is extremely tight, you might have to move the lever back and forth, a little less each time, until the pin is untwisted when the string is in tune.

If you flatten the string, gradually raise it until the tone is beatless, and then keep pushing, it will start to beat again. The beats will increase as you get sharper and sharper. Now the string is too sharp, and you have to lower it to the correct pitch. Detune and tune A49 until you can make it beatless. Remember:

1. Play loudly to settle the string tension.
2. Detune the string to the flat side.
3. Raise the pitch slowly until the string is slightly sharp.
4. Release your push on the lever; pull slightly to set the pin.
5. Don't jerk the lever; always move it smoothly.

After you tune the left string, mute it and practice on the right string, again using the center string for a reference. Don't adjust the center string, which will be your reference pitch until you get through the next few exercises. Practice for no more than fifteen minutes per session at first. You'll learn faster in several short practice sessions than in one long, tiring one. When you can tune the A49 unison accurately, proceed to exercise #2.

Tuning Exercise #2

PURPOSE: *To tune any unison beatless.*

Now that you can tune the A49 unison accurately, practice the same exercise on A37, an octave lower. Then proceed toward the treble, one note at a time. The higher the pitch, the more difficult it is to tune the unisons, for several reasons: it takes a smaller movement of the lever to eliminate beats, the sound fades away faster, and the higher strings have more false beats (this is discussed later in the text). Repeat each note as rapidly as necessary to sustain the tone, up to about twice per second in the highest treble octave. While you practice this exercise, don't adjust any of the center strings of the unisons, as mentioned in exercise #1.

After practicing on treble unisons, start with the G# below middle C and work your way toward the bass. You won't need any mutes for the bichord unisons. Practice detuning and tuning the left string of each bichord unison, leaving the right strings alone. Don't try to tune the monochord (single string) unisons yet.

Tuning Exercise #3

PURPOSE: *To learn to tune octaves.*

As stated earlier, the octave (any octave) is the most pure sounding interval in the piano. It is also the easiest interval to tune. Tune each unison in the temperament octave beatless. Leave the center strings of each unison in the temperament octave alone for now, tuning the outside strings only.

Mute off the two outside strings for F45 (F above middle C), then play F33 (F below middle C) and F45 simultaneously. Flatten the upper note, listen for beats, and raise it gradually into tune. Set the pin by raising the string slightly above pitch and easing it back down into tune. When you can tune the F33-F45 octave beatless, continue tuning octaves up to the top of the piano, and then from E32-E44 to the bottom.

As you go progressively higher, the octaves become harder to tune. Sometimes, it might be helpful to play the new note a fraction of a second after playing the reference note. Turning your head at a different angle sometimes helps too. If you can tune the high unisons beatless, you'll learn to tune the high octaves beatless with some practice. High treble tuning is discussed in greater detail later in this chapter.

In the bass, each octave has two or more prominent beats of different speeds that occur simultaneously. If you eliminate one beat, the other is offensive, so the place to tune the string is between these two points. Both beats should be slow, but neither is as bad as it would be if you eliminated the other. Tuning the bass is also discussed in greater detail later in the chapter.

By this time, you should be able to hear beats, tune unisons beatless, and tune octaves to sound good, at least in the middle of the piano. Your next challenge will be to learn to judge the speed of beats. All intervals within the temperament octave beat, but none should beat so fast as to be objectionable. To set the temperament, you must learn to judge the speed of beats and tune certain intervals to their correct beat rates.

Tuning Exercise #4

PURPOSE: *To learn to judge the speed of beats.*

Beat rate is measured in **beats per second (bps)**. To tune the temperament accurately, you must learn to recognize certain beat rates. There are several different meth-ods of setting the temperament, each requiring you to memorize different beat rates for your "foundation" intervals. The first method described below requires you to memorize seven, eight, and nine beats per second.

Set your metronome on 105 MM (MM is the standard designation of ticks per minute used in all metronomes) and count four beats per tick of the metronome (105 x 4 = 420 beats per minute, or 7 bps). Stop the metronome, try to keep the beat going in your head, and then turn it on again to check yourself. Practice this until you have a good mental idea of what 7 bps is. For a test, have a helper adjust a metronome without your looking at it, until you think it is set at 105. When you can do this accurately, proceed.

To practice recognizing 8 bps, set the metronome on 120, and count four beats per tick. If you've ever played in a marching band, you should have some idea of 120 "march tempo," and this should help you.

To learn 9 bps, set the metronome on 136 and count four beats per tick.

For your "final exam," have your helper set the metronome to the three different beat rates at random to see how accurately you can identify them. It isn't really cheating to look at your digital watch to identify 120 (60 x 2).

Tuning Exercise #5

PURPOSE: *To learn to tune A49 (A440) to the tuning fork.*

It is difficult to tune A49 directly to the fork, but once you're adept at hearing and matching beat rates, it is simple to compare the fork to another note — one that beats against it — and then to tune A49 to that note at the same beat rate. The comparison note is F21. It doesn't matter if F21 is in tune, as long as it is close enough to produce a usable beat rate. If you have successfully completed the above exercises, you may now practice on the center strings of the unisons, which you were supposed to leave alone for reference until now.

Mute off the two outside strings of A49. Hold the fork by the handle, tap one tine against your knee, and hold the end of the handle on the keybed. Play F21, and listen to the beats. Then play F21 and A49 simultaneously, and tune the center string of A49 to beat at the same rate the fork did. With practice, you should be able to duplicate the beat rate, for an accurate A440.

Tuning Exercise #6

PURPOSE: *To learn to set three important temperament intervals to beat at the correct speeds.*

Fold the last half inch (or about 1.5 cm.) of your felt temperament strip over, and push it between the E32 and F33 unisons, with the folded end facing the bass. Insert it about halfway between the hammer and v-bar (vertical), agraffe, or capo bar (grand). Form a small loop and another fold, and push the next fold between F33 and F#34. Continue looping, folding, and inserting until you've muted off all outside strings from F33 to A49, leaving all center strings unmuted. In a grand, lift the dampers with the sustaining pedal as you insert the felt, so you don't harm the soft damper felt by squeezing it as you deflect the strings.

In this exercise, you'll learn to tune three very important temperament intervals: F-A (approx. 7 bps), F-D (approx. 8 bps.), and Bb-D (approx 9 bps.). Using A37 as your reference pitch, tune F33 to it so it is beatless. Then gradually *flatten* F33, listen for beats, and adjust the pitch so the interval beats at 7 bps. Check the beat rate against your metronome, and correct the tuning as necessary. When you can reliably tune this major

third, go to the next interval.

Using F33 as your new reference pitch, tune D42 to it so it is beatless. Then gradually *sharpen* D42, listen for beats, and adjust the pitch so the interval beats at 8 bps. Check, make corrections, and practice until you can tune it correctly. While tuning, compare this major sixth to the F33-A37 major third, to make sure the sixth beats faster than the third.

Using D42 as your new reference pitch, tune A#38 to it beatless. Then gradually *flatten* A#38, listen for beats, and adjust the pitch so this interval beats at 9 bps. Check, correct, and practice. Compare all three intervals to hear that each beats faster than the previous one.

Two of the above examples are major thirds, and the other is a major sixth. How did you tune them? You *widened* all three of them, by flattening the lower note of F-A, sharpening the upper note of F-D, and flattening the lower note of A#-D. This follows the rule explained on p. 214 that all thirds, fourths, and sixths are a little wide of beatless, and all fifths are a little narrow.

When you can accurately tune these three intervals and hear that they beat at approximately 7, 8, and 9 bps, respectively, you are ready to learn to tune the temperament.

Tuning the Temperament

Through the years, tuners have used variations of two main methods of tuning the temperament. Many older tuners, older tuning texts, and the first edition of this book taught the "fourths and fifths" system of setting a temperament. In that temperament, you tune the slower-beating fourths and fifths to specified beat rates, and check your progress with the faster-beating thirds and sixths. If thirds or sixths don't sound right, you go back and retune the fourths and fifths until everything sounds right.

Since the first edition of this book was published in the mid-1970's, several fine tuning teachers have encouraged the use of a temperament in which you tune and check your progress mainly with the faster-beating thirds and sixths, because these are easier for most beginners to hear. You do not tune the slower fourths and fifths; you only check them as you proceed, to make sure they sound good. The first method described below, the *Defebaugh F-F Temperament,* was taught to the author personally by the late George Defebaugh after the writing of the first edition of this book, and is used here with the permission of his daughter, Lynn Defebaugh Eames. George generously spent much time teaching and promoting his method at Piano Technicians Guild conventions and meetings across the United States for many years, and he deserves credit for helping many technicians to become fine tuners.

The second method described below, the *Potter F-A Temperament,* also uses thirds and sixths, but expands the temperament from an octave to an octave and a third. It was developed and copyrighted by Randy Potter of the Randy Potter School of Piano Technology, and is used here with Randy's permission.

This chapter includes the Defebaugh and Potter temperaments for those interested in trying two different methods. For further instruction, refer to the videotapes available on tuning (see the Appendix).

Before practicing either temperament, strip mute the entire center section of the piano with your felt temperament strip. In the following text, the note that you tune always appears in bold face type.

The "Defebaugh F-F" Temperament

1. Tune A49 to the fork, as in the above tuning exercise #5.

2. Tune A37 to A49 as a slightly wide 4:2 octave. That is, tune A37 so its 4th partial is just a little flat of the 2nd partial of A49. To check the tuning, compare the F33-A37 major third, and the F33-A49 major tenth. It doesn't matter if F33 is exactly in tune yet, if it is close enough to create an audible beat with A37 and A49. F33-A37 should beat about one half bps slower than F33-A49. (In the theoretical temperament described in Chapter 6, it was stated that the octave is the only interval that is tuned beatless. In the present temperament, this tiny amount of extra stretch in the octave won't really hurt the sound of the octave, but will help the other intervals to sound a little smoother.)

3. Tune F33 to A37, about 7 bps flat, as in the above tuning exercise #6.

4. Tune D42 to F33, about 8 bps sharp, as in the above tuning exercise #6. Check A37-D42, which should be no more than 1 bps wide.

5. Tune A#38 to D42, about 9 bps flat, as in the above tuning exercise #6. Test F33-A#38, which should be no more than 1 bps wide.

6. Tune C#41 to A37 (sharp), slightly slower than A#38-D42.

7. Tune G#36 to C#41, less than 1 bps flat.

8. Tune C40 to G#36 (sharp), slightly slower than A37-C#41. Test F33-C40, which should be about ¹/₂ bps narrow.

9. Tune F#34 to A#38 (flat), slightly faster than F33-A37. Test F#34-C#41, which should be about ¹/₂ bps narrow, and slightly faster than F33-C40.

10. Tune D#43 to F#34 (sharp), slightly faster than F33-D42.

11. Tune B39 to D#43 (flat), slightly faster than A#38-D42. Test F#34-B39, which should be no more than 1 bps wide, and slightly faster than F33-A#38.

12. Tune G35 to B39 (flat), which should fit into the progression between F#34-A#38 and G#36-C40. Test G35-C40, which should be no more than 1 bps wide, and slightly faster than F#34–B39. Test G35-D42, should be about 1/2 bps narrow, and slightly faster than F#34-C#41.

13. Tune E44 to G35 (sharp), slightly faster than F#34-D#43. Test C40-E44, B39-E44, and A37-E44, which should fit into their respective progressions.

14. Tune F45 to G#36 (sharp), slightly faster than G35-E44. Test C#41-F45, C40-F45, A#38-F45, and F33-F45.

Test the entire temperament for smoothness by playing a succession of chromatically ascending (or adjacent) major thirds, then major sixths, then fourths, and then fifths. For each type of interval, the bps should increase smoothly as you go up the scale, although here and there you'll find nonconforming intervals due to inconsistent inharmonicity in the stringing scale.

For a final test, check the "inside thirds and outside sixths." Compare the major third G35-B39 to the major sixth F33-D42. The sixth should beat nearly the same, or a small amount faster, than the third. Move up a half step at a time, and repeat the test, until you check the entire temperament octave. If any intervals stand out, with badly out of tune beat rates, make corrections as necessary.

The "Potter F-A Temperament"

The "Potter F-A Temperament" is reproduced here from Randy Potter's course training manual *A Complete Course for Beginning and Intermediate Students in Piano*

Tuning, Repairing, Regulating, Voicing, Apprentice Training and Business Practices Copyright © 1987-1992, and is used with his permission. For further information, refer to the Appendix.

Symbols and Definitions

Several symbols are used in the "Tune" and "Test" sections of the Temperament below, to make it easier to read and refer to.

Three arrows (<<<) or (>>>), in the "Tune" section, are used to tell which note to tune from which note. The arrows point *to* the note being tuned.

The abbreviation bps stands for "beats per second."

The "equal" sign (=) in the "Test" section, means that the intervals on either side are equal, that they beat at the same beat rate. An example of this is in Step 1, where the A fork is compared to the F21 (a 17th interval below), then the A49 note you tuned is compared to the same F21. If the A49 was properly tuned, the two intervals will have the exact same beat speed.

The "less than" sign (<) means the beat speed of the interval to the left of the sign is *slower* than the interval on the right. The "greater than" sign (>) means the interval to the left of the sign beats *faster* than the interval on the right.

The "equal to or less than" sign (≤) means that the beat speed of the interval to the left of the sign is either equal to or less than the interval on the right. We use this with the 3rd-10th test interval for the octave. In step 2, for example, the A37-A49 octave is proved by comparing the F33-A37 3rd beat rate with the F33-A49 10th beat rate. Some tuners say the 3rd and 10th are equal, though most say the 10th should be slightly faster than the 3rd. (Slightly faster means perhaps .25 bps fast to .50 bps faster.) At any rate, because of varying rates of inharmonicity between one piano and another, this rate will vary from one piano to another.

The term "ladder," as in "ladder of thirds," "ladder of fourths," etc. refers to adjacent, successive, or chromatic intervals played up or down the keyboard (C-E, C#-F, D-F#, etc.).

The term "pivotal" means the same thing as "contiguous" or "stacked" intervals, in which the top note of one interval is the same as the bottom note of the next (C-E, E-G#, G#-C).

Setting the Temperament

1. Tune: A49 (A-440) to a tuning fork.
   Test: F21-A49 = F21-Fork
2. Tune: A37 <<< A49 (Octave)
   Test: F33-A37 ≤ F33-A49 (3rd-10th test)
3. Tune: F33<<< A37 (3rd) (6.9 bps theoretical)
4. Tune: F33 >>> F45 (Octave)
   Test: C#29-F33 ≤ C#29-F45 (3rd-10th test)
5. Tune: A37>>> C#41 (3rd) (8.7 bps, theoretical)
   Test: four pivotal thirds for progression

The F33-A37 beats about 7 bps, the A37-C#41 about 9, the C#41-F45 about 11 and the F49-A49 about 14. These are close approximations, because the actual beat rates will vary from one piano to another. However, the lower F33-A37 will be the slowest interval, at about 7 BPS, and the intervals will increase at a rate of about 4-to-5 going up, meaning that in the space of time it takes the F33-A37 to beat four beats the A37-C#41 will beat five times. The A37-C#41, then, has the same 4-to-5 ratio to the C#41-F45, and so on. While tuning we constantly compare one interval to another, listening for the sense of the beats, the feel of the beat speed.

Pivotal Tones Set

You now have your four pivotal thirds set: F-A, A-C#, C#-F and F-A. Notes on pivotal tones follow the end of this temperament.

6. Tune: F33 >>> D42 (6th) (8 bps, theoretical)
   Test: F33-A37 (3rd, 7 bps) < F33-D42 (6th, 8 bps) < A37-C#41 (3rd, 9 bps)
   Test: A37-D42 (4th) and D42-A49 (5th) are acceptable
7. Tune: A#38 <<< D42 (3rd) (9.2 bps, theoretical)
   Test: Compare to A37-C#41 < A#38-D42
   Test: F33-A#38 (4th) and A#38-F45 (5th) are acceptable
8. Tune: F#34 <<< A#38 (3rd) (7.3 bps, theoretical)
   Test: Compare to F33-A37 (3rd)
9. Tune: F#34 >>> D#43 (6th) (8.4 bps, theoretical)
   Test: Compare to F33-D42 (6th)
   Test: A#38-D#43 (4th) acceptable
10. Tune: B39 <<< D#43 (3rd) (9.8 bps, theoretical)
    Test: Compare ladder of 3rds from A37 up
11. Tune: G35 <<< B39 (3rd) (7.7 bps, theoretical)
    Test: Compare ladder of 3rds from F33 up
    Test: F33-D42 (6th) = G35-B39 (3rd), which is the M6-M3 test (or more fully, the "Major 6th - inside Major 3rd test")
12. Tune: G35>>> E44 (6th) (8.9 bps, theoretical)

Test: Ladder of F33-D42, F#34-
      D#43, G35-E44 (6ths)

Test: B39-E44 (4th) is acceptable
      (1.1 bps, theoretical)

Test: E44-A49 (4th is acceptable)

13. Tune C40 <<< E44 (3rd) (10.4 bps,
    theoretical)

Test: F33-C40 (5th) and C40-F45
      (4th) are acceptable

Test: A37-C#41/C40-E44 progres-
      sion is smooth

14. Tune G#36 <<< C40 (3rd) (8.2 bps,
    theoretical)

Test: G#36-C#41 (4th is acceptable)
      (.9 BPS, theoretical)

Test: Ladder of 3rds

Test: Ladder of 6ths

Test: Ladder of M6-M3 tests

Test: Ladder of 4ths

Test: Ladder of 5ths

The final three steps extend the temperament from F33 to A49.

15. Tune A37 >>> F#46 (6th)

Test: M6th-M3rd test

Test: Ladder of 3rds

Test: Listen to ladder of 4ths

Test: Listen to ladder of 5ths

Test: 3rd-10th test

16. Tune: A#38 >>> G47 (6th)

Test: M6th-M3rd test

Test: Ladder of 3rds

Test: Listen to ladder of 4ths

Test: Listen to ladder of 5ths

Test: 3rd-10th test

17. Tune B39 >>> G#48 (6th)

Test: M6th-M3rd test

Test: Ladder of 3rds

Test: Listen to ladder of 4ths

Test: Listen to ladder of 5ths

Test: 3rd-10th test

Notes on tests

There are many tests given here, mostly for reference. It is not expected that you will use every test for every interval every time. George Defebaugh used to say, "If you are not careful, you can test yourself right out of business. You can spend all day tuning one piano if you do every test. Pick a couple tests for each interval that work for you and use them."

Notes About Setting Pivotal Thirds (Steps 1-5)

For any successful temperament system, we must have a basis, or foundation. At any time during the tuning we must be able to return to that foundation as a "check" to see that we are on track. If our foundation is one note, such as the A49 tuning fork, we can check that note for accuracy, but may have a little more difficulty verifying the remaining notes that follow. By making our foundation the five notes that comprise our four "pivotal thirds," we have a broader foundation against which to check all other notes.

Using this system of pivotal thirds, we can check our A49 against our fork, then the notes in steps two through five using the tests listed above, in about 20 seconds — at any time during our tuning of the temperament. If these notes have held, meaning the aural tests (or checks) prove they are still where they are supposed to be (in short, the lower F33-A37 third will be the slowest, at about 7 bps, with each third beating at a progressively faster rate and the upper F45-A49 third beating the fastest, at about 14 bps), then we can immediately verify that any discrepancy in our temperament is with the subsequent notes. With a proper understanding of aural checks it then becomes a fairly quick and easy process to identify which note(s) are correct and which note(s) need to be corrected.

Notes on Extending the Temperament to a 10th (Steps 15-17)

Most temperaments are one octave wide, usually from A-A, F-F or C-C. I have chosen to make my temperament a tenth. It allows the use of four pivotal thirds, rather than only three, which allows the tuner to more accurately account for the inharmonicity present in the particular piano being tuned.

The final three notes, F#46, G47 and G#48, are tuned as sixths, though they could be tuned as octaves as well. I tune them as sixths, because it helps carry the feeling of temperament into the tuning, whereas octave tuning is more the duplication of the lower part of the temperament (F#34, G35 and G#36) into these upper notes. It also allows the tuner to continue to use one hand on the keyboard for the main checks, that of M6-M3 and ladders of 3rds, 4ths and 5ths. Finally, one can use the 3rd-10th test, which requires removal of the tuning hand from the tuning hammer. Only steps 2 and 4, the tuning of the A37-A49 and F33-F45 octaves, require two-hand checks. All other steps require only one hand, the playing hand, for checks and tests, allowing the tuning hand to remain on the tuning hammer — which speeds up tuning time. (This concludes the information by Randy Potter.)

Finishing the Midrange of the Piano

After tuning the center string of each temperament note, tune the rest of the center strings in the midrange section of the piano by octaves. First, tune the strings toward the treble, up to the treble break, and then tune from the temperament down to the low end of the treble bridge. Test by playing a succession of major tenths up and down the scale, adjusting the tuning to smooth the progression of beat rates as necessary. When you're happy with the tuning of the center strings in the midrange of the piano, remove the temperament strip one string at a time, starting at the bass end of the midrange. Tune the left string to the center one, unmute the right string, and tune the right string. If you have a hard time tuning the third string of a three string unison, temporarily mute the second one with a rubber wedge mute. Always finish by listening to the combined result of the three strings, to avoid leaving the left string a little flat and the right string a little sharp, or vice versa.

Tuning the High Treble

After you finish tuning the midrange section, either strip mute the treble with a narrow temperament strip, or insert rubber wedge mutes, one note at a time, leaving the center string unmuted. As you progress into the high treble, it takes less and less movement of the tuning lever to change the pitch. Also, the tone dies out more quickly, making the beats harder to hear. Play each note loudly and repeat it rapidly enough to prevent the tone from dying away. If you're uncertain about whether a treble string is in tune, detune it slightly to the flat side until it is obviously flat. Then slowly raise it up to pitch again, without going too far. Repeated practice should improve your skill. If you get lost when tuning the highest treble notes, try plucking the string, to help distinguish the pitch.

For fine tuning, test each note against the major tenth, double octave, and seventeenth. When you tune the treble to produce beatless octaves, the double octaves will sound a little flat. If you stretch the octaves too much, the double octaves will beat. The correct amount of stretch is somewhere between these two points, verified by a smooth succession of major tenths and seventeenths.

In many pianos, it is awkward or impossible to mute the outside strings of the unisons on either side of the treble break, where the plate strut passes between the midrange and high treble sections. If this is the case, mute the unison immediately to the left of the strut by inserting a thin wedge mute between the left and center strings, and tune the right string first. Then remove the mute, insert it between the left string and the next unison to the left, and tune the center string to the right string. Then remove the mute and tune the left string. Use this procedure in reverse for tuning the unison immediately to the right of the plate strut. In many pianos, especially in those with a large notch in the bridge for the plate strut, the notes immediately surrounding the treble break are the least stable because the soundboard and bridge are more flexible in this area. After you tune six or eight notes above the break, check the tuning of the two or three notes on either side of the break. Retune them if they have changed.

Tuning the Bass

The upper partials of low bass strings correspond to the fundamentals of notes near the middle of the keyboard. These partials are loud enough that you can hear them easily when you play a bass note with the corresponding higher notes. Because the partials are not "equally tempered," bass strings produce prominent beats when played with certain other notes. For example, compare the theoretical partial series of

Theoretical partial series of C16		Name of note whose fundamental pitch is closest to harmonic of C16	Theoretical frequency of fundamental pitch of note in column 2
6th Partial	392.436	G47	391.995
5th Partial	327.030	E44	329.628
4th Partial	261.624	C40	same
3rd Partial	196.218	G35	195.998
2nd Partial	130.812	C28	same
Fundamental	65.406	—	—

7-5. A comparison of the partial series of C16 to various other notes. See text for explanation.

C16 with corresponding higher notes on the keyboard (see illust. 7-5).

Although the octave, double octave, etc. are theoretically in tune with the equally tempered scale, the other partials are far from it. Therefore, when you play C16 simultaneously with any of these other notes, you will hear a very distinct beat. But, if you tune C16 beatless to any of these notes, the other intervals become very offensive.

Because each bass string has several prominent partials that have different beat rates from those of their corresponding pitches in the scale, you must tune each bass note to compromise these beat rates, so that no interval sounds more offensive than the others. As you descended toward the bass end of the treble bridge while tuning the low end of the midrange, you tested the tuning with the major tenth test interval. As you continue to tune lower into the bass, test each note with the fifth, major tenth, and seventeenth. When these tests get too muddy, use the seventeenth, which is two octaves and a third. In the lowest octave, test each note against two octaves and a third, and two octaves and a fifth, always tuning for a smooth progression of beats as you play up

Note Being Tuned	Comparison Chord Notes						
C28	G35	C40	E44				
B27	F#34	B39	D#43				
A#26	F33	A#38	D42				
A25	E32	A37	C#41				
G#24	D#31	G#36	C40				
G23	D30	G35	B39				
F#22	C#29	F#34	A#38				
F21	C28	F33	A37,	also	C40	F45	A49
E20	B27	E32	G#36,	also	B39	E44	G#48
D#19	A#26	D#31	G35,	also	A#38	D#43	G47
D18	A25	D30	F#34,	also	A37	D42	F#46
C#17	G#24	C#29	F33,	also	G#36	C#41	F45
C16	G23	C28	E32,	also	G35	C40	E44
B15					F#34	B39	D#43
A#14					F33	A#38	D42
A13				E32	A37	C#41	
G#12			D#31	G#36	C40		
G11		D30	G35	B39			
F#10	C#29	F#34	A#38				
F9	C28	F33	A37,	also	C40	F45	A49
E8	B27	E32	G#36,	also	B39	E44	G#48
D#7	A#26	D#31	G35,	also	A#38	D#43	G47
D6	A25	D30	F#34,	also	A37	D42	F#46
C#5	G#24	C#29	F33,	also	G#36	C#41	F45
C4	G23	C28	E32,	also	G35	C40	E44
B3	F#22	B27	D#31,	also	F#34	B39	D#43
A#2	F21	A#26	D30,	also	F33	A#38	D42
A1	E20	A25	C#29,	also	E32	A37	C#41

7-6. Helpful bass tuning chords. Experiment with other inversions in different octaves, to see what tests help you the most for tuning various pianos.

and down the scale in these intervals.

You also will find **major chords** to be useful for testing the accuracy of bass notes. A **chord** is any combination of three or more notes played simultaneously. A major chord consists of a note and the major third and fifth above that note, in any combination of octaves. For example, C-E-G, C-G-E, C-C-G-E, C-G-E-C-E and any other combination of these three pitches played in different octaves, are all C major chords. To test the smoothness of the bass tuning, use the sequence of descending major chords listed in illustration 7-6. As you go down the scale, you will get to a point where the chords become too muddy and have many nearly-coincident partials, making it hard to hear the correct tuning of the bass note. At that point, play the chord an octave higher, as listed in the illustration. This chart spells all chords with **tuners' sharps** instead of using the musically correct enharmonic sharps and flats.

The longer the bass strings are, the easier they are to tune. It would be helpful if every beginning tuner could learn to tune by practicing on a concert grand piano. Small spinets with short bass strings are the hardest to tune in that register.

Raising the Pitch

Many pianos that go untuned for a long time go flat by a quarter step, half step, or even more. Some tuners leave these pianos at the low pitch, tuning the temperament, unisons, and octaves to A-420 or whatever it happened to be. A piano with its string tension too low sounds dull and lifeless, and lacks brilliance. It is impossible to play with other instruments, and it hampers the musical progress of any student who regularly practices on it. To tune a piano to the wrong pitch is hardly better than not tuning it at all.

The following is one of the most important sections in the entire book. If you pay attention to the following principles, every tuning that you ever do will be easier, less frustrating, and will take less time.

1. When you raise the pitch of a piano, you add tension to the strings.

2. When you add tension to the strings, they push harder on the bridges, forcing the soundboard down a little. They also pull harder on the plate and frame, flexing them a little.

3. When the strings push the soundboard down and flex the plate as you raise the tension, other strings go out of tune a little.

4. Therefore, when you raise the pitch, *you throw the rest of the piano out of tune.*

If a piano is flat and you tune it to A-440, raising the pitch as you go, when you're done most of the piano will be flat again. Many tuners think the piano must undergo a "settling period," and use this as an excuse to come back in several weeks for another tuning. Often, the same thing happens, to a lesser extent, during the second tuning, supposedly requiring another settling period and a third tuning.

Actually, this effect occurs *during tuning*, and the results are immediate. Any violinist knows that adding tension to one string immediately causes the pitch of the other three to fall, as the body of the violin responds to the change of tension. Before you fine tune a piano or set the temperament, check the pitch. If the whole piano is flat, or if any part of it is flat, raise the pitch with one or more fast rough tunings. *If you fail to do this, you will waste the time you spend on a fine tuning as the piano continues to go flat while you tune it.*

If the strings are rusty, let each string down a little until you hear a "tick," before pulling it up to pitch. This will break the bond of rust between the string and the termination point. Set your temperament very quickly, without taking the time to make it accurate, so each note is approximately the right pitch. Then roughly tune the piano, following your usual sequence, but spending no more than twenty minutes to finish the whole job. Until you have a lot of experience, don't raise the pitch higher than A-440.

When you're done, the piano will be flat again, but not as flat as it was. Give it another rough tuning, and another if necessary, until you can go through the whole piano without having the pitch fall again. Only then should you fine tune the piano. Even if it needs two or three rough pitch raises before you can fine tune it, you'll

231

spend much less time doing this than you will if you give it two or three fine tunings. Your results will be just as good, even when you learn to complete the job in a few hours.

In a piano with a good pinblock and strings, you can raise the pitch a little higher than A-440 without damaging the strings. If the whole piano is about 50 cents (or 50/100 of a half step) flat, and you rough tune the temperament 20 or 25 cents sharp to compensate for this during your first pitch raising, the midrange will fall approximately back to A-440 by the time you finish raising the pitch, saving you an extra pitch raising. *Note: If a piano has rusty strings, don't raise the pitch above A-440.*

With extensive tuning experience, you'll learn how high to raise the pitch above A-440 in each section of the piano during the first pitch raise, and how far various types of pianos will fall during the pitch raise, depending on how flat they were before you started. Having a good understanding of pitch raising and observing how various pianos react will help you to become a much more efficient tuner.

Before raising the pitch of an old piano, always make sure the bass bridge is still glued to the apron, and the pinblock in a vertical is still glued to the back structure. If the bass bridge or pinblock is coming apart, you can't tune the piano until you repair it.

Lowering the Pitch

If a piano is sharp and you tune it to A-440, lowering the pitch as you go, most of the piano will be sharp again when you're done. This is exactly the opposite of what happens during pitch raising. Before attempting to fine tune a piano that is sharp, lower the pitch until the tuning is close enough to A-440 so it won't change again during fine tuning. Set the temperament about half as far

below A-440 as it was *above* (for example, if it was 50 cents sharp, set it about 25 cents flat). Taper off the amount of flatness toward the treble end, and tune the last half of the highest treble octave to the correct pitch. Tune the bass just a little flat, again tapering off the amount of flatness as you finish the low bass. When you finish lowering the pitch once, the piano should be close enough to A-440 to be fine tuned in one tuning. As in pitch raising, extensive tuning experience will help you to know just how flat to tune each section of each type of piano, depending on how sharp it is to begin with.

Tuning Problems

If all pianos were theoretically perfect, and followed the acoustical laws, tuning would be much easier than it really is. Unfortunately, very few pianos come close to acoustical perfection, and most of them have various faults that cause problems for the tuner. Some problems are inherent and can't easily be corrected; others develop with age or environmental abuse, and are correctable. The following discussion omits obvious mechanical problems like loose tuning pins, wobbly hammers, etc. These are discussed in the chapters on repairing and rebuilding.

False Beats. The false beat is one of the tuner's worst enemies. This is a beat within a single string that you can't eliminate by tuning. A string with a false beat sounds like two strings that are out of tune with each other. False beats occur most commonly in the upper middle register of the piano, from the treble break up to the middle of the top octave.

If either end of the vibrating part of the string doesn't make good contact with its termination point, this will cause false beats. Termination points include the bridge, the capo bar, agraffe, and v-bar. In grand pianos, false beats commonly occur because the strings aren't seated firmly on the bridge. If you find this problem, seat each offending string by gently tapping it down to the bridge, just next to the bridge pin, with a 3/16" brass rod and small hammer. It doesn't take much force to seat the string. If the problem occurs because of lack of down-bearing on the bridge, this cure will be short lived. Many pianos have false beats because the bridge notches aren't aligned with the center line of the bridge pins, as discussed on pp. 114-115. To solve this problem, loosen or remove the strings and reshape the notches. In many grands, the strings form small grooves in the capo bar, causing false beats, buzzing, and ringing noises. To correct this, loosen or remove the strings and reshape the capo bar.

Other causes of false beats include rusty strings, kinked or twisted treble strings, and strings that were stretched too much during stringing, pitch raising, or tuning. If you see a kink or bend in the speaking portion of a string, try to straighten it by burnishing with a steel rod. If this doesn't work, loosen the string and straighten it carefully with smooth pliers. If it still sounds bad, replace it.

The only way to "tune" a string having false beats, is to detune it to the flat side until the real beats become obvious. Then, slowly raise the pitch, concentrating on the real beats and ignoring the false ones, until you have tuned the string as close to beatless as possible. At first, this will be one of the most difficult parts of tuning, but with extensive tuning experience, you'll learn to ignore the false beats and tune the treble just as quickly as the midrange.

Sympathetic Beats. Occasionally you will notice a very soft, confusing beat that isn't in the string that you are tuning. Some-

times during pitch raising, the strings in the high treble that have no dampers resonate with the strings that you are tuning. This problem disappears after you tune the high treble more closely. Sometimes a temperament strip or rubber wedge mute fails to dampen a string completely, allowing it to vibrate sympathetically. If this occurs, insert the mute farther up or down the length of the string. In some pianos, the duplex scale causes beats during tuning. If this happens, stick a strip of drafting tape to the duplex string segments during tuning, or lay a piece of felt across them, and remove it when you're done.

Tuning Instability. You will occasionally encounter a grand piano that has tight tuning pins and is up to pitch, but in which one end goes out of tune as you tune the other end. Repeated tunings make no improvement. This condition can be caused by a loose pinblock. As you change the tension, the pinblock shifts or rocks on a high spot against the plate flange, throwing everything out of tune again. Tightening the plate screws in the pinblock area often helps to correct this problem. In more extreme cases, you may have to glue shims into the space between the pinblock and plate flange, as described on p. 101.

Difficulty in Equalizing String Tension. If you have to move the tuning lever exceptionally far before a string begins to change pitch, and then the pitch suddenly changes too much, the pressure bar might be screwed in too far. This causes too much friction between it and the strings. If the strings are bent at an unusually large angle by the pressure bar, compare it to other similar pianos, and if it is screwed in too far, raise it a little. This will help to equalize the string tension along the entire length of the strings. Don't raise it so high that any of the strings slip sideways. If the pressure bar screws are extremely tight and hard to turn, lower the string tension before adjusting them. Never try to tighten the screws to lower the pressure bar with full string tension on the piano, or you probably will break a screw. In a grand with no means of adjusting the counterbearing, check the shape of the capo bar. If the string termination point is too sharp, lower the string tension enough to push the strings aside, and round the termination point a little with a file. Don't make it too blunt, or there won't be enough friction.

Tuning the Back Duplex Scale

The **duplex scale** is the name given to the non-speaking segments of the strings in some pianos; the **back duplex** refers to the segments between the bridge and hitch pins. While many pianos have this section of each string muted with stringing braid or felt, fine-quality pianos have this section unmuted, so these string segments may ring sympathetically with the speaking portions, adding brilliance to the tone.

According to most piano manufacturers, the duplex scale shouldn't be tuned per-fectly. If it is, certain high treble harmonics can ring excessively. With the duplex scale a little out of tune, these harmonics won't predominate, but the duplex will add just the right amount of brilliance and carrying power to the tone.

The aliquot bars in some pianos have pins that fit into holes in the plate. Other aliquot bars are held in place only by the string tension. When you restring a piano, mark the locations of the aliquot bars or plates and put them back in the same places, as described in Chapter 8. If you believe that they are in the wrong places, contact the manufacturer or a fine piano rebuilding shop for consultation regarding where they belong.

Tuning the Mason & Hamlin Screw Stringer Piano

Many, if not all, screw stringer pianos had a little pouch or compartment built in to hold the special tuning wrench. If the original wrench is missing, obtain one from a piano supply company. Tuning a screw stringer is no more difficult than tuning an ordinary piano, but the feel is different

7-7. Tuning a Mason & Hamlin duplex scale aliquot bar by gentle tapping. A small dowel or 3/16" diameter brass rod is better than a screwdriver for this purpose because it won't scratch the aliquot bar or damage the plating.

because there are no tuning pins to bend back a little when you release them. In the author's experience, it is easier to bring a string up to the desired pitch by tightening the tuning nut than to lower it accurately, so you might find it desirable to lower each string a little and then bring it up to pitch.

If the screw stringer guide combs are cracked or broken, preventing the piano from being tuned, try to find a machinist who can make new ones. This is neither an easy nor an inexpensive task, because of the curved shapes involved.

Tuning Two Pianos Together

If all pianos were acoustically perfect, any two pianos tuned to A-440 would be perfectly in tune with each other. Because of string stiffness, though, a piano with short strings has different inharmonicity than a piano with longer strings. This means if you carefully tune both a spinet and a concert grand to A-440, all notes except A-440 will be out of tune between the two pianos. Therefore, it is impossible for two pianos of different stringing scales to be in tune with themselves and each other simultaneously.

When two pianos are used in concert together, they should be of identical stringing scale (i.e., identical brand and model).

Tune each piano separately. Then, with the help of an assistant, compare the two pianos one note at a time, correcting any discrepancies.

When two "identical" pianos can't be obtained, use two pianos having stringing scales as close to each other as possible. Tune each piano separately; do not make one piano out of tune with itself to make it more in tune with the other.

Tuning a Piano to an Organ

Pipe organs change pitch drastically with changes in temperature and humidity. This is because warmer or damper air is thinner and vibrates faster in the organ pipes, producing a higher pitch. The pitch of some electronic organ circuits also changes with temperature or humidity variations. Therefore, it is essential that the temperature in the room, and in pipe organ chambers, be the same as it will be during the performance. Select an 8' diapason stop on the organ. Make sure you don't use a stop marked "celeste," and make sure all tremolo or vibrato effects are turned off. Use A-440 for comparison, and then tune the piano to itself in the usual way. Don't try to tune a piano to an organ one note at a time; this will result in the piano being out of tune with itself.

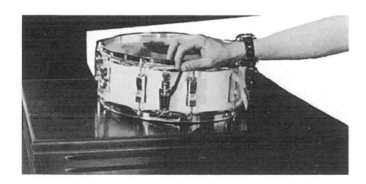

7-8. Releasing a snare.

Tuning a Piano on a Bandstand

If a snare drum is near a piano, the snares will vibrate sympathetically when you play the piano, causing an annoying buzzing sound and making it difficult to tune the piano. Most snare drums have a lever to release the snare moving it away from its head, which eliminates sympathetic vibration.

Tuning Victorian Pianos

Most American pianos made between the late 1800's and the early 1920's were designed to be tuned to the old A-435 pitch standard. Tune a Victorian or early-twentieth-century piano having a three-quarter plate to A-435 (from an A-435 fork), to avoid possible damage. Tune the temperament as usual; the beat rates will be very slightly slower than in the A-440 temperament. If you use an electronic tuning device, calibrate it 20 cents flat (A-435 is 20 cents flat of A-440).

If an old piano is heavily constructed, with heavy wooden bracing and a full iron plate, and is in good condition, you probably can successfully tune it to A-440. If you break a string in the temperament octave — an area where strings rarely break — be aware that you might not be able to raise the pitch to A-440.

Some Victorian grands have oblong tuning pins that require a special tuning lever tip or adapter. Obtain one from a piano supply company.

Electronic Tuning Devices

Several types of electronic tuning devices are now available to help make the tuner's job easier. Each converts musical tone into a visual pattern. All electronic tuners have several features in common: a control for setting the tuner to the desired pitch, a microphone — built-in or external — and a display that shows whether the pitch is sharp, flat, or in tune. The visual displays incorporated into the best known brands of tuners include stroboscope discs (Peterson and Conn) and circular or straight-line patterns of lights or LED's (Sight-O-Tuner and Sanderson Accu-Tuner, and the Yamaha PT-100, respectively). When the note is out of tune, the visual display moves in one direction or the other. When the note is in tune, the indicator stands still.

If pianos were acoustically perfect, it would be simple to calibrate the tuner to A-440, tune each note on the piano to the tuner, and finish with a perfectly tuned piano. Because of inharmonicity, however, the intervals must be stretched as explained earlier in this chapter, with the treble notes sharp of their theoretical pitches and the bass notes flat. If you tune a piano to an electronic tuner without compensating for inharmonicity, the treble will be flat and the bass will be sharp, with the other intervals somewhat compressed as well. Therefore, it is necessary to find the amount of inharmonicity of each note and compensate for it when you use an electronic tuner. Many beginning technicians try to use electronic tuners as shortcuts to good tuning, without understanding inharmonicity. The poor results thus produced have lead some piano owners and professional tuners to the false belief that it is impossible to tune a piano correctly with an electronic tuner. It is possible to tune a piano with an electronic tuner, *if you follow the proper procedure.* The electronic tuner is also a valuable learning tool, as long as you don't let it become a crutch.

To tune a piano competently with an electronic tuner, you must be able to tune any unison beatless. You also must have the same dexterity with the tuning lever as you would need if you were tuning by ear, to set the pins and set the strings so the piano will remain in tune for a reasonable length of time.

Adjusting the tuner to compensate for inharmonicity involves measuring certain partials of each string, and adjusting the calibration of the tuner accordingly. There's nothing particularly difficult about doing this, but it does involve a lengthy process of recalibration throughout the tuning. In each step of the tuning process described earlier in this chapter, recalibrate the tuner to accommodate the inharmonicity of the significant coincident partial for the interval that you are tuning.

The following is a simplified electronic tuning method that will produce acceptable results for most people, although a fine "ear tuning" is a little cleaner. Calibrate the tuner to A-440 if necessary. Strip mute the center section of the piano. Set the tuner on F or F33, tune F33 beatless to the tuner, and then measure the second partial. Divide the amount of stretch of that partial by twelve, and sharpen each successively higher note in the temperament by that amount by recalibrating the tuner for each note. This will divide the inharmonicity of the F33 fundamental-second partial among all the notes of the temperament. It won't be perfect for a scale with inharmonicity that changes substantially from one note to the next, but it will help you tune a temperament that sounds better than if you don't recalibrate at all.

To tune the treble above the temperament section, proceed as follows: Set the tuner to F#46 (or watch the appropriate band on the disc of a stroboscopic tuner) and play F#34. You are now reading the inharmonicity of the second partial of F#34. Recalibrate the tuner so this partial registers *in tune*. Then tune F#46 to the tuner. The fundamental of the upper F is now in tune with the second partial of the lower F, and the octave is beatless. This procedure appears lengthy on paper, but once you memorize the routine, it doesn't take long. Follow the same procedure for every note in the treble of the piano, calibrating the tuner to compensate for the inharmonicity of the lower note, and then recalibrating it for each next pitch. For a more clear sounding treble, test with other intervals like the major tenth, double octave, and seventeenth, as in aural tuning.

To tune the bass, use the opposite calibrating procedure. The first note below the temperament octave to be tuned is E32. Calibrate the tuner so it is in tune with the fundamental of E44. Then play E32 and read its second partial on the tuner. The second partial of E32 is the same pitch as the fundamental of E44. Tune E32 so the second partial is in tune. The fundamental is then stretched properly. To tune the next note, D#31, recalibrate the tuner so it is in tune with the fundamental of D#43, and repeat the procedure. As you go lower, test with the other intervals discussed in the above text on tuning the bass by ear.

It would be impossible to include here a perpetually updated review of new electronic tuners, but a few comments on those in production at the time this is written will give you an idea of several important types on the market. Regretfully, the author can't provide current advice on purchasing an electronic tuner. For more help, refer to the service manuals for the electronic tuners, attend Piano Technicians Guild meetings, subscribe to the *Journal*, and discuss this with other technicians.

The Peterson and Conn devices feature a stroboscopic disc with several bands that show the tuning of several partials at once. This makes it easier for you to see the inharmonicity of the string than in a tuner in which you must reset the controls to see each partial individually. If you learn to raise the pitch of a piano without using mutes, the strobe wheel helps you to see both the pitch of the string you are tuning and the pitch of the untuned strings of that unison simultaneously, something the rotating light tuners don't do very well. A more expensive model of the Peterson also has a tone generator that some technicians find useful for tuning organ pipes.

The Yamaha PT-100 has a straight-line display of little bars that move to the left or right if the pitch is flat or sharp. It has the advantage that it displays any note, from low bass to high treble, with the same easily read pattern. By comparison, the strobe disc tuners show high notes with very narrow, closely spaced bars, and bass notes with broad, widely separated bars. The PT-100 has 24 individual pre-programmed tunings built in. Eight are in equal temperament, eight in Mean Tone and eight in Werckmeister III, for assisting in tuning a variety of modern and historic temperaments.

The Sanderson Accu-Tuner (S.A.T.) has the most capabilities of any tuning device made at the time this is being written. Its display consists of a circular pattern of LED's. It contains a computer that measures inharmonicity and adjusts the temperament accordingly. It has the capability of "listening" to any piano — for example, a piano that you have just tuned by ear — one note at a time, and committing the tuning of each note to a self-contained memory. You can use that memory to tune the piano by using the visual display next time, making the job easier on your ears. You also can purchase stock tunings for the memory, based on fine tunings of specific models of pianos. After tuning a piano and playing the tuning into the S.A.T.'s memory, you can unload the tuning into a computer, modify it, load it back into the S.A.T, tune the piano, and hear what it sounds like. At this time, the Piano Technicians Guild uses the S.A.T. to test new applicants, by playing the finest possible ear tuning into the S.A.T.'s memory, and using that memory as a yardstick for measuring the applicant's tuning.

The Hale Sight-O-Tuner has the same type of display as the S.A.T. It is less expensive, has different circuitry, and has fewer computerized memory functions.

Other brands of tuners incorporate a meter with a needle that stays in the middle when the note is in tune, or deflects to one side or the other if the note is flat or sharp. Because of the brief lag in needle response compared to the instant response of other displays, many technicians find this type to be less useful. Inexpensive "pocket" tuners might help you tune organs, guitars, violins, and other string instruments, but most technicians think they are too simple and inaccurate to be useful for fine-quality piano tuning.

Why Does a Piano Go Out of Tune?

As explained throughout this book, piano strings are under a great deal of tension that is supported by the frame, plate, pinblock, tuning pins, bridges, and soundboard. Anything that affects the position of any of these parts will cause a change in tension and make the piano go out of tune.

Humidity Changes. Although a soundboard has a coating of varnish or lacquer, moisture from the air can seep into and out of the wood, mainly through the end grain, causing the crown to increase and diminish. This is the most important factor that causes a good piano with tight tuning pins to go out of tune. A piano goes flat, particularly in the midrange, in the early winter when the dry heat of the furnace draws moisture out of the soundboard, diminishing the crown. It goes sharp again in the spring when you turn the furnace off for the season and moisture from rain enters the soundboard, increasing the crown. This seasonal pitch change is noticeably absent from a piano kept in a climate controlled (temperature *and* humidity controlled) environment.

When the midrange goes sharp, some people listen to octaves in the treble and bass, and think they are flat and try to adjust them accordingly. But what you should do in this situation is to lower the pitch of the midrange to A-440 where it belongs. Don't raise the extremes above A-440 to compensate for the midrange going sharp.

Temperature Changes. Fluctuations in room temperature surrounding a piano cause less of a change in tuning than humidity changes do. However, direct sunlight or heat from stage lights is so intense that it can cause rapid changes in the tuning.

Stretching of the Strings. New music wire has a lot of elasticity, and it begins to stretch as soon as you pull it up to pitch. New strings stretch the most during their first few years in a piano. Because of this stretching, many new pianos sink a quarter step flat within a few months after each tuning, for the first two or three years. Then the stretching decreases, and the pitch remains stable for longer periods of time. Some piano makers and rebuilders stretch their new strings with a small roller immediately after pulling a piano up to pitch. This procedure

helps, but if overdone it is harmful to the strings. The louder and more frequently you play a newly-strung piano, the faster the strings will stretch, and the sooner they will stabilize.

Slipping Tuning Pins. This factor doesn't enter into the tuning of a good quality new piano, in which the pins should be so tight that the string tension doesn't cause them to turn. In an older piano that has been exposed to regular seasonal humidity changes for many years, however, the pinblock loses its tight grip on the pins. When the pins get looser, string tension causes them to rotate slowly, over a period of months, allowing the pitch to go flat.

Playing. The louder and more often you play a piano, the faster it goes out of tune by a small amount. This is due to equalization of tension along the length of the strings. The better you "set the strings" during tuning, the less this happens.

Summary. Every piano is subject to one or more factors that will make it go out of tune, including humidity and temperature changes, stretching of the strings, slipping of the tuning pins, inadequate setting of the pins and strings by the tuner, and hard use. How often should you tune a piano? This depends upon its condition, the environment in which it is located, and the musical demands of the owner. A piano used mainly as a piece of furniture probably won't "need" to be tuned more than once a year. A piano that is played used regularly and is in good condition might get by with being tuned twice a year, each time the seasonal humidity changes. A piano given a daily workout by a professional musician or serious student might need to be tuned monthly or even more frequently.

Improving Your Skills

If you become seriously interested in piano tuning, you'll undoubtedly want to learn to improving your skills and efficiency, so you can work faster without sacrificing quality. Following are some suggestions for accomplishing this.

1. Learn to set the pin and string with as few movements of the tuning lever as possible. Learn to find the correct tuning pin more quickly each time you move your tuning lever.

2. Learn to raise the pitch without using mutes. To do this, you must learn to tune two strings of a trichord unison beatless while the third string vibrates a quarter or half step out of tune. Although difficult at first, you can learn this quickly by raising the pitch of many pianos that are a half step or more flat. An incidental benefit of learning this skill is a vastly improved ability to tune strings with false beats as well as possible in a minimum amount of time.

3. Tune a lot of pianos. There is no better way to improve your tuning efficiency than to tune several different pianos a day, five or six days a week.

4. Learn to read music and to play the piano. Having these skills makes the tuning job more interesting even if it doesn't contribute directly to tuning proficiency. Being able to demonstrate a piano after tuning it will help you to establish a professional image.

5. Join an active chapter of the Piano Technicians Guild (see the Appendix for further information on the Piano Technicians Guild). Read *The Piano Technicians Journal*, attend PTG meetings, seminars, and conventions, and associate with other technicians. The PTG has a great deal to offer tuners, technicians, rebuilders and everyone else interested in helping to elevate the quality of pianos and piano music everywhere.

Chapter Eight

Complete Restoration:
Rebuilding a Piano in the Shop to Perform and Look Like New

Rebuilding a piano means making major repairs to each component to restore the instrument so it sounds, works, and looks as much like new as possible. Typically, in order to accomplish this you will completely disassemble the piano, remove the strings and plate, replace the pinblock (unless it is in unusually fine condition), repair or replace the soundboard and bridges, repair and refinish the cabinet, repaint the plate, replace the strings and tuning pins, replace all felt, cloth, and leather in the keyboard and action, including the hammers and damper felts, and completely regulate everything during reassembly.

When you simply repair a piano, you remove the loose dirt and polish some of the parts as thoroughly as possible without completely disassembling the piano. When you rebuild, you'll go far beyond this, making every part look just like new.

Fine-quality rebuilding requires the use of power tools, and if you expect to become a proficient rebuilder, plan to learn a lot about wood, woodworking, and woodworking tools and their safe use. Besides power tools, you'll need appropriate storage space for cabinet parts, the plate, the action, the keyboard, and rebuilding supplies during the job, which might take you several months' worth of spare time. For basic woodworking information, review the beginning section of Chapter 4. For more advanced in-depth study, read as many books and magazines as you can find on the subject, beginning with those listed in the Bibliography.

Because rebuilding usually requires a large expenditure of time and money, you'll need to weigh several factors carefully before "taking the plunge." How good will the piano be after you rebuild it? Will its market value be more or less than the total rebuilding cost? Does it have sentimental value beyond its actual market value? Do you want to restore a family heirloom to new condition even if it costs more than the instrument will be worth, or do you want to keep the piano only for a few years until you can "trade up" to a better one, in which case a complete rebuilding job might be impractical? Or do you want to rebuild a piano for the educational experience, in which case you'll be happy to make a little profit in return for increasing your skills? If you're contemplating a partial rebuilding job, do the general condition and quality of the instrument justify it?

It is usually worthwhile, for example, to replace a grand pinblock if necessary. But a vertical pinblock is built into the cabinet, making it harder to remove, and good quality verticals often are available at a cost lower than that of a complete rebuilding job. If there is evidence that an inexpensive vertical piano has a cracked or delaminated pinblock so even oversized pins won't hold it in tune, rebuilding usually isn't advisable. Exceptions to this are fine quality or exceptionally beautiful uprights and any reproducing piano, coin piano, or orchestrion, all of which are worth enough to make this large job economically practical. Whatever the circumstances, always evaluate the potential musical and market value of the instrument before making a quick decision regarding rebuilding.

If a plate is cracked or broken, the piano probably isn't worth rebuilding. For every fine welder who "could fix that crack so it will *never* come apart again," there is a piano technician who has seen one that did come apart. Consult with a mechanical engineer to see if a reinforcing brace is likely to withstand the many tons of string tension without causing the plate to break somewhere else. A brace might look strong, but the stress will be transferred from the area of the crack to the area surrounding the reinforcement, and there is a strong possibility that the plate will crack again *next to the brace*. This might happen during restringing, a month after you pull the strings up to pitch, when you move the piano, a year later, or at any other time. If you obtain an "identical" plate from a junk piano of the same make and model, be aware that you probably will have to relocate the screw holes in the wood, and you undoubtedly will have to make a new pinblock to fit the different plate. If you're absolutely sure that you can have the plate repaired successfully, go ahead and rebuild the piano, but don't be surprised if you have to consign your rebuilt piano to the junk pile after spending a lot of time and money.

If you are a beginning technician, you should rebuild as many old uprights or junk grands as it takes to learn to do fine quality work before attempting to rebuild a valuable grand, reproducing piano, coin piano, or orchestrion.

Preparation

Rebuilding requires removing the strings and plate from the piano. The height of the plate over the soundboard is very important, because it determines the amount of downbearing of the strings on the bridges. This has a major effect on the tone quality. Therefore, during disassembly, you should measure the downbearing before and after removing the strings, and you'll measure the height of the plate over the soundboard. This information will help you to decide on the ideal height when you reinstall the plate.

Before disassembling the piano, tune it, noting the tightness of the tuning pins and whether the tone is appropriate for that type and size of piano. If downbearing is inadequate but the strings are still in good condition, the tone is usually weak but long-sustained. If downbearing is excessive — a rare condition in an old piano — the tone is usually loud and short-sustained. When evaluating tone quality, take the condition of the strings and hammers into consideration.

Note: Before restringing a Baldwin grand having "Acu-Just" hitch pins or the threaded perimeter bolt plate suspension system, consult with the Baldwin company for instructions for that specific piano.

Disassembling the Cabinet

The Vertical. In a vertical, first remove the front panels, upper pillars, lid, music shelf, fallboard, name board strip, key slip, key blocks, action, and keys. Then lay the piano on its back. If you have a piano tilter, available from piano supply companies, you can lay a small vertical on its back by yourself. Push the tilter against the back of the piano. Hold the piano upright with one hand and rock the tilter back with the other until the prongs barely begin to lift the piano, tak-

8-1. Using a folding piano tilter. This one folds to a small enough size so you can carry it in your car. Suppliers also sell a larger one that is sturdier, for shop use. If you tilt a piano as large as the one in this picture, have a helper stand in front to keep the bottom from kicking out.

ing the weight off the back casters. Then tip the piano back against the tilter and rock it back until the tilter rests on the floor. By prying upward on the bottom of the piano with the tilter before tipping the piano back, you will keep the piano from rolling away from you.

When using a tilter for a large heavy upright, don't use the prying method described above; you might break the prongs or welded joints off the bottom of the tilter. Instead, have a helper stand in front of the piano and push the bottom of it toward you to keep it from kicking out. If you don't have someone do this, the piano might roll forward and crash to the floor. Rock the tilter and piano together. Once you rock the tilter enough to take the weight off the back casters of the piano, your helper can stop pushing against you.

If you don't have a tilter, you will need at least two helpers — two people behind the piano to tip it down to the floor and one or two in front to keep the bottom from kicking

8-2. The two screwdrivers hanging from this piano show the locations of screws holding the front leg assembly. In the piano illustrated, the half pilaster flush with the cabinet also has two screws holding it from inside the cabinet.

forward. Before tipping the piano, place a large block of wood on the floor where the pinblock will rest, so your fingers won't get caught beneath it.

Remove the front legs from a spinet, or the pillars from an upright. This will expose the keybed screws. In most verticals three large screws attach the keybed to the cabinet

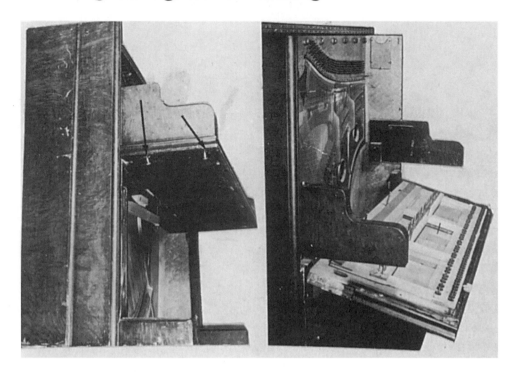

8-3. Left: Arrows show two of the three screws that usually hold each end of the keybed.
Right: Removing the keybed.

arms, and one or two screws attach the keybed to the plate. After you remove all the screws, lift the keybed out of the piano, or stand up the piano, and pull the keybed out like a drawer. Leave the key frame and bottom action ball bolts in place on the keybed.

Remove the screws from the perimeter of the piano bottom, that hold it to the back, sides, and toe board. In some pianos, you can remove the bottom with all pedals and trap-work still attached. In others, you must remove some or all of the pedal mechanisms first. The piano should now look like illustration 8-4, ready for you to measure and remove the strings.

The Grand. In a grand, remove the key slip, key blocks, fallboard, action, music desk, music desk guide rails, lid and lid prop. Tip the piano on its side. For a 5' or smaller grand, use two very strong helpers or three

8-4. The upright ready for string measurement and removal.

average ones. For a larger piano, add one weight lifter or two average helpers for each additional foot of length. (For every piano mover who might scoff at having ten or twelve people on hand for tipping over a concert grand, the author knows at least ten or twelve folks who would be very unhappy to have a piano dropped on their feet.) Select cooperative, attentive helpers who will follow a designated leader. If some helpers ignore what the others are doing, there is a danger of people getting hurt, as well as of the piano being damaged.

Begin by removing the pedal lyre assembly. Then place moving pads or thick blankets on the floor under the bass end of the keyboard. If the piano has fancy molding around the outside of the rim, pad the floor under the whole piano to avoid damaging the molding. If the molding projects so far that the piano won't stand up straight, insert blocks under the pads as necessary. With your helpers stationed along the keyboard and bass (flat) side of the rim, unscrew the large screws for the bass front leg. Have your helpers lift the piano just enough for you to remove the leg. If the leg has large alignment dowels, pull it straight down. If it has an iron leg plate, you'll have to slide the leg — usually toward the front or back, but sometimes toward one side — to unlock the plate, and then remove the leg. If it won't slide, hit the top of the leg with your palm, or pad it with a blanket and hit it with a soft rubber mallet.

After you have removed the first leg, lower the front bass corner of the piano all the way to the floor. Have one helper take some weight off the treble leg when you do this to avoid breaking it. Spread more blankets on the floor where the piano will come to rest. Then tip the piano all the way up on its flat side on the blankets, with at least one helper lifting some weight off the back leg.

With the piano lying on its side, you can take your time to remove the other two legs. If you can't find numbers on the legs, number them and their positions in the body of the piano now.

With the legs and lyre removed, tip the body of the piano back down to the floor or, preferably, place it on sturdy sawhorses at a comfortable working height.

Make a damper storage rack by drilling a row of 75 holes, about 3/4" (or 2 cm.) apart, in a long narrow board; mark "bass" on one end. Unscrew the damper wires from the damper levers. Pull the dampers out of the piano one at a time, number them starting with #1 in the bass, and place them in order in the storage rack. Store the rack where they won't fall out.

Remove the damper stop rails, lift tray, and underlever mechanism, making note of the exact location of each part before you remove it. Remove the sostenuto mechanism if it is mounted in the body of the piano.

The piano is now ready for you to measure downbearing and to measure and remove the strings.

Measuring the Downbearing Before Removing the Strings

Measure downbearing once before lowering the string tension and removing the strings, and again afterward, and keep a list of the measurements for reference during rebuilding and reassembly. Measure it at each end of each bridge, and at two or more intermediate places along the treble bridge, as shown by the arrows on illus. 8-5.

To measure downbearing, stretch a piece of carpet thread tightly across the bridge and plate bearing points to see how much the thread bears down on the bridge. Have a

8-5. The arrows indicate places where you will measure downbearing in a grand or vertical, once before lowering the string tension, and again after removing the strings.

helper press one end of the thread against the plate, next to the lowest hitch pin in the bass. Draw the thread across the bridge, pull it tight next to the lowest bass string, and align the other end horizontally with the hole in the agraffe. If there is no agraffe, rest the thread on the string termination point next to the lowest bass string.   Have a helper watch the thread where it passes over the bridge, as you gradually lift the free end away from the termination point or above the agraffe hole. At the moment your helper tells you the string lifts away from the top of the bridge, measure the distance that you have lifted the thread. Have your helper call

out "touching," "not touching," etc. as you raise and lower the thread, until you know the precise distance that the end of the thread is above the agraffe hole or termination point, and record this distance in your notes. Make another measurement between the thread and termination point at the hitch pin end. Repeat the procedure at each end for each bridge, as shown in the illustration.

A piano with good soundboard and bridges should have a positive downbearing reading at each measurement place. An old piano with a flat soundboard and loose ribs will have no downbearing, or even **negative downbearing.** When there is negative downbearing, the thread floats over the top of the bridge without touching it when you press the thread ends against the termination points.

A more sophisticated way to measure downbearing is with a **Lowell Component Downbearing Gauge**™, shown in illus. 8-6. This clever, compact device incorporates an adjustable, precisely graduated bubble-level vial, which provides actual measurements of front bearing, rear bearing, and net bearing (front plus rear), expressed in terms of the string deflection from a straight line. By plugging the angle measurements into formulae provided in the instructions supplied with the tool, it is possible to determine the actual amount of downbearing of each string on the

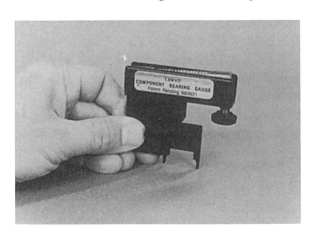

8-6. The Lowell Component Downbearing Gauge.™

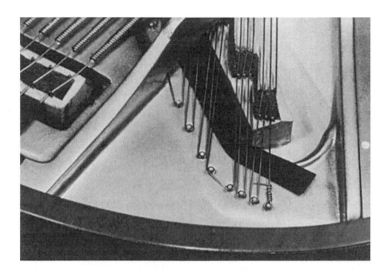

8-7. Always sketch odd stringing patterns, such as this one in a Cable grand, before removing the strings.

bridge, including downbearing force in pounds. If you want to learn as much as you can about fine-quality rebuilding work, this gauge will provide you with important information not obtainable with other methods.

Recording the Stringing Scale

Examine how the treble (non-wound) strings loop around the hitch pins, and make a sketch of the stringing pattern, showing single tied strings, strings that loop around more than one hitch pin, and extra hitch pins.

Make a list of all treble wire sizes, from the high treble down through the low tenor. Except for single tied strings, every two unisons have three separate pieces of wire attached to six tuning pins. Piano makers never intentionally use two different wire sizes for one unison, so every two unisons must always have the same size wire. This means you only have to measure the first wire of every two unisons, plus all single tied strings, which usually occur only at the end of a section. Lower the tension of each string that you are going to measure, by turning its tuning pin counterclockwise one half turn. Pull the string away from the soundboard, and measure a straight spot using a microme-

ter or music wire gauge. Polish the wire with 4/0 steel wool if necessary to remove rust, to ensure an accurate reading. Make a list showing how many unisons the piano has of each wire size, noting the wire diameter in thousandths of an inch. After your list is complete, add another column translating the measurements into music wire sizes.

If you encounter a section of wire that is halfway between two actual wire sizes, make note of this in your list, and when you restring the piano, use wire .0005" (half a thousandth) larger. It is common for wire to decrease in diameter by this much when it remains under tension in a piano for a long time.

Examine the wound strings. Is there adequate space between the end of each winding and the bridge and agraffe or capo bar? Are the windings the same length on all strings of each unison? Are most of the strings original? If so, you can send the original strings to a string maker to have new ones made. If not — if windings touch the bridge, agraffe, or capo bar, or if the strings of a bichord or trichord unison have windings that are more than 1/16" different in length, or if many strings appear to be incorrect replacements — then you should make a paper pattern, which will help the string maker do a better job. If the ends of some windings are too close to their strings' termination points, measure each gap and record it in your notes. Also, make note of odd strings and other problems. The text explains how to make the pattern later, after you remove the strings.

Lowering the String Tension

Removing the strings from a piano is a job to be taken seriously. The average string tension is 160 pounds (72.5 kg.) or more, adding up to a total of 18 tons (16,300 kg.) in a medium size piano. When dealing with tensions of this magnitude, as you do any time you rebuild a piano, try to keep the stress uniform to avoid the possibility of damaging the soundboard or cracking the plate. If you change the tension suddenly on one part of a piano, there is a risk of damage.

Measure the height of the pressure bar over the plate, and the space between the wire coils on the tuning pins and the plate. The overall height of the tuning pins is irrelevant, because not all pins have the holes located the same distance from the end. Check each section of pins, and the height of the pressure bar in several places, and record these dimensions in your notes for reference during restringing.

Use a tuning lever, T lever, or ratchet wrench equipped with a tuning pin socket to let the tension down on the left-hand string of the lowest three-string unison. Turn the tuning pin counterclockwise one full turn, just enough to remove all the tension from the string without disrupting the coil. Proceed all the way up the scale, lowering each left hand string. Then go to the bass section. Lower the left-hand string of each two-string unison, and then lower every other single-string unison. Go back to the treble and lower the middle string of each three-string

8-8. Lowering the string tension with a ratchet wrench equipped with a tuning pin socket.

unison. Then loosen the rest of the bass strings, and finally the right-hand string of each treble unison. Following this sequence will take you longer than going directly from one end of the piano to the other, but will reduce the possibility of damaging anything.

Removing the Wound Strings

Remove the wound strings first. Wearing proper eye protection in the event of flying broken pieces of wire, turn each tuning pin counterclockwise just far enough to pry the becket (the bend in the wire where it enters the eye of the tuning pin) out of the pin with a screwdriver. Slip the wire coil off the pin. The best tool for turning the tuning pins during this procedure is a ratchet socket wrench with a socket wrench tuning pin tip. If you don't have one, use a regular tuning lever.

Hang the strings in order by their hitch pin loops on a piece of solid copper electrical wire with a large knot tied on one end. If there are missing strings, place a cardboard or cloth front rail punching on the wire for each one, to show its location in the scale. After you thread all the wound strings onto the wire, tie the ends of the wire together, form the whole group of strings into a loop about 18" (or about 450 cm.), and tie the bundle with more solid electric wire or mechanic's wire. Attach a tag with the following information: your name and address; the brand name, style or size, and serial number of the piano; how many strings are single-string unisons, how many are two-string unisons, how many are three-string unisons, and how many (if any) lie on the treble bridge. Note how many front rail punchings there are for missing strings, and whether you think any of the existing strings are incorrect. Package the strings in a sturdy box and send them to a string maker for duplication.

Making a Pattern for the Wound Strings

If you observed that the ends of any windings were too close to the termination points — agraffes, capo bar, or bridges — before you lowered the string tension, ask the string maker to make the new strings with slightly shorter windings. Make a pattern showing the relative positions of the hitch pins, bridge pins, and agraffes or capo bar. Measure the distance from the capo bar or agraffe to the bridge pin for the first and last bass strings, and note these on the pattern.

Lay a piece of brown paper large enough to cover the entire bass section on the strings. Sand the paper across the hitch pins until they all show through, and press it down over the pins so it touches the plate. Stretch it tightly across the bridge pins, and do the same thing, so it rests on the bridge. Make sure the paper has a clean hole for each hitch pin and bridge pin. Then stretch the pattern over the agraffes or upper plate pins, and sand it enough to show their locations. In an inexpensive grand with a capo bar in the bass, trim the sides of the pattern as necessary to pull it under the capo bar. Rub the bottom side of the paper with a pencil to show the location of the bar. Remove the pattern from the piano, and then trace the rubbing through to the top side of the paper. Include the pattern with your sample bass strings, noting on it the area where you think the windings should be made shorter.

Removing the Treble Strings

Before removing the treble strings from a vertical piano, remove the pressure bar. If all the screws are identical, put them all in a small container. If not, poke a row of holes representing the pressure bar screw positions in a piece of cardboard. As you remove the screws, insert them in the holes to keep them in order. Tap the bar with a mallet and dowel rod if necessary to break it loose from rusty screws. If a screw is rusted into the pinblock, heat the screw with a large soldering iron, being careful not to damage the wood.

Again wearing proper eye protection, start with the lowest plain steel string. Turn the tuning pin counterclockwise until you can pry the string out of the pin. Repeat the procedure for the other end of the string at the next tuning pin. Remove the string from the piano, form it into a loop about 6" (or 15 cm.) in diameter, tuck the ends in and discard it.

If the piano has a duplex scale, and if the aliquot bars or plates don't have guide pins that fit into holes in the plate, mark the position of each aliquot with a tiny scratch on the plate. Number aliquot plates to keep them in order, or attach aliquot bars to double-sided tape in the correct order for reinstallation.

8-9. Upright piano with pressure bar removed and treble strings loosened.

Measuring the Downbearing After Removing the Strings

After you've removed all of the strings, measure the downbearing again with a tightly stretched thread at each point where you measured it before. In a piano with a good soundboard, you should get higher measurements, because without the strings bearing downward on it, the soundboard should rise a little, particularly near the center. List all the measurements next to your previous ones.

Removing the Tuning Pins

The quickest way to remove tuning pins is to use a half-inch variable speed reversible electric drill, with a special tuning lever tip made for a drill chuck. Don't even try to use a smaller drill; it will burn out rapidly if you subject it to the torque involved. *Don't apply any sideways pressure on the pins; this will ruin the pinblock.* Lift the drill with the pin as the pin unscrews, to keep the weight of

the drill off of it. If the pin scorches the wood, you are turning the drill too fast and not allowing the heat to dissipate enough; turn it slower. If you don't have a large variable speed drill, or in any piano in which you believe the new oversize pins might be only marginally tight in the old pinblock, use a hand brace with a tuning lever tip made for it.

Note the length of the tuning pins, and measure their diameter with a micrometer, dial indicator, or tuning pin gauge. If any of the pins were replaced previously with oversize pins, note their size and location on a sketch of the pinblock.

Some technicians like to spin the tuning pins out and remove the strings simultaneously, breaking the strings off as they go, to speed up the process. Some broken pieces of wire spin around with the tuning pins when doing this, putting circular scratches in the plate; other pieces go flying through the air. Some strings don't break, but instead wind around the pins backward, and have to be unwound again in the other direction. To the

8-10. Removing tuning pins with a half-inch reversible variable-speed drill, after removing the strings. Although the piano is standing up in this picture, you'll reduce the chance of damaging the pinblock by enlarging the tuning pin holes if you lay the piano on its back.

8-11. Removing the pins with a hand brace.

author, this speed is a waste of time, because of the extra time it takes to repair the damage.

Removing the Plate

Obtain four small pins, such as balance rail pins, and select a drill bit of the same diameter. Drill four index holes, one near each end of the pinblock, and another near each bottom corner in a vertical or each back "corner" of a grand, all the way through the plate and at least an inch deep into the wood behind it. Insert the pins just to make sure they fit, and then remove them and save them for later use. You will use these pins and index holes to ensure that you install the plate in its original position.

In a grand piano, cut four thin wooden wedges, and insert them between the plate and soundboard around the perimeter. Wedge them gently into place by hand, and

8-12. Storing the screws in order on a piece of cardboard.

draw a pencil line across each one showing where the plate touches it, as a record of the plate height. Make a sketch showing where you inserted them, and save it with the wedges for later reference.

Make a rough sketch of the plate on a piece of cardboard, and poke holes in it for the plate screws. As you remove each screw, insert it in its proper position in the cardboard for future reference.

In a vertical, number the four top action bracket bolts by filing one mark into the bottom of the first one in the bass with a small file, two marks in the second one, etc. Measure how far each one sticks out from the plate, and remove them.

Unscrew the plate over the pinblock first. Then remove the nose bolt nuts, and then the screws around the rim (in a grand) or the sides and bottom of the cabinet (in a vertical). With the help of several strong friends or a suitable winch attached securely to a sturdy beam in your building, lift the plate out of the piano. In most verticals, you'll have to slide the plate out through the top or bottom of the cabinet sides; if you lift the plate with a winch, roll the piano and tilter out from under it. Don't drag the plate along the bridges, pinblock, or cabinet, and whatever you do, *don't drop the plate*. If you drop a plate even as little as a few inches, it might break; cast iron is very brittle.

Obtain restringing instructions from the Baldwin company before removing a plate from a Baldwin grand with plate perimeter suspension bolts.

Ordering Parts and Materials

Each part of this chapter discusses how to order parts and materials for one section of the piano. If you wait to order these parts until you begin working on each section, you'll spend more time waiting than work-

ing. You won't necessarily anticipate every need in advance, but the more parts you order at the start, the fewer interruptions you'll have later. See the Appendix for information on where to obtain parts and materials for restoration.

For a typical restoration, you'll need a supply of music wire, custom bass strings, a pinblock, tuning pins, custom hammers, damper felt, center pins, key frame punchings, back rail cloth, a variety of felt and cloth to "dress" the plate, tuning pin bushings, name board felt, and for a vertical, backcheck felts, bridle straps, hammer butt springs, spring rail felt, jack springs, and hammer rail cloth, You'll also need soundboard shims, a fallboard decal, gold and clear spray paint for the plate; shellac and varnish, or sanding sealer and lacquer for the soundboard; and refinishing supplies, rubber head tacks, rubber bumpers, and other miscellaneous supplies for the cabinet.

Also, you might need new hammer butts and flanges for a vertical, shanks and knuckles for a grand, buckskin for grand backchecks or vertical butts and catchers, new wippens, other action parts, key frame pins, bridge pins, white keytops, sharps, black paint for grand damper heads, a fallboard decal, and other supplies described throughout this chapter.

Use German wire and bass strings for restringing a German piano. The author knows of several old German pianos with high tension stringing scales, in which American music wire of the same diameter as the original German wire could not be pulled up to pitch without breaking, implying that the German wire has higher tensile strength. German Röslau wire is available in two types: polished and tinned. Technicians generally agree that the polished wire sounds better, and the only reason to use the tinned wire is to avoid rust in locations with such high humidity that the polished wire rusts very quickly. When restringing a piano made somewhere other than America or Germany, ask the manufacturer or other technicians with experience restringing that type of piano which is the best wire to use.

Finish reading this chapter, then examine your piano and decide what repairs you plan to make. Order as many parts, supplies and materials as possible now. Then refer to each part of the chapter as necessary, as you progress through the various stages of restoration.

Restoration Cosmetics

When restoring each part of a piano, consider what it looked like originally, and try to restore it to look like new. Many parts had shellac, varnish, or lacquer sprayed on them; others were unfinished. Don't add finish to unfinished parts, such as action parts, the top of the keybed, the sides of grand dampers, the sides of keys, the key frame, etc. Finish applied on only one side of a piece of wood can cause it to warp during humidity changes.

If a part was painted black, clean it to see whether it had a dull, satin, or shiny finish. Try to find black aerosol paint of the same sheen. Typically, satin black paint looks better than either high gloss or dull paint on mechanical parts.

To clean unfinished wooden parts, scrape them carefully with a cabinet scraper, utility knife blade, or single-edge razor blade. This removes less wood and leaves the surface flatter than sanding often does.

Usually, you'll need to have some parts replated. Most silver-colored plated piano parts originally had nickel, not chrome, plating. Nickel has a warm, mellow hue with a hint of yellow color; chrome is brighter with a hint of blue. If you want your piano parts

to remind you of 1950's automobile parts, use chrome. If you want them to look like beautiful piano parts, use nickel. If you live in a place where poor air quality turns nickel cloudy, lacquer every nickel-plated part with good quality metal lacquer to keep it bright. Disassemble portions of the piano as necessary, to extract and list the parts that need to be replated.

Take the parts in for replating right away, so you'll have them back from the plating shop when you need them. Find a shop that specializes in fine-quality replating of antiques, piano parts, or other precision items, instead of a shop that spends most of its time replating motorcycle parts and automobile bumpers. Many shops in the latter category will buff away the details, round off sharp edges, and elongate screw holes.

In a typical vertical piano restoration, you'll have the following parts replated with nickel, only if they had plating *originally;* the large lag screws and washers for the top of the plate, the pressure bar, pressure bar screws, piano plate screws, action brackets, top action bracket nuts, pedal rods, pedals, and any nickel-plated cabinet hinges and other parts. If the pressure bar for a vertical has grooves on the back, file and sand them off, being careful to maintain the original rounded shape, before sending it out for replating. In a grand, replate only the parts that were originally nickel plated.

Don't plate unplated screws; polish and lacquer them. Don't plate gold-painted parts like action brackets. Instead, repaint them with gold spray lacquer, followed by a coating of compatible clear lacquer. This will dull the gold color a little, but will protect it from turning green or black.

If a piano had brass plating on some parts, have new brass plating applied, but note that you can't buff brass plating much, or you'll rub through it. Check all "brass" hinges and other parts with a magnet to see if they're solid brass, or plated steel or cast iron. If old lacquered brass plating still looks good, leave it alone.

Good quality grands have many solid brass parts, including nose bolt nuts, short lid props, hinges, pedals, pedal lyre rods and braces, leg sockets, lock and pedal escutcheon plates, and casters. *Polish these parts carefully to avoid rounding the sharp edges and scooping out the screw holes.* Then apply a coat of high quality metal lacquer to keep them bright.

Rebuilding the Cabinet and Frame

Inspect the body of the piano for loose glue joints. It is uncommon for the rim or frame members in a grand to come loose. It is common, however, to find loose glue joints in the back frame of old vertical pianos. To repair these parts, clean out as much old glue as possible from the glue joint. Fill the crack with aliphatic resin glue or epoxy, and pull it together as tightly as possible with large C clamps or pipe or bar clamps. Remove the excess glue.

If a cabinet side has pulled loose from the back of a vertical, first clean the dirt out of the glue joint. Then clamp the side to the back post in its original position with several large C or bar clamps, and temporarily install the keybed, toe rail, and bottom. Align the side with the back post, carefully observing all clues like old glue particles, scratches, flush surfaces, etc. Drill sideways through the back post into the side for three tight-fitting index pins, which will keep the side from sliding when you reglue it. Temporarily insert the index pins, and then drill for and temporarily install three large flat head

screws. If you rely on screws alone, with no index pins, the side *will* slip out of its correct position. Remove the bottom, toe rail, keybed, and side.

If you have to repair the soundboard or pinblock, do this before you permanently reattach the side, for easier access. After finishing that work, prepare the glue joint by regluing any large veneer splinters, removing large pieces of old glue, etc. Apply glue to the side and back post, assemble them, insert the alignment pins, install the screws, and attach large clamps to pull the parts together tightly. If you think you might have an alignment problem between the sides and keybed, install the keybed before tightening the clamps.

Occasionally the pinblock in a vertical piano separates and pulls forward from the back structure. If the pinblock is still good enough to hold the piano in tune, clean as much dirt out of the crack as possible, then insert aliphatic resin glue or epoxy, and clamp the entire assembly back together. If the individual laminations of the pinblock have separated from each other, you'll have to install a new pinblock.

If the lag screw holes for the top of the plate in a vertical are stripped, drill the bad wood out from the back of the piano with a 1" or larger Forstner bit. Make plugs of hardwood or pinblock material on a lathe, and glue them with epoxy. After the glue dries, drill through the original hole in the pinblock into the plug for the threaded part of the lag screw. This makes a better looking repair than drilling all the way through and installing bolts and nuts.

Carefully check all grand legs and leg plates. If you aren't sure whether you have the skill to make them structurally sound by regluing cracks, plugging loose screw holes, replacing rotten wood, etc., take them to someone who does. *You don't want the piano to fall off its legs.* Reglue any loose glue joints in a grand pedal lyre.

If the screw holes for the casters in grand legs are stripped, drill for and install longer screws. If the surrounding wood is cracked, reglue it with epoxy first.

Many old upright casters — especially the back ones, which bear most of the weight — are bent, so the wheels drag on the bottom of the piano, preventing the casters from working. Buy a set of high quality double wheel casters with ball bearings in the spindle and wheels, from a piano supply company. If necessary, knock out bad spacer blocks from between the back posts, and replace them, or remove bad sections of wood with a router. Glue the new wood, and glue all splits and cracks together, with epoxy. Then use a router to cut the wood out to fit the new caster socket if necessary, and drill for long screws. Temporarily install the bottom, to see if the new back casters will drag on it. If so, remove wood from the relieved areas for a little clearance. Make sure that the caster sockets are absolutely vertical; any deviation will make the piano track smoothly in only one direction. Remove the bottom.

To repair a broken vertical piano bottom, refer to p. 144-145 in Chapter 4. If the bottom is in such bad condition that it will be easier or better to make a new one, keep the old one on hand, even if its poor condition makes it look like it won't be an accurate pattern. Although you'll find the exact locations for the pedals and other hardware on the new bottom by holding them in their correct places while drilling the screw holes during assembly, the old bottom might provide a few clues that will make your job easier.

If the corners of a grand music desk are split around the hinge screws, reglue the wood with epoxy. Clamp the wood together while redrilling the holes to avoid breaking it again, and use longer screws if possible.

The Soundboard

Rebuilding the soundboard includes drying it, regluing all loose glue joints, shimming any cracks, and refinishing the board, including replacing the decal if it had one.

Dry the board slowly for about a week, to open the cracks as far as they might ever open in the future. By doing this and then shimming them carefully, you'll decrease the chance that the board will crack again for a long time, unless you expose the piano to severe humidity changes. Before drying a grand board, carefully remove any molding from around the perimeter and lay it aside. Stand a vertical piano up, or a grand on its side, and place two heat lamps in photographic reflectors on tripods four or five feet (1.5 meters) away from the front or top side of the board. Use three or more lamps for a 7' or larger grand soundboard. Make a list showing the length and width of each crack. Insert wooden wedges between the ribs and posts to push the soundboard out about 1/16" (or 1.5 mm.) at the center. This will help the heat to spread the cracks open without damaging anything.

Warm the board gently with the heat lamps, and check it once every few hours for the first two days to see what happens to the cracks. Feel the board; it should feel very warm, but not hot. If it feels uncomfortably hot when you press your hand against it, move the lamps a little farther away. If you dry the board too quickly, you'll cause needless cracks and loose glue joints. If you dry it slowly, you can open the existing cracks just the right amount. Move the lamps closer to or farther from the board to control the heat. Aim them so the broadest area of heat falls on the two largest areas of the soundboard, one on each side of the treble bridge, which will concentrate the heat on the areas with the longest cracks. There will be enough peripheral heat to dry the edges of the board adequately. After two or three days, measure the cracks again, and note the new dimensions on your list. Keep observing the progress, and sometime within about a week, the cracks should stop opening any further.

If you have access to an electronic moisture meter, insert the probe in the wood before you begin drying it, and make note of the moisture content several times a day until the cracks open enough. Ideally, the moisture content of the wood should be around 4%, but in a fairly stable humid environment, there is no need to make the wood that dry. Besides, only the best quality moisture measuring tools register that low with accuracy.

In a very humid environment, you might have to use a small space heater, air conditioner, or room dehumidifier to help dry the board enough. Some rebuilders place the piano and heater inside a partial plastic tent. Obviously, the heat source must be safe, gentle, and reliable so it doesn't start a fire. If the humidity in your locale is high in the summer and low in the winter, consider restoring the soundboard during the winter, so you can dry the board without using a space heater. There is always a chance that if you heat the whole piano inside an enclosure, you'll weaken and separate glue joints that are otherwise in good condition.

You'll see dirt in the portions of the cracks that have remained open during years of dry seasons. But when the heating process opens the cracks beyond where they ever opened during seasonal humidity changes, you'll see clean wood inside the ends of the cracks. When you can see this extending for an inch or two at each end of each crack, the board is dry enough. During the process of

8-13. As the crack opens, the soundboard separates from the ribs.

regluing and shimming the board, which might take several days, keep the heat lamps and wedges in place, so moisture from the surrounding wood and air doesn't begin to close the cracks again.

When the soundboard is dry, go around the back side of the perimeter, pressing hard with both thumbs, and try to pop the board loose from the inner rim, or liner and pinblock. Be careful not to fracture the ends of

8-14. Drilling through the crack and rib from the front of the board, after marking the location with small index card flags.

8-15. Pressing a block of wood behind the rib to keep the drill bit from splintering the wood.

8-16 (below). A simple soundboard clamp for gluing separated areas of the board to the rib.

extremely thin ribs. If the board breaks loose, clean old glue and dirt out of the glue joint, insert aliphatic resin glue, and clamp it back together. The best way to clamp the board around the perimeter is with overhead planks and little go-bars, shown in illus. 8-23.

As the cracks in the board become longer and wider, the board will separate more from the ribs along both sides of each crack. This separation must take place as the wood shrinks and the cracks open.

Inspect the back of the board along each rib to find all places where it is loose. At each place, insert small index card "flags" on both sides of the rib, to show you the location of each rib from the front of the soundboard. Drill a #60 hole through the crack, all the way through the rib, between each pair of flags. To keep from splintering the back of the rib, have a helper hold a block of wood

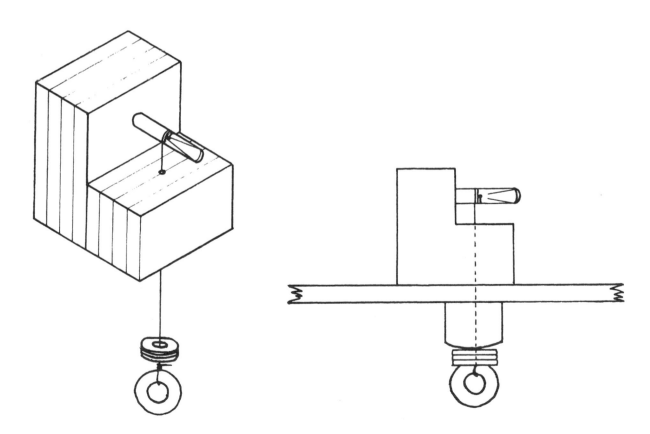

8-17. Inserting glue between the board and rib with an artist's palette knife.

8-18. A row of soundboard clamps in place, which clamp the board all the way down the length of one crack while it is being glued.

against it while you drill. (See illus. 8-14 and 8-15.) After you drill all necessary holes, remove the sawdust and old dirt from between the soundboard and ribs with self-adhesive sandpaper stuck to an artist's palette knife.

Make enough soundboard clamps, as shown in illus. 8-16, to glue all the loose spots on the longest rib at once. For each clamp, glue two pieces of pinblock material together, and sand the bottom flat and smooth after the glue dries. Drill a hole for a tuning pin in the upright part, and a $1/16$" hole for a piece of music wire in the horizontal part. Tie a 12" long (or 30 cm.) piece of #12 music wire to a washer, and thread several more washers or a thin strip of hardwood plywood on the wire, to cushion the rib.

Work some aliphatic resin glue between the soundboard and rib with a palette knife. Insert the clamping wire through the hole in the rib from the back and thread the clamp over it on the front of the soundboard. Cut off most of the excess wire, and thread the wire into the eye of the tuning pin. Tighten the wire by turning the tuning pin with a tuning lever. With practice, you'll learn just how much tension to put on the wire to pull

the parts together without breaking the wire. Have your assistant wear eye protection and gloves if necessary for protection against flying bits of wire when you occasionally break one. This method of regluing the soundboard to the ribs produces a repair that is invisible from the front of the board, and causes negligible damage to the ribs.

After you tighten each clamp, wipe the excess glue off the back of the soundboard and rib before it dries. Keep drying the board, and keep the wedges between the ribs and back posts. After the glue has dried for 24 hours, remove the clamps.

Shimming the Cracks. The next step is to fill the small cracks with v-shaped spruce **soundboard shims.** Obtain a supply of soundboard shims from a piano supply company, and a shimming tool similar to the one pictured. Grind the sides of the point to the same shape as the cross section of the shim. Make a **stop collar** from an appropriate machine nut, with a threaded hole for a set screw in one side. While you dry the soundboard, lean your shims against it to dry them simultaneously.

Adjust the stop collar so about $1/8$" of the point of the tool sticks out, and tighten the

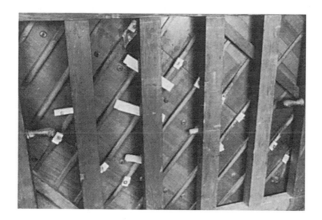

8-19. The same soundboard repair viewed from the back, showing the wedges pushing the soundboard out from the back posts, and the clamping washers padded with thin little blocks of hardwood plywood.

8-20. A soundboard shimming tool and stop collar for opening small cracks. The end of the small shim is shaped like the prow of a boat for precise fit into the end of the crack.

set screw. Insert the tool in the crack, and draw it toward you from one end of the crack to the other, shaving the sides of the crack open a little. Hold the handle so the cutting blade is perpendicular to the soundboard from side to side, and so the point leads the rest of the blade as you draw the tool toward you. Use moderate pressure to hold the stop collar against the soundboard to keep the width of the cut even. Draw the tool down the entire length of the crack several times, until you can feel that it isn't removing any more wood. Increase the cutting depth by adjusting the stop collar, and draw the tool through the cut again until you have opened the crack to a uniform width down its entire length.

Remove only as much wood as necessary to make the shim fit snugly into the crack. Trim the shim to length. Often, one or both ends of the shim should be shaped like the front end of a boat's hull, to fit the tapered ends of a crack.

If you do much soundboard shimming, obtain a supply of both the narrow and wide shim material sold by some supply companies, and shape a separate tool for each size.

Use the narrow shims and tool for the smallest cracks, and the larger ones for cracks over 1/8" (or 3.5 mm.) wide.

The wider and deeper you open a crack, the harder it is to make the shim fit perfectly. If you have a problem shaping the wood just right in some places with the shimming tool, use a sharp chisel, a utility knife, or any other tool that helps you create a uniform shape. Keep trying the fit of the shim as you proceed, but don't push it in too hard, or you'll break it. If your shims fit poorly down their entire length, something is wrong with the shape of your shimming tool.

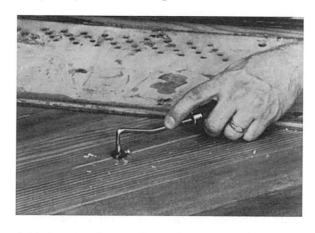

8-21. Scraping the wood out of a small crack with the shimming tool.

8-22. A small shim trimmed, dry-fit, and ready to be glued in place.

Clamp a large plank over each crack in the soundboard with pipe or bar clamps holding the plank to the sides in a vertical or the rim in a grand. Cut a number of little "go-bars" to press the shims in place. Make each go-bar about 1" by 1/8" (or 25 by 3.5 mm.) and a little longer than the space between the shim and plank. Make sure your wedges are still in place between the back of the ribs and the back posts, to keep the board from being pressed down by the go-bars. Then heat the shim and crack with a hair dryer, coat the sides of the shim with a thin layer of hot glue, and press it in place. Lay a thin wooden clamping plate on top of the shim. Bend the first go-bar and place it near the middle of the shim. Be careful to apply pressure straight down so you don't tip the shim sideways and crack it. Then add more go-bars, about one every three or four inches (7.5 - 10 cm.), making sure that they press the shim into the crack evenly. As you add more go-bars, the plank will spring upward, but the curve of the go-bars will keep them from falling out. If the plank is too weak to hold all the go-bars, brace it with another board clamped to it on edge. A pinblock blank makes the best, strongest plank for supporting go-bars.

After the hot glue sets enough to be rubbery, but not completely dry and brittle, peel the excess glue off the soundboard next to the shim with a narrow chisel. If you do this too soon, the glue will smear, and if you wait too long, it will be hard to remove. Removing it at just the right time will save you the trouble of having to chip away brittle glue later without damaging the shim.

Let the glue dry overnight, then remove the go-bars and plank and trim the shims down with a small plane. In some places, the grain will descend into the soundboard, and in others, it will rise. Always plane in the direction that the grain rises, or you'll tear narrow strips of wood out of the shim below the surface of the soundboard. If you trim the shims before all moisture from the glue evaporates out of the wood, they'll shrink below the surface of the board as they continue to dry, leaving a slightly indented surface down the length of the shim. Be careful not to cut into the surface of the soundboard with your plane. If you leave a little of the shim sticking up from the soundboard, you can sand or scrape it flush when you refinish the board.

Repairing Large Cracks and Damaged Areas. The above method works only for filling small cracks that have never been

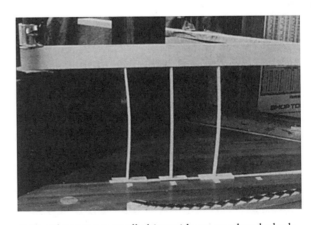

8-23. Clamping a small shim with an overhead plank and go-bars.

260

8-24. Left: Trimming a shim with a block plane. Right: The completed repair.

repaired before. But you'll often encounter areas in a soundboard where a series of small cracks veer off sideways, preventing you from making one long neat cut with the shimming tool. You'll also find old shims with new cracks on both sides, multiple shims jammed in next to one another, crushed wood, and other areas where a single new shim is insufficient to repair the old damage. To repair this sort of damage, make your own spruce shims and cut a larger slot with a router or special plane.

Before routing the slots, obtain some quarter sawn sitka spruce at least as thick as the soundboard, from a large specialty wood supply company or a piano rebuilding shop that makes new soundboards. Dry the spruce under the heat lamps while you dry the soundboard.

Measure the thickness of the soundboard every 6" along the length of each crack. Obtain a 1/4" or other appropriate diameter straight router bit, and adjust its depth in your router to cut through the soundboard. Many soundboards are thicker in some areas than others, so be very careful to remove just the right amount of wood without cutting all the way through the board. Be particularly careful not to cut so deep that you cut into any of the ribs.

Use small brads to fasten a wooden straightedge to the soundboard next to the damaged area. Drive them in at an angle sloping down away from the crack, so that as you bear against the straightedge with the plane or router, you won't push it loose. Locate the straightedge the same distance from the center of the crack as the center of the router bit is from the edge of the base. Rout a slot in the board the full length of the crack, removing all old shims, meandering bad areas and old crushed wood. At the edges of the board under the plate where the router won't fit, carefully finish opening the ends of the cracks by hand with a sharp chisel or one of the other methods described here.

Using a table saw with a sharp rip blade, cut a shim for each routed slot. Start by making the shim a little too wide. Then take off a tiny amount at a time until the shim fits into the slot snugly from one end to the other. After cutting and fitting all the shims, clamp planks to the piano, make enough go-bars for the job, and glue the shims in place with hot glue.

A hand-held motorized tool mounted on its own little router base is handy for cutting slots in a soundboard. The small diameter of the tool and base makes it possible to cut the ends of the slots much closer to bridges and the edges of the soundboard, necessitating less hand fitting of the ends of the slots. If you use this type of tool, obtain the best

8-25. Routing out a badly-damaged area of the soundboard with a $^1/_2$" bit for a new $^1/_2$" shim. Usually a $^1/_4$" bit and shim is wide enough.

quality, most powerful model available and use it very slowly with a sharp bit. An inexpensive model will burn out if subjected to this kind of work, as will an expensive one with a dull bit.

The Sorensen soundboard plane is a valuable tool for the professional rebuilder. It features a $^1/_4$"-wide cutting blade that you can insert in either front corner, enabling you to hand plane the slots almost all the way to the edge of the board. Although this beautifully constructed tool isn't inexpensive, it is one of the author's favorite tools for soundboard repair. (See "Suppliers" in the Appendix).

Filling Soundboard Cracks with Epoxy. Some technicians use epoxy to fill soundboard cracks that are $^1/_8$" or even as much as $^1/_4$" wide, because it is easier and faster than using wood shims. Unfortunately, when the old wood surrounding a hard epoxy "shim" expands and contracts with humidity changes, the epoxy often breaks loose, leaving a new crack down its length on both sides, so this is not recommended.

The Bridges

Repair small splits and cracks in the treble bridge with epoxy, as described on p. 102. If the top of the bridge has long continuous cracks, recap it. This is a very precise woodworking job, and you should practice on several inexpensive old vertical pianos before attempting it in a fine-quality piano. If it looks like it will take more precision or patience than you have, hire an expert to do this job for you.

8-27. A variety of planks attached to the piano with bar clamps, to hold the go-bars for shimming all the cracks in a soundboard at once. This is also a very effective method for gluing a soundboard around its perimeter.

8-26. Fitting a large shim into the routed slot.

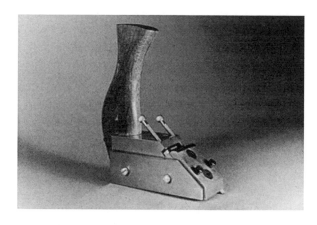

8-28. The Sorensen soundboard plane, for cutting parallel-sided slots in a soundboard all the way to the edge. To make this photograph as clear as possible, the plane was positioned with the blade down and touching the bench. In actual use, always lay a plane on its side to keep from damaging the delicate cutting end of the blade.

To recap the bridge, begin by removing the bridge pins. Carefully measure the height of the bridge every 6" (or 15 cm.), and the angle of the old bridge pins, and record this information. Make a pattern of the old holes and notches by attaching a strip of paper or thin mylar to the top of the bridge and rubbing with a pencil. Attach bolts to the base of your router like stilts and rout off enough of the bridge to remove the cracked portion. Be careful not to rout so deep that you run the router bit into a screw coming in from the back of the soundboard. If there is any possibility of doing this, remove the screw, even if it means drilling a small hole in the back post for access.

Glue shoe pegs or small dowels into any remaining bridge pin holes. Make a new cap of quarter-sawn hard rock maple, 1/8" (or 3.5 mm.) thicker than the wood you removed. Glue it in place, using the plank and go-bar method of clamping described in the previous section on soundboard shimming. Shape the edges of the new cap flush with the remaining old part of the bridge.

Install the new pinblock, and temporarily install the plate, as discussed later in the text. After deciding on the ideal height for the plate, tighten enough plate screws to hold it in place.

Stretch a thread across the new bridge cap and check the downbearing, which should be far too much because of the extra thickness of the new cap. Compare your measurements to those that you recorded while disassembling the piano, and removing the strings.

At each place where you measured the height of the bridge before routing it, cut a shallow slot across the new cap with a hacksaw to represent the finished height of the new cap. Check the downbearing at the bottom of each slot by stretching a thread through the slot and across the plate bearing points, and carefully cut each slot to just the right depth so you have a little more downbearing than you will want on the finished bridge. Then plane the whole cap down to the bottom of the slots. Keep checking the downbearing as you go. When the new cap is flat and smooth, with just a little too much bearing throughout, finish the job with a cabinet scraper. Refer to the sections on adjusting the downbearing on pp. 272 and 274-275.

When you have planed and scraped the new cap to the right height, attach the pattern that you made from the old one. Stretch your thread across from each agraffe (or the v-bar) to each hitch pin, and see if the side bearing will be too great. In many pianos, excessive side bearing is what caused the bridge to crack in the first place. Mark the positions of the new bridge pin holes on the new cap with a center punch, compromising between the old positions and the ideal positions of the strings if necessary. If you move the string positions on the bridge sideways to eliminate excessive side bearing, you might have to adjust the positions of the hammers later, so be aware of what you're getting into before making any major changes.

Select the longest available new pointed bridge pins, and drill the holes two or three thousandths of an inch smaller than the pins. Carefully copy the angle of the original pins as recorded in your notes. Sharpen your best chisel, and cut the notches according to the pattern. *Cut each notch perfectly down the center line of the bridge pins, and perpendicular to the line of the strings.* If you're sloppy about this, the piano will have false beats and will be impossible to fine tune. The hardest part of doing a beautiful job of notching a bridge is learning how to put a razor sharp edge on a chisel. If you keep your chisel sharp, the rest of the job will be easier.

Repair the bass bridge as necessary. If the cap is cracked, make a new one or send it to a supply company to have it duplicated. If the piano has a shelf or apron for the bass bridge, replace it if it is broken. The string downbearing on the bass bridge is very important. Many technicians lower the plate height to optimize downbearing on the treble bridge, and then leave the bass bridge far too high. Too much bearing on the bass bridge is a common cause for a piano sounding dead in the high treble. If you find this condition, adjust the thickness of the apron or new cap to reduce the bearing to a desirable amount (see p. 272).

After you've repaired the bridges, scrape the top of each one smooth, and burnish it with a mixture of alcohol and graphite, being careful not to smear any onto the notches. Clean up any residue, and then scrape the notches and sides of the bridge clean. Apply one coat of four-hour rubbing varnish to the notches and sides of the bridges with a small brush. Be careful not to spill the varnish into the pin holes or smear the graphite. Let the varnish dry completely.

Install the new pins. At this time, your wedges should still be in place between the soundboard ribs and back posts, to provide support for driving the pins into the bridges. Tap each pin to the bottom of its hole, using a pin punch and small hammer, but don't drive the pin so deep that you risk cracking the wood. Finish by filing the tops of the pins flat like they were originally. Some technicians flatten the tops of the bridge pins with a small hand-held belt sander. If you do this, be careful not to heat the pins so much that they become loose. Blow and vacuum the filings away.

Refinishing the Soundboard

Remove the old finish by scraping the soundboard with a cabinet scraper, which is a simple rectangular blade made of thin tool steel, available from woodworking supply companies. New cabinet scrapers are not sharp; so learn to sharpen the scraper, and keep it sharp. By bending the scraper a little, you can keep the corners from scratching the soundboard. A cabinet scraper is also useful for removing excess glue from around the shims. Scrape the board with the grain until you have removed all the original finish, and the entire board looks as much like clean new wood as possible. Then block sand it with 120 aluminum oxide sandpaper. Clean off all traces of sawdust and sanding grit, and sand it again with 220. Clean it again, and sand with 320, always with the grain. It is important when sanding any wood with increasingly finer sandpaper to remove all particles from the previous sanding. If you leave some grit from coarser paper on the wood, the finer paper will pick it up and keep scratching the wood with the coarser grit. Don't use steel wool on the bare wood, as the steel dust will leave behind a slightly gray color.

Regardless of how much you sand an old soundboard, some of the old shellac or other finish that penetrated into the pores of the spruce will always remain. Even if the unfinished wood looks like new when you're done sanding, which it usually does, uneven blotches of old finish will reappear like magic as soon as you apply new finish with a brush, causing the board to have unattractive dark patches and stripes. New finish, whether varnish or shellac, is so wet when it's brushed on that it soaks in, magnifying the problem. To eliminate most of the problem, spray the new finish on the board instead of brushing. Before spraying, *mask the bridges.*

Obtain some fresh white shellac, and brush a little on a scrap of wood to make sure it dries properly; stale shellac remains

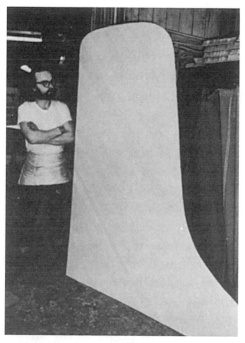

8-29. Andrew Nicholas showing a new spruce soundboard ready for installation in a 9' Mason & Hamlin concert grand piano at the old Aeolian-American factory in East Rochester, NY.

sticky. Dilute it 50/50 with alcohol, and spray a very thin mist coat on the board with a spray gun. If you spray a thin first coat, the material won't soak into the board like it does when you brush it, and the board will have a much more uniform color. When spraying shellac, you should use all the same safety precautions that you should use when spraying lacquer—the mist of shellac and alcohol in the air is every bit as explosive. Let the first coat dry, and spray on another slightly wetter coat for thorough coverage. After the second coat dries, rub it with 4/0 steel wool. Make sure the steel wool has no oil in it; if it does, wash it in lacquer thinner and let it dry before using it.

Clean your entire work area to eliminate as much dust in the air as possible and use a tack rag to remove the shellac dust from the soundboard. Apply a coat of "Four Hour Rubbing Varnish™" available from specialty woodworking suppliers. Use a good-quality china bristle brush or an inexpensive foam throw-away brush, and always work under strong light so you can see that you're covering the wood properly. Apply the varnish to a small area, brush it once across the grain to even out the flow marks, and then tip it off with the grain. Work quickly, to blend the overlapping areas together without any obvious lap marks, and then leave it alone. If you have trouble leaving brush marks, thin the varnish a little with the solvent recommended on the can. Leave the room until the varnish dries, to keep dust to a minimum.

Let the varnish dry overnight. Unmask the bridges. *Remove the wedges from between the soundboard and the back posts.*

Some rebuilders use sanding sealer and lacquer instead of shellac and varnish, because these are easier to apply and dry faster. If you do this, resist the temptation to apply too many thick coats, which will eventually crack and check. Apply no more than two thin coats of sanding sealer and two thin coats of lacquer. No matter what you use, don't apply it to the tops of the bridges.

Installing the Soundboard Decal

Installing the soundboard decal is a tricky operation, especially if the decal is a large one. Two types of decals are available: varnish transfers, and rub-on decals.

Varnish transfers are less expensive and harder to apply. Until you become expert at installing them, order two or three of each decal, because you probably will ruin the first one. Varnish transfers are not water decals; they are applied with varnish. Follow the instructions that come with the decal, or apply it like this: After the first coat of new varnish applied to the soundboard is completely dry, clean the decal area with a rag dampened in naphtha. Fold one corner of the decal back about 1/4" (or 5 mm.), and peel the heavy paper backing away from the decal at the corner only. With a camel's hair artist brush, apply tacky varnish to the lettering and gold work of the decal, but not to the spaces between. Allow it to dry for about five minutes or until it gets tacky. Position the decal over the soundboard and apply it. Locate it carefully; sliding it around on the wood more than a tiny bit will ruin it. Carefully peel the heavy paper backing off the decal, starting at the corner previously separated. With a small clean dowel rod or your finger, roll the air bubbles out from under the decal, working from the center to the top and bottom, until it is perfectly smooth. Don't get any varnish on top of the decal. Leave it until the varnish is completely dry. Then wet the thin paper backing, and peel it away.

Rub-on decals cost more than varnish transfers, but if you're careful, you have a better chance of doing a perfect job the first time, so you might not need two or three of them. Practice with smaller rub-on lettering available from a good graphic arts supply store. Then position the soundboard decal in the right place, and apply it, using the rubbing tool and following the instructions that come with it.

After you install the decal, and after a varnish transfer is completely dry, apply another thin coat of four hour rubbing varnish to the entire board. After it dries, you can leave it glossy, or if you prefer a satin finish, you can rub it with 4/0 steel wool and steel wool wax.

Replacing the Soundboard

A soundboard can have many cracks, bulges, and bad glue joints and still be repairable, but when a board falls apart, or when it has many old cracks, with shims inserted on both sides of older shims, the time finally comes when installing a new board is better than trying to fix the old one. Making and installing a new soundboard requires the use of a large heavy press for gluing the ribs to the board in a concave shape. In a humid climate, it also requires a hot box or drying chamber to dry the blank and keep it dry during construction, until you install it in the piano. Several shops in the United States specialize in making new soundboards for piano technicians. They supply you with instructions for removing the old board. You send them the old board with ribs and bridges still attached, and they return a new board with new ribs, and with new bridges if desired. (Refer to the advertisements in a recent *Piano Technician's Journal* for current suppliers of replacement soundboards.) If you're interested in learning how to build new soundboards, read everything you can on the subject in *The Piano Technicians Journal.* If possible, get a job working for a large piano rebuilding shop that makes soundboards.

The Pinblock

In a grand piano, if the original tuning pins were still tight, and if you can see no separation of the pinblock laminations, keep the original pinblock and use pins two sizes larger in diameter. Most pianos made in the United States have 2/0 tuning pins, while many pianos made outside the U.S. have 1/0 or even smaller pins. In a Bösendorfer grand with its original 1/0 tuning pins and tapered holes in the pinblock, new 2/0 pins might be tight enough. It is especially important to use a pinblock jack for restringing one of these pianos, to avoid damaging the block.

If the pins were very loose, or if the piano has already been restrung once, or if the laminations are coming apart, install a new pinblock. In a vertical piano, replacing the pinblock is such a large job that it is worth doing only if the piano is valuable.

Making and Fitting a Grand Pinblock

For a grand piano to stay in tune, the pinblock must fit snugly with the plate so the two act like one piece in the piano, and the tuning pin holes must be drilled very precisely, so the pins will stay tight for a long time. Making a new pinblock and fitting it to the plate requires careful, precise work, but a careful job is well worth the time it takes, because it will give the piano a long life of tuning stability.

Remove the original block. In some grands, the block isn't screwed to the inner

rim, and it comes out with the plate. In many others, the ends of the block are screwed to the inner rim, and you can unscrew the block and lift it out of the rim after you remove the plate. In some Steinway and some Mason & Hamlin and other grands, the pinblock is mortised and glued into the rim, and doweled around the perimeter into the rim and cornice.

Before removing a glued-in block, take careful measurements of every dimension, including the thickness of the block, the distance from the top of the cornice to the top surface of the block, the distance from the top of the outer rim to the top surface of the block, the distance from the back of the cornice to the back of the block at each end, the thickness of any shims, and everything else that you can measure. Take more measurements than you imagine you could possibly ever need. It never hurts to have too many measurements, but it might cause you extra work if you forget one.

If the block is only doweled to the cornice and rim, locate the position of the dowels. Drill a large hole down through the top of the block, almost touching the back of the cornice, to drill out most of each dowel. Then use a small saw or chisel to cut the rest of the dowel loose. If the block is glued to the cornice, you'll have to saw the glue joint apart, to avoid splitting the veneer on the cabinet. Drill a series of small holes down through the pinblock near one end, flush with the back of the cornice. With a sharp chisel or hacksaw blade, connect the holes to form a slot long enough to insert a hand saw. Using a small crosscut saw, cut the pinblock loose from the cornice from one end to the other, being careful not to mar the back of the cornice. If you leave a little extra wood on the cornice, you can remove it easily after you remove the pinblock. The 9 point/15"

"Stanley Short Cut Tool Box Saw™" or equivalent is handy for this job.

Order a new pinblock blank from a piano supply company, or send the old block and have a new rough cut pinblock copied from the old one. Several types of pinblock material are available. The traditional material has thick laminations, like those found in most old pinblocks, made of hard maple. Another

8-30. The photographs in this sequence show Andrew Boisvert fitting a pinblock to a new Knabe piano in the old East Rochester, N.Y factory of the Aeolian-American Corporation. In this picture we see a pinblock such as would be supplied rough-cut to a technician by a supply company.

type has about 15 laminations per inch (or 6 per cm.) made of European beech; one brand name for this type is "Delignit™." A third type, known as "Falconwood™," has even more laminations per inch. The author's favorite material is the Delignit™ type, as it is neither as soft as the traditional type, in which the pins tend to come loose, nor as hard as Falconwood™, which must be drilled with greater precision to get the best results. This book describes how to use the Delignit type of material, but each type has its advocates. For a thorough education in various pinblock materials, discuss the subject with other successful technicians who favor the other types.

If you buy a blank and cut your own pinblock, measure the thickness of the old block, and obtain a blank of the same or slightly greater thickness. Cut a slightly oversize rectangle out of the blank, and run it through a surface planer if necessary to plane it to the right thickness. Leave the ends long enough to accommodate any **snipe** (a small concave cut at the end of the stock) produced by the planer, or feed a second scrap board into the planer to prevent snipe at the end of your blank. It is important for

8-31. Applying blue chalk to the plate flange.

8-32. After clamping the block to the plate flange at its narrowest point, the technician prepares to tap the front edge of the block toward the flange to transfer chalk from the plate to the high spots on the block.

the pinblock to be the right thickness. If it's too thick, the piano action might not fit in the piano, or the drop screws or flange screws might rub.

Lay the straight front edge of the old pinblock flush with one edge of the blank, and trace the ends and the largest dimension of the back edge on the blank. The back edge of the pinblock usually has a taper or slope; you should trace the edge of this slope that sticks out the farthest. Cut carefully along the pencil line with an accurate band saw. Remove wood to match the taper or slope of the back edge of the old block, using a plane, hand-held belt sander, hammer and chisel, spoke shave, wood rasp, or other appropriate tools, until your new blank is approximately the same shape as the old pinblock. At this point, your blank is similar to what a piano supply company would provide if you sent the original block in for duplication.

Lay the plate upside down on sturdy sawhorses, and punch out the tuning pin bushings if present. Vacuum and blow the dirt off the bottom of the plate, wash the bottom with a scrub brush and water with a little detergent, and let it dry. Rub blue carpenter's chalk on the entire plate flange, lay the pinblock on the plate, and clamp the narrowest point to the flange. Tap the pinblock against the plate with a mallet until all high spots on the block are colored with the carpenter's chalk. Remove the block from the plate, and shave a little wood from the high spots with a spoke shave or wood rasp. Add a little more chalk to the plate, and repeat the procedure until the entire surface area of the pinblock has chalk on it when you remove it from the plate. It is important that the edge of the block make good contact with the plate flange, because this area bears much of the string tension. If the pinblock will be glued to the cornice, keep careful track of the dimensions so you don't make the new block too small.

8-33. Inspecting the edge of the pinblock for high spots revealed by chalk.

8-34. Removing wood from high spots with hammer and chisel.

8-35 (above, left and right). Using a spoke shave for more delicate work as the shaping progresses.

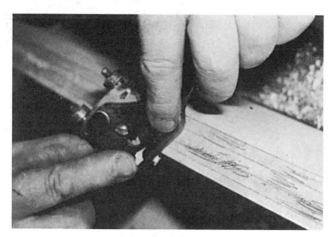

8-36 (above). Closeup of the spoke shave.

8-37 (right). After removing, shaping, and replacing the pinblock many times as shown in this sequence of pictures, the technician makes a final inspection for a close fit.

After shaping the block, lay the plate and pinblock in the piano. If necessary, cut the ends of the new block to leave a small gap between each end and the rim. Then insert shims after locating the plate and block in the correct place. The accompanying photos show the installation of a new pinblock in a piano in which the block is fastened only to

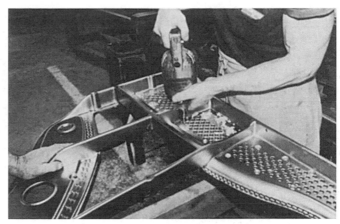

8-40. Drilling the plate screw holes.

8-38. Coating the pinblock with shellac before fastening it to the plate.

8-39. Clamping the pinblock to the plate before drilling the plate screw holes.

8-41. Fastening the pinblock to the plate.

the plate. When the pinblock is also screwed to the rim or glued to the cornice, don't drill the plate screw holes in the pinblock until after you adjust the downbearing and locate the pinblock in its final position in the piano.

271

Adjusting the Downbearing in a Grand

After repairing the soundboard and bridges and making the new pinblock, the next step is to adjust the height of the plate and pinblock in the piano to optimize string downbearing on the bridges. (In a piano with new bridge caps, you must set the downbearing and then adjust the final height of the new caps; see the above section on recapping the bridges.)

To adjust the downbearing of the plate in a Baldwin grand with "Acu-Just" hitch pins and the perimeter bolt plate suspension system, obtain restringing instructions from the Baldwin Piano and Organ Company for the particular model and serial number.

Position the plate and pinblock in the piano, and insert the alignment pins to locate the plate in its original position in relation to the inner rim. Drill new alignment pin holes through the pinblock area of the plate into the new pinblock, and insert pins. Insert shims under the pinblock where it rests on the inner rim, if necessary, so the plate rests solidly on the original supports without rocking. Temporarily insert the wedges that you made during disassembly around the perimeter of the plate. The pencil lines on the wedges will tell you if the plate is at the same height as it was.

Pull a piece of strong thread across the plate and bridge at the same places that you did before removing the plate, and compare the downbearing now to what it was then, as recorded on your list of measurements. Typically, the measurements will be the lowest when the piano still has string tension on it, a little higher after you remove the strings, and a little higher after you have rebuilt the soundboard. If you have less downbearing now, check the plate supports and the new pin-block; something might be holding the plate up higher than it was originally.

Ideally, you should be able to lift the thread a little above the point at which it rests on the hole in the agraffe or on the capo bar or other termination point before the thread lifts off the top of the bridge. What is "a little"? At each end of the treble bridge, and all along the bass bridge, about $1/32$" (or a little less than 1 mm.) is adequate. A little more than this at the top end of the treble bridge is good, but this rarely occurs. At the center of the treble bridge, from $1/16$" to $3/32$" (or about 1.5 — 2.5 mm.) is good.

In an old piano with little crown in the soundboard, any amount of downbearing up to the amount recommended here is good. It is a rare old piano that has more than this, except when the bass bridge is too high. If the soundboard has a lot of crown — more than $1/8$" near the middle when you pull a thread across the back touching the soundboard near both ends of the longest rib — a little more downbearing is desirable.

To increase the downbearing, lower the plate. Shave a little wood off the support dowels, or turn the support bolts or screws down around the perimeter of the plate and turn the nose bolts down. Remove shims from between the pinblock and inner rim if necessary. If you must trim wood from the bottom of the pinblock over the inner rim to lower the plate, check the fit of the action and plane the pinblock a little thinner if necessary for clearance of the hammer flange screws or drop screws.

To decrease the downbearing, raise the plate. Replace the support dowels with slightly longer ones, or turn support bolts or screws up around the perimeter of the plate and turn up the nose bolts. Add shims between the pinblock and inner rim as necessary.

If the pinblock is attached only to the plate, insert shims between the bottom of the pinblock and the inner rim so everything will be snug when you screw the plate into the piano. If the ends of the old block were screwed to the rim, locate and drill the holes in the new block very carefully. If the block was glued to the rim, inner rim, or cornice, pay close attention to the measurements that you made before removing the old block, to ensure that the new one will fit properly after you fit it to the plate. This will require installing and removing the plate and new block several time, to coordinate the fit of the rim, block, and plate, and it might require removing a little wood from the bottom of the pinblock where it meets the inner rim or adding shims between it and the rim.

Make sure the plate doesn't touch either bridge as a consequence of adjusting its position. If it does, chisel a little wood off the bridge as necessary, and apply varnish to the unfinished wood after you remove the plate.

After adjusting the downbearing and simultaneously fitting the pinblock to the case, draw alignment marks on the inner rim, cornice, and pinblock, and remove the plate. Carefully locate and drill the screw holes in the pinblock for the inner rim, and screw it down. Install the plate, install the alignment pins again, and mark and drill the plate screw holes in the pinblock. Insert and tighten the screws.

To summarize your progress up to this point, you have rebuilt and refinished the soundboard and bridges, but you haven't refinished the piano cabinet yet. You've made and temporarily installed a new pinblock, adjusted the plate height for optimum downbearing, and screwed the plate and pinblock into the cabinet. You still have to mark and drill the tuning pin holes in the pinblock, repaint and reletter the plate, and install the pinblock and plate permanently.

Making and Fitting a Vertical Pinblock

Replacing a vertical pinblock is hard work. Most vertical pinblocks consist of three thin laminations glued to the front of a thick beam. A new pinblock blank is thicker than the three top layers, but not as thick as the beam, so you have to remove enough wood with a large, powerful router to create a cavity in the piano just the thickness of the new pinblock. One way to do this is to rout and chisel out the entire old block to the desired depth. Another is to remove only the sections of tuning pin holes, and epoxy sections of new pinblock material into the three large holes.

To replace the whole block, obtain a new $1^1/2$" thick pinblock plank, and cut it to the length and width of the old block: length of the pinblock = width of the piano; width of the pinblock = dimension from top of the piano down to the plate flange. Lay the piano on its back on a tilter, and clamp several large support boards to the back, extending outward from and underneath the top of the pinblock. Lay another thick, flat plank across these supports, extending outward from the top of the old pinblock, and shim it up so its top face is flush with and parallel to the face of the old pinblock. Clamp it to the supports. This flat extension board will support the router as you slide it around after you remove most of the old pinblock.

Before routing, mask or shield the soundboard, the piano cabinet, and any other objects sitting near the piano with something substantial enough to protect them from flying wood chips. Wear face and ear protection. A router powerful enough to remove an old pinblock is noisy enough to cause hearing damage, and it will throw small wood chips hard enough to embed them in drywall six feet away. Routing out an old pinblock is one of the most dangerous procedures in piano rebuilding. Careless handling of a router can cause serious bodily damage or damage to the piano. Fingers and other body parts allowed to come into contact with a spinning router blade will sustain instant irreparable damage! If you don't have the expertise to handle a router safely, hire a professional to do this job for you.

Use two routers, each with a 1/2" collet and 1/2" straight bit. Set one bit to a depth of 3/4", to cut out half the thickness, and the other to the full 1 1/2", to remove the other half. Trying to cut through the whole thickness at once is asking a lot of a router — even a large, powerful one. You will make cuts from the bass end all the way to the treble end. Make a wooden straightedge from a 1"x4", a little shorter than the length of the old pinblock, and use this for a router guide. Temporarily nail the guide to the block so your first cut will remove the bottom edge of the block — the edge that rests against the plate flange — without cutting into the soundboard.

Make a shallow cut from one side of the piano all the way to the other with one router, followed by a deep cut with the other one. Then nail the straightedge 1/2" closer to the top of the piano, and make another cut. Keep moving and renailing the straightedge, or continue cutting freehand once there is no danger of running into the soundboard with the router. When you've removed so much of the old block that the router begins to be supported by the extension board, make sure the cut is still the right depth, and adjust the extension if necessary. After you finish routing, a narrow strip of old pinblock will remain along each side of the piano where the router base ran into the cabinet. Remove these pieces with a hammer and sharp chisel.

Test the fit of the new pinblock blank in the cavity. Use blue chalk to show high spots as in fitting a grand pinblock to the plate flange. Chisel, rasp, sand, and scrape the bottom and sides of the cavity until it is flat, and shape the new block as necessary for a snug fit. Dry fit the new pinblock and drill the plate index pin holes all the way through the new block and into the back. Now adjust the downbearing. Then drill the plate screw holes, pressure bar screw holes, and upper action support holes, and install and tighten the plate screws. Don't glue the block in until after you drill the tuning pin holes, as described below.

The second method of replacing a vertical pinblock is to rout out only the sections surrounding the tuning pins, leaving the perimeter of the old pinblock in place. Do this only if you're sure that the screw holes are good and that all old glue joints are still tight. Rout out each section of wood. Make an oversize paper pattern and rub around the edge with a pencil; transfer this pattern to the new blank, and cut it to size on a band saw. Shape the edges of the blank for a snug fit, and scrape or chisel any rough spots in the hole so the blank fits flush with the surrounding wood. Glue the new sections in with epoxy and let it dry, then install the plate and tighten the screws.

Adjusting the Downbearing in a Vertical

In most vertical pianos, the adjustable range of height over the soundboard is far less than in most grands. The top portion of the plate rests on the pinblock, so you can't lower the top of the plate without planing down the whole pinblock. In addition, the plate flange usually presses against the top perimeter of the soundboard, so you can't lower the plate unless you remove wood from the soundboard, where it shouldn't be made thinner. Around the sides and bottom, most vertical plates rest on wooden shims or on lugs cast into the back of the plate. These lugs or shims can be sanded thinner, so at least you can lower the plate a little around the bottom to increase bearing on the back side of the bridge.

Fortunately, if you rebuild the soundboard as described earlier in this chapter, you'll increase the crown by a little bit. This, combined with thinning the shims or lugs around the sides and bottom of the plate, is usually enough to provide minimal downbearing.

In many old uprights, when you remove the strings and loosen the plate screws, you'll see a gap between the plate and pinblock all the way across the width of the piano just above the plate flange, in the lower portion of the tuning pin area. Sometimes this gap is 3/16" or more, and you'll wonder how the plate screws could possibly have held the plate tightly against the pinblock without cracking the plate. In pianos with this condition, you can't check the downbearing until you tighten all plate screws. *Don't try to pull the plate down with only a few screws, or you might crack it* — you must distribute the stress across as large an area as possible.

Thinning the shim under the bottom of the plate, or thinning the lugs will let the bottom of the plate come to rest closer to the soundboard, and will help to alleviate this situation somewhat. Usually, this also will provide just enough bearing on the treble bridge to produce good tone quality; but it will cause the bass strings to have so much downbearing that you must lower the height of the bass bridge. Failure to do this will ruin the tone of the piano. *Many piano rebuilders do all the work necessary to make an old upright sound good, and then ruin the tone by leaving the bass bridge sticking up so far that the excessive downbearing dampens the entire treble end of the soundboard.* After you lower the plate by thinning the shims or lugs, be sure to lower the bass bridge accordingly by recapping it with a thinner cap or by replacing the shelf with a thinner one.

Make sure the plate doesn't touch either bridge. If necessary, chisel a little wood off the bridge, and varnish the bare wood after you remove the plate.

Before you decide to increase the downbearing on the treble bridge by grinding down the v-bar, consider the potential value of the piano. If the piano is valuable enough that someone might install a new soundboard in it in the future, don't alter the plate irreversibly. The new soundboard will have ample crown, but you won't be able to build up the v-bar again.

At this point, you have rebuilt and refinished the soundboard and bridges, but you haven't refinished the piano cabinet yet. You've made and temporarily installed a new pinblock, adjusted the plate height for optimum downbearing, and screwed down the plate. You still have to mark the locations of the tuning pin holes on the new pinblock, refinish the cabinet, drill the tuning pin holes in the pinblock, repaint and reletter the plate, and install the pinblock and plate permanently.

Marking the Locations of the Tuning Pin Holes on the New Pinblock

With the plate and pinblock screwed together, mark the centers of the tuning pin holes on the pinblock through the holes in the plate. Use a snug-fitting center punch or a punch made specifically for the purpose, available from a piano supply company. You will drill the holes at a 7° angle toward the front of a grand or the top of a vertical, so lean the punch in this direction when marking the centers. After marking the hole positions, remove the plate and pinblock from the piano.

Refinishing the Cabinet

Why wait until now to refinish the cabinet, rather than doing it earlier in the rebuilding process? Because throughout the process of rebuilding and refinishing the soundboard and bridges, and making and fitting the pinblock, you run the risk of damaging the finish every time you use a sharp tool or lift heavy parts in and out of the cabinet. Then, why not wait until after you install the pinblock and plate? Because if you have made a new pinblock, you should wait to drill the holes until immediately before you're ready to restring the piano. This way, the new holes won't be exposed to weeks of possible humidity changes or contamination during the refinishing process. Also, it's easier to refinish the inside of the cabinet without having to mask around the plate, and it's much easier to move the piano around the shop during refinishing without the weight of the plate.

Mask the entire soundboard all the way to the perimeter, to protect it from stripper, sanding scratches, stain, filler, and lacquer overspray. Use large sheets of paper, and stick the tape around the edges of the paper to the smallest possible area of wood, so you won't leave large patches of adhesive residue after the tape has been in place for several weeks.

When refinishing the front of the vertical keybed, remove the key frame but leave the bottom action ball bolts in place.

Clean and lacquer the bolts without disturbing their adjustment, as they will provide the reference point for reinstalling the action later.

Refinishing a piano cabinet is a *lot of work*. Many piano owners who have refinished a whole house full of antique furniture are amazed at the amount of work it takes to strip a piano and apply a beautiful finish. For further information, refer to the Bibliography.

If you decide to have this job done by a refinishing shop, ask to see other pianos that they have refinished, to make sure you'll be happy with their results. A professional refinisher should be willing to provide you with a sample of wood with the same type of veneer, showing the color, amount of filler (for smoothness of the surface), and amount of sheen (dull, satin, or gloss), and guarantee that the finished piano will match the sample as closely as possible, considering variations in the wood used in different parts of the piano. This will protect you from the refinisher doing something that you don't want. Conversely, it will protect the refinisher from you changing your mind after you agree on a certain finish. The best refinishing shops apply stain, sealer, paste filler, additional sealer, and then the finish coats in separate operations. If the refinisher mixes stain and filler, and applies them simultaneously, the grain won't be as distinct, and the final results won't be as good. If the refinisher builds smoothness with heavy coats of sanding sealer instead of using paste filler, you may end up with a cloudy finish or a finish that checks and cracks prematurely. Beware of refinishers who brag about using a large number of coats of finish. Try to find a refinisher who attains beautiful results with fewer coats; a thinner finish is less likely to chip or to develop checks and cracks.

Any experienced piano refinisher knows how to apply fallboard decals. Ask the person who will be doing the work how many decals you should order — even the most experienced refinisher might want you to supply two or three decals in case something goes wrong. If any decals are located in the corner of a fallboard, or in any other location other than the exact center of the board, give the refinisher a sketch showing the location of each decal.

After refinishing the piano cabinet, remove the masking from the soundboard and refinish and install the molding (if there is any) around the perimeter of a grand soundboard. Install the grand damper guide rails exactly where they were, according to your notes or alignment marks.

Drilling the Tuning Pin Holes

Make a wedge-shaped platform for your drill press table, to support the pinblock at a 7° angle for drilling. Attach a compressed air hose to your drill press, with the air stream aimed at the end of the bit. Obtain a set of 2/0 x 2$^1/_2$" nickel/blued tuning pins from a piano supply company, or shorter pins if the thickness of a grand pinblock requires them.

It is impossible to recommend one size of drill bit that will produce ideal results for all technicians in all types of pinblock material. Variables that will affect the results include the moisture content and hardness of the wood, the rpm of the bit, the feed rate (the speed at which you force the bit into the wood), the initial diameter of the bit and its sharpness, the amount of runout in your drill press spindle, the amount of time you take-between drilling one hole and the next, and the amount of cooling effect of your air hose, among other things. Until you gain enough experience drilling pinblocks to predict what works best for you, bore sample holes with various bits in a scrap of pinblock material,

and test the tightness with sample tuning pins.

Use a torque wrench to measure the tightness of each sample pin, and select the bit that produces the desired tightness. If it takes less than 50 inch-pounds to turn a tuning pin smoothly in its hole, the pin will be too loose to hold the piano in tune for an acceptable length of time. If the pin is in the range of 50 to 75 inch-pounds, the piano will be very easy to tune. As the tightness increases up to 125 inch-pounds, the piano will stay in tune longer, but it will be increasingly difficult to tune. From 125 up to 250 inch-pounds, tuning will vary from difficult to impossible; over 250, the pins might break. A reading from 95 to 110 inch-pounds is ideal.

You should find one of the following bits just right for drilling holes for 2/0 pins, depending on the type of pinblock material and other variables: $^1/_4$" (.250"), F (.257"), G (.261"), H (.266"), 2/0 tuning pin bit (.271"), I (.272"), 3/0 tuning pin bit (.276"), or 7.1 mm. (.279"). Softer pinblock material will require a smaller bit, while the hardest material with many thin layers will require a larger one. Always measure the diameter of the cutting flutes of each bit with a micrometer or dial caliper; bits are frequently off by several thousandths of an inch, and the flutes are often slightly larger than the shank. The heavier the bit, the better, and a bit that is solid all the way to the edge of the flutes is better quality than one with raised edges along the outside of the flutes.

The author has produced consistent results with 2/0 pins measuring 100 inch-pounds of torque in a Delignit block, by using a slightly undersize 3/0 (measuring .274") brad point high helix, or fast spiral, tuning pin bit available from piano supply companies. By comparison, a friend of the author, using slightly different technique with the same drill press in the same shop, produced similar results in a different scrap

8-42. A high helix, or fast spiral, brad-point bit. Bits sold by piano supply companies for use in a drill press don't have the step in diameter shown in this old drawing.

of Delignit using a 7.1 mm. bit.

Hold the pinblock firmly in place on the wedge-shaped support on your drill press, facing so the tuning pins will lean toward the front of a grand, or the top of a vertical. Use clamps or a floor stand or a helper to support one end, if necessary. Wear ear protectors to block the noise of the compressed air directed at the bit. Starting in the treble, center the point of the drill bit carefully on each mark, and drill each hole with a uniform feed rate. Use a speed of approximately 1500 rpm, and feed the bit into the wood at a consistent rate. Feeding the bit slowly into the

wood will create a smaller hole; a faster feed rate will cause more friction, more heat, and a larger hole. Feed the bit halfway through the pinblock in about three seconds, withdraw it to remove chips and then drill through the rest of the block in about three more seconds. Withdraw the bit again, and let the compressed air blow on it for about ten seconds while you move the pinblock to the next hole position. When you get to the bass section of the pinblock, drill with a slower feed rate to make the pins a little tighter, since the pins typically don't go into the block as far and often have higher string tension in this section.

Regardless of which drill bit, feed rate, spindle speed, and pinblock material work best for you, be consistent with each motion, and you should have consistently tight tuning pins.

When drilling a grand block, keep a clean, flat piece of wood under the pinblock, so the bit doesn't chip or tear the wood when it breaks through the bottom. When drilling a vertical block, stop short of drilling

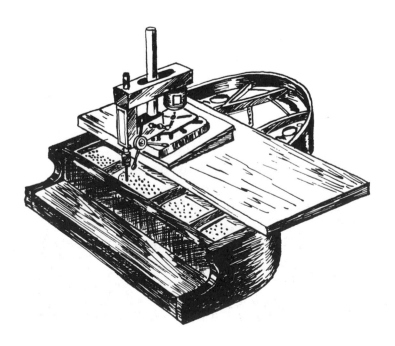

8-43. Drilling the tuning pin holes with a drill press inclined at a 7° angle.

all the way through, so when you glue the block into the piano, the glue won't squirt up into the tuning pin holes. If the holes aren't quite deep enough, drill them deeper with a slightly undersize bit in a hand-held electric drill after you glue the block into the piano and the glue dries thoroughly.

An alternate way to drill a pinblock is to work with it in place in the piano, as shown in illus. 8-43. If you choose this method, drill the pinblock before refinishing the case. Pad the rim with cardboard, and clamp a double-width pinblock blank or other large, flat board in place. Make a wedge-shaped platform for the drill press, to drill the holes at an angle of 7° toward the front of the piano. Wax the top of the large board and bottom of the platform to make it easier to slide the drill press from one hole to the next. Turn the head of an ordinary table-model drill press around backward, and fasten the base to the platform. Place several boxes of tuning pins on the platform toward the back of the piano if necessary, to keep the drill press from tipping forward. Use a pinblock support jack to press a piece of wood against the bottom of the block, so you don't splinter the wood when the bit breaks through. This method is likely to produce holes a little larger than those drilled with the same bit on the drill press table, because of the tendency for the drill press to wobble as you feed the bit into the wood.

To drill a vertical piano block that is already glued into the piano, lay the piano on the floor and insert blocks under the pinblock to create the 7° angle. Place the drill press on the floor, with the head turned around as in illus. 8-43, and slide it along the floor to drill the block. Use a hand drill with an undersize bit to drill the holes that can't be reached with the drill press. Then carefully ream them with a 2/0 spoon bit from a piano supply company. For consistent results, let the reamer cool between drilling one hole and the next.

Drilling an Open Face Pinblock

If a grand piano has an open face pinblock, in which the plate doesn't cover the tuning pin area of the block, you will need a template for locating the correct positions of the tuning pin holes in the new block. After fitting the new block to the plate and piano and drilling the plate screw holes, remove the plate and block from the piano. If you can pry the top lamination off the old block in one piece, and if it fits the new block perfectly, tape it to the new block around the edges and center punch the new tuning pin holes through the old ones. If there is any risk of the top lamination falling apart, make a pattern. Cut a piece of brown package wrapping paper or mylar (available from a graphic arts supply store) to the exact size of the top of the old pinblock, and tape it down around the edges. Rub over each hole with the side of a sharp pencil, as in making a coin rubbing. The holes will show up on the rub-

8-44. Making a paper pattern of an open-face pinblock.

bing as light spots with black outlines. Tape the pattern to the top of the new block, center punch the position of each hole through the pattern, and then remove it and drill the block as described above.

If you replace an open face pinblock in a vertical piano, make the pattern when you measure the old block, before routing it out of the cabinet. Mark the locations of the tuning pin holes, apply finish to the face of the block, and then drill the tuning pin holes before gluing the new block into the piano.

The Plate

Lay the plate on sawhorses outdoors and wipe it with a clean rag. If it has any artwork — pinstriping, rubber-stamped flowers or scrolls, or other fancy details — photograph it. To avoid glare from sunlight or a flash, photograph it on an overcast day, or in the shade. Lay a small ruler next to each design to show the scale. Measure the length of each rubber-stamped design, and keep the measurements with your other notes. File your photos of hand painted artwork for later reference. Enlarge a photo of each rubber stamping on a copy machine so an artist can trace it neatly in black ink on tracing paper. Then reduce each tracing to the correct size per your measurements, and give it to a rubber stamp maker to have a new unmounted stamp made.

If the plate has agraffes, make a pencil rubbing on a large piece of paper showing their alignment. Unscrew them and string them on a wire to keep them in order. Be very careful to keep any agraffe washers or shims with their correct agraffes. Remove any remaining strips of felt or action cloth, and keep them for later reference. Punch the old tuning pin bushings out with an appropriate dowel rod or pin punch and hammer.

If you made the decision to repair a cracked plate at the beginning of this chapter and you haven't yet made the repair, do so now. If you install a brace, make sure it won't interfere with surrounding parts.

If the capo bar of a grand plate, or the v-bar of a vertical plate has grooves, file and sand it just enough to remove the grooves, while maintaining the rounded edge. If you make it too flat, the strings will slip sideways, will be hard to tune, and might jangle or buzz; if you make it too sharp, the strings might break. Remember that removing metal from the capo bar of a grand *reduces* downbearing, while removing metal from the v-bar of a vertical plate *increases* it.

Wash both sides of the plate with warm detergent water and a scrub brush. If you think the old paint might be oily or greasy anywhere, clean it with naphtha. Don't bother doing anything to the back of the plate beyond removing loose rust and washing off the dirt. Rinse well. Where you scratched around each aliquot bar or plate, cut a piece of masking tape and stick it to the plate. Make round masking tape punchings the diameter of the agraffe shoulders, and stick one over each agraffe hole. Apply a narrow strip of masking tape along the string bearing edge of the v-bar or capo bar.

Refinishing the Plate

There are several alternatives for lacquering a plate. One is to mix your own metallic lacquer — using "bronzing powder" and the appropriate lacquer and solvent from a piano supply company or large industrial paint supply company — and to spray it with a conventional spray gun. Another is to go to an automotive paint supplier, choose a color from their extensive sample books, and have them mix it for you for use in your spray gun. Another is to use aerosol lacquer available

8-45. Spraying the piano plate from a Link keyboardless-style 2-BX orchestrion outdoors, using a spray gun and air compressor. Regardless of spraying location or method, always use a respirator with filter made for the specific product that you spray.

from a hardware store. Some brands of "bright gold" aerosol lacquer are close to the color used on many old American plates, and some "antique gold" matches the darker, more orange color of some modern Japanese and Korean plates.

After applying several thin coats of gold lacquer, apply several thin coats of clear lacquer to protect the gold from tarnishing wherever you touch it. By spraying on just a little clear lacquer at a time, you'll avoid creating dark spots by dissolving previous coats and pushing the metallic particles around with the force of the spray.

Manufacturers of paint and lacquer occasionally have to reformulate their products to stay within increasingly strict environmental protection regulations, and this undoubtedly

will continue in the future. In the event that high quality spray products become unavailable for amateur use, take the plate to an auto body shop for lacquering.

If the old paint is flaking, peeling, or badly checked, the only way to do a fine job of lacquering the plate will be to remove the old paint, first with paint stripper. Before doing this, lay tracing paper on the plate and trace the locations of the aliquot bars or plates. Some plate castings are smooth; others are very rough and are filled with a hard black undercoat, and sanded smooth before the gold and clear finish are applied. This undercoat will dissolve when you strip the paint, leaving you with a rough casting that will look bad unless you fill it and sand it smooth again before you lacquer it.

To make the plate smooth again, obtain a can of lightweight sprayable body filler (catalyzed polyester primer surfacer), such as **Evercoat Feather Fill**™ or equivalent. Following the instructions on the can very carefully and, using the correct respirator, spray a thin coat on the plate. Let it dry, and fill any large voids with spot and glazing putty or lacquer putty. Both products are available from auto body paint supply companies. Sand the surface down to the bare metal, and repeat if necessary until the casting is smooth. Don't build up too much thickness, or the filler might crack or check later. For a final undercoat, spray on a coat of compatible metal primer. Sand it with increasingly finer sandpaper, until you give it a final sanding with 600 wet or dry paper. Finish the plate with gold and clear lacquer, as described above.

Remove all masking tape from the plate. Gently polish the agraffes without rounding the sharp edges, and screw them into their holes, leaving them turned perpendicular to the string line or as shown on the rubbing that you made before removing them. The

281

agraffes in Steinway pianos between #230,000 (1925) and #265,000 (1930) aren't threaded all the way to the shoulder. Be extra careful not to break them when screwing them back in. Polish or replate the aliquot bars or plates, and lay them aside, in order, until you restring the piano.

Paint the lettering cast into the plate, using gloss black model enamel and a small brush from a hobby shop. You can do a faster job with a sharp black marking pen, or by applying appropriate rub-on lettering over the cast letters, but nothing else matches the beautiful look of shiny black enamel lettering.

Obtain a two-sided stamp pad made for fast-drying ink, such as a 'Mark II™' made for 'Aero Brand™' #1250 ink. Mount your plate artwork rubber stamps on little blocks of wood band-sawed to the outline of each stamp, and stamp an impression in each place where the plate had one originally. Practice on a piece of lacquered sheet metal to learn to transfer just the right amount of ink to the stamp and then to the plate. If you smear or blotch a stamping, quickly wipe it clean with naphtha, which shouldn't dissolve the clear lacquer on the plate, and stamp it again.

If the plate had pinstriping, find a sign painter who specializes in this art. Shops that specialize in custom van conversions often know of someone who is good at pinstriping. Have the pinstriper replace the striping and any other art work on the plate according to your photographs, using sign painter's enamel. Using oil base enamel makes it possible to wipe off mistakes with odorless paint thinner without damaging the lacquer.

Final Installation of the Pinblock and Plate

In a grand with the pinblock screwed to the rim or glued to the cornice, install the pinblock now. Glue it to the cornice with aliphatic resin glue, using felt-covered clamping blocks to avoid damaging the finish. In a grand with the pinblock attached only to the plate, screw it to the plate. In a vertical, glue the pinblock to the back with epoxy, using the long alignment pins to locate it perfectly. Let the glue dry.

In a Baldwin grand with "Acu-just" hitch pins and perimeter bolt plate suspension system, follow the instructions from Baldwin for installing the plate.

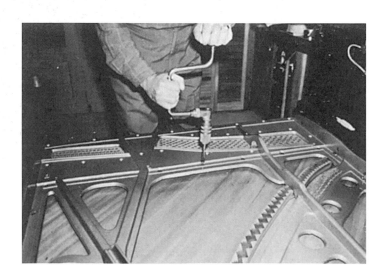

8-46. Tightening the Link orchestrion plate screws with a large screwdriver bit in a hand brace.

If you took the plated screws and other parts in for replating, as recommended on p. 253, you should have them back, ready for installation. If you didn't already do so, wipe them with a soft rag dampened with lacquer thinner, and apply a coat of nitrocellulose metal lacquer to keep them from turning dull.

You have already adjusted the downbearing and fitted the pinblock to the plate, so everything should be ready for assembly. Install the plate, check to see that it rests on all supports without rocking or bending, make any necessary final adjustments of the supports, and tighten the screws. Be sure to use an appropriate screwdriver so you don't damage the screw heads.

Draw all screws snug, and then tighten each one a little at a time, going over all of them several times until they're all tight.

Restringing

Restringing tools include the usual string repair tools (see p. 104) plus a tuning pin crank, tuning pin punch, coil winder, bushing punch, small sledge hammer, pinblock support jack (for a grand), a pair of cotton gloves if your hands sweat, and sometimes, a pinblock reamer and tuning pin bushing punch.

If you can't obtain a coil winder from a piano supply company, make one. Cut a 4"

long piece of 1" diameter dowel rod, and drill a $^5/_{16}$" hole down into the top 2" deep. Then drill a $^9/_{32}$" hole all the way through, and drill a small hole for a $1^1/_4$" x 10-24 round head machine screw into the top, as shown. File the threads off the machine screw $^1/_4$" under the head. Screw a 3" long, $^5/_{16}$" hex head machine screw up into the bottom.

Determining the Correct Size of the New Tuning Pins. If you installed a new pinblock, you drilled the holes for 2/0 x $2^1/_4$" nickel blued tuning pins. If you left the original pinblock in place, the size of the new pins will be determined by the tightness of the old ones. If the old pins were uniformly tight, use new pins one size larger in diameter. If the old pins were uniform but barely tight enough to hold the piano in tune, use new pins two sizes larger. Some Japanese pianos have very small tuning pins — smaller than 1/0 American pins, in some cases. When restringing one of these pianos

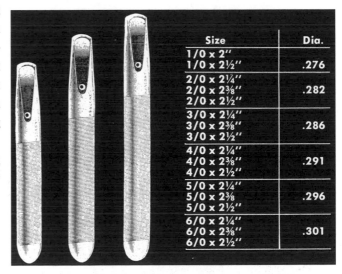

Size	Dia.
1/0 x 2"	
1/0 x 2½"	.276
2/0 x 2¼"	
2/0 x 2⅜"	.282
2/0 x 2½"	
3/0 x 2¼"	
3/0 x 2⅜"	.286
3/0 x 2½"	
4/0 x 2¼"	
4/0 x 2⅜"	.291
4/0 x 2½"	
5/0 x 2¼"	
5/0 x 2⅜	.296
5/0 x 2½"	
6/0 x 2¼"	
6/0 x 2⅜"	.301
6/0 x 2½"	

8-48. Tuning pin sizes.

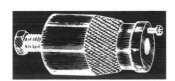

8-47. A coil winder, used with the tuning pin crank for winding neat coils of wire before driving the pin into the pinblock.

8-49. A pinblock reamer or spoon bit.

with larger pins, drill or ream the pinblock as necessary.

The Use of the Reamer. Pinblock reamers for use in an electric drill are available in various sizes, one for each diameter of tuning pin. The use of a reamer for this job is controversial, however; some technicians believe that it is neither necessary nor desirable. If the old tuning pins were uniformly tight, or if you have installed a new pinblock, don't use a reamer. If some old pins were much tighter than others, use a slightly undersize reamer to make the tightness of the new pins more uniform in an old pinblock. Let the reamer cool after drilling each hole, to keep it from expanding and reaming some holes bigger than others. Check the sharpness of your reamer, and try it in one hole to see if it

8-50. Driving tuning pin bushings in place in the factory. Normally, you will do this after you install the plate in the piano, and just before restringing. Bushings are made in various lengths, to suit various plate thicknesses.

overheats. If it isn't sharpened properly, it will burnish the hole instead of reaming it. Obtain a sharper reamer, or have someone experienced in sharpening specialized bits sharpen it so it shaves the wood clean.

Preparation. Lay out your old scraps of understring felt and cloth, and cut new pieces to the right size. Apply a thin bead of burnt shellac to the plate for each strip of felt, and gently press the felt in place. Install new hitch pin punchings if the plate originally had them.

If the plate had wooden tuning pin bushings, measure the thickness of the plate at the tuning pin area, and use bushings of the same thickness and diameter. If the exact thickness isn't available, use bushings that are a little too short rather than too long. Drive the bushings into the holes until they seat on the pinblock, with a hammer and dowel rod or bushing punch. In a grand, use a pinblock support jack.

Bore the new bushings out with an undersize pinblock reamer or ordinary drill bit, not with a brad point bit, and don't push the bit into the pinblock unless you're reaming the block. The pinblock reamer does a good job, and its rounded end makes it less likely to damage the hole in the pinblock due to misalignment of the bushing with the pinblock, than the spiral fluted end of a regular bit. Don't worry if the hole in the bushing is a little smaller than the tuning pin; the bushing will compress when you drive in the pin. Blow and vacuum out the wood shavings.

Refer to your stringing scale made during unstringing, and figure out the diameter of any missing strings by interpolation and extrapolation. Write each different wire size on a small piece of masking tape, and stick these to the tuning pin holes on the pinblock or plate where the wire changes size. Another handy indicator is a short piece of player piano tracker bar tubing slipped over each hitch pin where the wire changes size. If you want to try to improve the stringing scale, refer to the other materials on this subject listed in the Bibliography.

Restringing Procedure. If your hands perspire, use talcum powder or cotton gloves while restringing, or the strings and tuning pins will eventually have rust spots where you handled them. In a grand piano, always support the pinblock with a support jack wherever you are driving pins. The block of wood supplied with the jack will support an area of anywhere from a half dozen to a dozen unisons. Move it with you when you approach the edge of the support block.

Always wear safety glasses during restringing.

In any overstrung piano, you will obviously install the strings on the treble bridge first, and then string the overstrung bass section. It is better to drive the tuning pins in than to turn them. Driving them in roughens the wood a little, increasing the friction; turning them in generates more heat, compressing the wood and possibly enlarging the hole a little. Right-handed technicians prefer to hold the hammer in the right hand, in which case it might be more convenient to go from right to left, starting in the extreme treble in a grand and the low tenor in a vertical. (Because a vertical piano is strung while lying on its back, the high notes are on the left.) Most "lefties," including the author, prefer to string from left to right, holding the hammer in the left hand.

Decide where to start, and find the correct wire size by referring to your stringing scale. Unwind enough wire from the new coil for the entire string plus a little extra. Insert a new tuning pin in the coil winder, and insert the end of the wire into the pin so the wire sticks out by $1/32$" (or .5 mm.). The end of the wire will pull into the pin a little when you wind the coil. If the wire sticks out of the pin after you make the coil, the piano will look sloppy. If it doesn't go all the way through the pin, it might slip out of the hole later. Adjust the height of the tuning pin in the coil winder so the string lines up with the guide screw. With the tuning pin crank, turn the pin clockwise $2^{1}/_{2}$ times to wind $2^{1}/_{2}$ neat coils on the pin. Remove the pin from the coil winder, and drive the pin into the pinblock with a hammer and tuning pin punch. The punch will keep the hammer from battering the top of the pin.

Refer to the measurement that you recorded in your notes prior to removing the

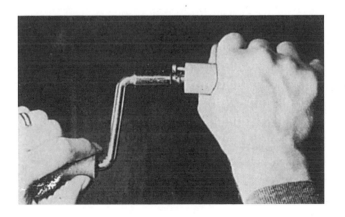

8-51. Turning $2^{1}/_{2}$ neat coils of wire onto a tuning pin.

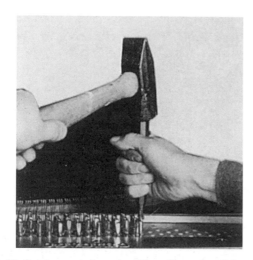

8-52. Driving a tuning pin. When the tops of the threads are flush with the surface of the plate or pinblock, you've driven the pin far enough in most pianos.

pins to see how far above the surface of the plate the wire coils on the pins were. Drive in the new pins so the new coils are just a little higher than this, to allow for turning them in another half turn when you raise the tension later. In most pianos, each pin has about 3/16" (5 mm.) space between the bottom coil and the plate *after the string is brought up to pitch.* The space between the wire coil and plate or pinblock is more important than the height of the tuning pin, because various sets of pins have the holes in slightly different places. In many pianos, the pins are just the right height when the top ends of the threads on the pins are flush with the surface of the plate. Beware of the tendency to drive each pin in a little farther than the last, resulting in a gradual downward slope.

Thread the string through the agraffe, if present, and across the bridge. Pull it tight and bend it around the hitch pin. As you form the loop around the hitch pin, bend the wire farther than 180°, and then let it relax into a parallel shape. By doing this, you'll minimize or eliminate the need for pinching with pliers, as shown in illus. 8-56.

Thread the remaining portion across the bridge and lay it next to its tuning pin hole. Measure 3" (75 mm.) beyond the hole, and cut the string from the coil. Most technicians use the technique of holding the wire across the width of their hand, using their fingers as a 3" ruler. This is a quick, accurate way to measure the precise amount of wire needed for the tuning pin if you always hold your fingers the same way. Thread the second half of the string through the agraffe, if present, and wind 2 1/2 coils onto another tuning pin with the crank and coil winder. Drive in the pin to the right depth.

After you install both pins, snug each coil with the coil lifter. Turn each pin clockwise to add just enough string tension to hold the coil in position, using either a ratchet socket wrench with a tuning pin tip or a regular tuning lever. If you add too little tension, the coil will spread out and you'll have to snug it again later, wasting a lot of time. If you add too much tension, you won't be able to install the pressure bar in a vertical, and you'll stress the soundboard improperly. The correct sequence is described below, under "Raising the Pitch."

Squeeze the becket with pliers, as illustrated, and add a little more tension if necessary. If one pin has more wire on it than the other, loosen one and tighten the other to pull a little wire around the hitch pin, until both coils are the same when both strings have approximately the same tension. This will help all the beckets to line up with each other after you raise the piano up to pitch and tune it.

If the piano has aliquot plates or bars, install them as you go, positioning each one before and after you add tension to the strings. You can drive the aliquot into position with a hammer and small wooden dowel if raising the string tension pulls it out of position.

8-53. Adding tension to the string after both pins are installed.

8-54 (right). Tightening the becket, or bend in the wire, where it enters the pin.

Instead of using the above method, you might prefer the following: Count six whole wires ahead, and measure the total length of the longest of the six. Add about 5" (or 12 cm.) for each tuning pin coil, and mark the overall length on your bench. Cut six pieces of wire off your supply coil to this length. Bend each wire in half at the midpoint to form a hitch pin loop. Cross the wire over itself near the bend to tighten the loop by hand to the right diameter. Lay the wire on the plate around the hitch pin, and thread it across the bridge and through the agraffes. Cut each end 3" beyond its tuning pin hole, using the width of your fingers as a ruler. Wind a pin on each end of the wire, and drive both pins into their holes. This method wastes a few inches of wire per string, but it can save time, particularly in a piano with agraffes.

With practice, you'll feel if a pin is looser or tighter than average while driving it, and

again while adding string tension with the ratchet wrench or tuning lever. If you encounter a loose pin, substitute a pin one size larger in diameter. If you encounter an extremely tight pin, remove the wire and turn the pin out of the pinblock. Removing the pin usually enlarges the hole enough that another pin of the same size driven in is just right. If it's still too tight, ream the hole with a pinblock reamer, as necessary.

Repeat the above procedure for all treble strings. Refer to your notes to copy odd stringing arrangements, such as single treble strings tied to their hitch pins, strings that skip a hitch pin, and strings that go around two hitch pins.

String the bass from the highest note down to the lowest. Hitch each string on its hitch pin, and thread it over the bridge and plate spacer pin or through the agraffe. Cut off the new end 3" (75 mm.) beyond the pin hole, again measuring against the width of your fingers. Wind a tuning pin on the end, twist the string one full turn in the direction of the winding to inhibit the winding from coming loose in the future, and drive in the pin. Add just enough tension to hold the coil in place, but don't pull the string up to pitch yet.

After installing all of the strings, check the height of all tuning pins by looking at each vertical, horizontal, and diagonal row. Drive in any pins that are sticking up above the average height, using a pinblock support jack in a grand. A little time spent carefully leveling all the pins now will result in a nicer finished job.

If you pay close attention to small details, you can learn to install the strings so accurately that all beckets will face the same way when the piano is in tune, even when you work fast enough to string the whole piano in less than a day.

Installing the Pressure Bar in a Vertical. You should have filed and sanded any grooves off the back of the pressure bar before sending it out for replating. If you didn't have it replated, file and sand the back smooth now, polish the bar if necessary, and apply a thin coat of lacquer to the front and back of the bar.

Lay the pressure bar in place, and insert the screws in their holes. Turn all the screws down until they're snug, and then tighten them, drawing the bar down until it is at the height recorded in the notes that you made during disassembly. Go back and forth from one screw to another, tightening each a little at a time, to keep the bar level and to distribute the pressure evenly across all screws. Ideally, the pressure bar should bend the strings down from the v-bar enough to keep them from sliding sideways, but not so much that it makes the piano hard to tune. Examine new pianos to learn what various manu-

facturers consider to be the ideal amount of deflection.

Raising the Pitch and Aligning the Strings. The newly strung piano doesn't have an action, and the strings aren't necessarily aligned with the hammers unless the piano has agraffes throughout the treble, so the first pitch raising and tuning is done by plucking with a small chip of wood, and is therefore known as **chipping**. Place a cardboard balance rail punching on one tuning pin for each "C" in the piano. Unless you have perfect pitch or fine relative pitch, use a pitch pipe, another piano, or an electronic tuning device as a reference during chipping.

Using a regular tuning lever, raise the pitch in the following order, recommended by Steinway, to stress the soundboard properly. Start in the middle of the treble section, and proceed up to note #88. Then go to the lowest note on the treble bridge and proceed up to the middle of the treble section. Then go to note #1 and proceed up to the highest note on the bass bridge. By the time you finish the first chipping, most of the strings will have stretched and fallen several notes below their correct pitch, but the tension will be high enough to pull each string taut.

Install new stringing braid wherever it was used originally, by threading it over and under alternate strings. Thread the braid through the strings under the overstrung section by pushing it in and out with the side of a large needle. Secure each end by doubling it back over itself.

In a vertical, clean and lacquer the four top action bracket bolts. Screw them in to the heights recorded in your notes during disassembly. Clean the keybed, and repaint the underside if necessary, if you didn't do this during refinishing. Install it in the piano.

Now install the unrestored action. In a vertical, place the action on the bottom ball

288

bolts, and turn the top action bracket bolts so they line up with the brackets. If a top action bolt won't line up with its action bracket, bend the bolt so it does. Align the strings that have no agraffes with the grooves in the old piano hammers (and old dampers in a vertical), with a string spacer. Force the spacer down over the strings, and tap it sideways with a small hammer. Sometimes it helps to insert the spacer between the v-bar and pressure bar in a vertical, or between the capo bar and upper plate rest in a grand.

Remove the action. If necessary, squeeze each pair of strings above the hitch pin with pliers to ensure that the wires are parallel. Tap each string where it goes around the hitch pin to seat it on the plate. If you use a screwdriver as shown in illus. 8-56, hold the blade parallel to the string so you don't nick or bend the wire. Or, use a small diameter brass rod.

Chip the piano several more times, until each string is no more than a half step below pitch. As you add more string tension, the combined tension will add more and more stress on the plate and soundboard, causing the pitch of the strings already tuned to fall. It usually takes two or three chippings, followed by two or three rough tunings, before a piano will still be approximately in tune after you finish tuning it. New strings will continue to stretch for several months of

8-55. Aligning the treble strings to the hammers in a piano that has no agraffes. You will do this with the action in place, although it has been removed for purposes of illustration.

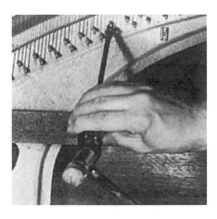

8-56. Pinching the strings parallel (left) and tapping the loop to seat it on the plate (right), hastening tuning stability.

hard use, or for several years if not played much. The more often you tune a piano during its initial stretching period, keeping the tension up where it belongs, the sooner it will stay in tune for long periods of time.

If you haven't done so already, stand a grand piano on its legs, and rebuild and install the pedal lyre. Rebush and repair vertical pedal trap levers as necessary; clean, repair, and refinish the bottom. Install the pedals and trap levers on the bottom. Then install the toe rail, front legs, and bottom on the piano.

Restringing a Baldwin with "Acu-Just" Hitch Pins or the Threaded Perimeter Bolt Plate Suspension System. Send the model and serial number of the piano to the Baldwin Piano and Organ Company for specific restringing instructions.

The Key Frame

Remove the old punchings and back rail cloth. Block sand or scrape the old glue from the back rail and the dirt from the rest of the wood. Clean the key guide pins with metal polish, or replace them if necessary. Polish the glides from a grand key frame. If you removed it previously, install the vertical key frame in the piano.

To order new back rail cloth, measure the thickness of the original cloth at one end where the keys didn't rest on it. Glue the new cloth to the back rail with hot glue, with only a narrow part of the cloth glued to the wood. Replace the cloth punchings with new ones of the original diameter and thickness, but don't add any paper or cardboard punchings yet. You will regulate the key height and level the keys during the regulating process later.

The Keys

If the old bushings are worn, allowing side play and rattle, replace them all. An **electric bushing remover** is a handy tool for this job. Wet each bushing lightly, and insert the heated tip of the tool. The heat will turn the water into steam, loosening the glue and the bushings. If you don't have one of these tools, wetting the bushing will be sufficient if the original adhesive was hot glue. Heating it with a small tool heated over a flame will help to soften other types of glue. Either method is preferable to taking a chance on soaking the whole front end of the key by holding it over an unfocused source of steam. Trim the old bushings and glue out of the key with a narrow sharp

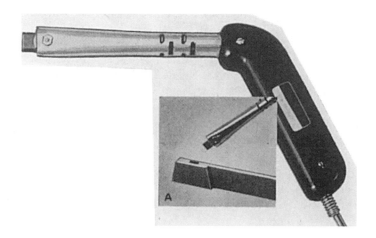

8-57. The Jaras electric key-bushing remover, available from certain piano supply companies.

290

knife, being very careful not to remove any wood.

Obtain a set of **key bushing cauls** of the right thickness. Key bushing cauls made of plastic, aluminum, brass, or wood are available in several sizes from various suppliers. If you have access to a milling machine, you can make them by milling a narrow tongue on a long aluminum or brass bar, and then slicing the bar into individual pieces.

Obtain a roll of new bushing cloth, being careful to get the same thickness as the origi-

8-58. Clamping a new bushing in place with a key-bushing caul. This is the best tool for precision key rebushing, as it forms the same size opening in every key.

nal. Cut or tear the cloth into long strips. Rebush and test the fit of one key before rebushing the entire set, to make sure the thickness is correct. Apply a small amount of glue on the sides of the hole in the key, and on the bottom of the key if the cloth was originally glued there. Insert the cloth, and clamp it in place with a caul. Be sure to insert the new bushings into the holes only as far as the original ones, to keep from adding excessive friction. After the glue sets, but before it gets brittle, trim off the excess cloth with a sharp knife, being careful not to cut into the key. Wash the excess glue off

with a slightly damp rag. Leave the caul in place until the glue is dry.

Check the key buttons; rebush them if necessary, and reglue any that are coming loose. Straighten any warped keys, using the method described on p. 118.

Check each key to see if any leads are loose. If so, lay the key on its side, supporting the loose lead with an appropriate small object on the bench. With a small hammer and center punch, tap on the lead around its perimeter to squash the lead tightly into the wood.

If the balance rail holes in the bottoms of the keys are loose, permitting the keys to rattle, try needling the wood and applying a little glue. If this doesn't help, replace the wood surrounding the hole with new material. Obtain a kit made for this purpose from a piano supply company. The kit includes a set of small phenolic washers and a special bit for cutting a flat bottom hole centered on the original hole. After drilling the hole just the right depth, glue the reinforcing washer in place, flush with the bottom of the key.

An alternate repair is to bore a 5/16" flat bottom hole 1/16" deep, centered on the original hole, with a Forstner bit in a drill press. Cut a sugar pine or poplar plug with a plug cutter, and glue it into the key, orienting the grain parallel to the grain of the key. After the glue dries, sand the bottom flat, and clamp the key between its neighbors to locate the exact center of the new balance rail hole. Drill the hole, and ease it as necessary with a small round jeweler's file held at an angle to thin the top surface of the insert without enlarging the hole. The success of your repair will depend on your accuracy in locating the new balance rail pin hole correctly in the plug.

Check to see if any capstans are loose in the wood. If so, plug and redrill the hole. Polish the capstans. If they are brass plated, replace them with a new set of solid brass capstans, or have the old ones replated.

Replacing White Key Tops. Several types of plastic key tops are available: molded key tops, imitation ivory key tops, and pyralin blanks. Each type has its advantages and disadvantages.

To remove old ivories, heat them with a warm iron and then cut them loose with a utility knife or sharpened 1" putty knife. If that doesn't work, heat them with a hot iron and then apply a cool damp cloth. Let them cool, and cut them loose. If that doesn't work, steam them with a damp cloth and hot iron. If your knife starts to tear wood loose from the top of the key, start at the other end. If you can't avoid pulling a piece of wood loose with a piece of ivory, let it dry, then cut the wood off the ivory with a sharp knife or chisel, and reglue it where it came from on the key. After regluing any wood splinters to the keys, sand the tops carefully, as shown in illus. 4-68. Remove as little wood as possible to make them smooth, and be very careful not to round the edges or sand them crooked.

To remove old plastic key tops, try cutting them loose, or heat them gently with a hair dryer, being careful not to melt the plastic or set it on fire. For a dramatic demonstration of just how flammable some old plastic key tops are, lay a small piece on concrete outside and light it with a match. It will immediately burst into flames.

Installing Molded Key Tops. Molded key tops have two major advantages: they're easy to install and they need little filing. Their disadvantage is that they're thicker than ivory or celluloid key tops, so they don't look like ivory. Also, the extra thickness might cause them to bump into the

name board felt. Many technicians cut down the tops of the white keys in a table saw so the total height will be the same as it originally was. Actually, most new molded key tops are only about $1/32$" (.8 mm.) thicker than the original key tops. They will usually fit in a vertical piano if you raise the name board strip and fallboard with shims between the name board strip and key blocks, or if you substitute thinner name board felt.

If there isn't enough clearance without cutting off the bottom of a vertical name board strip or grand fallboard, you'll have to cut or mill the tops of the keys down a little before installing molded key tops. If the sides of each key are perpendicular to the top *and parallel to the balance rail pin hole,* you can hold the keys in a milling vise for a drill press, and mill the tops down carefully with an end mill or a rotary planing tool made for the drill press. It might seem like a simple matter to cut the keys down with a homemade sliding jig in a table saw, but *it's easy to ruin a set of keys this way due to irregularities in their shape.* Whatever method you use, install each key in the key frame after surfacing, check the level of the top surface, and adjust your setup as necessary so the key tops are all level.

To install molded key tops, remove the action, remove the keys from the key frame, and prepare the white keys as described above. Install the white keys on the key frame, but leave the black keys out for now. Square and space the keys if necessary (see pp.157-158). Clamp a straightedge to the key slip, using wooden shims to bring it up to the level of the key tops. The key tops should overhang $3/32$" (or 2.5 mm.) from the front of the keys. Align the straightedge so there is exactly $3/32$" space between it and the fronts of the bare keys. If necessary, weight the keys in front so they will rest on the front rail punchings.

Molded key tops are made in seven different shapes, and each key top has the name of the note molded into the bottom. Apply a thin layer of professional quality contact cement to the top surface of one octave of keys at a time, and to the appropriate key tops. Let the cement get just tacky, enough so a piece of writing paper won't stick when you touch it lightly to the cement. Align the key top perfectly with the key and press it in place. Once the cement takes hold, you can't make any adjustments.

When all the white keys are done, remove the straightedge, and insert the black keys one at a time. File the notches in the white keys as necessary to make room for the sharps, with a medium rectangular file.

Installing Simulated Ivory Key Tops. Vagias simulated ivory key tops are thinner than ordinary molded key tops, and are made in white, ivory, and yellow colors, in glossy and satin finishes, plain and grained varieties. They look more realistic than thicker molded key tops, and they require a different gluing technique. Follow the gluing instructions that come with them, or score the backs with a utility knife and glue them with PVC-E.

Installing Pyralin Key Tops. Pyralin key tops are the same thickness as ivory, and if you install them carefully, they look realistic. Pyralin glue dissolves the plastic, so the

8-59 (above). The Oslund key-surfacing machine. Note the adjustable castings on the little sliding table that guide the bottom, side, and top of the key to hold it square.

8-60 (right). Surfacing the key.

8-61. White keys before and after surfacing.

wood must be perfectly flat or the key tops will be wavy. For the best results, pyralin key tops should be clamped. You can install these key tops by hand, but the best way to install them is with a set of Oslund key covering machines or other specialized power tools.

First prepare each key with the key surfacer. It produces a flat surface quickly and accurately.

Then apply a thin coat of pyralin glue to the key and the blank keytop. Allow the glue to soak into the wood a little, and lay the key top in place. Insert the key in the key clamp. The multiple key clamp has room for several keys, and after you surface and clamp the last key, you may remove the first one. This makes it possible to glue an entire keyboard without waiting.

After letting the glue dry overnight, trim the key tops with the key trimmer. Like the key surfacer, this machine does the job neater and faster than doing it by hand. Finish the job by rounding the corners and edges neatly

8-62 (above). Oslund multiple key clamp.

8-63 (right). An inexpensive home-made key clamp using pedal trap springs. The base must be clean, flat, and smooth to keep from marring the key tops.

8-64. (above). Oslund key-trimming machine.

8-65 (right). Closeup of the key-trimming machine with guide table removed to show the blades. The small blade trims the front and sides, and the large blade trims the sharp notch.

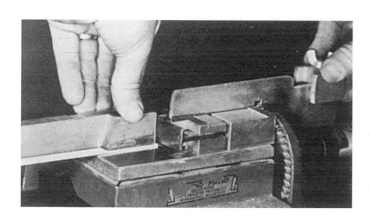

8-66. Using the small blade with the guide fence in place, to trim the front with the correct overhang.

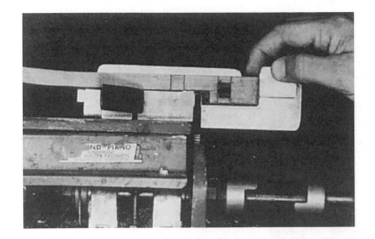

8-67 (left). Trimming the sharp notch. The adjustable stop, under the author's right hand in this and the previous picture, controls the distance from the front of the key to the notch.

8-68 (left). Using the small blade with the guide fence swung out of the way to trim the sides flush.

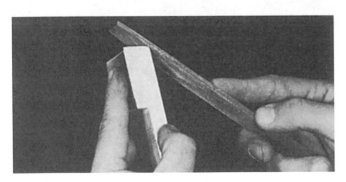

8-69. Hand-filing the corners.

8-70. A finished white key.

with a fine file. For a professional look, round the edges very carefully so they look just like the edges of ivories.

Some technicians who haven't been able to find a set of Oslund key covering machines have made their own ingenious tools for doing the same job.

The Sharps. If the original sharp keys are smooth but the black color is worn away, paint them. Make a jig like the one shown on p. 124, mask the bare wood behind the sharps, and spray them with high quality black lacquer. Sand and polish as necessary for a beautiful smooth finish.

If the sharps are pitted, chipped, or badly worn, replace them with new ebony or plastic sharps of the right length. After you have found suitable replacements, remove the old sharps with a sharp chisel, or cut them off, using a sliding jig in a table saw to hold them square. Glue the new sharps in place with aliphatic resin glue, and clamp them until the glue sets. Then use a utility knife to cut off the rubbery, partially dry glue before it turns brittle. Touch up the black color on the sides of the wooden key body with black stain or a marking pen as necessary.

Install the keys on the key frame, and ease them as necessary. You will level them and make other fine adjustments during the regulating process, as explained in Chapter 5.

Rebuilding the Action and Installing New Hammers

If an action needs extensive repairs, you have to decide whether to rebuild the old parts or install new ones. Rebuilding the old parts usually takes longer, but the cost of materials is less. If an action has obsolete parts, you'll have to rebuild them or make new ones. On the other hand, if good quality new parts are available, and if time is at a premium, the rebuilding job will be easier if you replace the parts. Always replace dark and brittle old wooden parts, even if the new parts need to have loose felt and buckskin reglued and other finishing touches completed. Talk to other rebuilders about the quality of available new parts or obtain samples to help you decide. If you decide to rebuild the old parts, consider how you'll make the plated wires — damper spoons, damper wires, backcheck and bridle wires, springs, etc. — look like new again. Will pol-

ishing and lacquering them be satisfactory? Or will it be better to replace them?

Rebuilding a whole action is nothing more than a large number of repair jobs multiplied by 88. For a thorough rebuilding job, repair or replace all parts of each type, even though the ones at the extreme ends of the action aren't worn as badly as the ones in the more heavily used middle section.

The importance of the correct striking point. One of the most important details of piano design is the point at which each hammer hits the strings. A vibrating string subdivides itself into many different fractions, which vibrate simultaneously to produce partials. Any point at which the vibrating string divides itself is called a **node**. The exact middle of a string is a node for the two vibrating halves; each point that divides a string into thirds is a node for the three vibrating portions, and so forth.

If a hammer strikes a string at one of its nodes, the striking action of the hammer will muffle the partial associated with that node. Thus, if a hammer strikes a string at one sixth of the string length, the resulting tone will have a weak sixth partial. The seventh partial and certain other higher partials are flat, compared to their corresponding pitches in the musical scale, so the striking point in most pianos is set at somewhere around one seventh of the string length. The actual measurement deviates somewhat from this theoretically ideal point, particularly in the high treble where the hammers are very close to the string termination point because of other factors, like string stiffness, which alter the partial series of the string. In any piano, the tone will be loudest and clearest when the hammers hit the correct striking point, particularly in the high treble. You can easily demonstrate the importance of the correct-striking point in a grand piano by loosening the action and sliding it in and out while playing and listening to the tone quality. You will find one point at which the tone is the best. In a high quality piano that hasn't been altered since it left the factory, this ideal point will be precisely at the location where the key blocks hold the action in place.

When you rebuild an action and install new hammers, be very careful to maintain the correct striking point. If the old hammers were installed carelessly, consult with an experienced piano technician to decide where to install the new hammers.

Rebuilding the Vertical Action

Number any sets of parts that you might reuse, starting with #1 in the bass, including the damper levers, wippen and sticker assemblies, and hammer butts. Number the two hammers at each end of each section with their respective note numbers, because you will use these as samples.

To order new hammers, send the first and last hammer from each section to a piano supply company for duplication. Be sure each is numbered as it lies in the scale. Include with the samples a list of how many hammers are in each section. Specify whether the new hammers will be used on the original or new shanks, so the duplicator will know what size to bore them. State if you want reinforced felt, for slightly more long lived resilience at a slightly higher cost. Specify the weight of the new hammers. Hammers are made in 12-, 14-, and 16-pound weights for small, medium, and large pianos, respectively. The weight refers to the weight of a whole sheet of felt from which several sets of hammers are made, and has nothing to do with quality. For the best tone quality, select new hammers whose weight corresponds to the size of the piano.

When you order new hammers, decide what other parts you might want to order as well, including possibly new hammer butts, hammer butt flanges, wippens, wippen flanges, jack flanges, damper flanges, damper levers, damper felts, hammer shanks, and miscellaneous action felts, springs, regulating screws, buttons, punchings, etc.

Many player piano and orchestrion actions have enlongated wippens for the stack pushrods. New wippens of this type aren't available, so you'll have to rebuild the old ones.

Prepare the action frame. Disassemble, clean, and replate or paint the action brackets. Plug and redrill any stripped screw holes. Rebush the hammer rail swing holes and damper lift rod hangers. Clean the action rails. Polish and replate the damper lift rod. Refinish the hammer rail if necessary, and replace the hammer rail cloth, using hot glue. Leave the upper portion of the new cloth unglued like the original. Replace the regulating screw punchings. If the regulating screws are rusty or hard to turn, replace them and their buttons. If the new screws are loose in the old holes, make new regulating rails of straight grained hard maple, or of beech for a European action.

Replace the hammer butt springs. Remove the old spring rail felt and glue by scraping and block sanding. Carefully remove several samples and lay them aside. Then pull on each spring to stretch out the coil. Clip the coil with a side cutter, and push the stump through the rail, pushing the glued end out of the slot. Compare the new springs to the samples to make sure they're the same length, and then discard the samples. Clamp the rail to the front edge of your bench with the slotted side facing up, so the new springs will hang under the edge of the bench as you install them. Grind the end of a large screwdriver blade perfectly flat and square. Insert the first spring in its hole, pull gently on the tail to hold the coil snug against the rail, and bend the tail down. Clip it off to the length of one of the samples, and push it down into the slot with the end of the screwdriver held parallel to the spring. Pressing the screwdriver squarely on the spring, tap it with a small hammer to drive the spring into the slot and simultaneously press the wood down around the spring.

As you continue installing the springs, insert a small rod through the coils to hold each new one in line. When you're done, tap any springs that popped loose back into their slots, and glue a new strip of spring rail felt in place with hot glue.

Polish all action screws and flange screws, and lacquer the heads if the piano is in a humid climate. Assemble the action brackets to the main rail and sticker rail. Install the hammer rail and damper lift rod, but don't install the spring rail yet. Bend the hammer rail swings sideways as necessary to eliminate any side play of the hammer rail.

Install the bottom of the cabinet, the pedals, and the trap levers.

Rebuild and install the dampers. In most actions, the damper levers are still in good enough condition to use. Cut or scrape the old damper felts off the heads, saving a few from each section for samples. If you have a hard time removing the cloth backing from the wood, wet the cloth until you can scrape off both it and the glue. Scrape the dirt off the tops and sides of the damper heads, or replace the damper heads with new ones as close to the original dimensions as possible.

Remove the spring punchings and glue, and install new punchings with hot glue. Don't use so much glue that it soaks through the punching. Let each damper spring clamp

its punching while the glue dries. Polish and lacquer the screws, and replace the flanges and springs if necessary. (See p. 141 for instructions for replacing the springs and cords in the old flanges.) Polish and lacquer the damper wires. Even if the wires aren't as shiny as new, they aren't very noticeable in the assembled action, and you'll save much measuring, bending, and adjusting by using the old ones.

Don't install stronger damper springs just because the old dampers didn't work very well; they'll make the touch too heavy. Instead, regulate the dampers properly. In the tenor section of many old uprights, the lowest eight or ten dampers don't work very well. To improve their damping, substitute trichord wedge felt for the original soft flat felt.

If you must replace the damper levers, lay the old ones in order on the bench, number the new ones, and bend and cut each new wire to match the old one as closely as possible. Install the damper heads on the wires.

Install the damper levers on the main rail, and install the action in the piano. Pull each damper head away from the strings to the point where it will rest when the new felt is in place, and bend the wire so the head is parallel to the strings in all planes. Check it from the side, the top, and the front. If you have any question about the correct alignment of the damper head with the strings, temporarily insert the damper felt without glue to make your final adjustments. Apply a thin layer of hot glue to the new felt, let it set, and apply another thin layer to avoid a dry joint. (With experience, you'll learn to apply just the right amount of glue in one slightly thicker layer.) Insert the felt between the damper head and strings, aligning it carefully with the head, and let the damper

8-71 (left). Installing new damper felts.

spring clamp the felt to the head while the glue dries.

If the tops of the damper heads aren't in a perfectly straight line, glue just the first and last damper felts in place. Stick a piece of drafting tape to the strings in line with the tops of these two guide dampers, and then align all the intermediate dampers to the bottom edge of the tape, for a neat looking job.

Install the dowel connecting the sustaining pedal to the damper lift rod, and regulate all of the dampers to lift simultaneously when you depress the pedal, as described on pp.171-173. If you are a beginner, this might seem like a tedious job, but it is much easier to do it now than after you install the hammers.

Prepare the new hammers. Unwrap the new hammers and number them on the bottom, starting with #1 in the bass. A new set of hammers has several spares. Lay aside those at the upper end of the bass section and the last few in the treble.

Prick a tiny hole centered in the shank hole all the way through each hammer molding with a sharp awl. This hole will let air and excess glue escape when you glue each hammer to its shank. Then give the hammers a "haircut" if necessary, trimming the fuzz off the edges with sharp scissors.

Installing new hammers on old

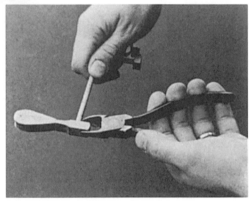

8-72. Splitting the old hammer from the shank, without damaging the shank.

shanks and butts. If you decide to use the old hammer butts and shanks, remove each hammer from its shank, except the second one from the end of each section. You sent in the end hammers from each section to have new hammers made. Now you'll use the second one at each end of each section as a guide to show you where to glue the new first one. To remove the hammers, cut each one with sharp side cutters, first vertically and then horizontally, and remove the pieces from the shank. Make several small cuts if necessary to keep from damaging the old shank.

Use a **shank reducer** in a combination handle to remove the old glue from the shank, but don't reduce the diameter of the wood (see illus. 4-104). Replace the spring punchings, rebush or replace the flanges, and replace the felt cushions and buckskin, if necessary. Obtain a set of plain bridle straps, cut them to the right length, and glue them to the junction of the butt and catcher shank.

Install all the old butts on the action. The second one from each end of each section will still have its original hammer, which will serve as a guide for installing the new end hammers. Travel the butts by papering behind the flanges, so each shank moves straight forward and back without veering off to either side (see p. 153). The more accurately you do this now, the less trouble you'll have when you align the hammers later.

Turn the action around with the back facing the front of your bench. Place each new end hammer on its shank. If the striking points of the new guide hammers are too high, trim the ends of their shanks down a little with a high quality dog toenail clipper of the type in which a flat blade slides over another blade that has a hole in it. Ream the holes in the hammers with a $7/32$" drill bit mounted in a handle, just enough so you can wiggle the striking point up and down $1/16$" (or 1.5 mm.). If the hammer is too tight on the shank, you won't be able to adjust the position of the striking point. If it's too loose, it won't stay where you put it when you wiggle it.

After adjusting the length of each end shank and the fit of each end hammer so you can align the striking point correctly, put the action in the piano and glue the first guide hammer in place. If you're good at using hot glue, use it. If you're inexperienced at gluing wood to wood with hot glue, use aliphatic resin glue instead. Squeeze a little glue into the hole in the first guide hammer, push the hammer down onto the shank, and rotate it from side to side to smear the glue around the shank. Wipe off most of the excess glue, but leave a small collar, to reinforce the glue joint.

8-73. The new guide hammers installed on the action.

Carefully adjust the position of the hammer. Look down on it from straight above to make sure it is perpendicular to the hammer rail. Look at it from both sides to make sure the striking point is at the correct height. If necessary, align the hammer butt from side to side. Until you become experienced at installing hammers, remove the action from the piano to compare the striking point of the new guide to the adjacent old hammer. Repeat this for each end guide hammer. Pay close attention to the striking point of the highest treble hammer; this should be no more than $1/16$" below the v-bar in most pianos, regardless of where the old hammer was. If you install the new hammer lower, the piano will have poor tone quality in the high treble.

Glue the rest of the guide hammers in place. Check and recheck each one while the glue sets, to make sure the alignment is correct. After the glue dries, remove the remaining old hammers from their shanks.

Place the action on your bench, and place all the new hammers on their shanks temporarily. If they're too high, measure how much each one needs to be lowered and cut the shanks down with your dog toenail clipper. Remove the hammers and lay them in

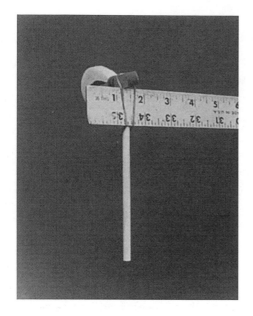

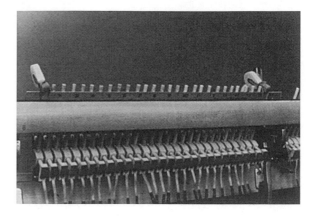

8-74 (left and right). Attaching a straightedge to the front of the guide hammer shanks in the bass section with rubber bands, as described in the text.

order on a clean piece of paper on the keybed. Install the action. Attach a straightedge to the front of the bass guide hammer shanks, as shown in illus. 8-74, with the top of the straightedge touching the bottom of the hammer tails. Cut away any glue that interferes with the straightedge resting snugly against the bottom of the hammers. Then loop a strong rubber band around the back of the shank beneath the straightedge.

Pull it up tightly around the front of the straightedge, then up over the top of the tail. Twist it, and loop it under and around the hammer head several times to take up the slack. This will hold the straightedge tightly against the shank and hammer without pulling the hammer out of line.

Find the middle hammer in the bass section and push it gently down onto its shank until the bottom of the tail touches the straightedge. Hold a second straightedge spanning the entire bass section *on top of the three hammers at their fattest point.* See if you can wiggle the striking end of the hammer up and down to bring it into line. If not, ream the hole in the hammer a little with the

8-75. Checking the alignment of the middle hammer.

8-76. Keep installing hammers halfway between each pair already installed.

8-77. The complete set of hammers, ready for final alignment with their strings, with the tails and striking points all in a perfectly straight line.

fluted reamer. Check the alignment of the hammer with its strings, and adjust the position of the flange if necessary. Then glue the hammer on its shank and wipe off the excess glue. Keep checking the hammer's alignment in all directions until the glue sets. Now you have three hammers installed in the bass section: one at each end and one in the middle.

Next, split the difference again. In other words, if you already installed hammers 1, 14, and 28, install 7 and then 21. Make sure the bottom of each hammer tail touches the top of the lower straightedge, and the top of the hammer barely touches the straightedge held across the top. The lower straightedge

8-78 (right, and two photos below). The completed set of new hammers.

ensures that the tails will all be aligned, and the upper one ensures that the heads or striking points will all be aligned. By continuing to install each new hammer approximately halfway between two others that you have already installed, you won't have any cumulative error. Also, the more hammers you install, the easier it will be to align the remaining ones.

When you finish the bass section, repeat this procedure for each remaining section. If you align each hammer carefully, your finished set of hammers will be in a perfectly straight line, as in a new high quality piano.

Installing new hammers on new shanks and butts. If you decide to replace the shanks and butts, you'll use a different procedure for installing the hammers. Check

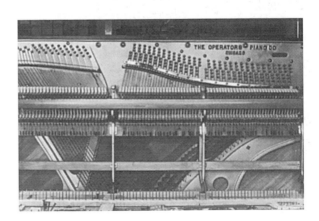

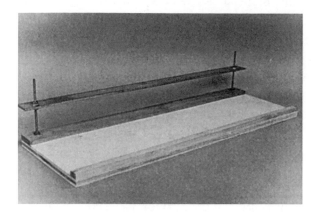

8-79. A hammer-head gluing jig.

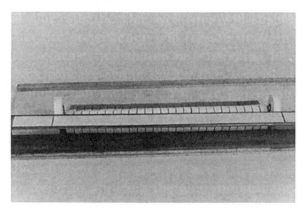

8-80. Masking tape in place on the straightedge, showing where to lay the section of hammers as you glue the shanks.

through the new butts and reglue any loose felt and buckskin, and check each flange and rebush any that you find to be defective. Thread the bridle straps through their holes in the catchers. Then install the new butts on the action rail, temporarily insert new shanks, and travel the butts. If a new shank wobbles because it's not snug, temporarily insert a small strip of paper next to the shank in the hole.

Make a hammer-head gluing jig like the one in illus. 8-79. Cut a slot in the straightedge for each machine screw. On each screw, place one nut under the straightedge and another on top, to allow you to adjust the height and the forward/back position.

Lay one complete section of hammers on the jig, so their sides touch. Mark the straightedge with a marking pen or piece of masking tape at each end of the section of hammers. The marks will show you where to lay the hammers on the jig as you glue the shanks.

Roll each new shank across a flat surface, and reject any warped shanks. Sometimes you'll have to go through two or three sets of shanks to find 88 perfectly straight ones.

Glue the hammer at each end of the section on a new shank. Draw a pencil line showing the grain orientation on the other end of the shank, so you can tell which way to turn it after you apply the glue. Squeeze a little glue into the hole in the hammer, and a little more around the shank. Rotate the hammer around on the shank as you install it to ensure good coverage. Turn each shank so the grain lines are parallel to the length of the hammer, to help keep the shanks from cracking. Then wipe off excess glue.

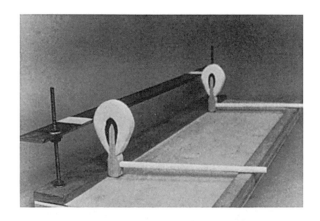

8-81. The straightedge adjusted so it touches the hammers at their thickest point, where the tails touch the back rail of the jig.

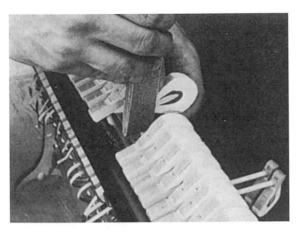

8-82. Sanding the sides of the bass hammer tails if they rub on the adjacent hammers.

With the end hammers in place between the alignment marks, adjust the straightedge so it barely touches the fattest part of each hammer when the tail touches the back rail of the jig. Tighten the nuts.

Leave the first hammer lying on the jig. Insert a shank into the next hammer, and lay it next to the first one. Ream the hole in the second hammer if necessary for proper alignment, then glue the hammer to the shank with the grain oriented correctly. Wipe off excess glue. Lay the second hammer and shank in the jig next to the first one, and adjust the hammer on the shank so the head just touches the straightedge when the tail touches the back rail. Continue this way until the entire section is glued. Keep checking previously glued hammers to make sure they don't pull out of line as the glue sets, and readjust them as necessary. Leave the hammers in the jig until the glue is hard enough to keep them from changing. Then lay them aside and glue the next section. When you're done, you should have a whole set of hammers glued to their shanks at the same angle.

Remove the second new butt from each end of each section, and temporarily install the old butt and hammer. Place each new

end hammer in its butt, measure how much too high it is, and cut that much off the shank with a dog toenail clipper. Insert the new end hammers again. Put the action in the piano, and check the alignment of the new guide hammers with the strings. Adjust the butt flanges if necessary. Glue the shanks in the butts and align the height of the hammers. As the glue sets, view the hammers from the front and side to adjust their height, and from the top to make them perpendicular to the hammer rail.

After the glue dries, place a straightedge under the tails of the guide hammers for the bass section, as in illus. 8-74. Then install the rest of the hammers. Cut enough off each shank to permit the hammer tail to rest on the straightedge. Don't shorten the shank any more than necessary, or you'll weaken it where it is glued in the butt.

If you can't align a hammer with its strings even after adjusting the butt flange, sand a little wood off the side of the shank where it fits into the butt. Thin the appropriate side of the shank by rotating it as you gently press it against a disc sander. This will allow you to lean the shank sideways, so you can align the hammer with the string while keeping it parallel with the other hammers.

After the glue dries, adjust the alignment of the hammers to the strings if necessary. If any hammer tails rub on adjacent hammers, trim the tails with a sanding strip or on a disc sander as necessary. If you traveled the butts and installed the hammers correctly, you should never need to sand the sides of the hammer heads.

Install the spring rail. Your action now has the dampers, hammer butts, shanks, and hammers installed. Remove it from the piano, and work the spring rail in from one end, being careful to jiggle the springs past the obstacles without bending the springs.

Replace any old cardboard front rail punching shims with new ones, and screw the rail in place.

Rebuild and install the wippen/sticker assemblies. Polish the damper spoons, polish and lacquer the bridle and backcheck wires. Remove the backcheck felts with a sharp knife. If you can't make a clean cut without marring the wood, just cut away as much of the felt as possible. Then apply water to the remaining felt and glue to loosen them, and scrape the wood clean. If the fronts of the backchecks are dirty or scratched, scrape off the old shellac, and wipe on a very thin coat of new white or orange shellac with a rag. Glue new backcheck felts to the backchecks with hot glue. Wrap a small rubber band around each to hold the felt in place until the glue dries, making the rubber band just tight enough to hold the felt without leaving an indentation.

Break the jack flanges off the wippens by rocking the flanges forward and back. If you rock them from side to side, you'll break the legs off the flanges. Remove the jack springs, and clean the old glue out of the holes with a jack spring hole reamer. Rebush and repin all flange bushings as necessary, and reassemble the parts.

Reglue the jack flanges to the wippens with hot glue. Seat each flange on the wippen carefully, so the jack doesn't lean off to the side. In most verticals, when the jacks are straight, they are centered on the backchecks.

After the glue dries, install new jack springs. Fill the spring hole in the wippen with hot glue, flush with the top surface of the wood. Place the large end of the jack spring in the hole, and seat the top of the spring in the jack. Loop a small rubber band around the backcheck wire and jack, pulling the jack forward just enough to put a little

tension on the spring while the glue dries. If the wippens have no stickers, stand them vertically in a row on the bench until the glue dries. If they have stickers, clamp a long slat of wood about 2" (or 5 cm.) away from the front of your bench, creating a 2" slot the width of your bench. After gluing each jack spring to the wippen, place the wippen so it straddles the bench and slat, with the sticker hanging down through the slot. The weight of the sticker will keep the wippen standing up straight while the glue dries.

If you install new jacks, observe which ones are relieved on one side to allow room for the letoff rail supports. If you install new wippens with new jacks already attached, observe that there are nine different combinations of jacks and spoons: jacks relieved on bass side, or treble side, or unrelieved, with spoons aimed toward bass, or toward treble, or with no spoons. Use the appropriate wippen for each note. If you need an extra wippen with the jack relieved on one side, sand the edge of the jack on a sanding disc. If you need a wippen with the spoon aimed in a different direction, you can usually bend the existing spoon and get it to work. If not, buy a few extra new wippens, specifying the type.

Install the wippen/sticker assemblies on the action. Center each jack under the hammer butt, and tighten the wippen flange screw. If you find you have to tip a wippen too far to one side, remove it, and reglue the jack flange in the correct position. If the front end of a wippen is off center, paper the wippen flange as necessary. Connect the bridle straps as you go. Use one hand to pull the jack forward and simultaneously hold the wippen up as far as it will go. Use the other to thread the bridle strap through the loop in the end of the wire and hook the tab over the wire. If any of the bridle wires are bent back so they allow the jacks to slip under the bottoms of the hammer butts, bend them forward just enough to keep the jacks in front of the felt butt cushions.

Install the action in the piano. Regulate the action and pedals as described in Chapter 5.

Rebuilding the Grand Action.

You will follow the same general procedure to rebuild the grand action as when you rebuild an upright action, except for the dampers. You'll rebuild them after you install the hammers. Rebush or replace flanges; replace felt, cloth, and buckskin as necessary; polish, replate, or repaint and rebush the action brackets, etc.; and assemble the action skeleton.

If the knuckles are flat and the shank bushings are worn, replace the shanks. Send a sample to the supply company to make sure the dimensions are identical. If you can't get replacement shanks, replace the bushings and knuckles. When you remove the old knuckles from the shanks, be very careful not to break the shanks. When installing new knuckles, feel the nap of the buckskin — it will feel smoother when you rub it in one direction than the other. Install each knuckle so the buckskin feels smoother as you rub *toward* the hammer; this will help the jack to slip back under the knuckle.

If the jacks are made in two pieces and some of them are falling apart, try to break all of them loose to reglue the whole set. Align the parts very carefully during gluing, and make sure they don't slip out of position if you clamp them while the glue dries.

If the repetition springs are corroded or bent, replace them with new ones of the same strength. If in doubt, send a sample to a piano supply company. Be prepared to spend a lot of time if necessary to adjust new repetition springs.

If most of the screw holes are stripped in a Steinway action, it is possible to drive out the wooden cores in the rails, insert new ones, and redrill the holes, or to obtain new rails from Steinway and solder them into the original action brackets. *Don't attempt either of these repairs until you have enough action rebuilding experience to recognize whether the geometry of the action is correct. If you inadvertently install a rail in the wrong place or orientation, you won't be able to regulate the action to work properly.* Instead of trying to do this yourself, take the action to an expert Steinway grand rebuilder, or send the whole action frame to the Steinway factory for replacement of the damaged parts.

Installing new grand hammers. Grand hammer installation is similar to vertical hammer installation, with a few exceptions. The hammers must form a 90° with the shanks; the tails must be shaped and roughened; and, because the hammers are drilled all the way through, the shanks must be trimmed if they protrude. As in a vertical, the striking point is very important; refer to pp. 297-298.

Prepare the hammers. Grand hammers must have their tails shaped so the backchecks will work and so the tails won't rub on the adjacent hammers. Unwrap and number the hammers. Insert a snug-fitting old shank in each hammer. The shank will form a handle and guide for sanding on a disc sander. Trim the sides of each tail by holding the shank parallel to the sanding disc, keeping the felt part of the hammer away from the disc.

Shape the back of the tail by resting the shank on a block of wood on the sander table, lightly touching the tail to the sanding

8-83. Sanding the sides of a tail so they are parallel to the shank, and they won't rub on adjacent hammers.

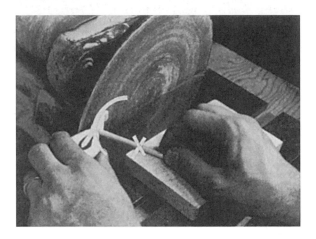

8-84. Shaping the back of the tail to make it parallel to the face of the backcheck. Rotate the hammer and shank about the center point as shown, to match the shape of the original hammer.

disc and moving the shank and hammer head in an arc, as in illus. 8-84.

For more accurate shaping make a simple jig with a support for the hammer attached to a wooden swivel clamped to the table of a disc sander, as shown and described in the October 1990 *Piano Technicians Journal*. (see Appendix).

Install the hammers. Install the old temporary guide hammers — the second one from each end of each section. If you're using new shanks, install, space, and travel them. If you're reusing the old shanks, remove the old hammers from them with a **grand hammer shank press**. Remove the glue with a **shank reducer**, but don't remove any wood. Install the new knuckles, and replace the bushings.

Fit each hammer to its shank by reaming the hole with a fluted reamer. Reaming makes room for glue in the joint and enables you to adjust the hammer slightly to form a 90° angle with the shank. Ream the hammer so it wobbles no more than 1/16" (or 1.5 mm.) at the striking point.

Install each new guide hammer—the first and last hammer in each section. Align its

8-85. The old second hammer from each end of each section — in this Steinway action, hammers 2 and 25 — temporarily installed.

8-86. Aligning the new end guide hammers, 1 and 26, with the old end guide hammers, 2 and 25, as you glue them on their shanks.

8-87 (left). The new guide hammers glued in place.

8-88 (right). Trimming the excess shank after the glue is dry. Roughen the wood a little, without altering the shape of the tail, for the backchecks to work properly.

striking point and tail to the old hammer, and simultaneously adjust the body to form a 90° angle with the shank.

After the guide hammers are dry, install the rest of the hammers. Usc straightcdgcs to align the tails and heads as in a vertical piano, and check the angle between each hammer and shank. If the shanks protrude from the heads, unscrew the shanks from the action after the glue dries, and sand the shanks flush with the tails on a disc sander. Roughen the backcheck mating area of each tail a little with a wire brush or coarse sandpaper, to match the roughness of the old hammer tails. If the tails are too smooth, the hammers won't check properly; if they're too rough, they will wear out the backchecks prematurely. After roughening the tails, reinstall the hammers and regulate the action.

For additional help with installing hammers, the **Jaras grand piano hammer installer, shank and hammer clamp,** and **vertical piano hammer installer** can be very useful, and can be purchased from certain piano supply companies.

Rebuild the dampers. Rebush the damper underlever flanges and the pivots for the damper lift rail. Install the damper action in the piano. Replace the felt on the damper stop rail or rails, and install them in a position a little too high. You will adjust them later.

Remove the old damper felt, being careful not to damage the wood. Dampen and scrape the wood, if necessary, to keep from

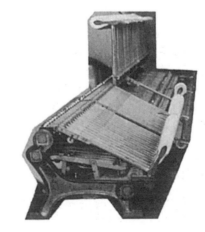

8-89. Careful work will result in hammers that are aligned perfectly, as in this picture.

gouging it. Refinish the damper heads if necessary, and polish the wires gently — with metal polish on a rag, not steel wool — so you don't hurt the thin plating. If you must replace the wires because the old ones are badly corroded. take the time to bend the new wires carefully, copying the old ones as closely as possible, to save time regulating them. Most damper wires are at right angles to the bottom surface of their heads before the felt is attached; draw a large "T" on your bench with accurate right angles, and lay the dampers on it for reference while adjusting the new wires.

Rebush the guide rail. Damper guide rail bushings should be the loosest bushings in the whole piano, so make sure the damper wires don't bind. Install the dampers in order and regulate them so they are parallel to the strings, with the bottom surface of each head level and centered over the strings.

Select the new damper felt carefully from the many types available from different supply companies. Copy the original configuration; for example, don't replace two short pieces with one long one. If you're rebuilding a piano made in another country, and you can't get the correct damper felt in your own country, get a catalog from a supply company in the country where the piano was made. They probably carry the correct felt. Cut the felt to the right length with a new single edge razor blade. Be careful to guide the blade as the felt compresses under it, so the finished cut will be perpendicular to the length of the damper. Apply hot glue to each felt, and glue it to the head. If you are inexperienced with using hot glue, coat the felt with a thin coat of glue and let it dry a little. Then apply a second thin coat to ensure a good joint. With experience, you'll know how much hot glue to apply in one coat. Bend the wire and align the felt as necessary so it rests squarely on the strings. After the glue dries, regulate the height of the damper levers so they won't interfere with regulating the action.

Install the action in the piano. Regulate it, as described in Chapter 5, and tune the duplex scale if necessary, as described in Chapter 7.

Finishing Touches

After you regulate the piano and pedals, the only remaining work is to reassemble the rest of the cabinet. Polish and lacquer all solid brass trim parts, and lacquer all replated parts. Install the name board felt. Attach all hinges. In a grand, install the lid prop. After assembling the fallboard, lid, and all other cabinet parts, examine the cabinet to see where it originally had rubber bumpers and rubber head tacks, and replace them. Sand the rubber heads down as necessary, to level cabinet parts. Move the piano to its new location, raise the pitch several times, and give it a fine tuning. Depending on your level of skill and patience, if you followed all instructions in this chapter and completed each part of the job carefully, you should have a piano that works, looks, and sounds as close as possible to the way it did when it was new.

Appendix

To repair, regulate, or rebuild a piano properly, you'll need certain tools, parts, supplies, and materials that are available only from piano supply companies. Some piano supply companies do business only on a wholesale basis to established piano technicians. Others sell at retail to hobbyists (or both at wholesale and retail). All have minimum order requirements, to keep from losing money on small orders.

The Vestal Press, Ltd., publisher of this book and the companion volume *Player Piano Servicing and Rebuilding* by the same author, stocks a variety of books on pianos, piano technology, and automatic musical instruments. *The Vestal Press Resource Catalogue* contains names and current addresses of suppliers, hobbyist organizations, correspondence and resident schools of piano technology, and sources of other books, videotapes, service manuals and periodicals, including materials that illustrate the tuning methods described in Chapter 7. Current sources for specific items mentioned in the text will be included in *The Vestal Press Resource Catalogue* as long as the items are available. Write to the Vestal Press at P. O. Box 97, Vestal NY 13851-0097 for further information.

The *Piano Technicians Journal*, the monthly publication of the Piano Technicians Guild, Inc., contains a variety of articles on all aspects of piano servicing, tuning and rebuilding, as well as display and classified advertising by major piano supply companies, smaller firms that specialize in supplying just a few items, and schools of piano technology. The Guild also publishes and sells its *Guide to Resources in Piano Technology*, which contains a large number of listings and advertisements for supplies and other resources. Write to the Piano Technicians Guild at 3930 Washington, Kansas City MO 64111-2963 for more information on these and other publications, and membership in the Guild.

The Randy Potter School of Piano Technology may be reached at 61592 Orion Drive, Bend OR 97702.

For current addresses of piano manufacturers, refer to *The Purchasers Guide to the Music Industries*, published by The Music Trades, 80 West St., P. O. Box 432, Englewood NJ 07631.

These references and addresses were correct at the time this text was prepared, but may of course change with time. If you need updated information, contact The Vestal Press at P.O. Box 97, Vestal, NY 13851-0097 (phone 607-797-4872) to purchase a copy of their current *Resource Catalogue*, which should provide the help you need.

DRILL SIZE CHART

Equivalency of fractional, metric, number, and letter drills to thousandths of an inch.

Inch	Mm.	Wire Gage	Decimals of an Inch
		80	.0135
		79	.0145
1/64			.0156
	.4		.0157
		78	.0160
		77	.0180
	.5		.0197
		76	.0200
		75	.0210
	.55		.0217
		74	.0225
	.6		.0236
		73	.0240
		72	.0250
	.65		.0256
		71	.0260
	.7		.0276
		70	.0280
		69	.0293
	.75		.0295
		68	.0310
1/32			.0313
	.8		.0315
		67	.0320
		66	.0330
	.85		.0335
		65	.0350
	.9		.0354
		64	.0360
		63	.0370
	.95		.0374
		62	.0380
		61	.0390
	1		.0394
		60	.0400
		59	.0410
	1.05		.0413
		58	.0420
		57	.0430
	1.1		.0433
	1.15		.0453
		56	.0465

Inch	Mm.	Wire Gage	Decimals of an Inch
3/64			.0469
	1.2		.0472
	1.25		.0492
	1.3		.0512
		55	.0520
	1.35		.0531
		54	.0550
	1.4		.0551
	1.45		.0571
	1.5		.0591
		53	.0595
	1.55		.0610
1/16			.0625
	1.6		.0630
		52	.0635
	1.65		.0650
	1.7		.0669
		51	.0670
	1.75		.0689
		50	.0700
	1.8		.0709
	1.85		.0728
		49	.0730
	1.9		.0748
		48	.0760
	1.95		.0768
5/64			.0781
		47	.0785
	2		.0787
	2.05		.0807
		46	.0810
		45	.0820
	2.1		.0827
	2.15		.0846
		44	.0860
	2.2		.0866
	2.25		.0886
		43	.0890
	2.3		.0906
	2.35		.0925
		42	.0935

Inch	Mm.	Wire Gage	Decimals of an Inch
3/32			.0938
	2.4		.0945
		41	.0960
	2.45		.0966
		40	.0980
	2.5		.0984
		39	.0995
		38	.1015
	2.6		.1024
		37	.1040
	2.7		.1063
		36	.1065
	2.75		.1083
7/64			.1094
		35	.1100
	2.8		.1102
		34	.1110
		33	.1130
	2.9		.1142
		32	.1160
	3		.1181
		31	.1200
	3.1		.1220
1/8			.1250
	3.2		.1260
	3.25		.1280
		30	.1285
	3.3		.1299
	3.4		.1339
		29	.1360
	3.5		.1378
		28	.1405
9/64			.1406
	3.6		.1417
		27	.1440
	3.7		.1457
		26	.1470
	3.75		.1476
		25	.1495
	3.8		.1496
		24	.1520
	3.9		.1535
		23	.1540

Inch	Mm.	Wire Gage	Decimals of an Inch
5/32			.1563
		22	.1570
	4		.1575
		21	.1590
		20	.1610
	4.1		.1614
	4.2		.1654
		19	.1660
	4.25		.1673
	4.3		.1693
		18	.1695
11/64			.1719
		17	.1730
	4.4		.1732
		16	.1770
	4.5		.1772
		15	.1800
	4.6		.1811
		14	.1820
		13	.1850
	4.7		.1850
	4.75		.1870
3/16			.1875
	4.8		.1890
		12	.1890
		11	.1910
	4.9		.1929
		10	.1935
		9	.1960
	5		.1969
		8	.1990
	5.1		.2008
		7	.2010
13/64			.2031
		6	.2040
	5.2		.2047
		5	.2055
	5.25		.2067
	5.3		.2087
		4	.2090
	5.4		.2126
		3	.2130
	5.5		.2165
7/32			.2188
	5.6		.2205
		2	.2210
	5.7		.2244
	5.75		.2264
		1	.2280
	5.8		.2283

Metric conversion chart for number, letter, and inch drill sizes. From *Modern Metalworking* by John R. Walker, published by the Goodheart-Wilcox Company. Reprinted by permission.

Inch	Mm.	Letter Sizes	Decimals of an Inch	Inch	Mm.	Letter Sizes	Decimals of an Inch	Inch	Mm.	Decimals of an Inch	Inch	Mm.	Decimals of an Inch
	5.9		.2323	21/64			.3281	35/64		.5469	1		1.0000
		A	.2340		8.4		.3307		14	.5512		25.5	1.0039
15/64			.2344			Q	.3320	9/16		.5625	1 1/64		1.0156
	6		.2362		8.5		.3346		14.5	.5709		26	1.0236
		B	.2380		8.6		.3386	37/64		.5781	1 1/32		1.0313
	6.1		.2402			R	.3390		15	.5906		26.5	1.0433
		C	.2420		8.7		.3425	19/32		.5938	1 3/64		1.0469
	6.2		.2441	11/32			.3438	39/64		.6094	1 1/16		1.0625
		D	.2460		8.75		.3345		15.5	.6102		27	1.0630
	6.25		.2461		8.8		.3465	5/8		.6250	1 5/64		1.0781
	6.3		.2480			S	.3480		16	.6299		27.5	1.0827
1/4		E	.2500		8.9		.3504	41/64		.6406	1 3/32		1.0938
	6.4		.2520		9		.3543		16.5	.6496		28	1.1024
	6.5		.2559			T	.3580	21/32		.6563	1 7/64		1.1094
		F	.2570		9.1		.3583		17	.6693		28.5	1.1220
	6.6		.2598	23/64			.3594	43/64		.6719	1 1/8		1.1250
		G	.2610		9.2		.3622	11/16		.6875	1 9/64		1.1406
	6.7		.2638		9.25		.3642		17.5	.6890		29	1.1417
17/64			.2656		9.3		.3661	45/64		.7031	1 5/32		1.1562
	6.75		.2657			U	.3680		18	.7087		29.5	1.1614
		H	.2660		9.4		.3701	23/32		.7188	1 11/64		1.1719
	6.8		.2677		9.5		.3740		18.5	.7283		30	1.1811
	6.9		.2717	3/8			.3750	47/64		.7344	1 3/16		1.1875
		I	.2720			V	.3770		19	.7480		30.5	1.2008
	7		.2756		9.6		.3780	3/4		.7500	1 13/64		1.2031
		J	.2770		9.7		.3819	49/64		.7656	1 7/32		1.2188
	7.1		.2795		9.75		.3839		19.5	.7677		31	1.2205
		K	.2810		9.8		.3858	25/32		.7812	1 15/64		1.2344
9/32			.2812			W	.3860		20	.7874		31.5	1.2402
	7.2		.2835		9.9		.3898	51/64		.7969	1 1/4		1.2500
	7.25		.2854	25/64			.3906		20.5	.8071		32	1.2598
	7.3		.2874		10		.3937	13/16		.8125	1 17/64		1.2656
		L	.2900			X	39.70		21	.8268		32.5	1.2795
	7.4		.2913			Y	.4040	53/64		.8281	1 9/32		1.2813
		M	.2950	13/32			.4063	27/32		.8438	1 19/64		1.2969
	7.5		.2953			Z	.4130		21.5	.8465		33	1.2992
19/64			.2969		10.5		.4134	55/64		.8594	1 5/16		1.3125
	7.6		.2992	27/64			.4219		22	.8661		33.5	1.3189
		N	.3020		11		.4331	7/8		.8750	1 21/64		1.3281
	7.7		.3031	7/16			.4375		22.5	.8858		34	1.3386
	7.75		.3051		11.5		.4528	57/64		.8906	1 11/32		1.3438
	7.8		.3071	29/64			.4531		23	.9055		34.5	1.3583
	7.9		.3110	15/32			.4688	29/32		.9063	1 23/64		1.3594
5/16			.3125		12		.4724	59/64		.9219	1 3/8		1.3750
	8		.3150	31/64			.4844		23.5	.9252		35	1.3780
		O	.3160		12.5		.4921	15/16		.9375	1 25/64		1.3906
	8.1		.3189	1/2			.5000		24	.9449		35.5	1.3976
	8.2		.3228		13		.5118	61/64		.9531	1 13/32		1.4063
		P	.3230	33/64			.5156		24.5	.9646		36	1.4173
	8.25		.3248	17/32			.5313	31/32		.9688	1 27/64		1.4219
	8.3		.3268		13.5		.5315		25	.9843		36.5	1.4370
								63/64		.9844			

CONVERSION TABLE
Millimeters to Inches

Millimeter	Inch Decimal
.1	.0039
.2	.0078
.3	.0118
.4	.0157
.5	.0197
.6	.0236
.7	.0275
.8	.0315
1.0	.0393 (7)
2.0	.0787
3.0	.1181
4.0	.1575
5.0	.1968
6.0	.2362
7.0	.2756
8.0	.3150
9.0	.3543
10.0	.3937
11.0	.4331
12.0	.4724
13.0	.5118
14.0	.5512
15.0	.5905
16.0	.6299
17.0	.6693
18.0	.7087
19.0	.7480
20.0	.7874
21.0	.8268
22.0	.8661
23.0	.9055
24.0	.9449
25.0	.9842
25.4	1.0000
44.5	1.750 (1¾)
47.6	1.875 (1⅞)
63.5	2.500 (2½)
66.7	2.625 (2⅝)

CONVERSION TABLE
Fractions of Inch to Millimeters

8ths	16ths	32nds	64ths	Decimal	Milli-meters
			1	.0156	0.397
		1	2	.0312	0.794
			3	.0469	1.191
	1		4	.0625	1.588
			5	.0781	1.984
		3	6	.0937	2.381
			7	.1094	2.778
1			8	.1250	3.175
			9	.1406	3.572

8ths	16ths	32nds	64ths	Decimal	Milli-meters
		5	10	.1562	3.969
			11	.1719	4.366
	3		12	.1875	4.763
			13	.2031	5.159
		7	14	.2187	5.556
			15	.2344	5.953
2			16	.2500	6.350
			17	.2656	6.747
		9	18	.2812	7.144
			19	.2969	7.541
	5		20	.3125	7.938
			21	.3281	8.334
		11	22	.3437	8.731
			23	.3594	9.128
	3		24	.3750	9.525
			25	.3906	9.922
		13	26	.4062	10.319
			27	.4219	10.716
	7		28	.4375	11.113
			29	.4531	11.509
		15	30	.4687	11.906
			31	.4844	12.303
4			32	.5000	12.700
			33	.5156	13.097
		17	34	.5312	13.494
			35	.5469	13.891
	9		36	.5625	14.288
			37	.5781	14.684
		19	38	.5937	15.081
			39	.6094	15.478
	5		40	.6250	15.875
			41	.6406	16.272
		21	42	.6562	16.669
			43	.6719	17.066
	11		44	.6875	17.463
			45	.7031	17.859
		23	46	.7187	18.256
			47	.7344	18.653
6			48	.7500	19.050
			49	.7656	19.447
		25	50	.7812	19.844
			51	.7969	20.241
	13		52	.8125	20.638
			53	.8281	21.034
		27	54	.8437	21.431
			55	.8594	21.828
	7		56	.8750	22.225
			57	.8906	22.622
		29	58	.9062	23.019
			59	.9219	23.416
	15		60	.9375	23.813
			61	.9531	24.209
		31	62	.9687	24.606
			63	.9844	25.003
8			64	1.0000	25.400

Bibliography

Note: Readers should recognize that many books and publications listed here are out of print and not readily available. Dealers in used books may be able to help readers who wish to acquire copies for their own libraries.

Acoustics

Helmholtz, Hermann. *On the Sensations of Tone.* 1885; reprint, New York: Dover Publications, Inc., 1954.

McFerrin, W. V. *The Piano—Its Acoustics.* Boston: Tuners Supply Company, 1972.

Business Hints for the Piano Technician

Boles, Don. *The Independent Piano Technician.* Atlanta: The Pinchpenny Press, 1968.

Music, General

Apel, Willi. *Harvard Dictionary of Music.* Cambridge: Harvard Univ. Press, various editions.

Blom, Eric, ed. *Groves Dictionary of Music and Musicians.* Ten volumes. London: MacMillan & Co., Ltd., various editions.

Scholes, Percy A. *The Oxford Companion to Music.* London: Oxford Univ. Press, various editions.

Piano Construction and Theory

American Steel and Wire Co. *Secrets of Piano Construction.* Original title: Piano Tone Building. 1916-1919 volumes; reprint, Vestal NY: The Vestal Press, Ltd., 1985.

Pfeiffer, Walter. *The Piano Key and Whippen.* Translated by Jim Engelhardt, 1978. Frankfurt: Verlag das Musikinstrument, 1955.

White, William B. *Theory and Practice of Piano Construction.* 1906; reprint, New York: Dover Publications, 1975.

Wolfenden, Samuel. *A Treatise on the Art of Pianoforte Construction.* 1916 with 1927 supplement; reprint, Old Woking, Surrey: Unwin Brothers, 1975.

Piano Consumer Information

Fine, Larry. *The Piano Book.* 2nd ed. Jamaica Plain MA: Brookside Press, 1990.

Gurlick, Philip P., Jr. *The Piano—A Piano Technician's Guide for the Piano Owner,* 3rd ed., ©1993, by Potter Press.

Leverett, Willard M. *How to Buy a Good Used Piano,* 4th ed., ©1994, by Potter Press.

Piano Dates and Serial Numbers

Herzog, Hans K. *Europe Piano Atlas.* Frankfurt: Verlag Erwin Bochinsky GmbH & Co. KG, various editions.

Michel, N. E. *Pierce Piano Atlas.* Long Beach: Bob Pierce, various editions.

Piano History

Dolge, Alfred. *Pianos and Their Makers.* 1911; reprint, New York: Dover Publications, Inc., 1972.

_____. *Men Who Have Made Piano History.* Original title: Pianos and

Their Makers, Vol. II. 1913; reprint, Vestal NY: The Vestal Press, Ltd., 1980.

Gill, Dominic, ed. *The Book of the Piano.* Ithaca NY: Cornell Univ. Press, 1981.

Loesser, Arthur. *Men, Women, and Pianos.* New York: Simon & Schuster, 1954.

Michel, N. E. *Historical Pianos.* Pico Rivera CA: N. E. Michel, 1969.

Roell, Craig H. *The Piano In America, 1890-1940.* Chapel Hill: The Univ. of North Carolina Press, 1989.

Piano Nomenclature

Mason, Merle. *Piano Parts and Their Functions.* Kansas City MO: The Piano Technicians Guild, Inc., 1977.

Schimmel, Nikolaus and Hans K. Herzog. *Piano Nomenclatur.* Frankfurt: Verlag das Musikinstrument, 1983.

Piano Regulating

Potter, Randy. *The PTG Piano Action Handbook.* 3rd ed. ©1991, The Piano Technicians Guild, Kansas City.

Many piano manufacturers supply service manuals containing regulating information to establish piano technicians.

Piano Servicing—All Aspects

Guide to Resources in Piano Technology, Kansas City, MO: The Piano Technicinas Guild, Inc., 1st edition 1992.

Howe, Alfred H. *Scientific Piano Tuning and Servicing.* Revised ed.Clifton NJ: American Piano Supply Co., 1966.

Howell, W. Dean. *Professional Piano Tuning.* Clifton NJ: American Piano Supply Co., 1969.

McMorrow, Edward J. *The Educated Piano.* Edmonds WA: Light Hammer Press, 1989.

Potter, Randy. *A Complete Course in Piano Tuning, Repairing, Regulating, Voicing, Apprentice Training and Business Practices Training.* Bend OR: Randy Potter School of Piano Technology, 1987-1991. (This extensive course includes a lengthy printed text, videotapes, action models, tools, and other materials covering all aspects of piano servicing.)

Stevens, Floyd. *Piano Tuning, Repair & Rebuilding.* Chicago: Nelson-Hall Co., 1972.

Travis, John W. *Let's Tune Up.* Takoma Park MD: John W. Travis, 1968.

White, William B. *Piano Tuning and Allied Arts.* 1946; reprint, Boston: Tuners Supply Company, 1953.

Woodman, H. Staunton. *How to Tune a Piano.* New York: Corwood Publishers, 1976.

Piano Stringing Scales and Rescaling

Donelson, James H. *Piano Rebuilders' Handbook of Treble String Tensions (And Other Characteristics).* Pleasant Hill CA: James H. Donelson, 1977.

Parsons, Tremaine. *PSCALE Piano Scaling Program* for IBM and compatable personal computers. Georgetown, CA: Tremaine Parsons, 1992.

Roberts, David. *The Calculating Technician.* Kansas City: The Piano Technicians Guild Foundation Press, 1990.

Travis, John W. *A Guide to Restringing.* Middleburg VA: Middleburg Press, 1961.

Piano Trade Information

Music Product Directory. Cincinnati OH: Ancott Associates. Updated twice yearly.

The Purchaser's Guide to the Music Industries. Englewood NJ: The Music Trades, published annually.

Piano Voicing

Dietz, Rudolf Franz. *Grand Voicing*. Frankfurt: Verlag das Musikinstrument; reprint, Clifton NJ: American Piano Supply Co., 1968.

Player Piano History

Bowers, Q. David. *Encyclopedia of Automatic Musical Instruments*. Vestal NY: The Vestal Press, Ltd., 1972.
_____. *Put Another Nickel In*. Vestal NY: The Vestal Press, Ltd.,1965.
Givens, Larry. *Re-enacting the Artist*. Vestal NY: The Vestal Press, Ltd., 1970.
Ord-Hume, Arthur W. J. G. *Player Piano*. Cranbury NJ: A. S. Barnes & Co., 1970.
Reblitz, Arthur A., and Q. David Bowers. *Treasures of Mechanical Music*. Vestal NY: The Vestal Press, Ltd., 1981.
Roehl, Harvey N. *Player Piano Treasury*. 2nd ed. Vestal NY: The Vestal Press, Ltd., 1973.

Player Piano Servicing

Givens, Larry. *Rebuilding the Player Piano*. Vestal NY: The Vestal Press, Ltd., 1963.
Ord-Hume, Arthur W. J. G. *Restoring Pianolas and Other Self- Playing Pianos*. London: George Allen & Unwin Ltd., 1983.
Reblitz, Arthur A. *Player Piano Servicing and Rebuilding*. Vestal NY: The Vestal Press, Ltd., 1985.

Refinishing

Gibbia, S. W. Wood *Finishing and Refinishing*. 3rd ed. New York: Van Nostrand Reinhold Company, 1981.

Woodworking

Feirer, John L. *Cabinetmaking and Millwork*. Peoria: Chas. A. Bennett Co., Inc., 1970.

Safety in the Work Place

Barazani, Gail *Coningsby. Safe Practices in the Arts & Crafts: A Studio Guide*. College Art Association of America, 1978.

Periodicals

The AMICA. News bulletin of the Automatic Musical Instrument Collectors Association.
Art Hazards News. Center for Occupational Hazards, 5 Beekman St., New York NY 10038.
The Bulletin of the Musical Box Society International. Periodical of the Musical Box Society International.
Fine Woodworking. The Taunton Press, Inc., Newtown CT.
The Piano Technicians Journal. Piano Technicians Guild, Inc., Kansas City MO. (Back issues of this publication constitute a vast library of technical articles written by some of the finest piano tuners, technicians, and rebuilders in the world. For information on ordering back issues, reprints of specific articles, a cumulative index, and other publications, write to the Guild at the address listed in the appendix.)

Photo Credits Not Attributed Elsewhere

Aeolian Corporation: 2-9

American Piano Supply Company: 4-35

Baldwin Piano and Organ Company: 2-6, 2-10, 2-21, 3-1, 4-49, 4-50

Dampp-Chaser Electronics Corporation: 4-119

Ginger Hein: 8-14, 8-17 through 23, 8-25, 8-26

Kawai Piano Corporation: 5-31

Harvey Roehl: 1-1, 1-10, 1-12, 1-13, 2-11, 2-12, 2-15, 2-18 through 20, 2-30, 2-32, 4-31, 4-48, 4-58, 4-70, 4-75, 4-77, 4-78 through 84, 4-95 through 97, 4-104, 4-107, 4-114, 5-5, 5-6, 5-54, 5-56, 8-29 through 41, 8-45, 8-46, 8-50, 8-71, 8-72

Schaff Piano Supply Company: 2-29, 2-33, 2-34, 4-20, 4-24, 4-73, 4-85, 4-92, 4-106, 7-4, 8-48, 8-57

Steinway and Sons: 1-3, 1-4, 2-36, 6-2, 8-5

Tuners Supply Company: 4-5, 4-38, 4-94, 4-100, 8-1

Index

Index

Index

Index

Index

326